P9-DGY-587

FLOATING
COAST

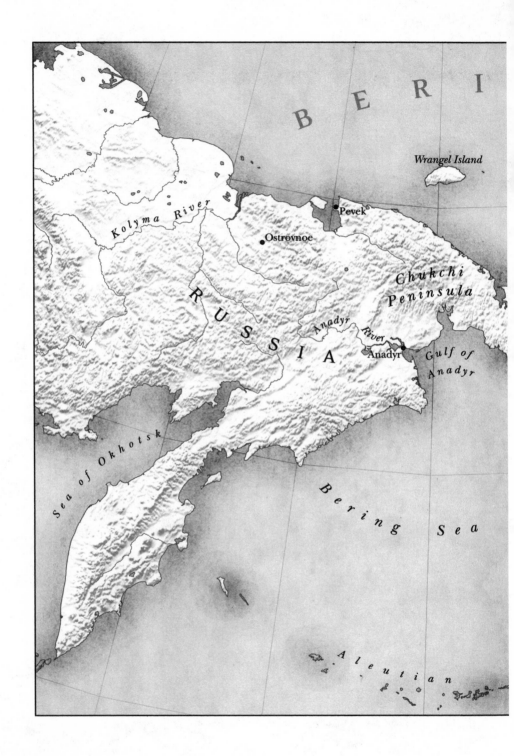

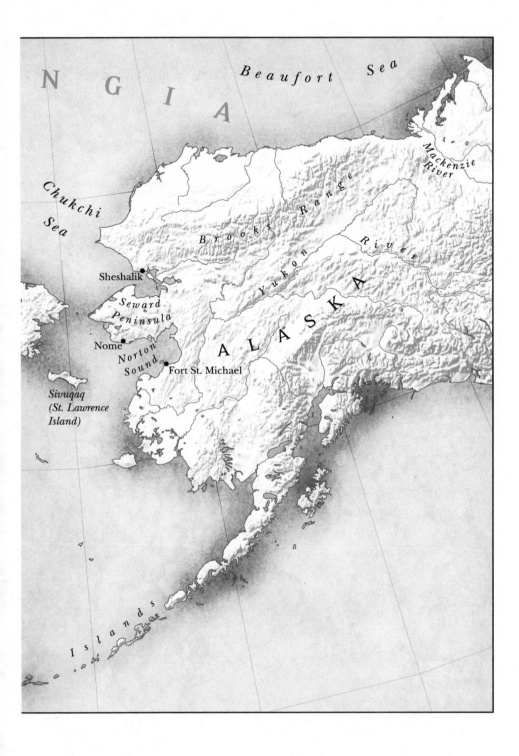

FLOATING
COAST

AN ENVIRONMENTAL HISTORY
OF THE BERING STRAIT

BATHSHEBA DEMUTH

W. W. NORTON & COMPANY
Independent Publishers Since 1923

"The Walrus and the Bureaucrat: Energy, Ecology, and Making the State in the Russian
and American Arctic, 1870–1950," *American Historical Review*, vol. 124, no. 2 (April 2019):
483–510. Reprinted with permission of Oxford University Press.

"Grounding Capitalism: Geology, Labor, and the Nome Gold Rush," in *A Global History of
the Gold Rushes*, Stephen Tuffnell and Benjamin Mountford eds. (Berkeley: University of
California Press, 2018): 252–72. Reprinted with permission of University of California Press.

For information about permission to reproduce selections from this book, write to
Permissions, W. W. Norton & Company, Inc., 500 Fifth Avenue, New York, NY 10110

For information about special discounts for bulk purchases, please contact
W. W. Norton Special Sales at specialsales@wwnorton.com or 800-233-4830

Manufacturing by LSC Communications, Harrisonburg
Book design by Chris Welch
Production manager: Lauren Abbate

Library of Congress Cataloging-in-Publication Data

Names: Demuth, Bathsheba, author.
Title: Floating coast : an environmental history of the Arctic / Bathsheba Demuth.
Description: First edition. | New York : W. W. Norton & Company, [2019] |
Includes bibliographical references and index.
Identifiers: LCCN 2019007096 | ISBN 9780393635164 (hardcover)
Subjects: LCSH: Arctic regions—Environmental conditions—History. | Human ecology—
Arctic regions—History. | Natural resources—Arctic regions—History. | Capitalism—
Environmental aspects—Arctic regions—History. | Communism—Environmental aspects—
Arctic regions—History.
Classification: LCC GE160.A68 D46 2019 | DDC 508.311/3—dc23
LC record available at https://lccn.loc.gov/2019007096

W. W. Norton & Company, Inc., 500 Fifth Avenue, New York, N.Y. 10110
www.wwnorton.com

W. W. Norton & Company Ltd., 15 Carlisle Street, London W1D 3BS

1 2 3 4 5 6 7 8 9 0

TO S. AND L. FOR THE WORLD,

TO S. FOR EYES TO SEE IT,

AND TO A. FOR MAKING IT HOME.

THE STRAITS

Ledum, Labrador Tea, *saayumik.*
A matted growth beneath the most shallow
depth of snow on record in all our winters.

Pausing upbluff from the edge of ice
I broke from branches leaves to pin
Between my teeth and tongue

until warmed enough for their fragrant
oil to cleanse you from me.

Somewhere in a bank of fog
beyond the visible end of open water,
alleged hills were windfeathered—

drainages venous. In routes
along the shore forever slipping

under, I am reminded—in the city
one finds it simple to conceive nothing
but a system, and nothing but a world of men.

Joan Naviuk Kane

CONTENTS

PREFACE:
ON NAMES

The people of the Bering Strait—Beringia—have many names for themselves. In translation, most signify that they are the true people. By the early nineteenth century, all the true peoples lived in many small nations. The term *nation* is imperfect, but captures the political autonomy, territorial sovereignty, and social distinctions that ordered peoples' lives. These nations came from three major linguistic groups: the Iñupiat (adjective and singular, Iñupiaq), the Yupik, and the Chukchi. This book uses those terms to refer to each people in general, and *Beringian* when referring to the three groups at once.

Everyone else is a foreigner. This term is deliberate: not all foreigners were racially white or ethnically European. Many were never settlers. In Alaska, not all were American by citizenship, just as in Eurasia not all were Russian by ethnicity or language. Norwegians, Poles, former African American slaves, Germans, Uzbeks, Native Hawaiians, and many others came to Beringia in the long twentieth century. What they had in common was an experience of

Beringia that, at best, spanned a few generations. Most had far less. I, too, am a foreigner, and write as one.

Places in Beringia also have many names. This book introduces those given by the original inhabitants first. They are replaced in the course of these chapters, as they have been on printed maps, by foreigners' names. The exceptions are large regional terms—Chukotka, Alaska, the Seward Peninsula, the names of seas, Beringia itself—that cross multiple linguistic boundaries. The original names will be strange to many, but then, strangeness is an experience of being foreign in a new land.

Below is a list of each original name and its colonial replacement.

Iŋanliq (Iñupiaq)	Little Diomede Island
Imaqłiq (Iñupiaq)	Big Diomede Island, Ratmanov Island (Russian)
Kiŋigin (Iñupiaq)	Cape Prince of Wales
L'uren (Chukchi)	Lorino
Qiqiktaġruk (Iñupiaq)	Kotzebue
Omvaam River (Chukchi)	Amguema River
Sivuqaq (Yupik)	Gambell, or St. Lawrence Island as a whole
Ugiuvaq (Iñupiaq)	King Island
Ungaziq (Yupik)	Mys Chaplino (later Old Chaplino), Indian Point
Utqiaġvik (Iñupiaq)	Barrow (now returned to Utqiaġvik)
Uvelen (Chukchi)	Uelen, East Cape
Siŋik (Iñupiaq)	Golovin
Tikiġaq (Iñupiaq)	Point Hope

FLOATING
COAST

Prologue

The Migration North

Each morning in spring, the sandhill cranes rise pair by pair from the fields and marshes where they rest, and turn their bodies north. They trill and honk on the wing, the sound filling the flyways of North America. By late April or May, they approach the Pacific Ocean's terminus, where the Seward and Chukchi Peninsulas reach toward each other across the Bering Strait. Twenty thousand years ago, during the last ice age, the water passing beneath them was land. People hunted mammoths and caribou across a corridor of earth. Now, cleaved by just fifty miles of ocean, a geological and ecological unity remains in the territory encircled by the Mackenzie and Yukon Rivers in North America, the Anadyr and Kolyma Rivers in Russia, and the oceans north of St. Lawrence Island and south of Wrangel Island. From river to river and sea to sea, geographers call this country Beringia.

I was eighteen when I first heard the cranes, standing on the runner of a dogsled eighty miles north of the Arctic Circle, on Beringia's eastern edge. I remember stopping by a lake to watch a pair dance. The light had come back, out of winter, running orange shadows onto the waning snow where the birds arched their necks, opened curtains of wing, and sang in throaty, chuckling harmony. We were both migrants from the Great Plains, the cranes and I. They came north to make from the brief fecundity of Arctic summer new feathers and new chicks. I came with less material longings: a Midwestern child raised on Jack London, I had visions of the Arctic as a beautiful but essentially static place to find nature untouched by people. My expectations were disciplined by an education that explained nature's past—geology, biology, and ecology—separately from human history, from culture, economics, and politics. It was a divide that endowed human beings alone with the power to make change; nature was the thing acted upon.

Living in Beringia collapsed this separation. I was apprenticed to a Gwitchin musher, a task that, in its specifics, was about sled dogs, but generally required learning how not to die. I did not know, when I arrived, that moose are dangerous when startled, or where to find blueberries, or the shape of an eddy where salmon congregate, or the color of the cloud that brings the storm in the season when bears leave their dens. Sandhill season. This did not mean people did not change things. Caribou died because we killed them. Dogs were born because we wanted their labor. We lived in a village built by people, from the cabins to the diesel generator that supplied electricity and the airplanes with their cargo of bread, soda, DVDs, tools. The village, by its very existence, was a testament to how people change each other; settlement, here, was a colonial figment, brought a century before by foreigners with their ideas of law, value, and the proper way to live. But those ideas, transformative as they were, did not alter the fact that the world I ran my dog team through was dense with action and transformation, only some of it human.

My host father and his country taught me two things I have carried in the years since. The first is that if we pay attention, the world is not what we make of it; rather, it is part of what makes us: our flesh and bones, and also our inclinations and hopes. In the Arctic, such attention is not an option but is necessary, and it yields appreciation for the precarity, the contingency, of simply being. The second is a question. In the north, I saw the power of people's ideas to change the Earth—to build villages, to legislate relationships with places and animals—while we simultaneously lived by rules whose origins were not only human. It left me wondering at the relationship between ideal and material, between human and not. What power do human ideas have to change their surroundings, and how are people in turn shaped by their habitual relationships with the world? Put another way, what is the nature of history when nature is part of what *makes* history? This question has been my companion across many subsequent migrations north. What follows looks to Beringia's past to find a way of answering.

*

It is good practice in the Arctic to know at the start of a journey what the way will be: the route you will take, how long you will be gone, and your purpose. Two days by boat, eighty miles down a river, to find caribou requires different tools and knowledge than dogsledding for a week to check traps.

The route of this book moves across the Chukchi and Seward Peninsulas, and through the territories of three peoples: the Iñupiat and Yupik in Alaska, and the Yupik and Chukchi in Russia.[1] In this wide country, the specific path is taken from the pattern of life made by the sun. For the past three million years, Arctic and subarctic Beringia has been so cold that ice and snow linger late into summer—and in places never retreat. The white surface refracts nearly two-thirds of sunlight back into space.[2] This pares down the land's productive ability. It is from solar radiation that photosynthetic bacteria and algae and plants take sunlight and, with water and air and soil, turn it into tissue. The energy in that tissue can then pass through the metabolisms of other organisms, from sedge grass to hare into the body of a wolf or a human. The death of one living thing becomes life in another. An ecosystem is the aggregate of many species' habits of transformation, their ways of moving energy from its origin in the sun across space and condensing it over time. To be alive is to take a place in a chain of conversions.

In the absence of solar gain, the chain of converting sun to flesh on Beringian land makes less energy than other terrestrial places; temperate grasslands fix three times more carbon, and forests over eight times as much.[3] But the seas are another matter. In their liquid seasons, the Bering, Beaufort, and Chukchi are some of the most productive ecosystems on Earth, home to organisms ranging from billions of microscopic plankton to hundred-ton bowhead whales. Some of this richness is only half marine, as walruses, seals, birds, and some fish build their bodies at sea and bring them to rest on the shore. Beringia has a particular geography of transformation, one where to note that the oceans are richer than the land is not metaphorical: a bowhead whale is so thick with calories, its body is forty percent fat by volume. A walrus is thirty. A caribou, maybe fifteen.

Human life in Beringia was shaped, in part, by the ways energy moved over the land and through the sea. An Iñupiaq nation like the Tikiġaġmiut killed enough whales to support a settled village, while the Nuataaġmiut, like my Gwitchin hosts who lived to the east, made a living on tundra where no one place had enough energy for stillness. Like the inland Chukchi, they were nomads. The borders between nations hummed with trade and war, moving the bounties of the coast inland, or the flint and caribou hides of the mountains to the sea.

Approximate territories of Beringia's nations, early nineteenth century.
Source: Ernest Burch Jr. Map by Molly Roy.

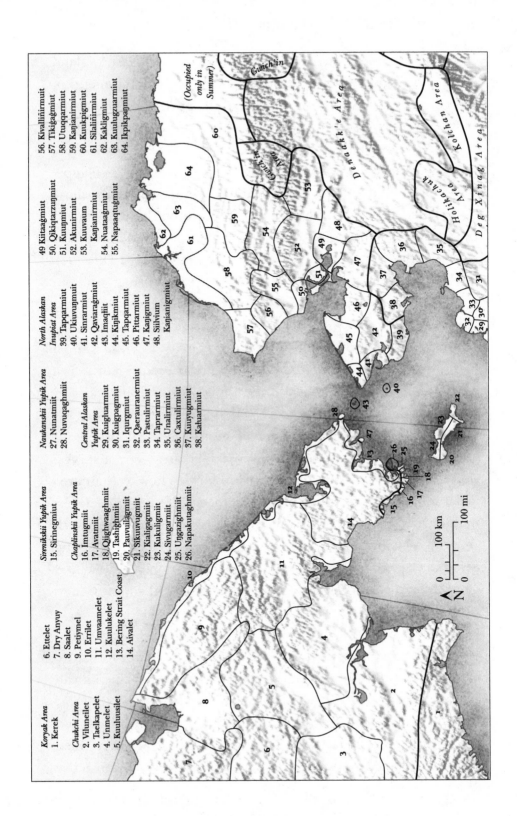

Koryak Area
1. Kerek

Chukchi Area
2. Viluneilet
3. Taelkapelet
4. Unmelet
5. Kuuluusilet

6. Ettelet
7. Dry Anyuy
8. Saalet
9. Petiymel
10. Errilet
11. Umvaamelet
12. Kuulukelet
13. Bering Strait Coast
14. Aivalet

Sireniksii Yupik Area
15. Sirinegmiut

Chaplinskii Yupik Area
16. Imtugmiit
17. Avatmiit
18. Qiighwaaghmiit
19. Tashighmiit
20. Pauvuilagmiit
21. Sikuuvugmiit
22. Kialigagmiut
23. Kukuligmiut
24. Sivugarmiut
25. Ungazighmiit
26. Napakutaghmiit

Naukanskii Yupik Area
27. Nunatmiit
28. Nuvuqaghmiit

*Central Alaskan
Yupik Area*
29. Kuighuarmiut
30. Kuigpagmiut
31. Iqurgmiut
32. Qaerauranermiut
33. Pastulirmiut
34. Taprarmiut
35. Unalirmiut
36. Caxtulirmiut
37. Kuuyugmiut
38. Kahuarmiut

*North Alaskan
Inupiat Area*
39. Tapqarmiut
40. Ukiuvuqmiut
41. Sinrarmiut
42. Imaqliit
43. Qaviaragmiut
44. Kijikmiut
45. Tapqarmiut
46. Pittarmiut
47. Kanjigmiut
48. Siilvium
Kanjianigmiut

49. Kiitaagmiut
50. Qikiqtarzugmiut
51. Kuugmiut
52. Akunirmiut
53. Kuuvaum
Kanjianirmiut
54. Nuataagmiut
55. Napaaquqmiut

56. Kivalliiniirmiut
57. Tikigagmiut
58. Uruqqarmiut
59. Kanjianirmiut
60. Kuukpigmiut
61. Silaliirmiut
62. Kakligmiut
63. Kuuhugzuarmiut
64. Ikpikpagmiut

*(Occupied
only in
Summer)*

Gwich'in

Denaakk'e Area

Kolchan Area

Holikachuk Area

Deg Xinag Area

Koyukon Area

N

100 km

100 mi

On that sea, in 1848, commercial whalers from New England crossed through the Bering Strait to kill bowheads for the energy in their blubber. The process they began is the focus of this book: the reduction of an ecological space, in all its complexity, to a source of commodities. When they had killed whales nearly to extinction, foreigners turned to walruses and foxes on the coasts. Then appetites moved inland, among caribou and reindeer, animals whose bodies eventually fed American and Soviet miners as they turned over the earth to find gold and tin. Foreigners followed in time the concentration of energy in Beringian space, and species. This book follows their pursuit of that energy, its five sections moving from sea to coast, coast to land, land underground, and finally back into the ocean.

The timeline of these journeys covers roughly a century and a half, beginning in the 1840s and ending near the present. It is a period as short as a wingbeat in Beringia's history: the seas and mountains here took millions of years to form; entire species— mammoths and beavers the size of bison—lived thousands of generations, then disappeared forever. Humans made a succession of societies across millennia, distinguished now by their artifacts: minute tools; carved figures with eerie, screaming faces; monuments made from bowhead whale ribs. In the thirteenth century, a civilization called the Thule spread from the Bering Strait to Greenland. Hundreds of years later, Iñupiat, Yupik, and Chukchi inherited their Beringian territory and filled it with new histories.

By the nineteenth century, each nation told that history differently, each with its own narratives of origin and transformative events. Generally, there were two kinds of past: what Iñupiat call *unipkaaq*, or myth and legend from a deep, indefinite, cyclical sort of time, and *uqaluktuaq*, or histories of wars, shamanic feats, and events in known, linear time. Both kinds of histories were filled with souls, beings of earth and sky and water that existed in active relationship with human persons. Some souls were animal, or animals who were once people; others were giants, or spirits without bodies, or rocks that spoke. All filled the world with action, leaving no neat cleavage between subjects who acted and the objects acted upon. Simply telling stories, which brought the past of these beings into the present, made both the teller and audience a conduit for souls.[4] A conduit of a past in which much of what made human history wasn't human at all.

What made the 1840s distinct in Beringia was thus not change, but new agents of transformation, the foreigners who arrived with their proliferation of ideas. From whalers killing for the market to bureaucrats trying to make borders between states to young Bolshevik evangelists promising utopia, foreigners came to Beringia with habits of mind born far away. They came as I had, familiar with temperate agricultural bounties and the industrial capacity to take the energy in things—trees, coal, oil—and turn it into propulsion and power. From these relationships of conversion, nineteenth-century authors from Karl Marx to Andrew Carnegie wrote new theories of time—theories in which objective laws moved human history from bare hunter-gathering life to the surpluses of settled agriculture, and onward to the possibilities for growth, freedom, and plenty unleashed by industry. This was the process of civilization, a telos of using ever more of static nature, ever more energy, to make things of cultural value. I was an inheritor of these theories, of a world in which entering the march of progress made a person human, and only humans made history.

On this, the particular human character of change, Marx and Carnegie and their diverse interpreters roughly agreed. They disagreed on much else. Their differences, after a period of market hunting, split Beringia between the ideological choices of the United States and the Soviet Union. The Chukchi and Seward Peninsulas, so alike in their hostility to agriculture and challenges to industry, thus hosted an experiment in how different human visions—Beringian, capitalist, socialist—met, mixed, divided.

Economies are a set of material relations, and also imaginaries of what is possible, desirable, and valuable. They are visions of how time operates, and what drives change. The foreigners who introduced markets to Beringia imagined progress as an upward historical trajectory, made by pulses of efficiency and innovation that increased growth. Profits, the measure of growth, were calculated in the short term: a quarter, a year, maybe a few years. Soviet socialists arrived in Beringia feeling both that they were behind capitalism and the need to eclipse it, to leap beyond into a world of greater liberty and bounty. Their means of acceleration was directed collective production, where plans broke down the next year or five into the number of tractors to be manufactured or walruses killed, each year with more than the last. Making more in the same period indicated speed, and suggested utopia was imminent.

In Beringia, these human ways of seeing time mixed with the times of the place itself, the lives of animals and cycles of seasons. Imported ideas of the future gave foreigners intentions about how to transform Beringia: to build a collective reindeer farm here, to claim a gold mine there. In the process, people rearranged land, dammed rivers, and altered the lives of whales, walrus, fish, caribou, and dozens of other creatures. From sea to tundra, the long twentieth century was filled with adaptations to the human intention to make a profit or fulfill a socialist plan. But to become action, to alter the world, human intention must leave the calm slip of the mind and voyage among other life. Whalers hunted bowheads, but over a few years, bowheads learned to avoid ships. Traders wanted fox furs, but every five years or so, the population crashes, taking the profits in their pelts with them. Over a decade, wolves eat the reindeer people planned to sell. Not all these ways of acting are the same; some had their own intents—the bowhead—and others, like flux in the climate, did not. But in

Tundra outside Egvekinot, Chukotka, August 2018. *Photo by the author.*

aggregate, they made humans but one subject among many acting in Beringia.[5] The scale of human transformations was often distinct, and faster than those initiated by other beings trying to convert energy from the land and sea. But even the grandest human endeavor was the mutual creation of peoples' ideas and the world around them. The capacity to act is *made*.

The following chapters trace what Beringia made of capitalism and socialism, and how modernity operates without the caloric ease of agriculture and industy. The critical events are not, mostly, wars or laws, but climate flux, or the life cycles of walruses and foxes. Looking away from what so often counts as history embeds people in the chain of energy conversions foundational to all life. From this perspective, capitalism and socialism are not laws of history that separate the human from the nonhuman; they are ideas about time and value that shape particular relationships with the basic matter of existence, matter that has its own influence over human ambition.

*

In autumn, the cranes take wing, each red-capped head turning south. On the hills beneath them, the brambles are crimson,
threaded with yellow where willows trace the course of streams.
The land is on the cusp of transformation by cold. Change came to
Beringia because the U.S. bought a territory called Alaska, because
Lenin took a train, because of world wars and world markets. But
change is always coming here, from the earthquakes that jumble
the Pacific Rim to the genetic drift of species over generations to
the seasons, rhythmic in their succession but abrupt in lived experience: one morning, you wake, and new snow has covered over
autumn. With or without people, there is no one moment when this
land and sea existed in some pure, unchanging balance.[6]

Yet this land and sea are also in the process of ceasing to exist in
the form we knew in the past. It is clear from whalers' logs and ice-
core samples and the open water that Yupik hunters see lapping
the Bering Sea coast in January that Beringia is warming. Like
earlier transformations brought by foreigners, climate change is
the unintended result of energy acquisitiveness, albeit for oil and
coal rather than whales and reindeer. The result is the problem of
intent writ large: people acted with the intent of driving a car or
bringing electricity to more homes. The sum of these actions now
alters the very bones of the Earth. But even if humans have collectively become a geological force, we do not direct the prospects
and dangers emerging from the diminished ice and permafrost.
"The earth," as Legraaghaq, born on Sivuqaq in 1912, observed, "is
faster now."[7] So fast that the land where I watched cranes not two
decades ago is no longer the same; the permafrost under the lake
where the birds danced has drained, its bowl filled with shrubs grown
lush in lengthening summers. Over the years spent writing this book,
my bodily experience of the place it describes has become its own

archive, a remembrance of consistent cold no child born today will experience.

The next ten chapters put this rapid present into the context of a less abrupt past. Each asks how capitalism, and the attempt to escape it through socialism, function when seen not just as human endeavors but ecological ones: What do the actions of whales, or the fate of mountains, tell us about the promises of modern economies? What do our ideas of time and progress do, out among other living things? It is, like any history, not the story but *a* story: many stories, in fact, as whales give different answers about modernity than mountains. And I write them as a foreigner, one who does not live in Beringia now, or speak for its many peoples. But if this history has a soul to pass on, it comes from the habits of mind learned amid northern seasons. First among them is to see the lives of other species and their habitats as worthy of our moral imagination and as inseperable constituents of our social worlds. To do so requires attention: to pay mind to the small scale—the sudden quiet before the bear breaks through the willow—as much as the large events, the season of wildfire or the turn in policy. It is in this play of people across Beringia's lands and waters, and the lands and waters playing back, that the past shows a full range of human relationships with the nonhuman. It is a vocabulary of consequences, and of possibilities.

PART I

SEA,
1848-1900

I seldom listen to only one voice.

dg nanouk okpik, *For the Spirits-Who-Have-Not-Yet-Rounded-the-Bend*

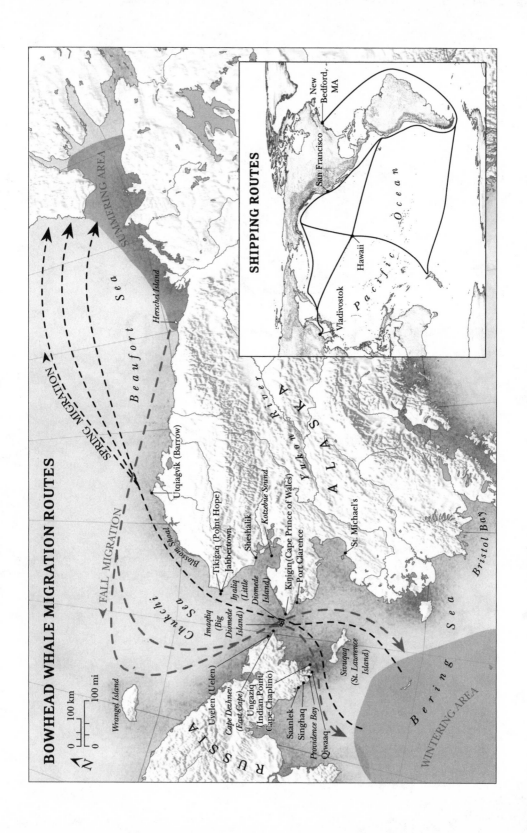

BOWHEAD WHALE MIGRATION ROUTES

N

0   100 km
0   100 mi

SPRING MIGRATION

FALL MIGRATION

SUMMERING AREA

WINTERING AREA

Beaufort Sea

Chukchi Sea

Bering Sea

Bristol Bay

Blossom Shoal

Herschel Island

Wrangel Island

Utqiaġvik (Barrow)

Tikiġaq (Point Hope)

Jabbertown

Sheshalik

Kotzebue Sound

Kiŋigin (Cape Prince of Wales)

Port Clarence

St. Michael's

Yukon River

ALASKA

RUSSIA

Imaqłiq (Big Diomede Island)

Iŋaliq (Little Diomede Island)

Uelen (Uëlen)

Cape Dezhnev (East Cape)

Ungaziq (Indian Point) Cape Chaplino

Saanlek

Singhaq

Providence Bay

Qiwaaq

Sivuqaq (St. Lawrence Island)

SHIPPING ROUTES

Pacific Ocean

New Bedford, MA

San Francisco

Hawaii

Vladivostok

1

Whale Country

Sometime at the end of the eighteenth century, a bowhead whale was born. It was late winter, the ice drawn far south in the Bering Sea by months of low sun and lower temperature. His mother had found an open place in the pack ice to deliver. In a shelter of air amid the inverted blue and crystalline ranges of ice, she lifted her pale calf for his first breath at the surface. All along the loose edge of the ice pack, other bowheads were giving birth. A quiet labor, a gush of blood, and a new whale slipped into seas that were home to over twenty thousand other *Balaena mysticetus*.

Spring sun moves the frozen edge of the Bering Sea north. The whales followed it, past the Bering Strait, the calf sometimes swimming, sometimes resting on his mother's back. Here and there amid the maze of solid water pushing down into liquid, they joined with small groups of other bowheads, the lead whale leaving a trail of exhaled bubbles to guide her followers. By June, mother and calf and their herd turned toward the Beaufort Sea, north of Alaska

and Canada, the passage of their backs marking the underside of
the sea ice. In the long, lazy days with no nights, the mother fed
and the calf played: a small breach, then swimming in expanding
circles. As summer drew down into September and October, the
whales turned again, westward to the Chukchi Sea, the calf grasping his mother's flippers as they moved. When the chill dark of
early winter thickened the pack ice, bringing the danger of sealing the mammals off from oxygen, the whales turned south. Half
a year into his life, the calf swam with bolder deep dives and long
gasps at the surface.

On this surface, the Beringian seas can seem barren—pewter
gray and raw with storms in summer, choked with ice through
sunless winter. But the Bering Strait is the terminus for the
world's deep ocean circulation. Water that began in the North
Atlantic arrives in the Bering Sea centuries later, dense with
nutrients shed by great rivers. Where the continents lean toward
each other at the strait, wind and undersea topography create
turbulence. Warm waters mix with cold, roiling iron, nitrogen,
and phosphorus upward. At the surface, these elements meet
with summer's abundant solar energy, with atmospheric carbon,
and with the organisms that make their cells from this mixture.
Where air touches water, over two hundred species of photosynthetic plankton give physical shape to sunlight. These algae and
diatoms are the Bering Sea's primary form of productive life.
Their teeming billions anchor one of the richest marine ecosystems in the world.

The work of plankton is the fundamental work of all living things:
to make more of themselves. Their cumulative transformation of
light into starchy tissue fills the sea with energy, the calories that
sustain over three hundred species of fatty, swarming zooplankton
in their many-splendored forms, from tiny shrimp and fish larvae
to mythology rendered in miniature: hydras, tentacled crowns,
things made of spines and sacs and jelly. The work of a whale is to

turn this diffused energy into hundred-ton bodies.[1] Their tools are their mouths, the jaws long as a rowboat and hung with sheets of baleen, more hair than tooth, to filter krill from water. In places, the plankton is so abundant that a whale can eat a quarter of what it needs for a year in six weeks.[2] It is from these tides that the bowhead mother grew her calf, making in fourteen months a ton of new life inside herself. After the calf was born, she labored for another year or more, turning sea to milk. She was not alone. Two hundred years ago, whales consumed half of the primary production of Beringia's seas.[3]

From all this energy, cetaceans took their own generative force: a bowhead makes many things in its marine world, among them, the communal lives of other whales. Even when swimming alone, the phrases of their songs hum and trill and groan, rasping like a creaking hinge, rumbling low, rising toward the high edge of birdsong. They may sing out to other whales when they find schooling krill, a small group forming a V-shape like a flock of geese, skimming forward with their great mouths bent to catch swarming copepods. Most of what they speak has no translation, no passage across the lines of species.

*

What does pass between the divisions erected by evolution is energy. With their flesh, bowheads made the lives of other beings. Some of the calves fed orcas.[4] And some fed people. Bowheads carry more calories per pound of flesh than any other Arctic species on land or sea. Even a year-old bowhead whale could nourish a village for six months. Yupik, Iñupiat, and coastal Chukchi in search of such sustenance were the first peoples to hunt the bowhead calf.

They were not the last. A bowhead can live for more than two centuries, and this calf was born when the United States had not yet purchased Louisiana and the Russian Empire owned Alaska, with Adam Smith's *Wealth of Nations* only a few decades old and the publication of Karl Marx's *Capital* more than fifty years in the future.[5] He would survive humans dreaming of utopia and courting nuclear apocalypse, the ideological and technological capacities of capitalist and socialist modernity trying to remake the world.

That the calf survived is remarkable, not just because two hundred years is a long time for a mammal to live. *Balaena mysticetus* were the lure that drew the industrial revolution and its ideologies into Beringia. Harnessing energy was the essence of that revolution. Commercial whaling ships were the vanguard, staffed with unlikely revolutionaries, men laboring to make a wage by transforming whale bodies into commodities. Their rituals of slaughter and profit are a study in the expectations of a growing market. They sailed into a place where whales were not for sale, but were understood as souls by the Iñupiat, Yupik, and Chukchi, who hunted them with expectations of a world constantly reincarnating and never easy to survive in. And there were the whales themselves, animals who, in the first years of this revolution, learned the danger of American ships and chose, with their behavior, to frustrate the desires of commerce.

I.

In late September 1852, two groups of whale killers met on Chukotka's northeast coast. A pair of Beringian hunters scouting the coastline near their fall camp sighted thirty-three ragged men limping southeast across the tundra. At first, the hunters kept their distance. They were outnumbered, without a common language. But Arctic desperation transcended speech. The crews' salvaged supplies—biscuits, rum, molasses, flour, the cooked remains of their pet pig, a makeshift tent—would not long stand the winter already bearing down from the mountains. The hunting party deliberated, observed, and opted for mercy.

The hunters knew something about the foreigners they divided between families in the walrus-hide tents of their winter village. Russian explorer Semen Dezhnev had sailed past in 1648. Vitus Bering landed a party down the coast at Singhaq eighty years later. James Cook and Joseph Billings explored the strait for the British Empire in the late 1700s, and two more Russian parties, led by Otto von Kotzebue and Mikhail Vasilev, came in the early nineteenth century. Cossack merchants traded at the Ostrovnoe rendezvous far to the west. And, for the past few summers, more ships floated off the coast, their sails like a new ice mirage over the water. But these pale, inefficient, shipwrecked sailors wanted neither war nor trade. Instead, they crouched in the winter tents, behaving oddly. Each morning, they tried to shave their growing beards. They recoiled from simple ceremonies with wild gesticulation. Their songs were hilarious. The village women had to sew their fur clothes and show them how to dress. Their stores of molasses and biscuit were delicious but insufficient. So the village housed them, clothed them, and fed them what the village had: whale.

The men were survivors of the wrecked *Citizen*, a ship come from New Bedford, Massachusetts, to join in the fifth season of commercial whaling. They were openly grateful to their hosts. Captain Thomas Norton later described them as showing "a degree of sympathy for us in our destitute and dependent condition wholly unlooked for, and altogether unexpected."[6] But gratitude did not make whale fat palatable. The American crew found the slippery, chewy stuff nearly unbearable, especially as they ate it raw, with no "further change in the promiscuous and offensive elements than what time itself would produce."[7] Taste—like attitudes toward bathing, sexual propriety, ownership, clothing, and religion—was one of many things Norton did not share with his hosts. Quartered close for dark months, examining each other through the smoke of seal-oil lamps, Norton and his rescuers were in the inaugural years of contesting which values guided life in Beringia.

*

The incommensurate ideals between whalers from New England and whalers from Beringia did not come from incompatible labor. Each made their living from whales' dying. The difference was in how they answered more elemental questions: What is a person? What is a whale? What is a whale's value? What will the future be? Norton saw that the whale was the "staff of life" for his hosts, but did not know how to ask much else. He did not even know what language they spoke.

Nor did Norton, sheltered in his tent, see how living in Beringia was an experience of constant change. One year, few geese come to their habitual lake. One winter, a storm surge brings the sea ice alive and pushes it hundreds of feet inland, crushing anything in its path. One moment, a hunter, crouched over a seal's breathing hole on the sea ice, is surprised by a polar bear. From experience of this temperamental material world, Yupik, Iñupiat, and Chukchi interpreted an incorporeal social realm, one in which few things had a permanent form, but most things had souls. Just as the future might be transformed by sea ice suddenly on land, souls could change their places. Shamans became whales and then people again; a person could start life as a walrus and grow into a boy; a powerful spell might make a man a polar bear for five days; caribou could have human faces. With no hard line between humans and other persons, land and seas were alive with sentience, judgment, and perilous whims. Existence depended on the cooperation of a will-filled universe.

Bowhead whales cooperated with human persons through a specific kind of transformation: by giving themselves over to die. Asatchaq, an Iñupiaq man born in the 1890s, explained eighty years later that whales watched people from their own country, or *nunat.* "'Those who feed the poor and the old, we'll go to,' the whales would say. 'We'll give them our meat.'"[8] They made this choice based on the moral worth and ceremonial care of the people who ate them.[9] Women spoke with the whales through solitary ritual, where the tongue of a particularly powerful shaman transformed into a whale's tail.[10] On Sivuqaq, Yupik brought meat to the sea, to feed the bowheads that fed them, while singing in low voices.[11] Without these preparations, the whales would tell each other that the humans were not ready, morally or practically. Unwilling to die for the unworthy, they would keep to their own country.[12]

If the whales left their country, they swam near Alaska in spring, and in spring and autumn along the beaches and headlands in Chukotka, where some Chukchi villages also hunted gray whales in summer. In these seasons, boat crews prepared the *umiak*, the walrus-hide boat that sheltered six or eight hunters on the cold sea. Each had a captain, often a man able, like his wife, to cast his soul into the country of whales, and skilled in the practical tasks of the hunt: making sure harpoons, ropes, floats, and spears were clean and bleached white, a color beloved of whales. Then the *umiak* crews went to watch, on the edge of the ice. Someone in the group always had an eye on the open water, where a black back might rise. A party could watch for weeks. They did not light fires or speak much. Each man wore new light-colored clothes so that they would seem to underwater eyes like part of the sky and ice. On Sivuqaq, women sent their husbands to sea with a prayer "that the hunters would go out as if transparent, casting no shadow."[13]

When a whale came, the hunters had minutes—seconds—to act. They knew the sharp hearing of bowheads, and so moved on muffled feet and with few words. An experienced captain might wait for the steamy rush of a whale's exhalation to mask the scrape of hulls against ice. As the boats stole toward the whale in silence, Yupik hunters watched for the animal to speak through its movement, signaling by the way it turned and dived how long the captain would live, and if it would choose to die.[14] Once the whale turned to dive again, the hunters addressed it. Paul Silook, who grew up hunting whales on Sivuqaq in the 1930s, described captains calling "out the name of the ceremonies, asking them to go ahead of the whale and stop it."[15] Iñupiaq men sang as their harpoons came in range.

If they closed on a large whale, the captain waited for it to offer a flank in the vulnerable moment of breath. Then the strike: the backward-curving barbs on each harpoon twisted a wound deep into the fat and muscle under the bowhead's skin. Bound by a cord to a sealskin float, dozens of harpoons held the struggling body to the surface, the whale's effort to escape working the points inward toward the heart or the spine. In a froth of frigid water and hot blood, killing the pinned animal might take most of a day. It was dangerous work. The whole great back could rise under an *umiak*, tossing its cargo into the cold spray. Gray whales, where they died for Chukchi hunters, were smaller but more dangerous. So hunters often killed yearlings or even calves of both species; a fast death, with one lance to the heart. Small female bowheads are so desirable, they have their own noun, *iŋutuk*, in Iñupiaq.[16] Sometimes, the chase ended with the whale living. The bowhead born at the end of the eighteenth century collected more than one harpoon in his first decades, carrying a museum of old weapons in his flesh for the rest of his life.

With the whales that died, hunters pinned still flippers to the corpse and pulled it toward the ice or land to butcher. Every person with an able back came, then, to haul it from the water. Once terrestrial, the body rose in a blue-black mound, blood leaching into the ice, leaving a tang of iron in the air as the whole village began working to separate skin from blubber from meat from bone. The tongue alone weighed a ton. Around the butchering, children chewed bits of blubber, their faces shiny with fat. Nearly all of a bowhead that is not bone was eaten, from the heart and intestines to raw skin that prevented scurvy.[17] Women packed meat into permafrost pits to last the summer. The blubber was stored to eat and

Iñupiaq whalers butchering a bowhead near Utqiaġvik, early 20th century. *Alaska State Archives, Reverend Samuel Spriggs Point Barrow Alaska 1899–1908 Collection, ASL-P320-06.*

burn in the lamps that warmed half-subterranean houses, some with rafters made from bowhead jaws.

As the great body came apart, it assembled social order. The carcass was divided according to rank: the choice fluke meat belonged to the first boat to land a harpoon, the flippers to the first and second boat, the lower jaws to the fourth and fifth boats.[18] Those with no share, the old and the unlucky and the widowed, were the responsibility of successful families, who gave of their whale as the whale had given itself—an act both practical and reverent, as it made a hunter and his wife worthy of leadership among people and worthy of future whale deaths. So did the days of feasting and ceremonies that followed the hunt, each nation with its songs and dances and particular offerings. Yupik hunters on Sivuqaq mixed the liquid from a whale's punctured eye with charcoal as paint for sacred designs on their whaleboats.[19] The Tikiġaġmiut nation in Tikiġaq offered the bowhead skull fresh water before rolling it to the sea, where its soul could journey home and transform, again, into a whale.

*

Around the same year that the bowhead calf was born, sometime at the turn of the nineteenth century, the Tikiġaġmiut nation itself nearly died. One summer, a boat filled with its people was ambushed by a party from Kiŋigin. Then the Tikiġaġmiut were attacked again, this time by inland people from along the Noatak River. The second battle was much worse. Half the Tikiġaġmiut, a hundred or more, died from spear and arrow wounds at a place they later called Iñuktat—"many people killed."[20] The survivors gave up much of their former territory.

The Tikiġaġmiut massacre was not isolated. Not long after, the island of Sivuqaq was raided from Ungaziq, less than forty miles across the sea on the Chukchi Peninsula. A man named Ngepaqyi assembled a thousand men in skin boats and "killed everyone, not even sparing the children," as Semen Iena told it.[21] Beringia was alive with political contest—for territory, trade, slaves, revenge, and over spiritual malfeasance. What else to do but war, when a powerful female shaman from a neighboring nation could kill by reaching a gloved hand into a special fire and pull the hearts of warriors from their chests? Or when Chukchi reindeer herders raided a Yupik village for slaves? Some of the violence was between nations of the same language; old women from the Iñupiaq Kiitaaġmiut nation were once cut into strips and left to dry on their own fish racks by men from the Kaŋiġmiut. Other times it was between languages, between Chukchi and Yupik, Yupik and Iñupiat, or Iñupiat and Chukchi. Along the Alaska coast, people still speak of Chukchi crossing the fifty miles between the continents to steal women. The history passed down through Beringian generations and foreigners' accounts in the 1800s is not one of primordial harmony, but of constant and violent transformation.

Eighty years after the battle at Iñuktat, Tikiġaq residents told a foreign whaler how difficult life had been in the aftermath, because "all the leading men, the great whalemen and skillful hunters" had been killed.[22] In communities that lived along bowhead routes, power within a village was constituted from the death and redistribution of bowheads. Political influence, the ability to take prisoners and territory, began with the human act of convincing whales to die, which bestowed moral authority and the practical good of caloric abundance. The survivors at Tikiġaq had to rebuild both kinds of power.

Over the next decades, they did: the younger hunters going out each spring, trying for whales. To hunt was "the acquisition, on each safe return with meat, of knowledge: the path of each journey, worked in with the knowledge pattern passed vertically down kin lines."[23] Time collapsed when hunting, as each participant, from the shaman calling the whale on shore to her husband with the harpoon, were the culmination of generations. Their gestures embodied a whole people's past in the service of the future. That, too, was part of the long answer Beringians might have given, had Thomas Norton been able to ask in 1852, to the question *What is a whale?* It made the darkness of the polar nights visible, the cold bearable, and stomachs satiable. It was a soul in life, a gift assuring human survival in its death, a means to power, a site of communal labor, a set of expectations and ceremonies, a theory of history.

II.

When bowheads part from solitude, they often congregate with whales close in size. When the whale born at the end of the eighteenth century left the company of his mother, he likely spent years migrating early into the ice field with other juveniles, the old bulls and cows coming behind.[24] In those decades, humans posed limited risk. People killed ten to fifteen bowheads every year in Chukotka and forty to sixty in Northwest Alaska.[25] No mind, human or otherwise, could imagine more. If the bowhead knew of human danger—if such warnings were carried in the refrains of his kind, or in his memories of his harpoon gorings—it was near shore. There was no menace in the open ocean. That is, until men like Thomas Norton came north.

A whale for the men on the *Citizen* had no soul or country. But a whale had value. If reduced to oil and baleen and shipped to New England, bowheads were commodities, natural objects just one sale away from currency. That currency could then become many things: personal wealth, regional power, investments in railroads or slave plantations or some concept of national glory.

The commodity value of bowheads came from the condensed energy in their blubber, primarily, and the properties of their baleen. In this, consumers of whales in New England and in Beringia were similar. But a whale killed by a Yankee ship in the nineteenth century was not desired as food. Instead, cetacean fats lubricated a mechanizing country: first, greasing sewing machines and clocks, and then the cotton gin and power looms. Baleen was useful for its "fibrous and elastic structure," employed in the manufacture of "whips, parasols, umbrellas . . . caps, hats, suspenders, neck stocks, canes, rosettes, cushions to billiard tables, fishing-rods, divining-rods . . . tongue scrapers, pen-holders, paper folder and cutters, graining combs for painters, boot-shanks, shoe-horns, brushes, mattresses," an array of consumer objects not yet satisfied by plastics or spring steel.[26] Refined whale tallow became fine-grade soap, a base for perfume, and filler for quality leather shoes. Orchards and vineyards used whale fat as an insecticide, as a wash to "prevent sheep from gnawing trees," and as a fertilizer.[27] The energy stored in blubber did not directly power industry—a duty serviced by waterwheels and the carbon stored in wood, coal, and petroleum—but whale products were critical to textile production. A single factory could use nearly seven thousand gallons—three sperm whales' worth—of oil in a year. Blubber was smeared on sheep before shearing, and on fibers to strengthen them for machine weaving.

Above all, the energy stored in whales became light. In New England, whale oil had been used as an illuminant since the 1630s. By the early nineteenth century, the demand for indoor lighting was growing alongside America's population, and the United States was not yet refining fossil fuels into lamp-friendly kerosene. Light came, for the most part, from animal fats or seeds. Whale oil, especially from sperms, produced the brightest light. There was no scent of bacon—a problem with pork tallow. Whale oil did not explode easily, like camphene. In the early sunsets and long winters of Boston, New York, Providence, and other eastern cities, whale-fueled lamps lit homes and factory floors, streetlamps and the headlights of trains. Whales guided ships home from lighthouses. Energy gathered from distant oceans became an intimate part of domestic and civic life for people who had never seen, touched, or tasted a whale.

What connected buyers of light to far-off whale corpses was the labor of thousands. By the nineteenth century, most of that labor originated on the Atlantic seaboard: Nantucket, Martha's Vineyard, Mystic, and especially New Bedford, Massachusetts, whose cobbled streets, brick insurance buildings, and split-shingled boarding houses launched several hundred vessels a year. Before he wrecked in Chukotka, Thomas Norton sailed from New Bedford. Like all the ships leaving the deep-water port, the *Citizen* was made of the surrounding country. Forests became planks and masts. Fields of hemp became sails. Iron became harpoons and knives. Fleece became felt to mat with tar on the hull, under a layer of copper to protect wood from sea worms and rot. The transformation of materials into a functional bark or brig or schooner—vessels classified by the number and position of their sails—required carpenters, caulkers, barrel makers, blacksmiths, rope makers, and sail weavers; organizing and paying them took agents, outfitters, and financers; sailing needed crews and captains; and processing the harvest was the task of refineries and buyers and marketers. In the 1840s and 1850s, twenty thousand people in New Bedford put their energies into work that was part of the dismembering and burning of whales.

All that blubber was money. New Bedford moved ten million dollars a year in raw product. Cetacean capital was never a huge part of the nation's production—despite what its boosters told Congress—comprising about one percent in the 1850s, and less by the 1860s. But it was the third-largest industry in Massachusetts, after the manufacture of footwear and cloth.[28] A few whaling families made fortunes from whale fat, and lent out their blubber revenue in industrial investments, in shipping, railroads, and textiles.[29] Concentrated energy became concentrated wealth. "Nowhere in all America," Herman Melville wrote of New Bedford, "will you find more patrician-like houses, parks and gardens," opulence that was "harpooned and dragged up hither from the bottom of the sea."[30]

*

As New England whalers harpooned their prey, nineteenth-century demand dragged them out across the globe's seas. By the mid-eighteenth century, New England crews could no longer find whales to kill near land, where the blubber was refined on shore. Shipbuilders adapted by making vessels able to render solid blubber into liquid oil at sea. The hunt then fanned into the Atlantic, ranging north and then south. In the early nineteenth century, the industry rounded Cape Horn to harrow the Pacific. Whalers reached Hawaii in 1819 on voyages lasting up to thirty months. Over the next twenty years, they moved north. In port, crews passed along rumors of good grounds in the waters off Japan and into Bristol Bay, then near Kamchatka.

Behind the whalers came the state. As one naval officer concluded, the American whaling fleet opened "to our commercial, and, of course, national interests, sources of great wealth" that the state then needed to shelter, as profit "cannot be brought into action without the protecting aid of government."[31] With Americans sailing—and sometimes wrecking—in exotic waters, the U.S. Navy moved forces into the Pacific. President John Quincy Adams told Congress in 1825 that this expansion was part of the United States encouraging "a flourishing commerce and fishery" and, through it, "assuming her station among the civilized nations of the earth."[32] Adams wanted the U.S. to muscle into the Pacific alongside the European powers that launched Cook and Bering, as an empire with growing knowledge of the globe. And in the Pacific, that knowledge came from whalers. In 1828, the Navy secretary compiled information accrued by whaling captains, a group "better acquainted with those seas than any other people."[33] When the government began an official survey of the South Pacific in 1838, with the goal of furthering "science, knowledge, and civilization," they did so at the urging of New Bedford captains who wanted better maps of seas in which they already hunted.[34] Fifteen years later, Commodore Matthew Perry arrived in Japan, following the lead of whale ships.

Being a whaling nation made the United States an imperial one, in the Pacific—an empire that saw civilization as having commercial potential, and commerce as having the potential to civilize. Whaling exemplified both, by introducing missionaries to "new spheres of usefulness" in "uncharted seas," and brought "the trade of the civilized world."[35] Making the world useful was America's divine cause. And so, whales and their killers made manifest destiny maritime. As the Navy secretary reported to Congress in 1836, "No part of the commerce of this country is more important than that which is carried out on the Pacific ocean. . . . It is, to a great extent, not a mere exchange of commodities, but the creation of wealth, by labor, from the ocean."[36] As labor improved land by farming it, in the theory of the time, so turning whales into oil improved the sea by making it yield currency. American oceans, like American land, were places of growth. For both the Massachusetts financer and the young republic's politicians, whale money was an abstraction that fed other, grander abstractions: commerce, national expansion, industrial investment, and a theory of history in which the past gave way to progress. Abstractions that hid the base fact that every dollar started in whale death.

*

Whales and their death were not abstract for men like Thomas Norton, whose labor made cetacean bodies into bottled light and distilled value. A voyage, to a whaler, meant years spent amid reek and risk. Whaling vessels wrecked. Sometimes, they caught fire. Ports of call featured strange languages, brawls, and unseemly diseases. Winds died and left ships fallow for weeks. Men's bones broke, wounds festered, scurvy threatened, bowels ran, and doctors were rare. Even taxonomic convention as to what their whale prey could *be*—fish? mammal? biblical terror?—remained open to debate.[37]

What was not in doubt was whales' value, the monetary worth of getting "a cargo of oil," as Captain Edward Davoll told his crew in the New Bedford harbor.[38] Responsibility for that cargo began with him; as captain, he was accountable for every barrel of rendered blubber rolled into the hold of the ship that he commanded but did not own. Most voyages in the mid-nineteenth century were funded by land-bound investors who diluted fiscal hazard by sharing ownership of a vessel and the expenses of outfitting a voyage. Captains were contracted based on their history of finding whales and managing crews. By mid-century, this meant knowing two oceans and the behaviors of any whales that could be boiled down into oil— rights, grays, sperms, and some humpbacks. Every decision the captain made was scrutinized, on his return to New Bedford, for its contribution to a profitable voyage. As Willis Howes, the bearded and sea-leathered captain of the *Nimrod*, wrote, "on the results . . .

hangs my Professional reputation as Master of a Whale Ship," a stress compounded by the fact that "the master is responsible for the misconduct or inferiority of every other man on board."[39]

Every other man on board could be any sort of man. Ships carried thirty-odd crew, of all classes, ranks, races, religions, and motives. Men from the Azores, Cape Verde, indigenous New England nations, and freed or escaped slaves met with New England sailors and crew native to the ports and islands visited along a ship's Pacific route.[40] "The crew seem to be somewhat of a mixed up mess 5 white 5 kanakas 2 portuguese [sic] 3 colored brethren with the cook who could be called black being the darkest one of all," wrote Mary Brewster, who sailed for the North Pacific in 1849 with her captain husband.[41] She was the only woman on board. Many ships had none. Experience also varied, as sailors were often recruited green. Walter Burns signed on as a member of the forecastle crew for the promise of "strange lands and climes, romance and fresh experiences," and "a pile of money."[42] Or, like Ishmael, they found no coin in their purses and nothing of particular interest on shore. These new sailors left in debt to the ship's financers for their oil-skins, utensils, shoes, and bedding, ignorant of route, duration, or expectations of the voyage to come.

What they found, often, was monotony; the days could be so similar, men marked them by the food they ate, itself a repeating cycle of bean day, codfish day, duff day, and bean day again.[43] Officers assigned men to smoke rats, scrub decks with lye, check the hundreds of yards of rope in the rigging, and patch sails. Shirking work, like swearing or drinking, caused the offender to be "seized to the mizzen rigging and flogged."[44] Sailors' chanties lamented oceans "sad and dreary," filled with whales "wild and ugly," and captains who yelled abuse—"let the buggers drown"—when crews failed.[45] The storms left men sick and, as one log described, feeling "like a tird [sic] in a pispot."[46] Many were homesick, carving stories of their desires in intricate scrimshaw.[47] "I wanted [a] little money," lamented the log keeper of the *Lydia*, "but I did not want it enough to come here and go through what I am now for it."[48]

It would be months before the *Lydia* returned to port. No captain would turn for New Bedford until their hold was full of oil, unless forced by calamity. Whaling labor was not paid as salary or wage. From the captain, down through the mates, blacksmiths, and stewards, to the greenest deckhand, each was paid a percentage of the cargo's value, or a "lay," upon the ship's return home. Captains received up to one-eighth of the net profit, while artisans and boat steerers received from an eighth to a hundredth. Cooks, experienced sailors, and other skilled crew might get a lay as large as a hundredth, while inexperienced seamen received as little as a two-hundredth share in the sale of their catch. Thus, each man had, as a report noted in the 1860s, "urgent, personal considerations to secure both for themselves and their employers the greatest quantity of oil."[49] To the crew, the value of a whale was in his share of its death. Every day without a whale was a day without even the promise of pay. Every day without pay was a reason to "*hope* ah yes *hope*," Captain Howes wrote, to find more whales, "that *hope* the Foundation from which springs all our aspirations."[50]

In 1848, a fifth of the world's whaling fleet was north of Hawaii, aspiring in seas already diminished to fill distant lamps.[51] Captain Thomas Roys, in the *Superior*, was among them. Three years before, Roys had been on Kamchatka, recovering from ribs broken by a whale fluke, when he heard a Russian naval officer describe plentiful whales to the north. Remembering this, Roys turned toward the Bering Strait.[52] Near Imaqłiq, his crew killed a new sort of whale: black, slow, exceptionally fat of body, and long of baleen. The *Superior* took sixteen hundred barrels of oil from just eleven kills. Six weeks later, Roys reported hope to the newspapers in Honolulu: cruising "from continent to continent, going as high as the lat. 70, [I] saw whales wherever I went."[53]

III.

Each year, bowhead whales sing new songs, filling the waters around the Bering Strait—the Bering Sea to the south, the Chukchi Sea to the north, and the Beaufort Sea to the northeast—with two or three distinct musical patterns. The bowheads mostly sing in winter, the seas gradually filling with the same chorus as whales dozens of miles distant pick up the notes. Such knowledge passed down through kin lines is the mark of culture.[54]

Humans can also move information rapidly across the sea. Roys's 1848 account brought fifty ships to the Bering Strait the following year. "The Arctic," Mary Brewster wrote, as the *Tiger* sailed north, "seems a long look, but from all accounts there are plenty of whale."[55] She found Roys did not exaggerate. On July 8, she recorded "a large number of whale," then "quantities of whale" on July 9, "plenty of whale" on July 10, "a great many whale" on July 11, "some whale" on July 13, and "any quantity of whale just come through the straits bound north" on July 14.[56] Later in July, the ship *Ocmulgee* was "Blubber-logged and whales in every direction."[57] The new "polar whales" were huge. A single kill might give 150, 200, or 300 barrels of oil, three times the yield of the average sperm whale, and sometimes three thousand pounds of baleen.[58] And the bowheads were "slow and sluggish beasts," often seen "moving leisurely," one captain's son wrote, "spouting with a regularity that indicated a peaceful state of mind."[59]

Yet, even with quiet whales, the labor of killing on the open sea was fierce, gory, and not always successful. It started with the watch, high in the rigging, waiting to "sing out for every thing [sic] that you see." Everything was every action of a whale: "There She Blows" at the sight of a whale's breath, "There goes Flukes," or "There She Blackskins" and "There She Breaches."[60] On the Bering Sea, sailors learned to look for "water . . . of a dark reddish cast caused by immense quantities of full grown shrimp," as whales congregated at these "greasy" places.[61] Some sailors claimed they could smell whales on the breeze.[62]

On sighting a whale, the crew lowered small wooden boats from the deck to the sea. Each was kitted with "irons," or harpoons, and sometimes bomb lances like giant rifles. As with bone or stone versions, metal harpoons might "point," or slip free, letting the whale go "off spouting good blood."[63] Whales dove. Or they fled with the boat dragging behind. "Be Careful not to hold on to your line hard," master Frank Horman ordered, "for by so Doing you will haul out the irons," but if the "whale is like to take your lines, then hold on hard."[64] One hunt on the *Francis* began with a strike at seven in the morning; then the whale "ran with [the starboard boat] so fast that the other boats could not catch them did not get him killed until 6.P.M. and they were then out of sight of the ship 14 to 15 miles to windward."[65] If a whale did not hemorrhage, it had to be killed at range close enough to "fire a bomblance into the region of the heart."[66]

Gunpowder made the work no less dangerous. "I have had my oar knocked out of my hand by a whale," wrote James Munger, "and the boat cracked and set to leaking, but I escaped."[67] Orson Shattuck considered his life "perilled [sic] every time that we are fast to a whale it requires great skill and judgment to kill one of those remorseless creatures," and "even the most skilled are sometimes killed."[68] Cephas Thomas, log keeper of the *Roman II*, met such a fate when "the Blow of the whale's flukes hit [his boat] edge ways which killed him instantly, the whale struck him the second time while in the water which sunk him."[69]

*

Despite the perils, it was usually the whale that died. As the crew towed a carcass to the ship and winched it half free of the water, they could assess what of its corpse would translate into a wage: a large "first-class" brown-skinned bowhead might get two hundred barrels of oil, while a "third-class" black-skinned bowhead only gave seventy-five.[70] To get the oil, the whale had to be flayed. With long-handled spades, the crew "cut in," paring blubber away from muscle. "The windlass squealed as the tackle raised the hook, the ship heeled over several degrees . . . and the blubber peeled off the carcass like so much birchbark," Ellsworth West recalled, "until all the blubber was stripped from the carcass."[71] The fat might be a foot thick or more, held as sheets by the dark skin. Whalers called these "blanket pieces." Suspended alongside oleaginous banners, slick with grease, the crew flensed but did not butcher, except when a calf looked "like nice beef" for supper.[72] Back in New Bedford or Boston, Americans had no appetite for whale meat. Other than blubber, only the "monster head" had value, for its "splendid bone"—the baleen hung "inside the mouth like a good sized room."[73] Once decapitated and stripped of lipid, the remaining tons, the muscle and organs and bones, were "set adrift to make a feast for the petrels, albatross and sharks."[74]

As the ship sailed away from the sinking wreck of whale, the crew faced days more labor to transform the fat piled waist-deep in the blubber room and a deck fringed with baleen into salable goods. They chopped whalebone into individual slats and polished off gummy flesh with sand—no woman wanted a corset smelling of rancid leviathan. Around the tryworks, the brick oven set into the ship's deck to render blubber, men took knives to the blankets of fat, cutting it so thin they called the pieces bible leaves, and fed them into the bubbling iron pots. Whalers had a taxonomy of fat: "dry skin" gave poor-quality oil; reddish-tinted or yellow oil was less valuable than clear white.[75] Young "green" whales had to be left "a day or two in the blubber room to ripen" before boiling.[76] Whales that were not flensed immediately or were found dead made for "nasty and stinking work" and yielded inferior black oil.[77]

Burning off water and straining out bits of skin from oil might take two or three days. Whalers sang as they worked—songs like

"Dixie" and "John Brown's Body" and songs about whiskey and Hawaiian women. They snacked on bits of deep-fried skin, which had "a rather agreeable taste, although it was much like eating pickled rubber."[78] All day and night, someone fed the fire with blubber scraps, melting down whale with its own flesh. Hoping for calm weather, as the trypots were a heaving wave away from spilling their boiling contents onto a deck already, West wrote, "awash with blood and gurry."[79] *Gurry* is the slime of offal and lard and remnant cetacean that oozed from sailors' labor. It made ship planks slick, as the men worked through the low sun of Arctic night, or when they burned fat for light in autumn. Over the sails rose a pall of boiling blubber and rancid flesh: "quite an offensive odor," one sailor wrote, "but I can bear it all first rate when I consider that it is filling our ship all the time and by and by it will all be over and we will go home."[80]

Home, and going there with money, was the common want of uncommon crews. When the *Francis's* log noted that "we are 9 months out have got nearly 800 bbls," and another "hundred cooking," it meant that safe harbor and wages were that much closer.[81] Whalers registered these desires in the ritual of the logbook: every day, a list of latitudinal and longitudinal distance from home; any day a whale was killed, the yield of oil and baleen, often with a stamp of the species inked into the margin. The combined thousands of barrels were eventually reported in industry newspapers and federal fisheries reports. Investors looked at such accounts to see if whaling had a future, if it would pay out for one year more.

Thus, from financier and nationalist booster through to cabin boy, the ceremony of bowhead commemoration was in tallying their reduction. It was a ceremony that also reduced the experience and knowledge of whalers. Crews were intimates of more than their own fear and suffering. The chase could be exciting and terrifying, but whalers also wrote of "the wild eye" of the "injured creature" they killed, and found the deaths "extremely painful" to watch.[82] Other sailors described the whales' "deep, heavy agonizing groan, like that of a person in pain" when struck.[83] The suffering was made worse, some whalers acknowledged, by their recognition of cetacean sentiments: crews described calves playing, mothers filled with nurturing affection, and whales manifesting "much sympathy for each other," choosing to "remain, usually for some time, with their dying companion" after a harpoon strike.[84] But knowledge of whale feelings, like whalers' own feelings, did not translate beyond the ship. No oil buyer on the New Bedford docks paid for emotion, any more than they paid for human injury. They sold light to people who could burn it with no knowledge of pain. Thus the "value of the prize," one whaler wrote, "cannot be sacrificed to feelings of compassion."[85] It was only as commodity that whales became useful to a sailor: a way to make a personal future, to buy another year's food and shelter. That was the value of a bowhead to Thomas Norton, his answer to the question *What is a whale?* It was the motto etched into many a scrimshaw: "Death to the living, long life to the killers, Success to sailors wives & greasy luck to the whalers."[86] *Greasy* luck to make greasy palms: whaler slang for money.

*

Sometime before the New Bedford ships came looking for grease, a man named Migalliq, from the Alaskan village of Tikiġaq, was captured by the Chukchi and taken across the strait. His captors did not kill him, but kept him long enough for him to see the copper they used for harpoon points. There was no such metal yet in Alaska, and Migalliq was impressed. But, the story goes, he told the Chukchi how slate from cliffs near Tikiġaq was far superior for making tools. That winter, before he walked home across the ice, he invited the Chukchi to come see for themselves. The next summer, they came, and gave rare copper in exchange for slate. It was a deception in value celebrated enough in Tikiġaq to be told down through the years, to the point that precise details—when? if?—are lost.[87]

Not lost is the wider sense of Migalliq's story: the importance
of exchange. Beringia's nations had wants beyond their territories.
Bowhead whale skin is delicious, but cannot make parkas, boots,
rope, tents, or boats. Places with many walruses have few trees. Caribou have excellent hides, but little fat. Trade turned blubber from
a whaling nation into soapstone for carving, wood for harpoon
handles, reindeer hides for clothing. And if ceremonies were a way
of asking hunted animals to return, trade was a way to compensate
if they did not, to take a season of plenty on the coast and help it
feed a lean autumn on the tundra. As war covered Beringia with
places of remembered violence and present danger, trade linked
nations in alliance and armistice. There were sites and times for
this exchange. At Sheshalik, in Alaska, hundreds of people came
by dog team and boat to feast, tell stories, marry, and meet surplus
with need. There were similar gatherings in Chukotka and on the
island of Imaqłiq. War ceased during the gatherings. To attack trav-
elers making their way with full sleds and boats was offensive.

It was through these trade routes and fairs that Migalliq's copper
came to Tikiġaq: it was Russian metal, likely from the trading post at
Ostrovnoe, on the western edge of Chukchi territory, hundreds of
miles from the sea. At the end of the eighteenth century, goods from
Ostrovnoe dispersed across Beringia; a Chukchi might exchange
furs for a knife manufactured outside Moscow, carry it east to barter
for foxes killed in the Alaskan interior on the island of Imaqłiq, and
sell the pelts back to the Russians for more metal. The knife might
work its way through Iñupiaq nations, while the Russians sold the
foxes to China. By the nineteenth century, there were other places to
trade for foreign things: Yupik living on the southern edge of Norton
Sound traded at the Russian fort of St. Michael Redoubt, and a few
rifles traveled into the eastern edge of Iñupiaq country, from British
posts far inland, along the Mackenzie River.[88]

It was this world that the Yankee fleet sailed into after 1848, expecting violence. Whalers' newspapers were filled with tales of cannibalism in the South Pacific, and they anticipated the same of the north. Some had read Frederick Beechey's 1820s description of Iñupiat "menacing our party," reprinted in Hawaiian newspapers.[89] So, when Mary Brewster was awakened, in 1849, by a sailor yelling, "the bloody indians are coming," she climbed up to the deck to find walrus-hide boats paddling toward the *Tiger* from the Chukchi shore and the crew assembling their weapons, "a few spades" and "four old muskets."[90]

The tension was unwarranted. "They wanted towack," Brewster wrote, meaning tobacco, for "they are all smokers & chewers even the children are extravagantly fond of it."[91] The men and women in their sealskin pants and caribou-hide jackets wanted trade, not war. In the first years of commercial whaling, the *Tiger*'s experience was not unique. Beringians approached with cautious interest, while whalers cultivated peace by giving needles and beads and other small things freely. The *Whalemen's Shipping List* called it insurance, so that vessels would have "[natives'] good will and aid in case any should be so unfortunate as to meet shipwreck upon their shores."[92] Trade exchanged things of value to Beringians with things useful to foreigners, in those early moments, even as the needs of each group remained invisible to the other: no Chukchi fingering a bolt of calico on the *Tiger* decks knew it came from a cloth factory with an endless desire for blubber, how the loom pedals ran smoothly from the same flesh that sustained Chukchi life. Just as Mary Brewster did not see, behind the demand for "towack," people assessing whether these new ships might be a reliable source for things they had used for more than a century, a way to gain leverage in trade. What came between foreigners and Beringians on the *Tiger*'s deck that day in June 1849, was "a large pack of ice coming." The ship was "up anchor" to avoid impact.[93]

IV.

Bowhead whales are animals of the ice. There are two main populations in the world, one in the North Atlantic and the other in Beringia, and both are adepts of polynyas and leads, the spaces where ice splits to reveal inky water to the sky. Bowheads navigate these rivers of air for breath. They sing out and listen for how the echoes of their voices map the frozen thickness above, warning of entrapment. When the frost catches them, bowheads will circle and splash, working to keep a channel open. If their way is filled by ice too solid to break, they retreat. These are their tools for living at the asphyxiating boundary of solid and liquid water.

Chukchi, Iñupiat, and Yupik hunters knew how to traverse the Beringian ice field: how to see in it the negative of what whales needed, the solidity to carry human weight rather than thinness that yields a whale's access to air. But for a copper-plated, wood-hulled sailing vessel, the ice was treacherous. In a night, a rime could grow over the ocean and clog the rudder. In a day, solid ice rumbled toward ships on wind and currents. "Early this morning the cry of land was heard which soon proved to be *ice*," Mary Brewster wrote, describing a few weeks later an "anxious day, for at one o'clock this morning the ice began to come upon us."[94] Sailors looked out onto ice hidden in April fog, or late-summer gales bearing icebergs able to pierce the thin shell holding up their home, their work, and their wealth. The whaling season was dictated by ice, beginning on its retreating edge in April, May, and June, tempting the gales that scoured its summer margin north of the strait into September. The bergs were "beautiful in the Rays of the Sun, as white as Alabaster or Snow, in all shapes," Eliza Brock wrote as her ship eased through loose ice, but "I shall feel quite glad when we get through it all."[95]

Amid that ice in 1849, fifty ships killed five hundred whales. The next year, nearly three times as many ships rendered more than two thousand bowheads into oil. For captains and crew, these tallies represented hope: the *Whalemen's Shipping List* proclaimed it doubtful "if so much oil was ever taken in the same period, by the same number of ships, and attended with so few casualties."[96] For boosters and officials like Secretary of State William Seward, the Arctic grounds confirmed the whale fishery was "a source of national wealth and an element of national force and strength."[97] Each year's growing tally of oil barrels was evidence of that future.

In 1851, more of the Yankee fleet sailed for the Bering Strait. They found different seas. The ice pack was thicker, slower to disperse in a cold summer. "Much ice in," one captain wrote. But more dramatic were the changed bowheads. The *Hibernia*'s log described "whales going into the Ice" when they lowered boats, repeatedly, on the 10th and 11th of June. Then, three whales evaded their hunters in the ice on the 22nd. Another escaped on the 29th. And so on.[98] Bowheads now identified whaleboats by sight; as a log keeper noted after a failed chase, the "Whale saw the boat and rolled away."[99] The *Whalemen's Shipping List* summarized the season as one of whales suddenly "few and wild."[100]

The next year was no different. If anything, the bowheads were wilder. The sounds of oars were "sufficient to throw [the whales] into a panic." When cornered, the animals dove away quickly, or swam backwards under the harpooner's boat. If struck, "the bowhead whale rubs that part of its body—in which the harpoons have been placed—against the ice."[101] Whales that had escaped a strike were especially canny; one recognizable for the steamboat-like whistle of his spout evaded whalers for years because he "always seemed to know when a boat was close to him" and would dive out of range.[102] Others, as the *Saratoga* log described, seemed to taunt their hunters: "16 boats charging one poor bowhead, who gave them all the slip, and went off shaking his tail at them as if to say 'oh no you don't.' "[103] The Yankee fleet began singing a new chanty, about bowheads "like spirits though once they were like snails / I really believed the devil has got into bowhead whales."[104]

Bowhead whales had learned that, against the Yankee fleet, evasion and ice offered an effective shelter. Only nine hundred were killed in 1851, half as many as the season before. A year later, Captain Norton disregarded reports of shy whales and assertive ice. His crew found bowheads "working quickly to the north," slipping from harpoon range into "loose, floating ice into which they went and shortly disappeared."[105] The *Citizen* was one of more than two hundred vessels the bowheads forced to sail close among the bergs. The fleet managed to kill over two thousand whales that season, but four ships foundered on the ice. Norton's crew was one; staying north of Chukotka in September, they killed their last whale in the early hours of the storm that wrecked their ship.

Nine months later, the *Niger* and *Joseph Hayden* rescued Norton and the rest of the *Citizen*'s crew after their winter in Chukchi huts. One sailor was overcome enough to drop to his knees and pray. The ships were deliverance: a return home, salvation from people with the wrong expectations of bowhead energy. The long winter had not eased the incongruence Norton felt among his saviors. Civilized people, he believed, did not eat whale; they killed them for profit and burned blubber to enlighten their homes. The Chukchi and Yupik devoured inch-thick bits of black skin with delight, but, Norton believed, had no mind to revenue, no "habits of industry" inducing them "to labor beyond their present necessities." They were confined to "listless and unprofitable" sameness, the mere "endurance of life."[106] Norton saw an immutable slog through blubber and grime. A people outside of time. That whales and their hunting contained history—a history of wars and ceremonies and trade alliances—did not pass the lines of cultures.

*

As Norton sailed home in 1853, several more ships passed too close to the ice and sank. A year later, only forty-five vessels sailed to the strait. A third of them ended the season having killed no

whales. The Yankee fleet retreated south. Over ten thousand bowheads likely remained in the Bering and Chukchi and Beaufort
Seas, and still died for Iñupiaq and Yupik and Chukchi hunters;
at least, the oral record contains no indication of whales fleeing
umiaks, and it is a record sensitive to such changes.[107] But no bowhead became commodity oil for the next two years. After three
summers of observing mass death, the value of the ice had changed
for a bowhead: the whales began using the floes as a tool against
slaughter. Their culture, at the surface observed by commercial
hunters, became one of choosing not to die for the market. It was,
perhaps inadvertently, a political assertion. Among people, there
was no shared answer to the question *What is a whale?* despite the
easy conversions of foreign tobacco to Beringian goodwill. Questions of value are political, containing arguments about how the
Earth should be valued and distributed in the present, and what
the future can be. They are human questions. But for a few years
in the middle of the nineteenth century, it was bowhead actions
that answered, rejecting market calculations that saw value only in
their blubber.

2

Whale Fall

No ecosystem is perfectly balanced, and all species develop tactics to survive change and avoid extinction. A diatom or small shrimp does so by replication and speed, making billions of creatures that live for weeks or months. Bowheads do so with care and slowness, by giving birth to few calves that they tend to for years. Their fat is an investment against shock; when production is rampant, they gorge; in a meager year, they eat less, and adjust their migration. By altering their consumption in space and over time, whales smooth the stochastic circulation of energy in the seas, so that places with whales are likely more stable than in their absence.[1]

By 1853, the bowhead whale born at the end of the eighteenth century was busy making more tons of himself. His life to that point likely spanned every American presidency and the reigns of six tsars, and seas grown dangerous with commercial hunters. Seven thousand bowheads had become oil in the first six years of dying for the market.[2] What neither the bowhead nor his various hunters knew in those ice-filled summers was how they were mere prelude to more profound change, to a revolution that would echo from the seafloor to the *iglu* roof. Over the next sixty years, industrial appetites drew down the number of bowhead whales to a mere three or so thousand. In their absence, a void: of calories for people to eat, of calves for orcas, of bowhead work in the seas. What filled this void, at least in human realms, was the state. Foreign sovereignty began in the absence of cetacean stability, as the first government patrols followed whalers north to police a transformed human world. The states of men came to replace a state of nature.

I.

In 1854, the American whalers were in retreat from Beringia's "fog, ice, and broken down hopes," as one whaler wrote, leaving bowheads to live and occasionally die for Yupik, Chukchi, and Iñupiat.[3] The commercial fleet turned to harrowing right whales in the Sea of Okhotsk, alongside a few ships newly financed by the Russian Empire. On calm days, captains sailed close to *gam*—a whaler's word for a social gathering of either people or whales. They talked about many things, according to their logs, from American politics to the morality of killing whales on Sundays. By the 1850s, they also discussed the future of whales, or whether whales had a future.

Commercial whalers believed, from their close observation, that whales were social beings with feelings, and had the intellect to try and keep their kind alive. As whalers hunted through the Atlantic and Pacific, they saw their prey learn. Right whales were "an utter impossibility" to kill, since "they hear a boat almost as soon as it strikes the water."[4] After a sperm whale stove in the *Essex* so badly it sank, in 1821, the species gained a reputation for vicious intelligence. Then there were bowheads, grown first "more and more shy," then "wild, restless, and suspicious," and finally seeking "refuge in the Polar basin."[5] It was this that made Willis Howes feel "a moral certainty that whale will be found [in the ice] as they are known to be north of us," rather than believe their numbers were reduced.[6] Facing such canny prey in so wide an ocean, many commercial hunters imagined whales not as decimated, but pursued into the awareness that would save them. The white whale, after all, survives Ahab.

Yet, by the 1850s, whalers were drawing another, less comfortable observation from the crow's nest and the killing boat. They knew whales had few offspring and grew slowly. They learned that when many "mere calves" were killed, a region would be "rendered useless as a cruising ground."[7] Shortly before Captain Roys sailed through the Bering Strait, a fellow captain warned that "the poor whale" was doomed by commerce "to utter extermination, or at least, so near to it that too few will remain to tempt the cupidity of man."[8] Charles Scammon, a whaler turned naturalist, wrote of cruising grounds "long since . . . abandoned, as the animals pursued have been literally exterminated by the harpoon and lance."[9] An 1850 editorial written from the perspective of a bowhead pled with whalers: "We polar whales are a quiet inoffensive race, desirous of life and peace. . . . I write on behalf of my butchered and dying species. I appeal to the friends of the whole race of whales. Must we all be murdered in cold blood? Must our race become extinct?"[10] Naturalists and sailors had witnessed the human termination of species before, from the dodo bird in the seventeenth century to Steller's sea cow in the eighteenth.[11] "Does the Whale's Magnitude Diminish?" asked a chapter of *Moby-Dick*. "Will He Perish?" In the 1850s, some gamming whalers might have answered *yes*.

Yet no one discussed ceasing the hunt. Much as whalers' observations of cetacean pain and social agony did not render into fiscal accounts, nineteenth-century legal and commercial ideas were not calibrated to the slow wildness of whale lives. The nouns for whales—bulls, cows, and calves—would have been familiar to English-speaking sailors as referents to livestock. But whales were not domestic, so there was no way to own one alive, to invest in its upkeep and harvest its progeny. All rights to claim them as property and sell them for profit occurred when whale parts became commodities. It made killing small whales, even calves "as practice for the boat crews," a sensible investment.[12] Thus, even with the words *extinction* and *extermination* in their conversations, the value of a whale was in present death. There was no entry in the accounting ledger for future cetacean lives.

But there was room, on that ledger or in the vision it gave whalers, to lean hard on the explanation of whale intelligence. It allowed captains to interpret absence as evasion, and evasion made absence into presence: a few whales somewhere signaled many others elsewhere. It was a theory in which whales had a future, and therefore so, too, did whalers' profits. More gams of whales, more gams of whalers. It just took learning to find them, a question of piercing what Melville called the "ultimate glassy barriers and walls" of the Arctic's "charmed circle of everlasting December."[13]

*

So, the men who killed bowheads for profit returned to Beringia in 1858. It was a particularly "cold, miserable, foggy place" that year, a foremast hand wrote, the ice never retreating north of the Bering Strait.[14] But more captains were sailing maneuverable barks, outfitted with light sails and better winches. With these ships, they began learning to move into the pack.

Then, in the 1860s, warm winds let the fleet sail in: dozens of ships, working their way into the Beaufort Sea, then westward close to Wrangel Island, north of Chukotka. They were nearly all under the American flag, again; Russian whalers never left the Sea of Okhotsk, for lack of the right ships, and they stopped whaling in 1863 for lack of right whales.[15] It was the Yankee fleet that learned to "steer clear, as much as possible, of large cakes of ice," Herbert Aldrich wrote, as a ship eased into a wide lead. Men hung off the rigging, "ready, at any instant, to wear or tack ship. As we wormed our way along there was a constant flow of commands: 'starboard!' 'steady!' 'port!' 'steady!' 'let her luff a little!' 'steady!' as we passed in and out among the cakes of ice."[16] Where the ice was too thick, whaleboats went ahead with small sails or paddled into crevices "in the ice that would just hold [the] boat" or allow them to pass through "soft, mush ice."[17]

In the early 1860s, such navigation converted over four thousand more bowheads to oil barrels. But learning the ice came with costs. In September 1871, autumn rolled down early, catching most of the Yankee fleet off the northern coast of Alaska. The chief officer of the *Emily Morgan* described "ice pressing in upon the land. All egress from our present position is cut off, both to the north and south, as the ice is driven up into 9 feet of water." Thirty-two other ships were "between the heavy masses of ground ice and land."[18] One, the *Roman*, was picked up, crushed, and dropped into the sea by two grinding floes, the sailors escaping with little more than their boots. Thirty-three captains, "having not provision enough to feed our crews to exceed three months, and being in a barren country where [there] is neither food nor fuel," abandoned their ships. Twelve hundred men dragged their whaleboats south along the frozen shore toward open water.[19] All survived, carried home by other vessels. Behind them sank $1.6 million in dead whale and rigging. Two dozen more ships would sink in the ice by the end of the decade.

The vessels that survived sailed south each fall with a profit below decks. It seemed like proof that technology, desperate ingenuity, and masculine courage would produce more oil. Or, as Captain Harston Bodfish wrote, "Success in whaling is entirely up to the man."[20] Bowheads had filled themselves with knowledge of human danger and icy shelter; the Yankee fleet, filled with need, countered. The *Whalemen's Shipping List* reported, in 1871, that the Arctic "was perfectly alive with whales. Hundreds of vessels could easily have been filled with them without perceptibly diminishing their number."[21] Half of Beringia's bowheads were, by then, reduced to profits and wages and piles of bone on the seafloor.

*

There were bowheads, but were there people to buy their blubber? In 1860, Captain Willis Howes, in a season of fogs and few whales, spent an evening gamming with Captain Low on the *Cynthia*. The two captains talked "about Pumping up Coal oil at the rate of 90 bbls per Day in fact Coal and its offspring oil was the all absorbing exciting topic of the day."[22] Whalers had been deriding the properties of camphene and pork tallow for years. But kerosene, refined from the petroleum deposits of the mid-Atlantic, provided a bright, stable flame. It did not smell. It burned in the same lamps that made light from blubber. And it was far less expensive than whale oil, and became more so as the price fell year over year.[23] By 1871, a gallon of kerosene in New York City cost twenty-five cents, between one-quarter and one-third the price of rendered blubber.

For people living on newly gaslit New Bedford streets and across the industrializing eastern seaboard, having a ready substitute for whale oil confirmed their faith in the progressive capacity of the market: for every lack or exorbitant expense nature generated— rare whales, expensive light—technical and commercial ingenuity supplied a solution. As the New Bedford boosters Zephaniah Pease and George Hough wrote, with the "inevitable decline of the whale-fishery . . . Fresh fields were sought for investment, and the capital for mills, factories, and foundries was at once forthcoming," a clear "manifestation of . . . enterprise and progress."[24] Petroleum allowed for growth, counteracting the "increase in population" that would have "caused an increase in consumption beyond the power of the [whale] fishery to supply" with "a source of illumination . . . at once plentiful, cheap, and good."[25] Whales, once they were barrels of commodity oil, had long been interchangeable with money. Now they were interchangeable with other forms of energy.

By the 1870s, petroleum caused whale oil prices to drop by half
of what they were when Roys sailed north.[26] *Vanity Fair* published
a cartoon of whales in evening gowns toasting "the discovery of
oil in Pennsylvania."[27] The *Whalemen's Shipping List* lamented that
petroleum had "a most ruinous effect" on New Bedford's primary
industry, but "the whales themselves will undoubtedly be grateful
for the discovery of oil which is fast superceding that hitherto supplied by themselves."[28]

Gratitude, for the bowhead born in the eighteenth century and
for his surviving kin, was premature. Fossilized sunlight replaced
much of the demand for blubber in the later decades of the 1800s,
but it did not do so completely. Some market remained, enough
that the *Whalemen's Shipping List* reported "no great change in the
consumption of oil" in 1879.[29] Most of all, there was baleen. "The

A sketch by A. Gabali showing bowheads, boat crews, sea ice, and
blanket piece being hauled onboard ship, 1906. *Courtesy of the New Bedford
Whaling Museum.*

inventive genius in vain has strived to supply an article which will fill the place of whalebone," one account described, "but none will answer the purpose."[30] The main use was corsets. As the industrial revolution liberated clothing from hand spindles and looms, fashionable dressing became a mass phenomenon. To be fashionable in postbellum America and Europe, a woman needed a corseted waist. Metal or cord worked for a cheap corset. But, as advertisers noted, strips of baleen provided the best "elegance of fit, style and shape."[31] The number of women wanting to buy the bourgeois propriety of an eighteen-inch waist surged—and with it, the value of bowhead "whiskers." The average set of whale jaws was worth nearly five thousand dollars in the late 1870s and early 1880s, "by far the most important feature of many whalers' cargoes."[32] Bowheads had not escaped distant desires.

II.

In the first decades of the commercial hunt, the Yankee fleet was of limited use and minimal threat to Beringia's nations. Sometimes, sailors gave away tobacco and beads; sometimes, they traded metal things for a few furs or fresh caribou meat; and sometimes, they required saving from their wrecks, but mostly they were too busy killing bowheads to spend much time at anchor. And if they threatened, Beringia's nations had reason to believe they could foil an attack.

They had before. Cossacks, the Russian Empire's hereditary military estate, built a fort on the Anadyr River in 1652 and raided northward in 1708 and 1711. "When they first came, our people were very afraid of them," a Chukchi man told the ethnographer Vladimir Bogoraz over a century later, because their "whiskers stood out like those of the walrus" and "all their clothing was of iron."[33] The cossacks were brutal, torturing prisoners and burning tents where Chukchi and Yupik refused to submit to imperial laws and taxes. The word for *cossack-like* in Chukchi became synonymous with cruelty.[34] Chukchi warriors allied with Yupik, and with Iñupiat from the islands of Imaqłiq and Iŋaliq, to try and repel the invaders. Hundreds died in battles during the 1730s; the cossacks, with rifles and metal armor, lost fewer than ten men.[35] But in 1742, two thousand Beringians, some with stolen Russian guns, routed the cossacks. Catherine the Great closed the Anadyr fort, too costly in blood and treasure to protect, and granted Chukchi and Yupik the status of "aliens not fully governed" under imperial law, allowed "to live and rule by their ancestral customs."[36]

Practically, the Chukchi and Yupik were sovereign. The same was true in Alaska, where the Russian-American Company rarely ventured north of Norton Sound, into the Iñupiaq country that Otto von Kotzebue warned could be dangerous.[37] Even exchange was on Beringian terms. Trade at Ostrovnoe, established after the cossack defeat, was invited by Chukchi wanting to buy metal and whiskey. In 1819, an American ship tried to barter on Imaqłiq, only to be driven away by Chukchi and Iñupiat uninterested in any disruption of their cross-strait trade.[38] By the time Roys killed his first bowhead, Beringians had spent two centuries forcing empires to recognize their values and convert goods on their terms. Why would it be any different with the "whisker boats," as the Chukchi called whaling ships for their beardlike rigging and hairy-faced crews?[39]

So, each April on Sivuqaq, hunters told each other, *Iya inglupiqaq atughanagniluku!* I will sleep with one eye open. Open for whales. Each whaling family made its offerings of codfish, roseroots, and walrus fat in ceremonial feasts where they ate whale from the last season, "fermented in the sealskin pokes" near the boat racks along the shore. It was, Lincoln Blassi remembered, "especially delicious."[40] No matter the whims of New Englanders, the value of bowhead flesh had not changed in Beringia. Baleen was part of that value; Chukchi, Yupik, and Iñupiat used it for sled runners, basket fibers, wolf traps, duck and ptarmigan snares, fish nets, snowshoes, parts of bows and arrows. Some was traded inland. But most whaling villages had piles of the pliable stuff carried over from year to year. With the prices of whalebone rising and whale oil uncertain in the 1860s, the racks of baleen leaning against walrus-hide houses were suddenly a reason to come ashore.[41] Whiskered men on their whiskered ships now wanted to buy the surplus whiskers of whales.

*

Trade brought a new kind of contact: sustained, face to face, with enough mutual vocabulary of word and gesture to establish intent. This much sugar for that much baleen, so many metal pots for a walrus tusk or a fox pelt. We "had to make a motion to understand each other," one Sivuqaq resident remembered, decades later.[42] In Chukotka, people had long practice in trading with foreigners at Ostrovnoe, so they arrived on whalers' decks with clear desires of the industrial world: rum, guns, tobacco, knives, other metal objects. On the North American coast, Iñupiat initially experimented with capture rather than exchange. At Tikiġaq, "the natives come on board us," Captain B. F. Hohman wrote, "and they were Very Noisey. They had some few walrus tusks and a good lot of Whale Bone and some skins for trade." On seeing they outnumbered the whalers, the Iñupiat became "Saucy" and "stole all they Could get hold of . . . and was in a fair way to take the ship." After losing the tobacco in their pockets and the buttons off their coats, the crew managed to clear the deck by gesturing with the "Big gun and pointed it at them. They hollered and went over the sides fast."[43] More than once, the Kiŋikmiut nation scoured vessels with small crews and "carried off whatever they wished."[44] But robbery was a short-term strategy. Negotiation could make ships' cargoes consistent, as a captain who traded without incident was more likely to return, bringing new riches from their country each summer.

The riches the Yupik, Iñupiat, and Chukchi wanted were those that did not come naturally to Beringia. Harbored at Port Clarence, near the place of the Sheshalik trade fair, the *John Howland* reported that "guns, rum, powder, knives, everything used in hunting is in good demand."[45] Firearms were prestigious and useful; whiskey titillating and novel. Most captains were not eager to trade in either. Carrying rum risked sailors' drinking, and carrying rifles risked sailors' mutinying. The few ships that did bring alcohol north in the early years of whaling found other hazards. "Rum was the cause," the *Whalemen's Shipping List* reported, of the first violent altercation between whalers and Chukotkans in 1852.[46] Near Kiŋigin, sailors blamed drink for a brawl on the *William H. Allen* that left the crew bleeding and fifteen or more Kiŋikmiut dead.[47]

It was also not entirely legal. In Chukotka, the Russian Empire still allowed cossack agents to trade whiskey for fur, but there were rumors of prohibition laws coming from St. Petersburg.[48] And by the 1870s, the Russian Empire only had foreign jurisdiction over half of the Bering Strait: Tsar Aleksandr II had sold Alaska to the United States in 1867. For the next decade, the territory was under U.S. military authority, which extended the Intercourse Act north. Written in 1843, the act regulated "trade and intercourse with Indian tribes," including banning the sale of repeating rifles—to prevent armed resistance—and alcohol. But whalers were unlikely to meet with patrols from either country. What stopped many captains, initially, was their belief that the liquor trade was immoral and unsafe. The "introduction of intoxicating liquors," one sailor warned, "does not advance the cause of civilization."[49]

But by 1875, commercial whalers had killed over thirteen thousand bowheads.[50] Rendered rare and hard to kill, whalers' methods showed desperate innovation: bazooka-like shoulder-loaded bombs, often unreliable in rough Arctic seas; a brief discussion of using poison.[51] The "enormous expense attending a whaling voyage in these times," the *Whalemen's Shipping List* wrote, "will require a much larger catch to make any favorable compensation for the owners of these vessels."[52] Baleen was becoming as hard to hunt as whale oil was to sell, except where it was piled in villages. This made the cause of civilization seem secondary to the cause of profit. Since the Chukchi, Iñupiat, and Yupik would not trade for what they did not value, ships began packing their holds with rum and whiskey in Hawaii.

Rum and whiskey, made from the fermented plant sugars of tropical climates, arrived in societies with neither the customs nor physiological tolerance that helped Russians and Americans somewhat moderate—or at least moralize—their consumption. In the Bering Strait, intoxication was new, desirable, and potently unpredictable. It could make whole villages dance for days and sing through nights. Or it could take the conflict between small nations and turn it inward, into what one man on Sivuqaq called "murder by drink." He remembered five-gallon liquor barrels rowed ashore, followed by sleepless nights keeping "very careful . . . watch" for people armed with rifles and a rage born of "terrible . . . whiskey."[53]

Terrible whiskey also bought other things from Beringians. Whalers wrote early and often of "extremely pretty" local women, "with glossy, coal-black hair, bright eyes, red cheeks, lips like ripe cherries."[54] It was not always an equal exchange of admiration. Men's beards made them look like "they were chewing muskrat skins," Mamie Mary Beaver recalled, "So the girls hid in the willows."[55] Other women had reasons—romantic, strategic—to seek the foreigners' advances, or might have folded crews into the local practice of exchanging or co-marrying husbands to transform ties of friendship into kinship.[56] Foreigners called this "wife-exchange" and viewed it with horror and titillation, but it was not coerced.[57] Nor was it remunerative sex. That concept was introduced by the Yankee fleet, which "induced [women] to go on board as the captains' or officers' woman" with payment in tools, cloth, and drink.[58] On the Chukchi coast, women learned to signal their availability by pressing their hands to their cheeks, mimicking sleep.[59] Some women carried more than calico and needles away from these encounters. One, named Pinanear, spent a season with the captain of the *Cleone*. The next year, the second mate described the whole fleet trying "to get a grimce [sic] . . . to see if the Child had any rezemblence [sic] to its Father."[60]

Not all women went with the whiskered men by choice. In 1913, J. G. Ballinger met an Iñupiaq woman who had been kidnapped as an eleven-year-old near Kiŋigin and "treated in the most revoltingly cruel manner" by the crew for a summer.[61] Her captor may have been E. W. Newth, whose habit of luring girls onto the *Jeanette* earned him the nickname "kindergarten captain" among other crews.[62] The wives of captains wrote with disapproval of ships that traded in women.[63] Newspapers reported that sailors were attacked in Alaska for being "unduly familiar with the native women."[64] Behind the euphemisms were other reasons to seek the oblivion of alcohol.

*

Even when consensual, relations between Beringian women and foreign whalers left behind a creeping, quiet violence: syphilis, a disease that sickened the newly born, weakened the healthy, and demented the old. In Chukotka, some communities had seen the disease among the Russians, and quarantined the infected. On the islands of Imaqłiq and Iŋaliq, people refused to sleep with whalers.[65] But these tactics were not universal. On the North American coast, whaler John Kelly reported that "the white people have introduced syphilis," causing "a blight that has almost swept some of the coast tribes out of existence."[66] A Russian doctor visiting Chukotka in the 1880s reported "syphilis, expressed in the most terrible forms," was common.[67] The Chukchi gave a syphilitic spirit the name *E'tel*. It took the form of small red people who pitched small red tents on human skin—or red foxes, returning to torment their trappers. The *E'tel* was not the only malignancy brought by sailors. Measles, scarlet fever, and smallpox crested and broke across Beringia, the final western terminus of the infectious trail of misery begun with Columbus. The diseases were so pernicious it was "no use to begin" ceremonies to "drive them away," one Chukchi shaman explained, "lest they grow angry and retaliate upon ourselves."[68]

Yet the diseases maintained their anger. And they came to villages where whales rose less often along the edge of the ice. Three decades of commercial harvests had taken the least volatile creature in the Bering Sea and made it rare, newly unpredictable. Even gray whales, killed in massive numbers far to the south, were scarce by the 1880s. Villages weakened by hunger were more susceptible to infection; infection made long, uncertain hunts less successful; lack of success made people hungrier. In some places, the compounding interest of the market's uncivil associates, famine and illness, tallied up to catastrophe. Most of the people in Chukotka's village of Qiwaaq perished, and in Saanlek.[69] In Alaska, the hungry and disease-filled years between 1881 and 1883 killed over half the Kivalliñirmiut nation.[70] The market had taken Beringian blubber and traded it back for empty metal pots.

Beringians knew of catastrophes—times of hunger, years when summer never came. Where they had the health to try, people looked for seals or caribou or hare to compensate for missing whales. Or they moved. But the market also traded back changed politics with its metal and tobacco. There were no longer enough coastal people to go to war—with each other or with foreigners. The sort of battles that repulsed the Russian Empire were things of the past, and with them went one Beringian tactic for surviving change. Grief was now the enemy. An enemy so great, some people reached for the oblivion of drink or suicide rather than face boats emptied of crews, unable to hunt in seas emptied of bowheads.[71] But most did what people in Beringia had always done: "in whatever way," as an Iñupiaq man explained decades later, "try and save themselves."[72]

*

Whaling ships saw the "ruined houses and depopulated villages" left like "a silent reproach to the white man, who came to the country bringing diseases in his wake."[73] One captain, shipwrecked in Chukotka, "felt like a guilty culprit while eating [the natives'] food with them, that I have been taking bread out of their mouths, yet although they know the whaleships are doing this, they still were ready to share."[74] If they killed a whale close to a village, whalers would often tow the flensed carcass to land. P. H. Ray described how the "American whaling fleet during the last twenty years has nearly exterminated" the bowhead, and "they will soon be classed among the extinct mammals, and with them will soon pass away many of the people inhabiting this shore."[75] But if whalers saw tragedy, they also saw the workings of fate: the end of whales and the perceived end of the "Eskimos" was part of a process that, if not exactly inescapable, was certainly irreversible. Even sympathetic foreigners could interpret the disappearance of people they considered "human anachronisms left over from the stone age" as part of some great historical evolution in which whalers were mere players.[76]

Players who embodied productive industriousness; whalers' labor made profit from the frozen seas, and their innovations made growth possible. For whalers and their boosters, this was as obvious as their ships. The center of Arctic whaling moved to San Francisco, where investors funded coal-fueled steamships to power into the spring ice in pursuit of more whales. Some crews chipped away at outcroppings of coal along the Alaskan and Chukchi coasts, but most burned fuel brought from Appalachia or the Rockies by train; importing one sort of energy to the Arctic even as they emptied whale oil out for Presidio lamps. A small refinery opened on San Francisco's Dogpatch wharf in 1883, its yard planted with ten-foot-high fronds of baleen waving dry in the sun, bound for eastern markets on the same transcontinental railroad that hauled coal west.

By the 1880s, the catch from steamships was more than twice that of vessels under sail. In these years, Harvard zoologist Alexander Agassiz warned that commercial hunting would render whales extinct within a half century.[77] But the steamships, like the light barks that first navigated into the ice two decades prior, made the hunt seem—possibly—not an issue of the "bowhead whale becoming extinct," but once again the evasive "northward movement of the whale."[78] Steamships followed that movement, hunting bowheads in the retreating spring ice, killing through the summer and long into the fall before icing into the Beaufort Sea near Herschel Island for the winter so that they could kill the first migratory whales in spring. Steam made whaling more efficient. And efficiency was the fulcrum on which progress was supposed to advance: it allowed for growth in profit, and profit allowed for further investment. It made whaling seem a business, one captain observed, like any other, governed by the principle of doing "whatever will make money or save money, that is the thing."[79] From this perspective, the coal-powered fleet showed that the whaling industry "has only just reached that secondary stage, common to all businesses, when circumspection, systematic information on prevailing conditions and rightful management" would assure profits.[80] If, as one San Francisco paper predicted, the "price of whalebone will go still higher," then "different methods of whaling shall be introduced."[81]

When the whaling industry was reduced to technology and demand, when whales themselves became mere obstacles to track through ice, what whalers saw on each cruise—the smaller whales, the days without a spout on the horizon, the starving villages— disappeared, at least for the world beyond Beringia, the world that demanded baleen. So the hunt went on, among bowheads now so diminished that even seasons of few dead whales and little profit were a gross cetacean loss.

III.

The habits of whalers long mixed the world: Atlantic Ishmael and Pacific Queequeg, pulling in common cause. As the commercial fishery ground itself against the ice, foreigners and Beringians mixed commercial and local ideas of work and trade. Foreign whalers, desperate to make their voyages less expensive, began hiring Beringian whalers: the men were experienced and did not have to be fed on the long journey in and out of the Arctic. Beringian whalers, desperate to make a living amid hunger and epidemics, joined to buy food and manufactured tools. In Chukotka, whalers became an easier source of rum and rifles and metal than Ostrov-

Beringian and foreign whalers scraping baleen aboard ship; the men in the foreground are wearing waterproof seal or walrus-gut coats; the girl on the left is eating the gum scraped off the baleen. *Courtesy of the New Bedford Whaling Museum.*

noe. "Shipped [hired] five Natives for the season," the *William Bay-lies*'s log noted in 1887. Five years later, the same ship paid a crew of Yupik whalers from Chukotka with "the old bow boat with an old sail and a set of oars."[82] Whole families might sign on with a ship, women sewing and cooking, men whaling. Some became permanent crew, their southern voyages making them the first Beringians to discover Seattle, San Francisco, Honolulu. On the Alaska coast, men would "sell themselves to the whale captains for whatever provisions they needed," one elder remembered, referring to the credit people would incur to buy supplies. "Then in April they would go back and whale to the person they sold themselves to."[83] In selling the self to kill the selves of whales, work became a thing divisible by units of trade and time, measured out in bags of sugar or rounds of ammunition.

If the value of a whale changed for some of the people killing them as paid labor, it did not end the rituals for most. The man named Ataŋauraq, who some in Tikiġaq said went insane after his child died, did stop observing whale ceremonies. But Ataŋauraq was distinct, a man known to rape and murder, to beat people into trading their baleen for just a little sugar. In the 1870s and 1880s, he curried favor with ships' captains by selling extorted whalebone until he alone controlled the supply of ammunition and flour in Tikiġaq. A leader, of sorts, but made so by violence, not from a successful hunt distributed among people. Ataŋauraq's behavior made him, as one villager described, "like a white man." He was eventually killed for his crimes.[84] Foreigners could not be repulsed now; they might even be useful. But there was a penalty for Beringians who did not live the values of their country.

Yet the new crept in. Peoples' mouths were full of strange words: *hana-hana* for *work* and *puti-puti* meaning sex, borrowed from Hawaiian; *mek-fast* for *fasten* and *spose* for *if*, from English; *kuni* from the Danish *kone*, meaning wife.[85] Foreigners renamed the Beringians they sailed with, substituting unfamiliar syllables with Cockney,

Samson, Big Mike, Sam Lazy—or the name of the ship that hired
them, making men literal hunting vessels: Thrasher, Rainbow, William Baylies.[86] Man and ship alike visited places named and named
again: Port Clarence, St. Lawrence Island, Cape Prince of Wales,
Shishmaref Inlet, Kotzebue Sound, Blossom Shoal, Providence Bay,
and Cape Dezhnev were all titles given by Vitus Bering, Otto von
Kotzebue, James Cook, and their imperial ilk. These were the titles
on whalers' maps, to which they added their own: Ungaziq became
Indian Point in English and Mys Chaplino in Russian. An Alaskan
river called the Hulahula, from the Hawaiian for dance. Beringian
names passed back, consonants smoothed off in passage: Uelen,
perhaps from the Chukchi *uvelen*, or "dark, thawed patch"; Kivalina, a Russian naval officer's misapprehension of the Iñupiaq
nation name Kivalliñirmiut. South of Tikiġaq, or Point Hope, killing whales named a whole new place: Jabbertown, after the many
languages of its residents—dialects of Iñupiaq, variants of English,
German, Portuguese, Hawaiian, and Tagalog.

Jabbertown was another commercial innovation, a settlement
foreigners established to kill whales from shore. The Tikiġaġmiut
refused to let sailors hunt whales from their village, so fifteen miles
down the coast, Yankee ships built sod-and-plank houses and hired
Iñupiat from the Seward Peninsula. It was not the only such whaling station; north, at Utqiaġvik, Charles Brower also bought baleen
and fur. And foreign whalers on shore needed help. As Clinton
Swan recalled, "those who know where to harpoon the whales"
and how to "put baleen in the water, soak it" were in demand as
hired labor.[87] So was the work of women: for the parkas, gloves,
and hats they sewed, the meals they cooked, the companionship
they provided. Whalers could be trouble—sometimes, they did not
pay; sometimes, they drank—but they could also become family.[88]
Joe Tuckfield married an Iñupiaq shaman in Jabbertown, adopted
an Iñupiaq child, and took on the name Yuuguraq.[89] Pausana
married whaler Heinrich Koenig. There are generations of Brow-

ers in Utqiag'vik. And Iñupiaq nations mixed, Kivalliñirmiut with Tapqarmiut and Imaqłiit. Converting labor to food and outsiders to family adapted old tactics of survival—trade and alliance—to new Beringian circumstance.

Some whalers looked at Jabbertown and other shore stations with moral reservation—over alcoholism, prostitution, miscegenation. Ataŋauraq was "a thorough terror."[90] But they also saw progress. The many things whalers found the Yupik, Iñupiat, and Chukchi to lack, from industriousness to cleanliness to a proper diet, could be solved with exposure to the market. Civilized people ate well in warm houses, wore new clothes, bought soap and books. They were enlightened by commodities. And commodities, at least when plentiful, came with a kind of independence: freedom from scarcity. Freedom from the need for whale flesh in particular: how was flour not just as good? Witness to new industrial marvels and the certainties of agriculture in their home ports, most whalers saw nothing revolutionary in making whales and wheat interchangeable. Independence from nature's particulars was a given consequence of civilization. Spreading commerce spread civilization, which made the world better by allowing more people more access to commerce. The logic was circular, but the concept teleological: a stark line of progress into the future. A line that allowed for the idea that people and whales were fundamentally separate beings, that whales had no country.

*

For the Russian Empire, whales did not have their own country, but they were, rightfully, a potential part of the tsar's. But along the Chukchi coast, "American ships engaged in whaling pay no attention . . . to where borders are drawn in the water," one regional official wrote, leaving "few whales on our shores." By the 1880s, Americans killing whales that should belong to Russians was cause for increasing imperial alarm. Russia had again tried to start a whal-

ing industry by giving a concession to Finnish captain O. V. Lindholm; his company built a small oil refinery on the Sea of Okhotsk,
killed a few dozen right whales nearby each year, and sold the
products in Japan and Hawaii. The industry could spread north,
except that the Americans' "ruthless destruction of sea creatures"
might foreclose on such profits forever.[91] As M. Vendenski wrote,
Russia had to protect "our stocks" before "it is too late to preserve
the possibilities for the Russian whaling certain to begin along our
Pacific coasts."[92] Imperial Russia, owner of Beringia in the eyes of
the wider world for over a century, was at risk of losing all "Russian
prestige in the far north," as one administrator wrote.[93] The empire
had already lost Alaska; now it lagged the Americans on its own
continent.

There was also a moral edge to the empire's critique of American whalers. Russian whales dying for Americans impoverished
Russians—or, at least, subjects who should properly, eventually,
and territorially be part of the empire. Yet, in Chukotka, Russia's
unconquered aliens suffered "illness by way of hunger, which origi-
nates in years with poor harvest of marine animals."[94] Alongside
famine were intoxication and the trade in firearms that might
arm peoples not historically friendly to the tsar. Americans "crept
into the Chukchi's trust," one regional official reported, "with
their spirits and guns, robbing and severely corrupting them."[95]
Another lamented how "American activity" on the Chukotka
coast "brings a huge quantity of hard liquor while slaughtering
whales."[96] Combined, the ships "completely depleted the land and
its inhabitants."[97]

Revolutions change who has power, and who sets value. The
whalers' revolution undermined Russian sovereignty: control over
law, space, fealty, prestige, energy, the meaning of the tsar's rule.
In 1881, a Russian gunboat sailed along the Chukchi coast, leaving bulletins written in English to inform sailors that it was illegal
to sell firearms or alcohol in imperial territory. Other patrols fol-

lowed, an attempt to excise the wages of whalers' values coming in from the sea.

*

To the U.S. government, a whaler in Alaska was not foreign. A whaler was not many things: a missionary, a statesman, a bureaucrat, a teacher, an explorer for God and country. A whaler was, however, a person with a reputation for drunkenness, brawling, and womanizing, despite "claiming the appellation of *civilized*."[98] Some hunted on the Sabbath. Ships were a Babel of languages and colors. Orson Shattuck, who shared the middle-class tastes of most government officials, shipped out on the *Eliza F. Mason* only to be dismayed by the crew—"as a class the most ignorant that can be found under American colors"—and a captain who "treated the laws of his country with contempt."[99] Whalers were commerce personified, willing to sell anything, hunt anytime, and buy the favors of local women. What kind of state followed such men?

The answer, for bureaucrats watching Alaska, was a state of anarchy. Calvin Leighton Hooper, on an early U.S. government patrol of the Bering Sea, reported that starvation was the result of excessive drinking and would "continue until some active measures are taken by the Government to remedy it."[100] Any temperance-minded official knew drunkenness was the adversary of development, especially as Yupik and Iñupiat were seen by the government as childlike at best, "primitive in their life and mental processes" much of the time, and "lazy, filthy, and worthless" at worst.[101] Washington bureaucrats, conditioned by nineteenth-century understandings of progress and race, classified Iñupiat and Yupik as "Eskimos," and Eskimos were a type of native, natives were in most ways like Indians, and Indians lived outside time, inside savagery, with inclinations to resist civilization. The federal government feared Alaska thus would follow the Great Plains into war. The whalers' practice of selling rifles "must inevitably lead to serious troubles, sooner or later," G. Otis reported to Congress in 1880. "Indian wars have been provoked by similar causes . . . the whites would go under unless aided by the military, and in the present state of the country there are no troops for the defense of Alaska."[102] Whaling ships armed a potential enemy within. So, in 1880, the U.S. government sent its own maritime patrols to enforce the Intercourse Act.

Whaling left a rent in Beringia's productive capacity, making an unpredictable world for both the United States and the Russian Empire: filled with hunger, untaxed whale oil, unregulated trade, an uncertain state monopoly on violence. All challenged basic assumptions of what a state was politically, what it should do practically, and its value as an agent of legal standards and moral progress. But neither government suggested an international moratorium on whaling. There was a model for an international treaty: the United States tried to negotiate protections for fur seals just to the south of Beringia in 1893, and Russia joined a treaty to shelter its own seal rookeries in 1911. But even in their national waters, the United States passed no laws to regulate whaling. Lindholm, shortly after he closed his company in 1885, called for protection of Russia's defenseless whales, but none came.[103]

In Russia, some of the neglect had to do with distance, a lack of quantifiable fiscal loss—the Russian whaling industry was minuscule and sporadic—and more pressing concerns closer to St. Petersburg: the assassination of Tsar Aleksandr II in 1881, financial instability in the 1890s, strikes and people reading Marx in the 1900s. To American bureaucrats, whales were a source—albeit a small one—of national profit. And to some, whale depletion and even extermination counted as a sign of progress. In 1898, the U.S. Department of the Interior compared whales to bison, "sacrificed for the fat that incased their bodies and the bone that hung in their mouths" to the point of the "destruction of the whale."[104] As the bison had surrendered to settlers moving west across the plains, the whales surrendered to ships moving west across the seas. There could be no protection from the inevitable.

Bowheads had brought stability to Beringians for centuries, their great bodies dependable in a volatile world. This dependence went unrecognized in the state response to the commercial harvest. The problem of whaling, for the United States and Imperial Russia, was not so much that it killed too many whales, but that it brought commerce while failing at civilization. For the U.S. government, that failure was the result of profits gone to the wrong things—guns, alcohol—and for the Russian government, the wrong things sold by the wrong people: the Americans. The solution was enclosure: borders that would bring an unruly market to sovereign heel. It was a human solution to problems both states saw only in human terms—alcohol, disease, even hunger could be solved by turning Beringia's wealth to better ends. Just as bowhead deaths were invisible to the people consuming them as light, bowhead life and the work it did was invisible to foreign governance—or, if not invisible, replaceable. Beringia did not need whales; it needed progress.

IV.

In death, either from old age or harpoon wounds, a bowhead sinks from the surface to the seafloor. A whale fall, bringing tons of fat and protein to a place of little light and scarce energy, sequestering the carbon in a whale's body away from the atmosphere. Over the carcass blooms a succession of organisms: sharks and hagfish first, then other small creatures, and finally bacteria specialized to feed in the anaerobic spaces of bone. Hundreds of species can make thousands of generations over decades on a single carcass, a whole world of lives. For part of the nineteenth century, these minute communities likely flourished on the skeletons left by commercial whalers. Then the whales ceased falling. Far below the human ken, commercial whaling left quiet, unsung extinctions.[105] What may also have died within the songs and culture of the bowheads is similarly submerged; humans can only imagine the loss of those eighteen thousand or more voices.

Before they were killed, the bowheads touched much of the life in Beringia's seas, the mechanical energy of their diving and the caloric energy of their bodies helping sustain beings ranging from bacteria to people. Commercial whaling was just one sort of production bound to whales, but one particularly unsuited to animals that give birth only a few times a decade. Despite the statements of faith regarding more whales just beyond the ice, bowhead time is slow. It takes years to strain the light fixed by plankton into tons of flesh. As a result, whaling could not obey the simple economic formula of innovation creating efficiency and efficiency leading to more production. With every technological adaptation increasing the speed, lethality, or range of the whaling kit, more whales died. More dead whales meant fewer future whales, which made future whale profits less certain. Efficiency could consume more, but not produce more. By the end of the 1890s, a good year for the industry was one in which fifty whales died. The remaining population was likely fewer than five thousand animals.

Yet, commercial whaling did not cease because the market recoiled from devouring the future of an entire species—and with it, its own prospects. The mechanism of capital had no such discipline: people buying corset stays and umbrellas were insulated from most knowledge of bowheads. Consumers did not know about whale time. What they saw was expense; the very rareness that came from so much death made baleen costly, so that in 1905, a season's take could pull in over ten thousand dollars. The *San Francisco Chronicle* called whaling "as big a gamble as Arctic gold mining. The profits are big when whales are found."[106]

Then, suddenly, there were no profits. In 1908, Charles Brower, who ran the shore whaling station at Utqiaġvik, tried to sell a hold full of baleen in San Francisco. He found no buyers. Later that year, in New Jersey, he toured a factory that made "thin steel, covered with rubber, vulcanized and polished." Spring steel, its manufacture worked out the year before, was a cheaper, industrial answer to the whalebone umbrella rib and corset stay. As had been the case for most uses for whale oil, baleen had become obsolete. It was "a grim truth," Brower wrote, that manufacturing had replaced whalebone, but also one that confirmed for him something about human ingenuity—the need for a "jolt . . . into trying out a new plan" for profits. The market's appetite for energy demanded whales in the early nineteenth century, then caused them to be hunted down until even their capacity to reproduce could not save them. And when bowheads became acutely finite, when growth became impossible, the market invented an inexpensive substitute that "worked as well as the real thing."[107]

It was the promise of American progress through commercial growth: for every lack imposed by, say, the absence of whales, engineering eventually filled the breach with petroleum and steel. The whaling industry became another footnote in the narrative of progress: more people had light, more people had umbrellas, fewer men died on Arctic voyages. The bowhead frontier could be empty so long as growth moved elsewhere. Nothing in that narrative reckoned with how whale profits were incommensurate with the cost their absence left in Beringia, in human lives and changed seas. Bowheads avoided extinction not because a new space opened in the accounting ledger to tally their worth alive. They survived because, in the world outside the strait, they ceased to have value at all.

Charlie Brower returned to Utqiaġvik and switched from selling whale to selling fox fur. He married a woman named Asiaŋŋataq. Their youngest son, Harry Brower Sr., was born in 1924. He would grow up in a transforming village, one where money replaced trade, the draft replaced shamans going to war, where the borders of the federal state replaced the borders of small nations; a village with churches and schools and government agencies. Harry Brower also grew up a whaleboat captain. In 1986, he became ill and was flown by airplane to the hospital in Anchorage. Far away from Utqiaġvik, he dreamed he swam with a bowhead. The whale explained how he had died, suffering from an explosive harpoon strike. When Brower woke, he told the story to his sons. In its details, it was the story of a whale the young men had killed the same night as Brower's dream, because "the whale gives itself to you," Brower explained. "If the good Lord wants you to catch a whale, He'll let the whale come right up to you."[108] Despite the transformations that had come to their village, Brower and his family still lived in whale country.

In Utqiaġvik, at the end of the twentieth century, one such hunt killed the bowhead born at the end of the eighteenth century. Among the Iñupiat, as among many Beringians, knowing a bowhead through the labor of its killing and the communion of its eating still has value. Nor have bowheads ceased to be. Their numbers are growing.

PART II

SHORE,
1870–1960

And, confronted by an unknown landscape,
what happens to our sense of wealth.

Barry Lopez, *Arctic Dreams*

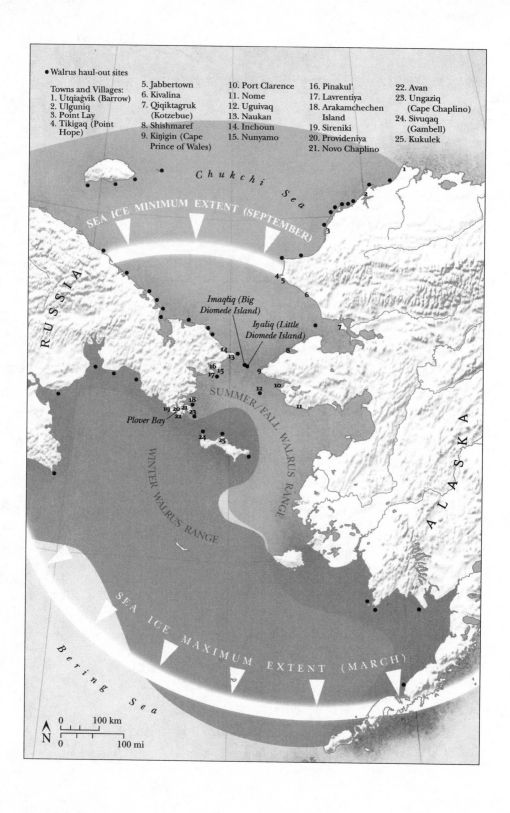

● Walrus haul-out sites

Towns and Villages:
1. Utqiaġvik (Barrow)
2. Ulguniq
3. Point Lay
4. Tikigaq (Point Hope)
5. Jabbertown
6. Kivalina
7. Qiqiktaġruk (Kotzebue)
8. Shishmaref
9. Kiŋigin (Cape Prince of Wales)
10. Port Clarence
11. Nome
12. Uguivaq
13. Naukan
14. Inchoun
15. Nunyamo
16. Pinakul'
17. Lavrentiya
18. Arakamchechen Island
19. Sireniki
20. Provideniya
21. Novo Chaplino
22. Avan
23. Ungaziq (Cape Chaplino)
24. Sivuqaq (Gambell)
25. Kukulek

Chukchi Sea

SEA ICE MINIMUM EXTENT (SEPTEMBER)

RUSSIA

Imaqtiq (Big Diomede Island)

Iŋaliq (Little Diomede Island)

SUMMER/FALL WALRUS RANGE

WINTER WALRUS RANGE

Plover Bay

ALASKA

SEA ICE MAXIMUM EXTENT (MARCH)

Bering Sea

N

0   100 km

0   100 mi

3

The Floating Coast

There is another kind of shore in Beringia, one in which the solid is not earth. Each winter, cold hardens the sea. Molecules lose energy, transforming liquid to solid. Ice crystals form, skimming the ocean's surface when the temperature drops to 28.6 degrees Fahrenheit. Wind and rising warm waters mix the crystals into suspension. As the cold deepens, crystals intertwine into a greasy film, thicken, and become slush. Sometimes, ocean swells ball the slush into lily pads of ice. Sometimes, the young ice rolls over the ocean's surface like an oil slick, still carrying enough brine to be elastic. Sheets of slushy ice slide and adhere to each other on the waves, condensing and exuding salt, until all that is frozen is fresh. A terrestrial brink floats outward over fluid water. It was these formations that Yankee captains feared: the slurry hardening around their hulls, then turning solid and opaque. Slabs of yearling ice will build four, five, six feet thick between October and May, hundreds of miles of sea covered over by a suspended coastline.

The transitions of water from liquid to solid to liquid again set the pulse of Beringia's marine and coastal production. In the ice, colonies of algae shelter in briny pools, piecing together cells from the sunlight that glints through. Krill graze these miniature marine pastures, even in winter. In spring, as the floating coast draws back toward land, fresh water melts off the ice, spilling krill into the sea. Algae blooms in the sun. Waves plunge minute life downward, feeding clams, transparent shrimp, red-armed brittle starfish, and pale and eerie king crabs, on into schools of cod, halibut, pollock, and mackerel. Up come some of these creatures in the bills of diving ducks.[1] Up come squid, their milky tissue caught in the mouths of bearded seals and walrus.

*

Walruses were the second sort of energy foreigners harvested in Beringia. In the late nineteenth and early twentieth centuries, commercial whalers killed walruses as a replacement for rare bowheads, taking yet more energy from the seas. Facing a deepening productive crisis, Iñupiat, Chukchi, and Yupik killed foxes and traded their fur for flour, expanding the revolutions begun by whaling, up onto the sea ice and out among fox dens, moving change from the sea inland.

It was over these changes that the United States and the Russian Empire tried what they had not with whales: to enclose energies and peoples with sovereign borders. They did so out of recognition that commerce, without a state to contain it, extracted too much energy and traded back profit too minimal to bring civilization. The market could not be trusted to make all values. Beringians also found value lacking in the walrus trade, and made their own borders and laws to shelter the herd from the restlessness of capitalism, from the quickness of its demands.

I.

Walruses are coastline embodied. They cannot eat without the sea, feeding a hundred or more feet underwater, where they root beds of clams and benthic worms from the mud. But they must breed and birth in the air. So the herds slide and wallow between, riding the edge of the sea ice south in autumn, then north through the Bering Strait in summer, sometimes leaving the ice to flop onto patches of sandy earth. Like whales, they concentrate rich seas in their bodies—over a ton for females, more than two tons for males. Walruses are not as fat as bowheads; the mussels they eat take their cut of the sunlight. But beneath inches of furrowed skin, a third of a walrus's body weight is blubber. They do labor no person can, transforming submarine muck into useful tissue and hauling it to shore, drawing a line of energy from the sea onto the solid world.

In Ulġuniq, in Alaska, and on the Beringian islands—Sivuqaq, Ugiuvaq, Iŋaliq, and Imaqłiq—and in Chukotkan villages like Ungaziq and Inchoun and dozens of points between, people tied their human being—their being alive—to the alchemy of eating walrus flesh. Walruses allowed people to live in seasonal villages in coves and bays and on barrier islands far removed from where bowhead and gray whales migrated near shore. In these places, walrus was a staple. And walruses were needed even where people did eat whale; families lived inside the hides of walruses stretched over the bones of whales, their homes made from what the sea gives the land and what death gives the living. Birth and laughter, sex and storytelling, dance and prayer, eating and dying formed a beating heart within these amalgamated coastal dwellings, reanimating skeleton and skin.

Walrus death, like whale death, began in supplication and ceremonies of welcome—what the Yupik called *Terre sek*, singing the animals closer to shore with "words about walrus, and the grunt is in the song."[2] Coastal Chukchi refrained from burning driftwood during winter, as the smell offended walruses.[3] The ceremonies were paired with watchfulness. In Ulġuniq, hunters looked for smudges of dirty-looking ice moving northward with the retreating pack, the brownish sign of a walrus herd at a distance. Before they went out in their skin boats, Yupik hunters in Ungaziq spat out the traces of old foods and borrowed a clean, respectful mouth from "the Old Woman of the Upper Sky."[4] Thus cleansed, Timofey Pangawyi explained, he could give the incantations of a successful hunt: "may my harpoon be flying right! May it reach [the walrus] quickly! May it hit the target. The birds, the wind, and the others that are near—may they not dare to interfere with this flight!"[5] Near the Chukchi settlement of Inchoun, men speared walruses on the pebbly beach. Around Sivuqaq, the shore men hunted on was the winter sea ice, crossed on foot or with boats dragged to an open lead. They harpooned walruses as they rose for air. "When first fresh meat was brought in everybody would be happy," Conrad Oozeva explained in the 1980s, "because everyone in Sivuqaq would get a taste of that new fresh meat. That's the way it was in those days when everyone lived together like one big family."[6]

Death had its rules. Before the butchering, hunters thanked each kill with offerings of fresh water and reindeer tallow.[7] Or bits of neck and head meat slipped back into the water "to turn to food near the walrus," in one shaman's words.[8] Once hauled home by boat or dogsled, women and men cared for the carcass. Flippers were put in a warm place to ferment, unleashing a thick organic reek. Organs were parceled out, each a delicacy, the blubber packed in permafrost ice cellars, the tough bits reserved for dogs. Women uncoiled and cleaned intestines, sewn later into waterproof coats and tent windows. The hides were so thick, most had to be split in two lengthwise.[9] Trade moved in boats and sleds bottomed with this skin. Men made war inside walrus-skin armor.

In quiet times, people carved tusk ivory into buckles, lures, fishing weights, combs, dolls, and amulets. Some tusks became invocations of their former selves, carved portraits of walrus-beings, many of whom were part human. The Yupik knew an old walrus woman, Myghym Agna, who controlled all life in the sea. Once, she kept the animals away from people out of rage over a broken tusk. The Chukchi called her Mother of Walrus. Keretkun, a black-faced, temperamental master of sea animals, ruled parts of the Chukchi coast.[10] On Sivuqaq, a woman named Agnaga went to live under the sea, in the house of rotund walrus-men, their faces naked of tusks in their cozy seafloor home. They wore their tusks only when swimming to the surface to die on the spear of a respectful hunter.[11] Walruses existed in a state of change: between human and not, between rage and sacrifice. Part of a universe in which, Nikolay Galgawyi explained in Chukotka, "Everything transforms into everything else—otherwise it cannot be."[12]

*

In the icy summers of the early 1870s, walruses began transforming into something new: money. The Yankee fleet waited on the southern edge of the pack ice, holds empty, staring across a suspended shore at walruses so numerous, "they looked like a vast herd of cattle resting after grazing."[13] Some knew that the *Cleone* had rendered oil from walrus fat in 1859, each carcass filling more than half a barrel. Working for oil when bowheads were absent could salvage a day otherwise wasted, in the terms of the logbook's profit tally, putting dollars to time. It took 250 walruses to equal a single bowhead, "hard work and how getting oil," the log keeper on the *Trident* wrote, "but it is all that can be done now."[14]

It took only a few years for the Yankee fleet to perfect the how of hard walrus work. At first, sailors tried clubbing, but the animals "flopped with surprising agility" into the sea.[15] Whalers then made spears and hooks, with more success.[16] At least until the herds learned of human danger: Walruses set sentries, animals that stayed awake to warn others in their sleeping piles of polar bears or orcas, and they learned to call out at the sight or smell of people. Walruses scarred from human attacks learned to "give warning to their neighboring associates," Charles Scammon wrote, signaling with "loud roarings, or if asleep, by pecking at [other walrus] with their tusks."[17] Mother walruses sheltered calves with their bodies. Sometimes, the "enraged animals," one sailor wrote, used "their heads like so many battering rams" against the approaching whale-boat, so "looking down we saw two pairs of walrus tusks protruding through the bottom."[18]

But the herd's tactics were limited. They could not cease need-ing air and water, so they could not flee their icy coast. They lay exposed when whalers learned to paint their boats white, wear pale clothes, and creep toward sleeping herds from downwind.[19] And they remained exposed when whalers began hunting with rifles. By the mid-1870s, crews killed hundreds in an afternoon with a bullet to each massive brain, guns so hot from firing that men dan-gled them in the sea "on a lanyard to cool."[20] The crack of gunshot did not even startle the walrus sentinels.[21] It sounded like fractur-ing sea ice.

As the rifle smoke blew off, sailors turned to cutting away blub-ber, chopping free tusks to sell as a poor man's substitute for ele-phant ivory, sometimes harvesting gallbladders to peddle in San Francisco's Chinatown as a treatment for silk.[22] For themselves, to feed their labor, whalers took a few hearts and livers, tongues for pickling, perhaps a bit of muscle to grind into sausage.[23] But most of each carcass was abandoned in blood-black heaps. The meat had no market value. John Muir, observing the hunt in the 1880s, compared walruses to bison, hunted nearly to extinction for their tongues.[24] Even after birds and bears and foxes gorged, a pall of rot rose off the ice.

It was not the only sort of industrial waste. Animals sank after being shot in the water. Sailors abandoned carcasses when seas "got so ruff," one log keeper described, that whaleboats could "not get

on the ice to skin."[25] Butchering spilled hot blood in such quantity
that the ice rotted from under dead walruses, slopping them into
the sea.[26] And commerce killed the future of the herds. Whalers
hunted mostly in June and July, when the ice floes were covered in
nursing females. When a crew killed a "whole herd of grown animals," one observer wrote, only "the little ones remain on the ice
hovering around the carcasses of their mothers until death from
starvation silences their moanings."[27] But there was no time, in the
calculus of the whalers, to let those mothers live; the pressure to
earn a wage on return to port required oil in the present. By 1886,
the Yankee fleet recorded killing more than 140,000 walrus, from
a population of some 200,000. Tens of thousands more died, the
sunken carcasses and starved infants becoming an untallied line
in the accounting books, in the mathematics that measured commercial growth.[28]

*

Far from Beringia, walruses were a minuscule part of imagining a
prosperous, mechanized future: as fan belts on power looms or grease
in factory cogs, or as the luggage for a train journey from San Francisco to New York or the tip of a billiard cue. Consumers saw no death
in their ivory buttons, unaware of the former creature that helped
enrich its ocean and might have expired defending its young. The
buttons were just one more sign of new wonders for purchase, of rising plenty. In Beringia, the tide pulled the other way, exposing a bare
shoreline. The market, having already made whale calories uncertain,
was doing the same with walrus. Any shock of weather or migration
now tilted coastal Beringians into precarity. The inaugural experience of industrial modernity in Beringia was one of profound loss.

Each place has its own story, its own etiology of how climate and
emptied sea and people formed into a tragedy. On Sivuqaq, a warm
winter in 1878 drove sea ice far from shore. "Everyone was short of
meat, on account of the poor year," James Aningayou explained

in the 1940s, so "everybody have a hard time."[29] The next year was cold, the ice too thick for walruses to surface near the island. Two years of hunger, and then an outbreak of dysentery. Of the fifteen hundred people who lived on Sivuqaq, more than a thousand died, either from hunger or illness or some combination of the two. In the village of Kukulek, whalers came ashore in the summer of 1879 to find people dead on the sleeping platforms in their homes. Some had collapsed while walking to the village grave site.

Sivuqaq was not singular. Along Beringia's coasts, hunger came to a village here, a nation there, across decades. In 1890, on Ugi-uvaq, an island whose two hundred or so people were sustained by walrus, Iñupiaq hunters killed only two. People ate their dogs and their boat covers and their boot soles, and still two-thirds did not see spring.[30] The Sighineghmiit nation abandoned three villages on the Chukotka shore for lack of living people.[31] The fate of whaling villages also became the fate of villages that relied on walrus. Forty years after Captain Roys sailed through the Bering Strait and gave the market its first bowhead, less than half of Beringia's coastal people remained.[32]

What explained this state change in Beringia? In Chukotka, a man named Ale'qat told Russian ethnographer Vladimir Bogoraz of a walrus-being who had for years brought abundant whales to people. Then foolish hunters attacked him. The walrus cursed his persecutors: "When you go to sea," he told them, "you shall be drowned. When you stay ashore, you shall die of starvation. When you have food enough, you shall be visited by the *tornaraks* [shaman's spirit] of the disease."[33] Walruses turned on their hunters because their hunters had turned against the order of things. On Sivuqaq, people knew the specifics of the violation, and kept its meaning clear across generations. In Kukulek, "Somebody [struck] a young male walrus," in Aningayou's telling, and pulled "it right on top the ice. Cut it up before it died. Kind of a cruelty, having a good time cutting that live walrus."[34] Estelle Oozevaseuk explained that "this thing they did had consequences." People in Kukulek dressed in their best clothes, went down to the shore, and told the sea they had been wrong. Then they crawled into to the bellies of their walrus-covered homes and died in their sleep. Their peaceful surrender, their deaths of repentance, turned "bad living to good living" for the next generation, with the lesson, as Oozevaseuk gave it a century later, to "never kill anything that is not eatable."[35]

Other nations had other answers. The Chukchi believed the foreign whalers were so foul, particularly their habit of burning driftwood, that they drove away the herds.[36] Iñupiaq parents told their children of bounteous harvests "before white men came to drive away the whales and walrus."[37] In 1901, a Yupik man explained to Bogoraz in broken English how people from Ungaziq went out for walruses, "seek em, hunt em, no nothing. By and by die." The reasons were Americans who treated walruses with disrespect, then sold liquor. "No good," he told Bogoraz. "American man plenty s[on] of b[itch]."[38] Foreigners killed too well, and not wisely.

Some of the American hunters agreed. "Carrying out this war of extermination" on the walrus, wrote Frederick A. Barker, a captain once saved by people in Uvelen after his ship was wrecked, "will surely end in the extermination of this race of natives." He vowed to never kill another walrus.[39] Crews debated the fate of whales—were they decimated or elusive?—but the absence of roaring, odiferous herds was obviously due to "indiscriminate slaughter."[40] Ebenezer Nye compared the walrus to the dodo bird. "I don't want or need money bad enough to go for the walrus," he wrote.[41] Calls for restrained hunting filled New Bedford and Hawaiian newspapers. But as the nineteenth century closed, whaling voyages risked returning with so little profit that crews earned a dollar each for years of labor.[42] The need for a wage required suspending the moral imagination. So, whalers repented in print and killed in person. Like fishermen and timbermen across the United States, their experience of modern plenty was restless, moving from one profitable species to the next.[43] The result, in Beringia, left both the mediators and survivors of market demand needing to replace the energy of the sea.

II.

An arctic fox wears its coastal disposition in its coat. Summers, their fur is dusky brown, fading to yellow-white at the belly—colors for a season spent trotting the beachside tundra, here snatching and sucking down a duck's egg, there whipping a lemming from its burrow, sometimes eating berries or seaweed. In winter, arctic foxes are brilliant white or pale blue-gray, the colors of the sea ice they follow as it expands. Their rapid paws skim over the jumbled landscape made by the pack. Then, a pause, to sniff: foxes can scent a half-gnawed polar bear kill from miles away or under feet of snow. If they are lost in winter, Iñupiaq hunters know to follow the blot of fox urine to where it marks the salvation of cached caribou or walrus, buried by blizzard. Ten or more foxes will track a carcass and congregate to eat the bones clean. The 1870s must have been a splendid time to be an arctic fox.

Even glutted with the market's dead, arctic foxes do not grow fat from their peripatetic scavenging. Most weigh less than twenty pounds. They sleep comfortably on the ice because of their pelts, dense at the skin and overlaid with silky guard hair. At the end of the nineteenth century, people a world away, in New York and Moscow, London and Beijing, desired these pelts. A sable cape or fox stole had long signified wealth, the luxury of constant warmth through drafty winters. In 1838, the Paris fashion house Revillon Frères expanded the fur market from the elite to the European and American middle classes with a line of ready-made fur coats. A decade later, Captain Roys reported the Bering Strait full of "valuable furs that could easily be purchased."[44] By the 1880s, walruses had dwindled like the whales; where hunters once killed fifteen or

Quwaaren (right) aboard ship, near Ungaziq. *Courtesy of the New Bedford Whaling Museum.*

even thirty thousand in a summer, they now took a hundred or less. Fur became a way to manage profits without blubber.

Quwaaren managed the whalers. He was a small Yupik man, born when Ungaziq was a small village, and had watched from his childhood the changing desires of foreign whalers. By the time Quwaaren had children of his own, trade in polar bear and arctic fox pelts was supplanting the whale and walrus oil harvest. In winter, he sold manufactured things—guns, traps, axes, knives, needles, flour, distilled spirits—to Yupik and Chukchi in exchange for ivory, baleen, and furs. In spring, when the ice pulled back from Ungaziq's pebbly cape, Quwaaren watched with a spyglass for whalers sailing in to exchange that ivory, baleen, and fur for more manufactured things. Some years, Quwaaren had tens of thousands of dollars in rifles, baleen, flour, ivory, rum, and hides in his three storehouses, their peaked wooden roofs and glass windows imported from San Francisco. There were profits enough to buy his daughters a gramophone and to dress his son in ankle boots and wool suits.[45] A son Quwaaren perhaps sent south to America, for school.[46]

All fur wealth began with fox labor: the long day trotting on the ice, the balletic headfirst leap into a drift at the sound of a vole. Transforming live foxes into commodities was Beringian labor. Foreigners did not harvest pelts. It was Yupik, Iñupiat, and Chukchi who dug pits in the snow and lined them with sharpened caribou antlers and bait, concealed by a thin piece of ice. Or set steel traps on land, where they would not drift away with the ice. Killing, skinning, stretching, and drying skins was an alternative to whaling for pay, but less disruptive than leaving for months at a time. Families could mix trapping with their usual ways of living: hunting seals, fishing, picking bitter dock and roseroot and berries.

Trapping was a new variation on the old pattern of trade; Quwaaren was a new variety of leader, one for a time when skill with foreigners was more important than war, when fur and what it bought mediated changing times. So, snares and deadfalls stretched from the haunts of arctic foxes out to the habitual paths of tundra animals: wolverine, sable, martin, wolf, red fox. Their skins were hauled back toward the sea by Chukchi reindeer sleighs, or by Iñupiaq families pulling a winter's take to the coast with their dog teams.

There were rules about killing foxes: their expiry could not be unthinking, or the animal's soul might cause a death in the killer's family.[47] But changing a fox's skin into something else useful was not considered waste, as the pelts became bread, ammunition, liquor. At Jabbertown and Utqiaġvik, Qiqiktaġruk, and all along the Chukchi coast, red foxes were the common denomination of this transformation: a pound of gunpowder was worth a full skin, a day of labor half a skin, a silver fox or set of tusks or a rack of baleen worth many. A pound of sugar: one-quarter of a red fox. A gallon of molasses: one and a half red foxes. A twenty-five-pound bag of flour: two red foxes.[48] Ivory carvers started making cribbage boards and curios for foreigners; an ivory dog team could equal many red foxes in its power to purchase other things. Through transmutations of flesh, men who trapped for trade, women who sewed clothes to fit foreigners, and children who learned to haggle in English, a fox killed fifty or eighty or a hundred miles from the sea replaced absent coastal energy. The demands of the shoreline were beginning to change the state of the land.

These transformations required learning the value of foreign calories. "When we were first introduced to white man's food," Robert Cleveland recalled, "everything tasted bad to us . . . we would smell their cooking and it did not smell good to us."[49] In Iñupiaq, terms for foreign fare were descriptive and disapproving: beans were *niliġuaq*, a thing that makes you fart; oatmeal was *siġri*, or dandruff; mustard was baby shit, and the word for bananas, *usuuŋnaq*, meant "like a penis."[50] Chukchi called mustard "bitterness," bread "powder-meat," and brandy "bad water."[51] But because it was what they could make, now, from the place they lived, people in Ungaziq and other villages survived on flour cakes baked in a bit of oil. Ataŋauraq, the violent leader in Tikiġaq, hired a Japanese cook off a passing ship for a week, so that the man could teach Iñupiaq women to bake.[52] Others began to make a soup of flour, molasses, and seal grease. By the end of the nineteenth century, thousands of pounds of flour and sugar came north each year, a trickle of calories back into an emptied sea.[53]

*

In 1886, Quwaaren bought a sixty-foot schooner, the *Henrietta*, off a whaler for two heads of baleen, a thousand pounds of ivory, five hundred fox skins, and three polar bear hides.[54] With a ship, Quwaaren could sail from Chukotka, hunt walruses at sea, buy furs in Alaska, and sell them back in Ungaziq. His plan never left anchor. While he was loading for his first voyage, the Russian gunship *Kreiser* sailed up the cape, found Quwaaren without proper documents, and seized the *Henrietta*.

The *Kreiser* was on its fifth annual patrol of the Chukchi Peninsula. The Russian Empire was alarmed by American whalers and wanted them out of territorial waters, but the fur trade was a more direct affront to sovereignty. It took place on land, and worse, it used animals that were the empire's historic source of power and wealth. Beginning in the eleventh century, much of the imperial treasury had been filled by selling sable, martin, ermine, fox, and any other desirable furred creature to the markets in Leipzig and Beijing. They were Siberian animals, trapped by indigenous Siberians: the Khanty, Nenets, Evens, and other "small peoples," as they were known in Russian. Their labor was generally compelled. Under imperial policy, cossacks and the trader-trappers called *promyshlenniki* found good fur country and took hostages— preferably someone important, or their children—from local peoples, demanding oaths to the tsar and annual tribute, or *iasik*, as ransom. The military trailed, building fortifications. "Small peoples" struggled to hunt what they needed while paying tribute and enduring the smallpox and syphilis and abuse that came with its extraction. When *iasik* depleted a region's furs and peoples, *promyshlenniki* moved east, tracking fur to the Pacific.[55] Making tribute for the tsar was as restless as making profit from the Bering Sea.

It was this way of enclosing empire that the Chukchi and Yupik repulsed in the 1740s. The post at Ostrovnoe was a compromise: the Chukchi agreed to trade if the Russians took no hostages, while Russian agents officially ignored how exchange was so "favorable to the Chukchee," it was "humiliating to the Russian Empire."[56] The stockade was the only place in Chukotka to press another imperial goal: that of civilizing "alien" subjects like the Chukchi by making them "Russian, not just in faith, but also in nationality" through Orthodox conversion, Russian education, and edicts not to over-harvest fur species while also paying *iasik*.[57] Imperial elites had long been concerned that Russia was backward, that it had come late and perhaps shabbily to European enlightenment. In the nine-teenth century, a generation raised on translations of James Feni-more Cooper saw in Russia's east a new world, a way to not imitate Europe, but transcend it by substantiating progress without capital-ist excess or immorality. Siberia could be Russia's American west, a place that made the empire's future by assimilating wild land and "complete savages" like the Chukchi, who lived in the "ignorance and degradation" of the past.[58] Ostrovnoe extracted wealth, but it was also the far edge of an aspiration.

In practice, Ostrovnoe was imperfect—there was "utter igno-rance" among the "aliens of even the basics of religion," one offi-cial wrote. But it was far better than the Chukotkan coast hundreds of miles to the east, where the empire had never managed to sta-tion an administrator. The few imperial officials to visit by ship in the 1880s sent alarming news. "Many of the Chukchi speak Eng-lish," N. P. Sokolnikov reported, "and along the coast there are many illustrations, Bibles, and other books of American origin."[59] Worse than the Bibles and rumors of Protestants proselytizing were rumors of Chuckchi armed with American cannons, preparing to invade Kamchatka.[60] Alcohol was everywhere. Furs and ivory "fell into the hands of those Americans passing by boat, or through their counterparts from the Chukchi," rather than going to Ostrovnoe.[61] Aleksandr Alexeevich Resin, who surveyed the coast in 1884, found "on average our shores are visited by thirty-one [American] ships each year, each vessel earning about 39,000 rubles" from trade.[62] Meanwhile, Beringians were starving or nearly starving. What tipped the balance toward not starving was, often, food traded by the very "foreign predators" who stole walruses and foxes in the first place. "The people who help us when we are hungry," the Chukchi told Nikolai Gondatti, "are not Russians. It is the Americans who trade flour and salt pork for our whalebone and ivory."[63]

Thus, the Russian Empire looked northeast and saw its aliens not fully governed, and at risk of becoming aliens governed by—and profiting—someone else. In 1879, Constantin Pobedonostsev wrote to the future Tsar Aleksandr III asking for naval patrols. "If we do not send Russian vessels to those shores," the councilor wrote, the Chukchi "will altogether forget that they belong to Russia."[64] The empire needed to replace English Protestant Bibles and Great Plains flour with Russian Orthodox Bibles and steppe flour.[65] Two years later, the *Kreiser* steamed north from Vladivostok on its first annual patrol. The ship was not tasked with preventing the walrus hunt or fox trapping, but with keeping Americans from landing to trade.[66] The Russian Empire did not want to stop commerce, but lessen its moral decay by changing its direction: ivory and fur should turn inland, to serve Russia's eastern frontier rather than become an extension of America's west. The empire needed to enclose the bodies of walruses and foxes and the people who killed them with the state.

*

On a clear day, when the *Kreiser* sailed along Cape Dezhnev toward Uvelen, the crew could see the state where the Protestant Bibles and Great Plains flour originated. Kiŋigin, on the spit of American mainland closest to Russia, was just fifty miles east. In 1890, two missionary couples, the Lopps and the Thorntons, arrived in the village. They called it Cape Prince of Wales, or Wales. Before them was a village of half-underground Iñupiaq houses and skin-boat racks on a low, grassy shore between the sea and a ridge stickle-backed with stone like some ancient animal. The reason to live so near the "vast, unbroken, terrifying silence" of the shore ice was to save "more than five hundred immortal souls," Harrison Thornton wrote, so "benefits may accrue to the world from their civilized and Christianized decedents."[67]

Missionaries came to northwest Alaska to change the state of Yupik and Iñupiat from damned to saved. They were paid in part by the federal government, a piece of an attempt to stabilize a coastline visited by few walruses or whales, but with excessive access to alcohol. Congress and missionaries wanted pupils "uncorrupted by ardent spirits," because ardent spirits turned furs and ivory into rotgut rather than into industrious, civilized trade in things like traps and soap and calico.[68] This effort was supported, by 1880, with United States Revenue Cutter Service vessels *Corwin* and *Bear*, which patrolled the Alaskan coastline each summer—looking for vessels that "traded liquors, breech-loading arms, and ammunition," G. W. Bailey wrote to the Secretary of the Treasury, "contrary to and in violation of law."[69] The federal prohibitions were, one Congressional report explained, necessary in Alaska, as, "armed with improved deadly weapons and crazed by drink, Indians are . . . converted into fighting men, prepared to make war between themselves and upon the whites."[70] So, the revenue service searched whalers' ships, when it could find them, and poured contraband whiskey over the sides.

On the shore, Ellen Lopp was supposed to teach resistance to the corruptions of rum in a white-painted mission house. Her teaching began with learning: she had to speak Iñupiaq, cook walrus, feed her children gruel squeezed from a length of seal intestine. As her Iñupiaq improved, she taught physiology, arithmetic, geography, and English. "We use seals for food, fueling, and cloth-ing," read one exercise she composed for her students. Followed by the phonetics of "Thou shalt have no other God before me."[71]

Converting Iñupiaq to English was the simple part of converting Iñupiat to Christian. In explaining the parable of Saul, Lopp wrote home, "I might have said he disobeyed God, but I don't know any word for disobey. These people don't use such a word much. They have no government to obey, or Bible."[72] She was not alone. Sivuqaq's missionary, William Doty, spent several weeks trying to explain "the sin of taking another woman for a wife," only to dis-

cover the "custom of having two wives" was stronger than his ora-
tory.[73] Iñupiaq and Yupik women went bare-breasted in the warmth
of their homes; soap was as novel as literacy; celebrations where
dancers gave "a hideous yell or screech" went on all night.[74] These
habits disquieted foreigners, who condemned them in their English
terms: witch doctor, devil, sorcerer, false sprits. The list of things
to change was long. In Qiqiktaġruk, Carrie Samms kept a tally of
ceremonies she saw disappear: the neglect of special huts in which
women gave birth; driftwood marking un-Christian graves burned
for heating fuel; fewer dances; less singing.[75] What one missionary
called "a blessed harvest of souls."[76] A log of moral dividends.

For the United States, the dividends were also fiscal. At the end
of the nineteenth century, federal policy toward Native people conflated Christianity with civilization, civilization with progress, and
progress with productive growth, which came from individuals taking raw nature and working it into valuable things sold for profit.
On the Beringian coastline, the market valued furs, fish, and ivory.
It was unlikely, Alaska's commissioner of education wrote, that
white settlers would labor at this harvest. But as a trapper or hunter,
"the native" could "assist the white man in solving the problems
of turning to use" Alaska's icy verge.[77] Leading Yupik and Iñupiat
out of "abject poverty, a burden to whites and a misery to themselves," and "toward self-support," required, according to Congress,
"careful supervision, instruction, and advice."[78] That was the missionary's task. It was why Congress helped fund their schools: to
stabilize trade, to teach the right reason to sell a fox. Individual
moral salvation made for national economic growth.

*

The revenue service stopped most years at Port Clarence, a comma
of land sheltering a deep harbor. One summer near the turn of the
century, as William Oquilluk told it, a shaman named Punginguhk
was arrested by the revenue service: the captain wanted "every witch

doctor" in "prison for all their life." Punginguhk knew the arrest was coming; he was the sort of man who knew things before they happened. But he went willingly aboard. The captain jailed him, after a trial in which Punginguhk "refused to let his evil spirits go." Then Punginguhk escaped: he flew through walls, dodged knives, made bullets fall from the air. When the *Bear* tried to sail away with Punginguhk, he called the winds to push the ship back into the harbor. Finally, the captain released him. In Oquilluk's story, it is a gesture of acknowledgement and respect.[79]

In this story, Punginguhk knew what the *Bear* wanted. The state, in order to be a state, had to seize power and set value. Missionaries and patrols came to supplant local ways of being married, criminal, wealthy, a good person. But to the revenue service, the tsar's navy, and missionaries—Orthodox, Protestant, or Catholic—Punginguhk's form of power was illegible; in the telling of the foreigners watching on the *Bear*, there was no flying, and no ship turned by command. They saw only "a rather lame affair" of a man who believed in false spirits, making a show of escaping some manacles.[80] Missionaries believed their message of earthly increase and heavenly salvation would inevitably replace such empty performing: after all, to its believers, Christian industriousness seemed universally true and transparently desirable. Who did not want more goods and more good life after death?

Yet Punginguhk was not alone among Beringians in his refusal of such enclosure. In Alaska, shamans threatened to kill other Iñupiat who converted. Some Beringians were reticent to share food with Christians or learn English. Along the northwest coast, there were prophecies that all the people who died in epidemics and famines would return as spirits to repulse foreigners.[81] Near Ostrovnoe, many Chukchi avoided priests and bureaucrats.[82] When Russian official Nikolai Gondatti told Yupik and Chukchi that he was their friend, "they shook their heads and asked, 'why do Russian vessels take from us guns, gunpowder and lead.' "[83] Some missionaries had a reputation for getting Beringian women drunk, to rape them.[84] In Tikiġaq, one word for the revenue service was *aŋuyaqti*: harmers.

Meanwhile, the wrong sort of commerce continued. People bought guns. They drank, sometimes with the very people who were supposed to police liquor, like the *Bear*'s captain, Michael Healy.[85] They drank, too, perhaps, to subvert foreign laws, to keep commerce on their own terms. The contraband was helped by distance and ice that allowed small trading vessels to escape the revenue service. Each spring, when the *Kreiser* sailed north from Vladivostok, it hit the wall of pack ice that ocean currents drove down the coastline; those same currents cleared the approach of vessels sailing from the east, out of Seattle and San Francisco, heavy with illicit goods. The ice helped men like Quwaaren, whose survival lay in turning foxes and ivory into rum and rifles, now made more expensive in Alaska by the revenue service's patrols.[86] Four other Yupik and Chukchi schooners began buying whiskey from Americans on the Russian shore in autumn, to trade for fur in Alaska come spring, when they, too, could sail east before U.S. patrols could clear the ice pack.[87] The same sea ice that was home to walruses and foxes, and because of them attracted commerce and its depredations, also repulsed borders.

III.

Much of what is an arctic fox begins as a lemming. Plump and gray, a lemming scurries from a patch of seedy grasses toward its tunnel; then, the fox snatches it. Or a seagull grasps the body in its talons. When an arctic fox eats a gull's egg out of a spring nest, it, too, is part lemming. Lemmings bear the Arctic by living quickly—always moving, dying after three or four summers. They eat and breed through the winter, so profligate that their numbers bulge outside the limits of Arctic vegetation every few years. Fox numbers follow the lemmings.[88] When there are few lemmings, foxes have small litters and their populations decline precipitously; when there are many rodents, a fox can birth a dozen kits in a summer. A female walrus might have that many calves over her forty-year lifetime. But walruses, when not hunted to the quick, build longevity into their fat bodies; born infrequently, they die slowly. Foxes were an erratic replacement for walrus. Stability did not follow the fur trade.

By the turn of the twentieth century, American missionaries and bureaucrats were aware that fur commerce, even if stripped of alcohol, did not prevent starvation. Ellen Lopp lamented that hunger periodically "hinders our work. Think of teaching the lesson about 'hungry and ye fed me not' to a Sunday School class, the members of which hadn't had half a dozen square meals since the Sunday before."[89] A missionary at Qiqiktaġruk reported a "great many calls for food."[90] In 1899, traders and missionaries in the village petitioned the secretary of the interior to send relief. It was a short year for fox, and with few "fur-bearing animals" or walruses, the Iñupiat faced "great destitution."[91]

Federal officials opposed direct material aid. "The experience of the Government in feeding the Indian tribes of the West," the commissioner of education replied to the petitioners, showed that "if the natives find that they can be relieved by the Government they will cease to do what they can to help themselves."[92] Dependence was expensive, and, in the late-nineteenth-century thinking of federal bureaucrats, it inhibited liberty. Some members of Congress wanted the Yupik and Iñupiat to kill their own calories, or buy them by selling valuable pelts and tusks. If "larger game animals from certain regions" disappeared in the process, one observer wrote, it was "but an evidence of the progress of civilization."[93] For some federal administrators, looking at Alaska from a distance, what the territory needed was just enough state to make the market morally stable, and then commerce would fill the absences commerce itself had made. A lack of fox or walrus was just an opportunity for the market to change species of desire, to find a new frontier of growth.

But, by the late nineteenth century, not everyone looking at Alaska from Washington, D.C., and New York saw a new frontier. Many saw a mirror of the last one—and, as such, a place that might need to be conserved rather than used. This, at least, was the view of the Boone and Crockett Club, a group founded by Theodore Roosevelt to promote "manly sport with a rifle."[94] Manly sport meant killing large game, but much of that game had been displaced by the restive market's previous desires. Hunting for profit, as club member Henry Fairfield Osborn wrote, had made America's "animal fortune" of bison, antelope, bear, and elk a "matter of history."[95]

Where such game was still present, the club advocated conservation: parks, preserves, and hunting limits. As a politician, Roosevelt was generally a utilitarian progressive, a promoter of "national efficiency"—putting coal and forests and rivers to their only rational use, that of sustained profit and American power.[96] But some animals were more a cultural resource than an economic one. Bears, deer, and walruses were not only "a matter of hide and meat," but to "the true sportsman, the scientific student" became "a subject of intense admiration."[97] In Alaska, club members saw the last example of the "primitive conditions approximating those of the whole country when first settled," the conditions that defined, for them, America's uniqueness.[98] Preserving this last frontier required protecting it from the market: a kind of rational use derived not from profit, but from maintaining a final theater for the masculine script of stalking, aiming, killing, and hanging evidence of grit and skill on the wall.

In Beringia, walruses *were* the walls, not their decoration. Boone and Crockett Club members, accustomed to killing that did not feed or shelter them, saw Yupik and Iñupiaq hunting as profligate and uncivilized. Foreign hunters, the few that remained as the whaling fleet dwindled, needed sanction. But foreign hunters were more rational than the "natives," Madison Grant wrote, driven to "hunt all day" rather than do "ordinary labor," and thus "a greater enemy to the life of the game than the average white man."[99] Grant wanted game species—bears, walruses, Dall sheep, moose, caribou—to be protected except for licensed trophy hunts.

John Lacey, a congressman from Iowa and a club member, also worried that "the dark chapter of the destruction of our large and small game in other parts of the United States" was repeating in Alaska. But he was additionally concerned about "starvation of the Indians." In 1902, Lacey introduced the Alaska Game Law to Congress.[100] It was a compromise between unrestrained market hunting and moratorium. Game species were subject to harvest limits and closed seasons; no person could kill more than two walruses, and only in September and October, unless they were facing immediate starvation. Selling ivory, skins, and blubber was illegal. Traders were fined for buying parts of any creature classified as game, walruses included. The United States government had concluded that neither the market nor "the native" could be trusted to value walruses rationally. Even as missionaries recognized how foxes could fail to feed whole villages, the federal government made them the only legal option. Ivory could not officially transform into anything else.

On Sivuqaq and Iŋaliq, in Kiŋigin and Ulġuniq, hunters went out as ever. How many walruses became boat covers and feasts went unrecorded. Officials from the Bureau of Biological Survey, the agency in charge of administering the game law, were hardly present enough to count every kill. It would be decades before they collected formal surveys. But the law did have an impact: in 1902, a man named Toonuk traveled thirty-five miles to Kiŋigin with ten walrus tusks, but found no buyers.[101] Bearskins and walrus hides were now contraband. In 1903, newspapers reported "the entire suppression of the fur trade" had "reduced the natives to a starving condition."[102] The Senate investigated. "During the open season," the trader P. C. Rickmers testified during hearings, walruses "are not present, because the animals follow the ice where they can't be reached at that time." Rickmers reported that people in Qiqiktaġruk "have nothing whatever now except salmon" to eat, because it was illegal to trade flour for black bear skins. The investigators concluded that "aborigines and Natives" should be allowed to sell game.[103] But for Boone and Crockett Club allies in Washington, walruses were too valuable to trust to commerce. A 1908 amendment to the Game Law reestablished that walruses could only die for subsistence.

What the Game Law ignored was how subsistence in early-twentieth-century Alaska required commodities. Need, desire, missionary tutelage, and the harvesting of foxes by the thousands to replace walruses absent in the hundreds of thousands made flour, sugar, tea, rifles, bullets, knives, metal pots, needles, cloth, and traps regular parts of most Iñupiat and Yupik lives. Fox pelts bought access, but only when the cycles of fox life and consumer desire matched. Some years, trappers could not meet demand for lack of furs. Other years, there were foxes, but no demand. As a result, even depleted walrus herds could be a more consistent way to make both food and cash. So, hunters walked the ice, past the three-mile limit of national jurisdiction, to hunt, and they sold illegal ivory in the back alleys of Nome.[104] Walrus bodies, tusks chopped clean, washed up on the occasional beach.[105] The federal government aspired to civilized stability, but had made a state of contradiction: having come north to involve Yupik and Iñupiat in the market to assist their survival, it spent the young decades of the twentieth century trying to regulate Iñupiat and Yupik away from the market for the survival of the walrus.

IV.

"My dwelling," Pavel Popov wrote in 1889, is "not excessive in its comforts, but is a safe haven from the almost polar cold in winter."[106] Popov was in Anadyr, site of the fort abandoned by the Russian Empire a century before, newly home to Popov and his small staff. The aspiration was to build "trading posts and a school . . . a mission and a church, and organize at least some medical care."[107] Popov was hopeful, given "the attitude the local Chukchi display towards us, that if in the years to come all essential goods were sent to me here, American influence will decrease on its own."[108]

The reestablishment of imperial presence in Anadyr did not entirely keep Americans away. Even after the Empire sent an administrator, and eventually a missionary, to the coast—Anadyr was 350 miles or more from where most foreign ships landed—the patrols were too few to seal the border. But Popov's hopes were not completely in vain. The missionary taught Russian to Yupik children. A pair of brothers from the Caucasus, Aleksandr and Fedor Kavaev, did brisk business from Anadyr, and other Russian subjects traded further north. In those years, if there were foxes, there were people to buy them. The trend of wearing a whole fox as a stole pushed the value of a pelt from ten or twelve dollars in 1912 to twenty or more in 1916, and nearly fifty by 1920.[109]

Selling foxes again shifted Beringians to meet far-off demands, this time moving to bays and inlets closer to Anadyr to trap. Vasilli Nanok remembered moving as a child to a camp with "many fur animals, foxes and Arctic foxes" on the Chukotka coast. His family was from Ungaziq, but Quwaaren, by then, was dead, and American traders sailed past to Anadyr for trade. Nanok's family was one of many to run traps out onto the ice and up into creek valleys. In the early twentieth century, a string of trapping camps stretched over a hundred miles from Ungaziq toward Anadyr.[110] Families still killed seals, and the occasional walrus, and traded for reindeer meat from inland. But the fox was the animal that oriented their lives.

At the Anadyr post, imperial administrators watched with worry and hope as people came westward from the coast and eastward from the tundra with their fox-fur bundles. The empire's border still leaked fur revenue—at least two hundred thousand dollars in 1911 alone.[111] American traders came to Anadyr with sacks of needed flour and the .30-30 rifles the empire had ceased trying to police.[112] But there was hope now that Moscow's new factories could make goods to compete. "Russian chintz," one officer reported, was "preferred to the American, probably due to its bright and bold colors."[113] But they worried, still, that dependence on American trade sank Yupik and Chukchi into debt, that debt provoked overzealous trapping, and such trapping violated the tsar's regulations. One administrator concluded that, with only four guards at Anadyr, "Chukotka should be classified as a region where no restrictions on trapping rights are possible." He hoped that in a country with so few people, there would be "no danger of exterminating" fur animals.[114]

Popov and his successors did worry about the extermination of walrus. They knew that, each year, American men like Charlie Madsen hunted on their ice.[115] In spring, Madsen would sail east from Alaska, stopping on Ulġuniq, which he called King Island, where he hired Iñupiaq hunters. Walrus skins were again in demand, to make bicycle seats and handbags, and the rough pelage of old bulls was used to buff silver jewelry. Some years, Madsen had contracts to deliver a hundred thousand pounds of walrus hide to a firm in Seattle.[116] The First World War caused a surge in demand, as the U.S. government bought walrus oil to make nitroglycerine and hides to polish ballistics.[117] Madsen's ship was one of several seeking walruses and fur, a reinvented remnant of the whaling years. Their hunt, Madsen recalled, was "confined entirely to Siberian waters" by the Game Law.[118] The ice floating on those waters was the habitual shelter of nursing walruses and their infants. The Game Law exiled commerce from American space, only to have commerce kill the future of the herds outside federal enclosure.

Sometime in the same springs when Madsen sailed from Nome, walruses stopped flopping onto the small sand spit at Ungaziq; it was this absence that pushed Vasilli Nanok's parents to trap foxes for trade.[119] The famine at Ungaziq was not isolated. In 1915, Captain Zilov sailed the *Yakut* north after years with no patrols—the 1905 Russo-Japanese War and its aftermath had kept the fleet to the south—and found the "marine Chukchi . . . who make their living hunting walruses, complain about the possibility of starvation soon."[120] Other imperial agents reported that Chukchi and Yupik were "eating the meat of dead dogs, the skins of marine animals, [leather] straps, bits of clothing and even human and animal excrement."[121] Near Uvelen, the herd abandoned its habitual beach. "The village headman," Zilov wrote, "requested every measure be taken to protect this important fishery for them."[122] American steamers, people in Uvelen said, were to blame. They enraged the souls of the walruses.[123]

Zilov had little assistance to give. His ship was slower than American vessels, and he was not sent north every year. An international treaty to protect the herds, which both Russian and American bureaucrats hoped for, never came to pass.[124] Inside the empire, law had not caught up with Beringia's species, making "no mention of walruses, seals and polar bears."[125] So, at sea, imperial captains could force Americans to buy trading licenses or expel them for selling liquor, but Russian authority did not extend to walrus bodies.

Word of Uvelen's barren shore spread up the coast to Inchoun. The village was near a large haul-out, a place to which walruses by the hundreds dragged their pebbled bodies to rest for days or weeks, the beach catching the nose from miles downwind, the air thick with fermenting mollusk and dung. The Chukchi who lived in Inchoun had seen their beach empty during the first wave of commercial hunting; in those years, their settlement was reduced to a few huts. Fearing a return of such barrenness, a man named Tenastze asked a shaman to speak with the walrus. What did their beings require to again shelter people? Tenastze took the walrus's reply and made rules for Inchoun. People killed with the wrong mind; the right mind required no alcohol. People hunted with the wrong tools; the right tools were spears. Each year, a man watched the beach for the first walruses to arrive. No one killed these animals, letting them call out to their fellows, telling them the sand was safe. When many walruses came, people went down and killed what they needed—quietly, and with ceremony, under the direction of Tenastze and the shaman.[126] By 1920, Inchoun hunters were able to help feed communities up and down the coast, but did not kill for trade.[127]

Inchoun was not the only Chukotkan village to protect walrus. In places where the animals hauled onto shore, away from the shifting sea ice, the "natives are exceedingly hostile to anyone who does not take their kill," wrote trader James Ashton, "they refuse to see anyone wantonly waste what is so vital to their life and prosperity."[128] Another trader angered Yupik for collecting tusks left as offerings to walrus.[129] Arakamchechen Island, with its large walrus beach, had its own local leader who directed hunters to use spears instead of guns. "The whole village," a man named Ekkurgen told a schoolteacher in the 1930s, "would hunt together."[130]

*

The terrestrial coastline forms where the energies of wind and tide use water to alter the shape of solid earth, a state of transition without conclusion. The floating coast is also made from transition, as liquid water goes solid, then back. Changes of state, in a chemical sense, are caused by transfers of energy. Unrestricted walrus hunting transferred too much energy away from the north and changed the state of Beringia's nations, empires, and commercial practice. It changed the lives not just of walruses, but of any creature whose fur could be traded as replacement for walrus flesh, and of people. But while dollar value might make fur seem the same as blubber or ivory, the rhythms that governed their creation were not equivalent; the market's habit of supplanting one desire for another did not apprehend how a fox would never live on the same time as a walrus. This left state-making in Beringia with two linked problems: how to harvest energy and how to enclose land so that the harvest did not deplete all life. Organizing energy and enclosure is at the core of politics; it requires decisions about change, value, and the allocation of the useful world. Sovereignty in Beringia was a political tool, a way to assert the value of walruses outside profit and, by doing so, to set limits on what the restless market could reach. It gave the shelter of time to walrus populations, to grow on their generational terms.

By the second decade of the twentieth century, young walruses began filling the shelter with noisy new bodies. Their infancy was protected by laws, local and national, and slack commercial demand, the accidental reprieve of desires turned elsewhere. A new herd began to form on the ice. Over the next fifty years, it would become central to a new state on the Chukchi coast: the state that Bolshevik revolutionaries were already forming, far to the west.

4

The Waking Ice

Sea ice speaks to itself, and to any being near, in groans and cracks; in rumbles that grind on for hours, percussive bangs and shrieks and silences, and then a snow-muffled roar. Sailors who overwintered their ships in the ice called it the devil's symphony. Beneath the surface, there were other instruments in the score: bowheads singing, and walruses, and bearded seals. Each male walrus has its own song, and each song lasts for days, filled with creaks, twangs, whistles, barks, and a rhythmic knocking.[1] The song of bearded seals belies their eight-hundred-pound bulk, with an eerie trill, a lost hum, and a moan.[2] Paul Tiulana described their song as "four notes and sounds like a musical instrument far down in the ocean."[3]

Tiulana was born on Ugiuvaq, in the Bering Sea, and as a child in the early 1900s he learned to hunt on the ice, following older men as they looked for walruses and bearded seals, which they called *ugruk*. Listening in on the world under the ice. *Ugruk* they pursued in winter, the ice a pale glow in the brief twilight that replaced daylight so far north, and on into spring. Walruses they hunted in late spring's thin but constant sun. A hunter might stalk a seal alone, but it would be butchered in company; a seal must be drawn before its intestines go green with sepsis. Breastbone, flippers, backbone divided up in walrus-stomach bags. Tiulana learned to carry even the blood-soaked snow back to Ugiuvaq, for soup.

To hunt on the sea ice and not die is an act of sustained, complete attention. Early in winter, ice still elastic with salt droops underfoot. Late in winter, ice is mountainous and chaotic, a landscape of bergs driven over and under each other by tides and winds, cut with snaking rivers of exposed water.[4] The ice is frozen, but never still. Tiulana hunted on a surface that drifted beneath him; too fixated on a rising seal, he might look up miles from home. His teachers told him to repeat the phrase "The ice never sleeps; the current never sleeps" as a reminder.[5]

It is movement that makes the ice sing. In forming, thawing, and shifting under the wind, ice steadies the circulation of the world's oceans, making them hospitable for living things. The white surface refracts sunlight off the Earth and seals in some of the solar energy absorbed by the ocean. Both movement and reflection moderate the Earth's temperatures, calming the intense gifts of the sun, doing work on a planetary scale.[6] An arctic fox determines the lines of trappers and shapes the world as lemmings know it—here, a danger. A walrus sets the season of hunters and shapes the sea where it eats, pluming nutrients as she roots for clams—above, a bloom of algae. The sea ice shapes being, human and otherwise, on this planet. From its groaning surface, the world as we know it is made.

*

In 1917, the Russian Empire was disquieted by the world that foreign commerce had made on its shores. For more than half a century, since the first Yankee ship started killing bowheads, borders had been elusive. In their absence, Americans tied Chukotka to a corrosive market, one that took ivory and pelts in exchange for alcohol and starvation. How to provide the material goods of civilization without such moral pillage? Imperial Russia was out of time to find a response. Over three thousand miles away, the Russian Revolution was making a new state.

The Bolsheviks had an answer—Marx's answer—to the empire's question: excise capitalism, take its industrial tools, and turn them to material liberation and moral transformation. For Marxist revolutionaries, the material and moral were linked by labor: under capitalism, poverty forced most people to sacrifice their ability to direct their own actions—to even *conceive* of directing them— because they had to earn the wages paid by the wealthy. Because life without conscious purpose deadened the soul, a worker became a thing, an object whose labor enriched someone else. But if all people worked according to their desires and ability and gained according to their needs, there would be no starvation and no reason to drink. It was a utopia of the exploited last becoming the enlightened first.

The vision of salvation the Bolsheviks brought to Chukotka required the elimination of private property and market exchange, as private property concentrated wealth unequally and markets aided such accumulation. Thus, after the Russian Revolution, two different ways of making an economy, moral and material, came to mediate foreigners' visions for the relationship between human and nonhuman in Beringia. Yet, on the shore, the United States and Soviet Union came to a similar accord with the creatures that fueled their productive faiths. Both used foxes and walruses as the economic base by which they would transform Beringians into Americans or Soviets. Both tried to farm foxes, in order to make inconstant populations—and thus production—predictable. Both found the porous, shifting shore hard to enclose; they uprooted and resettled communities that seemed at risk of drifting away ideologically or physically across the ice. And both concluded that the energy in walrus bodies was essential to the few people who lived on the Cold War border. Around walruses, both ideologies acknowledged their dependence: on plankton, sea ice, and blubber. The generation of wild walrus life became as valuable as the accounting of profit or plan.

I.

In the winter of 1919, Anadyr was a cluster of cabins, storehouses of fox and bear and wolverine pelts bundled for summer trading, the offices of a few American and Russian fur companies, and the imperial administrator's post. It was a village built on animal extraction. A village also built by a "capitalist system," Mikhail Mandrikov argued, a system that would "never save workers from capitalist slavery." Mandrikov and his colleague Avgust Berzin, like young Bolsheviks everywhere, saw capitalism as irredeemably exploitive, divided at its functional core between the owning rich and the laboring poor. The solution was not tsarist enclosure and reform, but collective ownership. In Chukotka, they preached liberation, a future where "every person . . . has an equal share of all the value in the world created by work."[7] Their revolution was already two years old in Petrograd when Mandrikov and Berzin took control of the Chukotkan administration, seized fur storehouses, and proclaimed the First Soviet Revolutionary Committee, or Revkom.

Six weeks later, most members of the Revkom were dead. Bolshevik speeches against American traders like Charlie Madsen and their lines of credit—debt that doomed the poor "to a cold and hungry death"—left the Revkom with many enemies.[8] But Anadyr's merchant class was only temporarily better armed. Bolsheviks sailed and walked and took dogsleds north from Kamchatka. Small, nasty battles erupted with remnants of the empire. It was 1923 before the Red Army declared Chukotka liberated from "White [Army] bandits and foreign predators and plundering armies," and part "of a new world, a new life of fraternity, equality, and freedom."[9]

Chukotka came into this new world just a year before Vladimir Lenin's death. East of Beringia, wartime state economic control and requisitioning had given way to the New Economic Policy, as the Soviet government temporarily let markets operate. Peasants sold their surpluses and retailers peddled without state direction. The step back was Bolshevik strategy: a chance to woo peasants disaffected by war and by communism's habit of seizing their cows, to build up industry impoverished by imperial policy, and do something for people still living on the first rung of history's ladder, like the Chukchi and Yupik. To help these potential Soviets, a group of Bolshevik faithful—many of them ethnographers experienced with "backward peoples"—formed the Committee of the North in 1924.[10] From Murmansk to Chukotka, the committee sent "missionaries of the new culture and the new Soviet state," as one member put it, "ready to take to the North the burning fire of their enthusiasm born of the Revolution."[11]

New worlds and missionaries and conversion: the stuff of the American coast for thirty years. Except the Soviet kingdom was one where heavenly utopia was completely of the Earth, and everyone would belong to it equally. Marxism, especially the variant interpreted by Lenin, promised complete liberty, an escape from both natural caprice—there is no freedom in hunger—and from political contention. After all, if all wants were supplied equally, what strife could remain? The state was a necessary initial guide to this change, but would wither away along with the haggling over want that is politics.

For the Bolsheviks, history made this future visible: a set of scientific laws that tied production to social evolution and evolution to the revolution, to the next step in profound state change. The Committee of the North had a plan for this transformation in places like Chukotka. Conversion—which the Soviets called enlightenment—would begin, as Lenin said, with the "victorious revolutionary proletariat" engaging "in systematic propaganda in [the natives'] midst." This was enlightenment through knowledge. Then, the government had to "assist them through all possible means"—that is, forge enlightenment through industrial development.[12] Such "economic organization," the Tenth Party Congress made clear, would transform "the toiling native masses from backward economic forms to a higher level—from a nomadic lifestyle to agriculture . . . from artisanal production to industrial-factory production, from small-scale farming to planned collective farming."[13] Utopia was a product—or rather, utopia was *in production*, organized not to benefit the capitalist few, but the communist all.

*

The power of communism as an idea was in its universality; dialectical materialism described a scientific process whereby the socialist future was inevitable. In their theory of revolution, Bolsheviks were just the accelerant. But everywhere they found the inevitable very difficult: among peasants, among less strident socialists, among those devoted to orthodoxies other than Marxism. And then there was Chukotka, where even the seasons were recalcitrant, with a "severe winter lasting almost all year long."[14] The Bolshevik missionaries found themselves living in "dark, windowless *yarangas* (tents), which are lit and heated by fat-burning lamps," G. G. Rudikh wrote from Cape Dezhnev. "The usual food was the meat of seals, walrus, whales—often raw. It was blatantly unsanitary . . . and [people were] hungry."[15] And the people! No one had "an idea about culture," one Bolshevik wrote.[16] Yupik and Chukchi practiced shamanism, or were under the influence of Lutheran missionaries from Little Diomede.[17] They lived in a time that human history was supposed to have surpassed, without literacy, temperance, science, gender equality. No proper food or clothing. No soap. The list of woes would have been recognizable to Ellen Lopp.

The cause of this backwardness, for the early Bolsheviks, was clear. First, there was that year-long winter. "The natives are still dependent on the elements," P. G. Smidovich wrote, and "starve after a bad season."[18] Communism was a product of workers mastering nature, so its opposite, backwardness, was a symptom of closeness to natural tempers. Then there was capitalist exploitation. "The Americans, having destroyed the creatures along their coasts," visited Chukotka "with inflated prices on highly desirable products, thereby forcing the natives to intensify and increase the number of animals killed." This produced "forced dependence on the kulak merchants," I. Krivitsyn wrote, who were "vitally interested in the natives being benighted, cowed, unable to struggle, and economically without power."[19] The president of the second, more successful, Anadyr Revkom explained to his comrades how "foreign firms ruthlessly exploit and rob the natives—the labor of a Chukchi is worth a box of biscuits. The Chukchi, as politically backward elements, do not understand. . . . If only they could eat." Without stable food, only the "voracious [capitalist] sharks gain."[20] And the Bolsheviks shared imperial concerns about "the predation of marine animals by American marauders for entire decades."[21] The vagaries of capitalism made the vagaries of nature worse. Thus, the Yupik and Chukchi lived in two pasts at once: the past of their own primitiveness, and the past of capitalist exploitation.

The Bolshevik missionaries came to make Chukotka part of one liberated future. Their means was the "Collectivization in the North," wrote one expert from the committee. Collectivization was the only way to "fully increase the productivity of the indigenous economy." Productivity would ease poverty, collectives would provide meaningful work, and both would enable conscious action. Because of northern conditions, collectivization had to "start with the simplest forms—associations for common use of land, *artels* (workshops) for the communal manufacturing of products—and ascend gradually to higher forms of the socialization of production."[22] Each *artel* would become a *kolkhoz*, or collective farm, where workers owned their production means and plans, and eventually a *sovkhoz*, a state farm, with centralized ownership and quotas.

In the Bolsheviks' theory, such economic restructuring would make more of whatever raw thing came under collective production. Freed of American predation, fox numbers would increase, as "the intensive destruction of sea animals influences the condition of hunting for fur-bearing animals, since arctic foxes eat the carcasses of sea animals that have washed up on shore."[23] Then, as a committee member wrote, "rational use and politically just valuation" would create "the conditions for raising foxes in model fox-farms," guaranteeing a "long-term fur supply."[24] Soviet marine biologists described a future in which "the fat of sea animals flows in a fast, broad wave into the tanks" of hunting *artels*.[25] The way to make more walruses was to collectivize their killing.

To do so, the Revkom concluded that its first priority was to supply "sufficient rifles and bullets" for the "spring run of walrus."[26] Not a huge step toward utopia; in the 1920s, the Committee of the North assumed that exiting two pasts at once was a gradual process. But even slow change required ammunition—along with flour, sugar, tea, potatoes, and other tools. The local purveyors were exactly the capitalists the Soviets were there to eject: American traders. The Bolsheviks began nationalizing their property—the warehouses of furs and goods.

Some traders chose to risk having their cargoes confiscated and kept sailing west from Alaska. Some, married into coastal families, stayed. But most of the fox and ivory traders left. Supplies in Chukotka dwindled. In 1924, the Revkom reported hearing "very often . . . from the Chukchi: 'yes, you are Russian, you say every year we are all a society, that soon we will have cheap Russian goods and schools and hospitals, [but] we see that with each year things are worse and worse for us.' "[27] People in Uvelen took a note to Iŋaliq, asking any trader passing to visit "and we will give you fox skins . . . we are very short of everything."[28] With frustration familiar to past imperial administrators, the Chukotka Revkom finally signed a five-year contract with an American trader named Olaf Swenson in 1926, exchanging continued access to Chukotka's ivory and fur for tons of supplies.[29] The revolution would be fed by the capitalist sharks, at least until the "proper organization of supply" allowed the Soviets "to keep the border" themselves.[30]

II.

Walruses are ever in company: fresh from the sea, a lone animal rocks toward the touch of others. They sleep flipper to flipper and communicate by twitching their whiskers, sometimes a bristly kiss. Roger Silook had an ancestor who joined this welcoming commune. First, the man walked out onto the floes and migrated south with the herd every autumn. Then, as Silook told it, "one day the walrus hair started growing on his body" and he joined the herd.[31] For years after, the ancestor barked to his family from the ice. In the 1920s, that ice was home to growing numbers of walrus. No government counted them in those years, but, dissuaded by American law and Russian revolution and low demand, the commercial hunt waned. When walruses died, it was for men like Paul Tiulana, killing a few at a time to eat and sell the occasional carved tusk.

Foxes had no such reprieve. The commercial value of fur was a fickle thing, changing quantity and species year over year. Demand declined in 1919, then surged in the early 1920s. When Jay Gatsby motored toward the American dream, his passengers wore fox fur against the cold speed of combusting fossil fuel. Car fashion helped make an arctic fox pelt worth fifty dollars. Blue foxes were worth four times as much. Each spring on ships, and later by airplane, buyers scrambled to reach Alaskan trading posts. The "grey haze" of Daisy Buchanan's fur collar might have begun as a fox near Utqiaġvik, now often called Barrow, where Simon Paneak learned to set traps.[32] Or it could have come from Sivuqaq, now often called Gambell, where children scouted for fox dens in the summer, marking the location for winter traps. Everywhere, people learned to shoot foxes when the tundra was overrun with lemmings and to set traps in leaner years. People still sold a few ivory carvings. But "when the price of fur got high," one trapper recalled, "everyone was happy."[33]

Born in 1906, Napaaq grew up watching her father trap foxes outside Gambell. Once, in camp, she met a "witch doctor" who could "travel high and swift" and knew the future through his songs.[34] She knew that animals judged their hunters. She sat through arithmetic lessons in a wooden building, sketching daily life in her notebooks: men hunting on the ice; women skinning seals or preparing berries outside a canvas tent with a metal stove.[35] Around her, a world filled with "spirits that live in wild place and are good," and those close to the village that "cause deaths."[36]

But the state of beings was changing. Along with shamans and walrus-people, there were Christians, and not just foreign ones. Near

An arctic fox caught in a metal trap, northern Alaska 1910. *U.S. Geological Survey, Ernest de Koven Leffingwell Collection.*

Nome, an Iñupiaq man converted because it promised everlasting life.[37] So did a man in Gambell. His father also became Christian, but to ward off deaths in the family.[38] Others joined congregations after epidemics or because shamans were seen as too powerful; even decades later, some hoped that shamans would "never come back. They bring death and trouble to people."[39] Punginguhk, the man who drove away the revenue service, gave up "doing crimes with false spirits" because he wanted to.[40] Much of shamanic practice, the singing and drumming and acts of war, eroded from daily life.

Yupik and Iñupiaq histories often explain Christian participation and commercial participation as a practical matter. *We converted because it offered life. We used outboard motors as they are fast. We went to the mission doctor when our medicine did not treat diphtheria. We trapped foxes to buy outboard motors.* And: *we distributed the meat from our kills to the weak among us, and treated a successful hunt as a gift, whether the result was eaten or sold or a bit of both.* Using an idea for its practical worth did not require absolute conversion, but adaptation. Doing so changed both practices, carrying shamanic trances to church altars and rituals of community giving to market transactions.[41] Napaaq drew a life where, out of the transformed sea and society brought by the market, people made a world from both Beringian ceremonies of reverence and imported ceremonies of exchange: a fox for so much ammunition, a soul for so much prayer.

The rite of the Eucharist, for Beringia's missionaries, was exclusive; to believe in Christ meant not believing walruses were once people. Holding the two ways of being together at once was impossible. The only kind of transformation officially tolerated by Lutherans or Catholics or Methodists was communion, and life becoming life after death. Yet the road to salvation was also earthly. In the 1920s, many missionaries in Beringia taught Christianity as a practice of making nature useful, and use was measured in profit. And profits tied people to a future made better through material accumulation, a kind of liberation from privation through growth.

It was a view shared by the Bureau of Indian Affairs (BIA), whose instructors worked alongside missions to teach "those things which will enable [the natives] to secure a livelihood," including carving ivory and harvesting pelts.[42] From these "little dabs of things," one Gambell teacher wrote, they could "accumulate thousands [of dollars] every year."[43] Christianity took care of souls and capitalism took care of bodies, and together they were a potent answer to the problems of life: to the needs of living tissues, and to tissues bound to pass into death.

The Bureau of Biological Survey had a different opinion of fox-based accumulation. In charge of tracking Alaska's animal life, the bureau reported that while "greater numbers of walrus . . . have been observed" in 1919, Alaskan "fur-bearing animals . . . not classed as game animals" were suffering the "high price now commanded by all classes of fur."[44] Where the BIA saw foxes helping assimilation, the Bureau of Biological Survey saw them as a common resource at risk of plunder by hunters in search of wealth. When Congress gave the bureau control over fur animal regulation in 1920, game wardens asked teachers—often the only government representatives in communities—to report "molestation of dens of foxes" and prevent "the extirpation of any kind of fur animal."[45]

Evidence of canid decline was thin; foxes breed quickly and tolerate substantial hunting.[46] And their cyclic populations made them hard to count. But in 1921, the bureau outlawed the shooting of foxes. Hundreds of skins harvested before word of the new policy reached remote villages were reclassified as contraband. The regulation was "a very serious hardship on the Natives," according to one trader, because the tundra was too flush for foxes to take bait in traps.[47] The following year, the bureau allowed guns, but banned metal traps. Frank Dufresne, the warden on the Seward Peninsula, snuck through villages to find Iñupiat in violation of the rule, "sweating them what I thought was a proper time" for their infractions.[48] Then Dufresne shortened the trapping season.

Point Hope's missionary wrote to protest the lost revenue.[49] So did Charles Brower, reporting that Barrow had "hundreds of fox tracks all coming in off the ice" after the hunt closed.[50] Yupik trapper Bobby Kava wondered at the sense of "such a short season."[51]

Instead of wild, trapped foxes, the Bureau of Biological Survey wanted farmed fox. Foxes bred from "intelligent selection of the right types of breeding stock."[52] Foxes raised in pens, killed at prime pelage, thus making profitable land that was of little "value for agriculture."[53] Fish and seal offal bought from local hunters would replace lemmings. With such steady food, stable populations would replace cycles of boom and crash. Enclosure would turn the fox into consistent income for owners and their employees. The inevitable demands of "expanding civilization" need no longer diminish "the supply of furs."[54]

Stability was expensive: farms required tens of thousands in lumber and wire and breeding stock. Such costs meant most farmers were foreigners. A "couple of white guys came off the boat" near Barrow, Adam Leavitt Qapqan remembered, "and they start a fox farm there."[55] Another opened in Kotzebue. Small hutches and runs proliferated around Nome. On Shishmaref, a trader named George Goshaw imported eighty blue foxes in 1924. Dufresne reported with satisfaction that a few "Eskimo" women earned thousands a year by owning hutches and pups, but they were an exception. Where Beringians profited from the farms, it was usually by selling fish or labor, not by ownership.[56]

The bureau saw fox profits—from trapping them, farming them, or by working for wages tending them in pens—as bound to keep growing. But the roaring demand for fur crashed with the rest of the American economy in 1929. Foxes lost more than half their value by 1930.[57] The progress preached to the Yupik and Iñupiat had shown itself to be full of temper: one year, prices for fur swelled; another they dipped. One year, fur farms bought salmon; the next, they closed. One foreigner championed salvation through profit; another restricted trapping. The state was one of contradiction. Commerce stirred demand in a place, then moved on, an inadvertent reprieve for once-demanded species that left poverty for their hunters. It cast people outside market time, far from the promises of growth.

*

Like Paul Tiulana on his island, Mallu learned as a child how not to die among the ridges and snaking leads on the ice near Ungaziq. He learned that wronged animals would seek retribution.[58] He also learned Russian from the Chukchi coast's lone Orthodox missionary. When the Bolsheviks came with their promises of "mastering the full use of resources" through "the socialist reconstruction of the northern economy," Mallu's comprehension was not limited by their terrible Yupik.[59] What he heard was an escape from winters "when we had hunger, because the sea animals did not come," leaving "children without fathers." So, he wrote later, "I decided to organize a *kolkhoz*" named Toward the New Life.[60] By 1928, Mallu and half a dozen other young Yupik men were elected members of the local Soviet administration. The Bolsheviks had converts.

Mallu joined the revolution just as the revolution lost patience. Lenin was dead, taking the New Economic Policy with him. Josef Stalin led the worker's state—a state Stalin found insufficiently revolutionary. There were still class enemies among the peasants and merchants, still spiritual enemies among the clergy. And there was still not enough production or industrialization. In 1928, Stalin's first five-year plan demanded that the country speed up: peasants would collectivize and produce more grain, grain exports would pay for imported equipment, and equipment would build industrial socialism by 1933. It was a task of urgency, of *Time Forward!* as a novel of heroic socialist labor proclaimed. In the north, there was no grain or factories, but there was a sense of haste. The truth of the Stalin revolution lay in its ability to transform any place at the same rate. The Committee of the North could no longer make allowances for people "who, because of their extreme backwardness, cannot keep up either economically or culturally with the breakneck speed of the emerging socialist society."[61]

But how to tell whether socialism was emerging? Utopia was in production, but what was the product? The five-year plan hurtled toward a future only vaguely described by Marx or Lenin. The Stalinist method of substantiation was quantification: how many new *kolkhozy*, how many new people joining the *kolkhozy*. This was much of Mallu's work: recruiting Yupik and coastal Chukchi by explaining that "a good life can only be built through a collective farm."[62] He also offered flour, ammunition, metal boats, and outboard motors. The capitalist sharks had finally been exiled from Chukotka, and the Soviets controlled supply, if imperfectly; even Mallu complained that there were no "cooking pots or needles."[63] But what the Soviets had, they gave to people in collectives. It was, Mallu admitted, an excellent reason to join a *kolkhoz*.

And the *kolkhozy*, rhetoric aside, did not look all that transformative. Members hunted walruses and seals in order to refine "fat which can be used for industrial purposes."[64] Yupik already hunted walruses and seals. The collective required hunting together and distributing the catch after the *kolkhoz* manager tallied it against the plan. Yupik already hunted in groups and distributed their catch. A collective wanted fox pelts in exchange for sugar and tea, an old rite of transmutation by 1930. No one in a collective could be substantially richer or poorer than anyone else. Among the Yupik and coastal Chukchi, no one was. Elsewhere in the Soviet Union, collectivization was a conflagration. Peasants by the millions fled, killed their livestock, fought with the Bolsheviks; Bolsheviks beat, robbed, and killed the peasants they called *kulaks* for wanting to own a horse. Elsewhere in Chukotka, reindeer herders acted like peasants. But on the coast, the breakneck speed of the five-year plan meant carrying *kolkhoz* ammunition on the spring hunt and hanging a portrait of Lenin in the *yaranga*; the material dictates of Stalin's revolution were not initially so revolutionary.[65]

The material form of the revolution had a cultural end—what the Bolsheviks called "consciousness," the state change from spontaneous reaction to full awareness of how each person furthered the laws of history. The mental part of conversion was not as simple as calling a hunting party a brigade. It required replacing all prior beliefs with those of a good socialist. The Bolsheviks "agitated that we ought to stop observing our festivals," Andrei Kukilgin recalled in the 1970s, ordering that "they had to be tossed out altogether."[66] Not everyone was willing. Some avoided Soviet participation in case it angered seals and other animals.[67] Others warned that walruses would stop coming if children went to Soviet schools.[68] Even Mallu still ritually fed decapitated walruses in the 1920s.[69] A few slipped out of Soviet borders. On Sivuqaq, Napaaq drew a portrait of the shaman Walunga when he arrived from Soviet Chukotka. Anders Apassingok's family crossed in 1928.[70] Most of the people on Soviet Imaqłiq, or Big Diomede, traversed the few miles of open water to American Iŋaliq.[71] As Yupik and Iñupiat had once tried to exile Alaskan missionaries, a man in Naukan named Nunegnilan created a set of rituals meant to drive away the Soviets. Wearing robes and crosses like Christians, his followers danced and avoided soap and its smell of being Bolshevik.[72]

Nunegnilan was arrested by the Soviet police. Shamanism, to the Soviets, was the open practice of living in another, lesser, time. It was deliberate rejection of the Soviet future. But Nunegnilan's was a rare arrest, on the coast; the purges among inland Chukchi herders stopped shy—mostly—of Mallu's followers. Mallu led a campaign against a woman who foretold the end of communism, and against a Chukchi man named Ekker, on Arakamchechen Island. Ekker had taken over the walrus beach, scaring away other hunters with his ability to "kill by casting a spell."[73] He was driven off his island by two boatloads of men.

In place of Ekker's spells, the Soviet state had its own rites: those of the plan. In the plan—a five-year plan, subdivided into a series of annual plans, further broken down into monthly plans—the state set production quotas for each factory or farm. The plan was a way to make speeding through history a material, sensory fact: the plan set out a number that indicated socialism was beginning to exist, to overtake capitalism. Exceeding the plan—killing twenty walruses where ten would have done—meant that socialism could arrive sooner, and made a person or a *kolkhoz* a hero of socialist labor. And the plans' quotas increased, year over year. More walruses, more seals, more foxes. Where the market measured success in general growth and tolerated abandoning species and places and people when desires shifted, the plan expected each person and every farm to show increase.

Yuri Rytkheu was born on Uelen's sandspit in 1930, into a world partly made by the plan. Or aspiring to it: that year, Chukotka's collectives killed under fifteen hundred walrus.[74] Fox harvests were a paltry few hundred, hardly enough to feed "an artisanal blubber processing industry" or the Soviet demand for fur, let alone the ideological need to exceed past capitalist production.[75] At *kolkhoz* and party meetings, foreign Bolsheviks lectured Beringian Bolsheviks: if it took "forty rounds [of ammunition] for a seal and fifty for a walrus," then "Eskimos and Chukchi shoot badly."[76] Beringian Bolsheviks complained of bad schools and worse police interference with travel along the coast.[77] Everyone wanted motors. But even with their complaints and worries over unfilled plans, such meetings and the rituals of tallying the year's fox pelts and blubber pounds substantiated the state of being Soviet.

When Rytkheu was five years old, Chukotkan *kolkhozy* harvested almost six hundred arctic foxes and a few more walruses than the year before. In *kolkhozy* meetings, people discussed how to make even more: better boats, improved trapping procedures, and faster butchering to improve the "quality of the products (hides and meat)."[78] Rytkheu learned from his uncle incantations for good weather and many walrus. He went to school—a hut with a blackboard and glass windows. From his teachers, he learned how to read and write and to condemn shamans and *kulaks.*

When Rytkheu was seven years old, brigades harvested nearly six thousand animals from metal boats. Two small ships, the *Temp* and the *Nazhim,* killed twenty-five hundred more at sea. Almost four thousand arctic fox pelts became tallies in *kolkhozy* logs. Rytkheu watched the first electrical lines go up along Uelen's single gravel road. A man cut a hole in the roof of his family's *yaranga* and attached a lightbulb, making real part of Lenin's dictum that communism was Soviet power plus the electrification of the whole country. It was a childhood, Rytkheu wrote later, "lived simultaneously . . . in many different times."[79]

One of those times was the time of people who became walrus. The other was the time of the lightbulb and the plan, a time in which the decision not to hunt more and more had become irrational. Soviet time moved so quickly, it forgot the devastation of overharvest the Bolsheviks had lamented only a decade before. Lack was a capitalist problem. In 1938, nearly ten thousand arctic foxes filled the plan. So did over eight thousand walruses. Only on Big Diomede did people ignore *kolkhoz* plans and limit their walrus kill.[80] At Inchoun, ceremonies of restraint dissipated with collectivization. Perhaps the idea of the plan and its certain future was welcome in the village. Perhaps the Inchoun ceremonies drifted from public life like so many others: without violence, but not without cost. Even voluntary conversion is loss.

III.

Each autumn, cold converts the Bering Sea to solid, and a frozen ghost of ice-age land stretches between the headlands of the continents. The ice is uneasy, without the deep repose of the submerged earth over which it floats. It can shift away from shore, suddenly, or take people. It took Paul Tiulana's father; gone out to find seal, he never returned. In 1936, it took a group from Chaplino. For days, they were stranded among the grinding floes, their mouths raw from drinking salty water. They were rescued by villagers from Gambell, Alaska, more than forty miles from where they started in the Soviet Union, across the International Date Line.

When the ice retreated that year, whaleboats from Gambell took the hunters home. Chaplino welcomed them with a celebration, and likely some suspicion from the police.[81] It was a rare visit, by then. Together, on the beach, sharing the relief of survival, the American Yupik and Soviet Yupik spoke dialects of the same language, ate the same succulent plants soaked in the same seal oil, looked for the same birds signaling spring. But in their respective villages, their missionaries now preached different kingdoms coming, amid economies that set different measures of value. In Chaplino, the *kolkhoz* took any walruses or foxes killed in exchange for supplies, even if those supplies were more likely to be posters of Stalin than sugar. In Gambell, the store had more sugar and no Stalin, but valued walruses and foxes erratically. Lived communism was consistent, if often insufficient; lived capitalism often bounteous but capricious.

In 1936, the American experience of caprice was particularly severe. Even in a year when foxes shadowed every snowdrift, their pelts gave just enough income, one trapper remembered, to buy at most "coffee, sugar, beans, canned vegetables, oatmeal, canned milk . . . and Sailor Boy pilot bread."[82] Not profits to buy timber to frame cabins, or boats and motors. Most fox farms, owned by foreigners wanting profits, closed during the Depression, taking with them the consistency of wages, and of foxes fed seal offal rather than lemmings. Whole villages bought their ammunition on credit. In the years when Yuri Rytkheu saw himself advancing toward a "new way of life, a just life" under "the banner of the Russian Revolution," Beringians just a drifting ice floe away hoped for a different future.[83] A future that looked like their recent past, with its generous fox profits and little debt.

The present of 1930s Alaska looked, in practice, more like an older past: one in which calories came off the ice or did not come at all. People in Gambell and Wales and Point Hope had eaten walrus and seal, no matter the price of fur, over the fox-rich decades because it was delicious, and because to not hunt was neglectful, a violation of a reciprocal connection that, if abandoned, would force the walrus to "return to their own kind to report on how they had been treated."[84] But in the 1930s and into the 1940s, stalking walruses and bearded seals singing under the ice was also, again, a necessity, the creatures more stable than those human demands that were mediated through money.

And walruses could also give small profits. The Department of the Interior, eager during the Depression to support "the economic welfare of the Indian tribes through the development of Indian arts and crafts," became a distributor for Yupik and Iñupiaq ivory carvers. Figures of dogs and polar bears sold particularly well in Anchorage and Seattle and beyond.[85] The demand only increased during the Second World War. Paul Tiulana, like many other English-speaking Beringian men, was drafted. At home, less experienced hunters were more likely to shoot, but not recover, their kills. After the bombing of Pearl Harbor and Japanese landfall in the Aleutian Islands, three hundred thousand foreigners came to Alaska. The military flew lend-lease planes out of Nome, and built installations on Sivuqaq, which they called St. Lawrence Island. The military imported many things: alcohol, overt racial segregation, tons of concrete and tin infrastructure—and demand for walrus. Everywhere the military went, a surging market "for both carved and uncarved ivory" followed.[86] Alongside the new profits came rumors of headless walruses washing up on Beringian shores and reports of bored soldiers shooting the herd from airplanes.[87]

Worried again about walrus extinction, Congress passed new legislation in 1941. As before, only Alaska Natives could hunt; killing walruses for their tusks was illegal, as was selling raw ivory.[88] But in the new law, the state protected sales of carved tusks, a concession desired by the BIA, which sought to protect profits from the worked-ivory market, a business that was worth a hundred thousand dollars by 1945.[89] The Department of the Interior also wanted to assure more walruses. Officers from the Fish and Wildlife Service, convinced the 1941 law still incentivized overhunting, sent letters to Beringian teachers, suggesting that "killing their year's supply [of walrus] with spears" rather than guns would reduce the harvest.[90] Their inspiration was an article, twenty years old by then, about the Chukchi practices at Inchoun.

Not so far from Inchoun, lend-lease planes from Nome landed in Egvekinot and Markovo with cargoes of truck parts and medical supplies and other assistance for the Red Army. An army, as N. A. Egorov wrote shortly after Germany invaded the Soviet Union in 1941, suffering from an "insufficient supply of fat."[91] Egorov commanded the Soviet whaling fleet, and saw in the oceans great stores of unused lipids, not just in whales, but in walrus. Walrus oil production, Egorov believed, could double. When Chukotka failed to meet these new plans—in 1942, walrus kills were less than half the goal—the fault was put with technology.[92] Their motors were "not designed for continuous operation with a heavy load," one *kolkhoz* reported, exposed to "rain and damp, not to speak of the storms which happen so frequently in the north-eastern sea."[93] The promise of the plans remained. In trying to meet them, even without the right motors, even with most ammunition and petrol allocated to the front, sixteen thousand more walruses became entries in *kolkhozy* accounts during the war. By 1945, the Beringian herd was reduced to sixty thousand animals.

*

In 1948, seventeen Iñupiat from American Little Diomede took their boats two and a half miles to Soviet Big Diomede. It was not an accident of drifting ice, but a planned visit. Each person had filed applications with the Soviet government months before for permission to cross the border.[94] But the party set off that summer in the midst of the Berlin airlift. Unknown to them, in their boats filled with food, their respective states' alliance against a common enemy was over. A Soviet patrol arrested the American Diomede residents. After weeks of detention, they were released with orders never to return.

The Cold War made the need for borders and assimilation a question of existential survival. The United States looked to the Soviet Union and saw an unnatural nation devoid of markets, frozen under leaders totalitarian and nuclear. The Soviet Union looked to the United States and saw a country with a long habit of invasion, committed to immoral exploitation in the name of commerce, now with an atomic bomb. All that lay between them was a strip of water that, for half the year, was as good as land. Before the development of intercontinental ballistic missiles, the Beringian shore was considered a logical site to stage an invasion or an air attack. Soviet authorities closed the village on Big Diomede, forcing residents to the mainland.[95] The Red Army installed heavy artillery in Avan, Yuri Pukhlouk recalled, after "we were taken away from there, so we wouldn't bother it."[96] Across the strait, military installations moved to Nome and Wales, to make Alaska a "bristling bastille and a major launching point in any future push-button war against any aggressor Nation in the northern hemisphere."[97] Beringians needed to be American or Soviet because, as one U.S. official put it, "the Eskimo . . . are the only people who can live within the Arctic, and the Arctic is even now becoming the frontier defense of these two governments."[98]

But were Beringians sufficiently patriotic to withstand socialist influence? J. Edgar Hoover worried that "the Eskimo" were not loyal Americans.[99] During the Cold War, being American meant being capitalist, and being capitalist required making nature valuable, as a wage laborer or proprietor or small farmer. Independence from the federal dole was ideologically and practically important.[100] As a result, many federal teachers, even prior to the 1950s, had no issue with market hunting for "large numbers of walrus, because they form a large part of the livelihood of these [Native] peoples."[101] Missionary Benedict Lafortune wrote that, "were it not for [the ivory] all the King Islanders would have to be put on relief. The seals give them their food and fuel, and the walruses give them their clothes and ammunition and outboard motors etc. etc."[102] The BIA ship *North Star* supplied village stores and bought carved ivory and a few fox pelts. Killing walruses for profit was a rational act, because profit made Yupik and Iñupiat economically free, and economic freedom was the ideal state of man. The alternative was socialist-seeming dependence on federal aid.

Yet the Bureau of Biological Survey, and after 1959 the Alaska Fish and Wildlife Service, frequently did not see Iñupiaq and Yupik hunting as rational. Their vision of walrus use was closer to that of the Boone and Crockett Club than to BIA hopes of self-sufficiency. As one report stated, walruses suffered from "the Eskimo's careless behavior" and the encouragement of the Department of Interior's ivory marketing program.[103] The BIA and the Fish and Wildlife Service were caught in a conundrum: only present walruses could help assimilation; assimilation demanded market participation; market participation demanded too many walruses. These contradictions were expressed in ever-changing state rules—Did walrus tusks need to be tagged? Were there limits to the walrus kill? Where could ivory be sold?—that penalized Yupik and Iñupiat for participating in the rites of commerce the state simultaneously demanded they join.

Then there was school, with its incongruities. Napaaq had attended because her father wanted her to. Literacy was useful. It was also more or less optional in the 1920s: children went to local day schools between months spent in trapping camp. But federal presence expanded in the 1930s, and especially alongside military infrastructure in the 1940s. William Iġġiaġruk Hensley moved to Kotzebue, away from his parents, to "attend school steadily enough so that the authorities left me alone." He remembered the welcoming warmth of the schoolhouse, but the teacher beat his knuckles when he spoke Iñupiaq, sending the "message that our language was inferior."[104] He, like many students, had to leave Beringia after eighth grade, for BIA boarding schools in southern Alaska, or in Oregon and California. The journey, even if parents and children desired it, was a rupture. Beringian experience was reduced to summers, not the long round of a year; Beringian languages to what words survived enforced English. Beringian parenthood was replaced by institutional brusqueness and, too often, abuse.

Like rules for hunting, education made foreigners' visions for Beringia unavoidable even for people who never left. In 1959, the government closed the school on King Island. Parents remember the BIA threatening to take their children if they did not stay in Nome for the school year. Over the next decade, Paul Tiulana watched his community trickle away from the place he learned to hunt—the place he still hunted, even with one leg amputated during his military service—until he, too, had to leave. How to stay? To be with their children, to raise a future, parents had to abandon the home of their long past—the "places," King Island Iñupiaq poet Joan Naviyuk Kane wrote in 2018, "that gave rise to highly specific dialects, stories, dances, and song that passed down knowledge that is absolutely necessary for survival of the body and the intellect."[105]

As an old man, Tiulana recalled contradictions the state offered. "On the one hand we are told that we have to go to school to make a living, more income, cash for our pockets to buy better things for ourselves," he remembered. All this meant more education. "But when we go to school, we lose our own culture." And the "only income we get from Native culture is food for our families. In the Native way, everything is given by nature. . . . Even the modern

society cannot compete with Mother Nature."[106] At issue, in Tiulana's words and all along the Beringian coast, was the incongruity
between assimilation based on profit, and profit based on changing live animals into dead. Convert too many of any species into
a commodity, and consumption exceeds reproduction. So, there
were regulations, an annual zigzag of quotas and restrictions.
But the ideal of capitalism is to outstrip death—each year, more
consumed! More profits! Growth is an incantation against mortality. To be American in the Cold War was to seek this ideal. To be
Beringian was also to face its impossibility, the fact that so much of
growth is built on accelerated entropy.

*

Being Soviet was a material state. A state antithetical to living in
hide tents, even with a lightbulb. It meant, by the early 1950s, not
traveling between times as Yuri Rytkheu did as a child, but living
in the same future. In that future, Rytkheu was a graduate from
Leningrad University and, in 1953, published his first short story,
"People from Our Shore." It begins with a Chukchi family in a village very like Uelen, trying to install glass windows in their *yaranga*,
and where the *kolkhoz* manager "recorded everything in his 'speaking leaves' (as the old people called all papers on which something
was written)."[107]

That same year, Stalin died. In 1956, Nikita Khrushchev vowed
to drive Stalin's ghost out of the country and quicken progress. A
series of Communist Party decrees ordered new housing, cultural
centers, schools, machinery for collectives, hospitals, and roads.
Across Chukotka, communism was under construction. Often slow
construction—"of the planned building for 1954 only four properties have been completed," one party report noted.[108] But it was,
for its boosters, a sign of enlightenment arriving—finally—in the
north. Even a *yaranga* with windows, Yuri Rytkheu wrote, "could not
satisfy the needs of present-day man," because there was no place

to put a table for reading and writing, for keeping the speaking leaves with their tallies.[109]

To be Soviet was to live in modern apartment buildings, with roads between them and water inside them, consolidated around schools and hospitals. The architects of Khrushchev's reforms saw no sense in dispersed settlements, in the string of small villages and camps scattered along the coast, but wanted people moved to town. To become Soviet by moving was not voluntary. The government did not speak openly about security, about ideological loyalty, but the people they moved first were the people closest to America.[110] Iñupiat from Big Diomede were sent to Naukan. Naukan was closed in the 1950s, its residents moved to Lavrentiya, Pinakul', and Nunyamo. Then Pinakul' and Nunyamo were closed. Chaplino was moved to Novo Chaplino. Between 1937 and 1955, the number of inhabited coastal villages in Chukotka dropped from ninety to thirteen.

Chukchi women butchering walrus for their collective, 1951. *Peter the Great Museum of Anthropology and Ethnography (Kunstkamera), Russian Academy of Sciences.*

The promise of the First Five-Year Plan, to make everyone live in one time, was finally becoming reality. Yuri Rytkheu celebrated these changes, writing that the "peoples of Chukotka have traversed a hard path together with the whole country . . . they have emerged from darkness to light."[111] Other coastal people were less triumphant. Nina Akuken left Naukan "crying the entire way," having not gone "to the graves to bid farewell" to buried ancestors. Her new village was filled with "unfinished houses. Nothing was plastered, and there was no stove."[112] At Chaplino, residents left so quickly, pots of soup still boiled on their abandoned fires. "Nothing was as it should be," Vladimir Tagitutkak recalled, because "I didn't hunt anymore."[113] Like many people moved by the state, he worked now in construction.

Contraction also had an economic end. Khrushchev's policy of *ukreplenie* (consolidation) merged small *kolkhozy* into larger *kolkhozy* or into *sovkhozy*, where plans and products were controlled more fully by the state. The number of Chukotkan collectives shrank from forty-six to twenty-six in the eight years following Stalin's death.[114] The new farms were organized to mimic industrial factories; small teams of metal boats still hunted walruses and seals, but more of the catch came from ships crewed by foreigners, able to kill on a mass scale far from land. Walruses were still butchered and distributed by the collective, but more of the catch was processed in mechanized blubber refineries.[115] Workers hauled leftover muscle and offal from the plant at Sireniki to fox farms. In long sheds filled with cages, foxes were fed "year round fresh sea mammals and vitamin feed."[116] Such enclosure was a product of fuel: petrol for motorboats to reach places with walruses and seals, coal for electrical plants and seafaring ships, diesel to run the refinery vats, imported energy to make energy.

For a few years in the 1950s, *ukreplenie* worked. The number of fox farms grew from a single breeding operation to nineteen by the end of the decade; liberated from the rise and fall of their wild numbers, fox production first became stable, then grew to thousands of pelts each year. And despite walruses trying to escape—the "females and their calves" diving from the sea ice "when the first shot was fired"—over five thousand were harvested by ships and boat brigades in 1955 alone.[117] It was an example of "Stakhanovite work practices in exceeding the annual production plans," named for Alexei Stakhanov, who proved himself the ideal socialist worker by mining fourteen times his daily quota of coal in 1935.[118] The coastal equivalent was in slaughter or skinning; the more animals become blubber and leather, the more proof there was that people in "traditional occupations," as Rytkheu described, were a "component part of the economy of the country in its building of socialism."[119]

The contributions were not just in oil and hides, but in art. Rytkheu began writing stories of socialism arriving in Chukotka. In Uelen, a collective of ivory carvers etched old legends of giants and walking whales into walrus tusks, alongside new legends of Bolsheviks bringing the word of socialism north. A carving of Lenin reclining on a stuffed sealskin was so celebrated in Moscow that Uelen avoided closure.[120] In that carving, like many others, the Soviet Union was drawn literally ahead of the capitalist world. History moved down the length of a carved tusk as in the panels of a comic book; past trade with Americans ended in a frame where the Soviets planted their flag, then new panels filled with helicopters and bathhouses and Red Army salutes began. Socialism was a different space, one ahead in time and sealed off from the rest of the strait.

The walrus recognized no such border. In the Bering Sea, some lived mostly in Soviet territorial waters and some in American, and some rode the ice back and forth between. Their way of being resisted enclosure. In the 1950s, out of concern for the decreasing number of walruses, hunters in Gambell passed a local ordinance stricter than state regulations.[121] Yet the source of the decline, as one Yupik man noted, was clear: "'it looks like we are saving the walrus for the Russians.'"[122] There were now fewer than fifty thousand Pacific walrus.[123]

IV.

Throughout their migration, walruses stir nutrients into the water column, especially nitrogen, that help photosynthetic organisms bloom, and those blooms feed squids and clams and small fishes and tube worms.[124] Without walruses, the productivity of dozens of small bits of life goes slack.

Soviet plans on the coast went slack just a few years after Khrushchev's reforms made them bounteous. Soviet marine biologists, who counted every walrus hauled into a *kolkhoz* beginning in the 1930s, now surveyed ice become conspicuously bare. There was no obvious technological reason; people were in collectives, and collectives had boats and refineries. Yet, of the "33 former coastal concentrations on the Chukotsk Peninsula," wrote biologist S. E. Kleinenberg, only three remained in 1954.[125] The result, the Academy of Sciences reported to the Council of Soviets, was "a significant reduction in the number of walruses, which has a very painful effect on the situation of the local indigenous population of the Chukchi and Eskimo."[126]

Walruses had stopped obeying the promise of socialist production, the utopia Marx indicated would arrive when humans bent the world completely to serve their freedom from material wants. Soviet practice conflated liberating people with increased production, whether the products were needed or not. On the tundra and in the open ocean and under Chukotka's mountains, Soviet planners continued to forecast unending reindeer growth, expanding whale production, and mines spitting forth ore at ever-faster rates. Generally, falling productivity signaled retreat. But even with ships and fossil fuels, Yupik and Chukchi communities were isolated from the "necessary food and household items" that walruses could pro-vide.[127] Ice cut off most external energy from October until nearly July. Chukotka without walruses risked a return to hunger.

Starvation was hardly what the Soviet 1950s were supposed to be about. Moreover, Khrushchev wanted the Soviet Union to lead the world not just in factories and missiles, but in international enlight-enment. "Capitalist and colonial countries," explained a report from the Commission on Nature Protection, experienced the "profound and irreversible depletion of natural resources . . . before they realized the need for conservation. The Soviet Union cannot and should not repeat this path."[128] The 1954 meeting of the Interna-tional Union for the Protection of Nature brought Soviet delegates together with American conservation biologists, now half a century into trying to reconcile modernist demands of production with wal-rus reproduction.[129] The Soviets, like the Americans, concluded that returning to old, Inchoun-like, limited hunts would allow walruses to flourish. Doing so, one delegate reported, had "high urgency and not just internal, but international, importance."[130] Glossing over the recent Soviet rate of killing, Kleinenberg noted how commercial hunting brought herds to a "catastrophic condition," while, in the USSR, walruses could be "preserved in bigger numbers."[131] Social-ism in the 1930s required more production to overtake the capitalist world; in the 1950s, it could also entail comparatively smarter pro-duction, able to leap ahead of the market's errors.

In 1956, at the urging of biologists from the Russian Academy of Sciences, the Soviet ministers of the Russian Soviet Federative Socialist Republic passed a decree prohibiting industrial walrus hunting at sea—even as plans for whales, foxes, reindeer, tin, and gold kept growing. Yupik and Chukchi *kolkhozy* could only kill wal-ruses for food and use the ivory in their carving workshops. The "purchase of fat and hide" by other organizations was prohibited, as was the killing of nursing females.[132] Gray whales took the place of walruses as fox food. It took several years for these regulations to make their way from ideal in Moscow to practice in Chukotka, but by the 1960s, only about a thousand walruses were killed each year in Chukotka.[133] The Soviet practice of always producing more was subsumed by the need not to consume too much.

*

Both the market and the plan tried to accelerate time: to increase the speed with which people consumed things, and thus generate growth, or overfill plans and thus bring about the future more quickly. Neither capitalist time nor socialist time fit the cycles of walrus life. But on the shore, both economies were able to change their cadence, learning within a few decades of their respective onslaughts to curtail the appetite of the market and the collective.[134] In 1972, the two countries formalized their similar compromises with walrus biology in the Environmental Protection Agreement. The accord managed walruses according to values other than escalating human use by limiting kills to indigenous subsistence. It made the floating coast a space apart, exempted from the market's roving paroxysms of demand or the plan's exponential plot of increase. Doing so protected the livelihoods of the few people the state could assume would live on the Beringian shore. Sovereignty depended on walrus energy, and walruses depended on protection from the ideology that each sovereign state wished to make universal. In an action far different from their treatment of whales, foxes, caribou, and wolves, both governments accommodated what a walrus is: a migratory animal, one that moves energy from sea into new flesh consistently, but not quickly. In the Arctic, constancy does not have the speed of fox lives.

For Beringians, walrus legislation kept the state present: to count the kill, to prevent hunting for ivory, and to keep preaching the contradiction that a growing market or growing plan made life better while curtailing such possibility with walrus. For walruses, regulations gave back time. A few thousand walruses a year died by human hunters, a number in line with Beringia's long historic norm—

before walruses became part of a plan or bottom line—allowing the herds to regain a population near that which existed before the century of slaughter. The population was healthy enough for the Soviet plan to expand, in 1981, to five thousand kills a year, prompting a Yupik woman to complain that her *kolkhoz* hunted walrus cows and calves for the fox farm, something that "should not be done" and would "destroy the spiritual base of our culture."[135] A year later, biologists found that walruses were thin, starving even, and in their desperation behaving like arctic foxes: scavenging seal flesh, their usual prey of mollusks chewed to bare mud by the swelling herd.[136] To consume beyond primary production is not only a human trait.

*

On the wall of the lodge in Gambell, where visitors stay, there is a framed letter: an apology from the Presbytery of Yukon to the people of the village. It repents for "failing to understand what the people of Gambell would have wished us to know," for contributing to Yupik language loss, for devaluing Yupik dances, and for confusing Yupik "identity in the world." Nearby are ads for fox-fur mitts and hats, and posters with the year's walrus hunting regulations. Kills for subsistence; ivory for sale only when carved. Those carvings remain one of the few ways to make money in Gambell; growth, in Alaska, has moved to the distant petroleum frontier.

Outside the lodge is beach covered in dark stones, dotted with the occasional white vertebra from generations of walruses become food. To the northwest, the hills above the abandoned village of Chaplino are visible across the water and the International Date Line. But people do not cross by boat. The border, like laws limiting Russian walrus kills, outlasted the Soviet Union. In fall, people on both sides of the strait watch the sea ice form a new floating coast, with new leads where the walruses come to breathe, new crystalline ridges of ice where the foxes wait. Every year is particular and temporary; all conversion is a loss.

The instinct of capitalism and communism is to ignore loss, to assume that change will bring improvement, to cover over death with expanded consumption. Such modernist visions are telescopic: from the present, each leaps into a distant world, a future place of freedom and plenty. The present must accelerate to reach that far country. Speed is quantified in what can be converted to material value for sale or the state. What exists in between, the mess of lives lived in shifting concert with tides and winds and the never-fixed mark of ecological complexity, slides from focus. These ideological habits make thinking in terms of generations, both human and nonhuman, difficult. But, as the walruses show, it is not impossible.

PART III

LAND, 1880-1970

Time is the flesh of the silent cosmos.

Joseph Brodsky, *Eclogue IV: Winter*

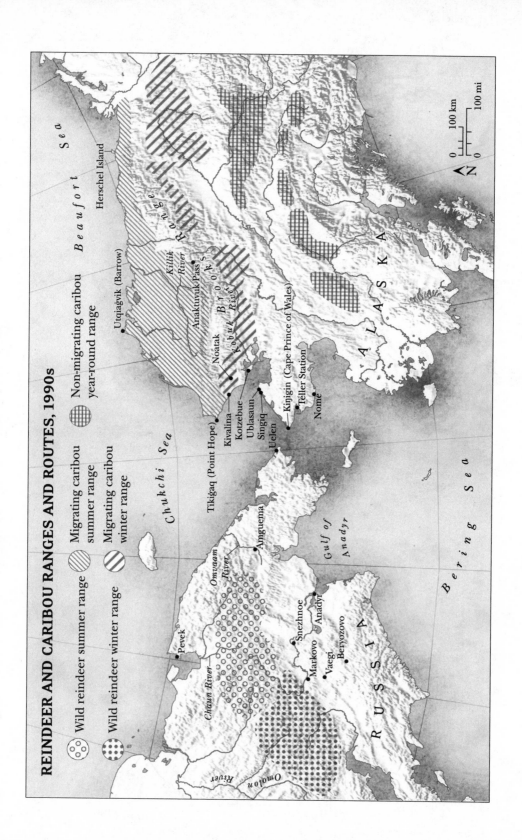

REINDEER AND CARIBOU RANGES AND ROUTES, 1990s

Wild reindeer summer range

Wild reindeer winter range

Migrating caribou summer range

Migrating caribou winter range

Non-migrating caribou year-round range

N

0   100 km

0   100 mi

Beaufort Sea

Herschel Island

Brooks Range

Killik River

Anaktuvuk Pass

Noatak

Kobuk River

Utqiagvik (Barrow)

Chukchi Sea

Tikigaq (Point Hope)

Kivalina

Kotzebue

Ublasaun

Singiq

Uelen

Kinigin (Cape Prince of Wales)

Teller Station

Nome

A L A S K A

Pevek

Chaun River

Omvaam River

Anguema

Snezhnoe

Markovo

Vaegi

Anadyr

Beryozovo

Gulf of Anadyr

R U S S I A

Omolon River

Bering Sea

5

The Moving Tundra

A t the northern edge of Asia and North America, the land rolls inland from the sea. Underfoot, Beringia is a patchwork of peat bogs, fields of ice-cored hummocks, shrub-covered plateaus, and lichen-furled rock. On the southern edge of the tundra, where it shades into taiga, there is enough sun and soil to grow black spruce and birch. Move north, and the sky presses down without the interruption of forest. The summer is only long enough for willows to grow a few hundredths of an inch each year.[1] Beringia is not a place where plants easily make tissue from light. Yet there are calories fixed in the lichens and moss, in the sedges and grasses. These truncated green things are the stuff of life for some of the largest herds of herbivores on Earth, the hundreds of thousands of *Rangifer tarandus*—gangly, long-nosed, but imposing, known in Eurasia as reindeer and in North America as caribou. Through their bodies, the tundra feeds wolves as large as men.

To be alive as a reindeer is to move: they walk within minutes of birth, walk while sleeping, walk while eating. In spring, pregnant

caribou move from lichen pastures in the interior toward the sea or
to mountain uplands. They arrive thin, coats patchy, and give birth
where breezes push away the summer's torment of mosquitoes.
Bulls and barren cows follow, seeking the open plains where wolves
rarely den and vegetation is thick.[2] In autumn, the vast commune
splinters and turns back toward winter pasture, their spadelike
hooves trammeling paths half a foot deep over years of passage. A
moving herd sounds gently percussive, the tendons in each hoof
slipping over the bone with a click.

Human beings have followed the beat of Rangifer migration for
tens of thousands of years, as far south as Europe during the last ice
age, where charging bulls are painted on the cave walls of Lascaux,
then back north with the glaciers' retreat.[3] Rangifer bodies were
of twofold use: hundreds of miles from the lush ocean, they transformed indigestible plants into protein and fat, and their hides
kept warmth close to the skin. A Beringian family needed at least
a dozen pelts per year for clothing, and more for the leather used
in sleds, tents, and the harnesses on their dogs.[4] Hunting was one
way to meet this need. But in western Siberia, people and reindeer
formed another way to live, and to die, near each other: the reciprocal relationship of domestication. Reindeer that stayed close to
people were protected from wolves, and people who kept reindeer
close were protected from starvation. The practice spread east,
reaching Chukotka a few hundred years before any Imperial Russian.[5] By the time foreigners arrived in Beringia, people in North
America lived with wild caribou, and with both wild and tame reindeer in Chukotka.

*

On the sea and on the shore, foreigners in Beringia anticipated
wealth from fur, ivory, and blubber, but they did not expect agriculture. Cultivating energy was a terrestrial pursuit. It was also critical
to the theories of history foreigners imported; from the biblical par-

able of hunter Esau and farmer Jacob to the predictions of Adam Smith and Karl Marx, taming plants and animals to human agricultural will turned wild nature into culture, offering the stability that allowed people to make their own future.[6] To domesticate and cultivate, to *grow*, was foundational to civilization.

Then there was Beringian land: too cold for corn, or wheat, or even, in most places, potatoes. Horses, pigs, and cows had no fodder. The tundra, to most foreigners' eyes, locked its people in timeless dependence on a land unpredictable and cold. But there were reindeer: animals that could be owned collectively or privately, with palatable flesh, running in herds that promised meat and leather by the ton. And domesticated herds also seemed, to the governments of Russia and the United States, a means of social conversion. Changing the relationship between reindeer and people—owning them privately as a small farmer, as part of a missionary education, or collectivizing them in a *kolkhoz*—could make Beringians part of sovereign visions. Beringia existed in a time apart. Reindeer would bring the land and people into history.

I.

In the 1860s, a Chukchi boy named Ei'heli grew up on the Omolon River, learning to route his years around the migratory turns of his father's reindeer herd. It was a pattern relatively new to the Chukchi. In the decades prior to the seventeenth century, people hunted reindeer on the peninsula. They learned from the Tungus how to capture reindeer and breed them to pull sleds.[7] Groups of nomadic families began keeping a few dozen animals, which they scrupulously avoided eating. Wild herds still clothed and fed people, along with the corpus of other things hunted and gathered. Yet, with the reindeer close, sometimes a herder would suck milk from the udder of a nursing doe, spit it into a bladder, and share it as a delicacy.[8]

Drinking reindeer milk was a prelude to a slow transformation—one that began, like many things in the north, with the climate. The eighteenth century was cool in Chukotka, conditions favored by reindeer. More does brought their fawns to term, and more fawns survived. For the next fifty to eighty years, the domestic herds grew, but the wild reindeer hunt continued. The Chukchi increased trade with their coastal neighbors, where hunting at sea was less productive in the cold.[9] Then, near the turn of the nineteenth century, the domestic herds foundered in wet springs and disease-ridden summers. So, too, did the wild reindeer. Driven by a need for meat and pelage, herders began to kill their stock. The practice continued when the herds increased again. Reindeer breeders found themselves with a massive surplus: enough animals to quadruple the number of people living on the tundra in four or five generations.[10] Enough for the Chukchi to field armies of over a thousand men.

Ei'heli came of age in a time of plenty, a child of the reindeer revolution. The benefits of that revolution were not distributed equally. Some herders had hundreds of reindeer, some a dozen, and some so few that they worked for the wealthy, or as trappers and traders, or moved to the coast and hunted from the sea. Five to ten percent of herders owned between half and two-thirds of the peninsula's domestic herds.[11] Reindeer came with prestige and power, the ability to give gifts and make war. Women married wealthy men and left them if their fortunes changed. Ei'heli's father, Amar'wkurgin, owned two large herds. By the late nineteenth century, Ei'heli had five herds and almost as many wives. It was a time, in the words of one Chukchi man, of peace, when "everybody thinks only of gain, and all tribes and nations intermingle."[12] As with the reindeer, so too with the people.

Domestic herds did not liberate the Chukchi from chance. A rich family could become poor in the space of hours, or days, or weeks—their herds lost in blizzards, to disease, or to the many beings, only a few of them human, that made mischief on the tundra. The Chukchi were surrounded, as one shaman said, "by hostile spirits who walk about us invisibly with gaping mouths." On the tundra were mushrooms stronger than human minds; fish the size of boulders; creatures that could shift shape. Such beings might master a reindeer herd and turn them feral, or command a destitute herder to murder a rich man.[13] At the end of summer, when a pastured herd returned to camp fat from grazing in the uplands or near the coast, its arrival was met with loud cries and a flurry of blunt arrows, to drive away any lingering, malevolent, invisible souls.

Out in those pastures, Ei'heli and the men he hired sheltered birthing cows from wind, separated trampling bulls from calves, culled animals infected with scabies or hoof rot, cut the velvet curl of calves' ears to mark them as a particular person's property. Herders gelded young bucks with their teeth, using them for draft animals to spare pregnant does. They moved the herds constantly. Dogs and men listened for the wolves that came with nights of heavy snow; teaching the animals over generations to ignore some dangers of predation.[14]

Tending the herd, especially in the rut or in the stampedes brought on by biting flies, was the work of the whole camp. Women spelled their husbands at watch during the dusky midnights of summer. Children as young as ten knew how to lasso a calf. And the labor came due. In early autumn, people moved from camp to camp for the ceremonies of slaughter, giving gifts and dancing, racing and gambling, eating bone marrow until grease rolled off their elbows, the shaman's drum punctuating the bustle with prayers of gratitude and elation.

*

In the early autumns of the nineteenth century, Iñupiaq nations were also on the move. Tuŋŋana and Kiktuġiaq were born in

Nuataaġmiut country, among the wide river plains and crumbling foothills of the Brooks Range. In their childhood, caribou herds were hundreds of thousands strong.[15] Every animal in them was wild: the revolution of domestication had not broken eastward into North America. Chukchi knew the power of tame animals and would not sell live reindeer. So, in Alaska, people did not move herds, but moved to find them, as well as the other things that made life: arctic hare, beluga whale, eggs, greens, moose, muskox, ptarmigan, roots, seals, sheep, walruses, the occasional bear. Variety and transience were features of human adaptation as much as of caribou. When Tunŋana and Kiktuġiaq were small, they waited with their mothers at a fishing camp, running between racks of *sulukpaugaq*, the grayling, and *iqalukpik*, arctic char. The hillsides above were lustrous with salmonberries and blueberries as the quickest people climbed among them to hunt.

There were many ways to kill a caribou. Small groups stalked them with bows and arrows. People built funnel-shaped corrals of stones and brush; the fastest runners, men and women, channeled part of a herd into the narrow point and snared or speared animals in their milling, white-eyed panic. Others killed swimming caribou from kayaks. A strong man on snowshoes could run down a cow.[16] As a boy, Tunŋana was taught that death was only part of caribou labor: each carcass had to be skinned, each section of flesh cut into sheets to dry or packed into a cleaned stomach to carry. The marrow bones were cached and split open in the lean months of late winter, women praying for plentiful grease as they boiled them.[17] Kiktuġiaq learned the precise uses of hide: the skins of fall-killed cows were best for parkas; bull hides with winter hair became beds; calfskins were soft enough for underwear. The thin hide peeled from forelegs made pliable mittens and boðt tops.

Before the 1850s, seven populations of Rangifer oscillated through northwestern Alaska, some half a million strong.[18] But even then, their hunters did not take abundance for granted. Rain might turn the tundra to knee-deep mush. Snow could linger, perturbing migration. There were valleys inhabited by wild babies, called *iraaq*, that tickled unsuspecting people to death. Once, a hunter was swallowed whole by a giant lake fish.[19] And caribou, some of them once human, based their willingness to give their flesh on the behavior of their killers. Years before they married, Tunŋana and Kiktuġiaq learned that familial harmony made hunting fruitful; that they must speak respectfully of the animals, or a black cloud would form over the hunter; that they should cut off the head of a dead caribou so the soul could return to its herd.[20] Good people knew what caribou valued about the landscape—the tender lichen, the slow rivers, the places of few bears and strong breezes—and what caribou valued in human beings. They behaved accordingly, for a successful hunt was a thing of joy.

II.

Tunŋana and Kiktuġiaq were just old enough to learn these things when the world of foreigners began its creep into Nuataaġmiut country. Inland from the coast came steel traps and guns, iron pots and alcohol, traded from whalers for caribou meat and hide parkas.[21] Inland, too, came disease: an outbreak of *qaviqsirut:* red sickness, measles.[22] Or perhaps the disease walked with other nations, the people trailing, hungry, across the Kobuk River and the tributaries of the Noatak because caribou had stopped coming across their fall tundra.

Around the Arctic, Rangifer were in decline at the end of the nineteenth century. Herds in the hundreds of thousands found dozens of ways to die, from wolves to starvation to infected hooves. In Alaska, the hunt began failing along Norton Sound and on the Seward Peninsula in the late 1860s and 1870s. Over the next ten years, the absence crept north: uneven in severity, but terrible in scope.[23] Between 1881 and 1883, nearly every edible thing was scarce, not just the animals killed by commerce, but also fish and birds. By 1900, the seven great caribou herds had collapsed into two.[24] And as with the caribou, so too with the people. Nations buckled into each other, the unlucky caught in a cascade of lack: the whales mostly gone, the walruses hunted poor, then the caribou. In search of sustenance, the Kivalliñirmiut nation went up the coast to Tikiġaq or Utqiaġvik, or inland toward Nuataaġmiut country, as did the Napaaqtuġmiut and scattered remnants of other nations. The survivors remember people collapsing in their tracks from cold and starvation.

Those survivors brought word of calamity to the Nuataaġmiut before the inland herds declined. With them came theories about the disaster. The aŋatqut, the shamans, some said, stole the herds. In Kivalina, a man named Ikaaqsaq tried to convince his people to move away from the increasingly barren coast to better country; when they did not follow him, he seized all the caribou. Others described forest fires that drove away herds and depleted mosses and lichen.[25] Some along the coast blamed the appetites of whalers, with their guns.[26] Qaviaraġmiut historian William Oquilluk, whose family fled from the Seward Peninsula to the whaling station at Jabbertown during the famine, told of three prior calamities. Each had its own cause: the first winter, long generations ago; a great flood in the lifetime of distant ancestors; a hungry year with no summer survived by his grandparents. Disaster was hardly novel, whatever the origin.

Nor were the solutions. William Oquilluk followed the history of each calamity with its recovery, earned through knowledge. Iñupiat first learned to think, then to make tools, then to have the powers of the aŋatqut. They also learned to move in times of catastrophe.[27] When the Nuataaġmiut heard from refugees that hunts were failing to the southwest, they decided not to wait for their caribou to wane. Stillness might mean starvation. In the 1890s, Nuataaġmiut scouts went north and east, and found places with sheep, fish, and other game. Their families followed. Tuŋŋana and Kiktuġiaq's first son, Simon Paneak, was born along the Killik River, far from old Nuataaġmiut country. By then, their nation had scattered over hundreds of miles, clusters of tents sheltering where there were still caribou among hills north of the Brooks Range.

The Nuataaġmiut now lived within reach of Herschel Island and Utqiaġvik. The Yankee whaling fleet, iced in over winter, waiting for whales, wanted to buy fresh meat and fox furs. Visiting the ships became a regular part of the Nuataaġmiut year. Thus, as whales and walruses fed distant markets, caribou fed the demanding work of killing at sea and on the coast. The extractive arm of commerce extended onto the tundra through displaced Iñupiat. Years later, Simon Paneak recalled how "everybody wanted to be caribou hunters, you know, because getting rich. . . . That's why all the Eskimos were moving up that way. The whalers pulled them up."[28] To the south, the village of Kiŋigin began trading reindeer hides from the Chukchi just across the strait. People needed clothing; commerce and climate had left the Seward Peninsula almost barren of caribou.

*

To many American observers, the tundra had never been a place full of life; "dotted with blackened skeletons of old ice," one whaler wrote, it was "an utterly desolate land."[29] For those Americans who interpreted westward expansion not as theft, but as putting unused land to productive purpose, the "impassable deserts of snow, vast tracks of dwarf timbers, frozen rivers, inaccessible mountain ranges" made Alaska seem frozen out of time, and thus "absolutely useless."[30] They viewed inland Iñupiaq nomadism as a sign of poverty, a lack rather than an adaptation. In so poor a wilderness, it seemed inevitable that people would starve.

Or maybe people were starving because Alaskan timelessness met badly with modern times. Michael Healy, on the revenue

service cutter *Bear*, wrote that caribou once "made yearly vis-
its. Now it is rare to find that the natives . . . have seen or tasted
deer meat."[31] Where Iñupiat blamed fires caused by lightning or
shamans, foreigners blamed firearms. Naturalist William Nelson
thought rifles enabled the "slaughter [of] deer with true aboriginal improvidence."[32] Sport hunters of the Boone and Crockett Club
mold imputed it to the "wholesale massacre perpetuated by the
natives."[33] Healy was more charitable, arguing that the "timid disposition of the deer" made them shy of guns, but he was horrified
that Iñupiat killed fawns and does.[34] Sheldon Jackson, Alaska's first
commissioner of education, had another theory: starvation was the
result of an immoral market. Walruses were nearly extinct because
"commerce wanted more ivory," he reported to Congress. Whales
had been "sacrificed" merely for blubber, and now rifles "killed off
and frightened away" the caribou.[35]

Whatever the cause—barrenness, backwardness, barrenness
made by a backward market—foreigners concluded the tundra
needed to be reclaimed from uselessness and its people salvaged
from poverty. The most influential plan for deliverance came from
Jackson. Too short and bespectacled to evangelize overseas, he came
of age as a missionary among the Choctaw. By 1885, when he became
Alaska's education commissioner, he shared the prevailing postbellum commitment to indigenous assimilation through Christian
education and market production.[36] His task, as he saw it, was "not
only to teach reading, writing, and arithmetic, but also how to live
better, how to make more money in order to live better, and how to
utilize the resources of the country in order to make more money."[37]
In Alaska, this required something that would "make valuable vast
areas of land otherwise worthless," and "take a barbarian people . . .
and lift them up to comfortable self-support and civilization."[38]

Jackson found his solution on the Russian side of the strait in
1890, where he sailed with Captain Healy. The revenue service
had orders to distribute gifts among the Yupik and Chukchi as a

sign of American goodwill. At harbor along the coast, Jackson met a group of inland Chukchi, people he described as "good-sized, robust, fleshy, well-fed," and even "half-civilized."[39] Their vitality, in Jackson's estimation, came from owning domesticated reindeer. Jackson proposed to Congress the idea of importing tame stock. Big game had gone the way of the bison. The ocean could not be restocked like a trout stream. Caribou were wild and implicated in a feral marketplace run by immoral gun and rum traders. But domestic reindeer could be *owned*. Jackson, like those who read his congressional reports, understood progress to be a function of production; hunting and gathering had to give way to an agricultural or industrial existence if Alaska were to be American. Private property was the foundation of farming and industry. Possessing reindeer, Smithsonian naturalist Charles Townsend wrote, would "render a wild people pastoral or agricultural," putting them on "the first step toward their advancement."[40]

Rangifer solved Alaska's agrarian barrenness as well as its human backwardness. It also offered redemption for U.S. Indian policy. The first skeleton of federal bureaucracy—courts, schools, mining laws—came to Alaska with the 1884 Organic Act, a few years after Helen Hunt Jackson published *A Century of Dishonor*, which catalogued federal moral and practical failures toward "people we have suffered . . . to remain savages."[41] The book helped sour Congress and missionaries alike on treaties and reservations as policies that created dependency and poverty. Sheldon Jackson hoped to avoid such mistakes in Alaska. Instead of reservations, mission schools operating with government support could use reindeer for market pedagogy. Once taught their value, Beringian owners could take space that was unappealing to whites, and make the land plentiful while attaining the "position of civilized, wealth-producing American citizens."[42] Jackson's ideal was the extermination of difference, but also penance. "In our management of these people," Townsend wrote, "we have an opportunity to atone, in a measure, for a century of dishonorable treatment of the Indian."[43] Redeeming the last frontier from immiserization would redeem the first frontier, or its heirs, from a history of brutality.

*

Redemption began on a rocky spit of land under hills scoured red and bare by wind, on the northern edge of Port Clarence, along a stream long used by whalers for fresh water. Jackson named the inaugural canvas tents and drafty cabin Teller Station, after his congressional ally, Henry Teller. In 1893, Jackson did not have many such allies. Congress declined his first request for reindeer funds. It took him two years to raise money from church groups, gain permission from Tsar Aleksandr III to import domesticated reindeer from Russia, to convince a few Chukchi to violate tradition and sell their stock, hire several Chukchi willing to move to Alaska as instructors, and load 171 reindeer into the *Bear* with a sling. In the darkless night of July 4, the domesticated *Rangifer* finally arrived, quivering and bruised, on a North American tundra green with familiar plants.

The reindeer walked out onto Iñupiaq land. For its people, the animals had to prove their utility. After decades of absent caribou, Iñupiaq nations on the Seward Peninsula bought hides from across the strait, traded their labor for flour, caught fish, seals, some walruses, birds, beluga whales.[44] Reindeer were not salvation from immediate crisis because the crisis had moved on. The reindeer might even *make* a crisis. The village of Kiŋigin, not far from Teller, controlled the hide trade from Chukotka and threatened to kill the Chukchi herders before they became competitors.[45] But the reindeer were also a curiosity. All winter, Iñupiaq men and women filed through Teller to inspect the small herd. Four stayed on, paid in clothing and food and the promise of owning their own animals, eventually, once they learned to lasso and corral and drive a reindeer sled. In the spring, they watched over the Teller does and sixty spindly-legged calves. That summer, Jackson imported more stock from Chukotka and distributed them among mission schools around Alaska, including the Yupik villages on St. Lawrence Island.

Jackson was of the same generation as Frederick Jackson Turner, who theorized that American distinctiveness was a product of first encountering and then cultivating the frontier. It was a transition from growth acquired as roving commercial appetites stripped territories of wild value—bison, or timber, or minerals—to growth that was domesticated, enclosed, able through innovation and efficiency to maintain profits in a particular space. It was a capitalism of property, not just extraction. And property gave owners political liberty—independence to speak and vote with their material security assured, while agriculture gave the market a stable future through owning and killing the same kind of animal. Proof that such steady increase was possible lay in the reindeer: born onto tundra nearly devoid of caribou, calves flourished on abundant lichen. Even wolves were rare. In 1897, the number of domesticated Rangifer in Alaska was over two thousand head. By 1901, the number had doubled.

III.

Moving north out of the taiga, with its windbeaten spruce and alder, patches of the tundra appear pale. Mats of greenish-gray reindeer lichen cling to dry rock and sandy soil, each minute, hornlike branch made from interdependent fungus and algae. Where water is held on the surface by permafrost, meadows of sedge and primrose are broken by mounds of undecomposed plants, a peaty home for shrub birch and cloudberries. Farther north, and up mountainsides, splays of red and yellow lichen cover the stone. Across these miniature biomes come the Rangifer herds, a composite of more than four hundred species of shrubs, sedges, grasses, mosses, and lichen. Their meat, made from such variety, tastes like no other ungulate—sweet and complex, the fat nutty.

In Chukotka, the reindeer moved with their minders, who rested their animals on good pasture, while leaving other places to recover from grazing. But the tundra did not always cooperate. In the early twentieth century, spring sleet covered the land in ice, pinning reindeer on poor fodder. Ei'heli's luck turned with an outbreak of hoof rot. Wolf packs grew. Some herders lost half their animals.[46] Imperial Russia's regional officers at Ostrovnoe knew that herd collapse brought hunger to people the tsar was meant to govern with benevolence. It also brought political instability that was confounding to the empire. In the 1860s, Baron Maydell tried to anoint hereditary chiefs among the Chukchi, choosing the richest reindeer herders in the hope that titles would extend the empire's influence. Ei'heli's father, Amar'wkurgin, was given medals to signal his new rank. Ei'heli inherited the medals, but lost many of his reindeer, and his prestige.[47] Leaders were as fluid as reindeer populations in Chukchi country. Without formal, permanent bonds of loyalty—or a monopoly on violence and commerce—the Russian state watched with little recourse as Chukchi-controlled furs were traded to American ships. Uncertain reindeer numbers were part of uncertain sovereignty.

Chukotka's regional administrators had an eye on Americans for another reason. Alaskan schools, one administrator wrote, raised both valuable reindeer and "consciousness on the part of their natives regarding their need for culture."[48] That culture, at least for Russian populists, was defined by agriculture; it was the peasant commune that gave Russia a model for progress separate from the depredations of Western capitalism. Reindeer could move the peasantry north. N. F. Kallinikov, who surveyed the Chukchi Peninsula in the early twentieth century, also visited Alaska. He reported that Jackson's program had "natives . . . working for the common good" after only a few years, a solution to "all the poverty we are witnessing" in Chukotka. Regional officials requested funds to "raise [the Chukchi] level of initiative and the transition to a more advanced use of natural goods," while "introducing Russian culture."[49]

Moral and sovereign ends were conveniently aligned; if only the number of reindeer would stabilize. And stabilizing herds seemed a more manageable and urgent task than finding teachers for "the very scattered population of the Peninsula."[50] In 1897, the military governor of Primorskaia Oblast requested 1,823 rubles for a veterinarian to study reindeer diseases in Chukotka. Over a decade later, the governor was still arguing for the necessity of veterinary assistance, since "the industry of reindeer herding, given [the region's] conditions, has such serious economic importance."[51] Finally, in 1911, two veterinarians went north, equipped with "the physical health permitting them to serve in the far districts," but without medical supplies or the visit to the Teller Station the regional administrator suggested.[52]

The young men found their task nearly impossible. The Chukchi did not want to discuss their herds' condition with foreigners. There were no roads. Even the etiology of hoof disease was unclear; U.S. specialists attributed the illness to bruising on rocky ground, and those in Russia believed it was infectious.[53] Four years after the veterinarians' arrival, the Chukchi Peninsula herds were in decline. More than three hundred thousand domestic animals died from disease, wolves, and starvation. Wild reindeer nearly disappeared completely.

*

In the experience of men like Ei'heli and his sons, to lose many reindeer was terrible. But then, many things on the tundra were, in a place where boulders were beings, rivers had their own masters, and wild reindeer were watched by a spirit who demanded care in the hunt. As one shaman explained to Vladimir Bogoraz, "Nothing created by man has any power."[54]

Bogoraz was told this at the turn of the twentieth century when, banished by the tsar for his populist socialist beliefs, he turned his Chukotkan exile into ethnographic fieldwork. He was the first socialist many Chukchi met. By 1917, Bogoraz was back in the West. He was not, at first, a Bolshevik—he was a milder sort of socialist, skeptical of professional revolutionaries—but he saw the Committee of the North as able to bring morally necessary change. Bogoraz shaped the committee's initial approach toward "small peoples," arguing that trained ethnographers should protect them from aggressive development, offer medicine and education, and then assist with the gradual transformation of "economic life" by "introducing new elements to ensure painless progress."[55] Those elements were collective farms, allowing people to "not only feed themselves but constantly improve their lives, become confederates in the worker's state."[56] And in a country with millions of reindeer in herds from Finland to Chukotka, these confederates would do important work. "Judging from the example of Alaska," one committee report noted, "reindeer herding can achieve significant development and deliver an important industry not only for natives of the north, but to the national economy as a whole."[57]

In St. Petersburg—now Leningrad—in cold rooms lit by oil lamps, Bogoraz trained some of Bolshevism's missionaries at the Institute of the Peoples of the North. But most who went to Chukotka were untrained volunteers inspired by Lenin, by the promise of adventure, by a salary. Tikhon Semushkin, a teacher from south of Moscow, was so moved by Bogoraz's descriptions of Soviet work in the Arctic, he took a train east, followed by the sea-sickening voyage northward from Vladivostok. Arriving in the strait, Semushkin found himself looking at the American west, where it sat in the past across the International Date Line. Chukotka, he wrote, was the meeting place of "two days—New and Old—and two worlds, new and old, socialist and capitalist."[58]

The new world was, Semushkin wrote, "hostile to construction," due to the "storms, cold rain, agglomerations of ice."[59] He found many of the same challenges as the Christian missionaries living to the east, in the past. In winter, the only transit was by dog team or reindeer sleigh; in the summer, the land was swampy—knee-deep in places. Insects were a torment. The Chukchi spoke no Russian, so Semushkin and his comrades learned Chukchi—a struggle that caused hilarity or horror when men spoke in the dialect reserved for women. Most of all, even in their own language, the tundra Chukchi were disinterested in Semushkin's explanation of how "all our people were making a new life, just as Lenin said." In his memoir, written a few years after arriving in Chukotka, Semushkin described trying to convince a Chukchi man named Tnayrgyn that his children should attend boarding school at the *cultbaz*, or culture base, in Lavrentiya. Pointing to a portrait of Lenin, Semushkin explained "how he that we see hanging on the wall taught that all peoples will live well only when they themselves make their own lives" by learning to read. Tnayrgyn responded: "What you say is nonsense. Doesn't [Lenin] know we make our own lives for ourselves?"[60]

Tnayrgyn's was a common sentiment. The secretary of the Chukotka Revkom tried to organize elected leaders among the Chukchi, only to be told the Chukchi had no "chiefs" and were "all equal," at least over time.[61] And no one wanted to discuss reindeer. "The Chukchi took me in and willingly talked about general, abstract themes and topics that do not affect the fundamental problems of the economy," reported a committee member tasked with forming collective farms. "But when issues began to touch on the deer and reindeer herding, the Chukchi became wary and stopped talking."[62] Semushkin and his colleagues debated whether this meant the Chukchi were not "primitive communists," as expected, but "primitive capitalists" who needed to be saved from themselves. "If it is possible to speak about the existence of class stratification on the tundra," wrote N. Galkin, "it is only among the reindeer herders. Here there are 'masters and workers.' "[63] Or perhaps not: "There is no stratification, as such, among the nomads," wrote another Bolshevik; fortunes changed so often, there could be no stable class structure.[64] Either way, it would take years to form collectives, as "these first steps are the most difficult."[65] But those steps, for the Bolsheviks, would inevitably lead to Soviet citizens: they offered a material salvation as transparently desirable, to them, as the life after death promised by missionaries across the strait.

The Bolsheviks preached liberation. But future liberation implies present oppression, and the Chukchi did not see themselves as oppressed. Lenin promised small peoples self-determination on the road to collective utopia. The Chukchi had been determining their lives for centuries, and knew the reindeer—the animal the Soviets took such suspicious interest in counting—helped them do so. Semushkin told parents that school was a useful and moral place; the Chukchi saw foreigners drinking, arguing, and cheating, and an outbreak of influenza that killed children. Semushkin himself was rumored to have spread gonorrhea.[66] Most of all, the Soviets promised to lift Chukchi from timeless stasis into conscious, historical action, failing to see in Chukchi histories of war and domestication a people who already understood the future as theirs to shape, at least politically. Nothing created by man had any power over the tundra as a whole—that was, to a Chukchi herder, nonsense—but the Chukchi had long exercised power over other people, and themselves. As Tnayrgyn explained, foreigners "do not understand our way of life" and had little to offer, as "they cannot live on the tundra."[67]

So, some Chukchi visited the *cultbaz* for the tea, radio, and films, but tundra participation in worker's committees was low. Most new Soviet believers came from coastal villages.[68] Even lower was the number of herders interested in joining *kolkhozy*. Conditions for reindeer were good in the 1920s, swelling the herds to half a million domestic animals.[69] But at the end of the decade, less than one percent were in collectives.[70] Where herders were convinced to merge their reindeer and listen to talk of the light Lenin would bring, *kolkhoz* herds were so small and supplies so short that, one organizer wrote, "We bought reindeer. We ate them all . . . So in reality there are no reindeer collectives."[71]

*

Even as they ate the stock of the revolution, Chukotka's Bolsheviks had clarity regarding the collective form their new economy would someday take. Across the strait, the American missionaries had sustenance, but declining certainty. Their problem was not reindeer: there were ten thousand or so domestic animals by 1905. Nor was the issue a lack of positive attention; Congress had begun funding the program, and reindeer appeared in the national press after a small herd was driven north to feed ice-stranded whalers at Barrow in 1897. At Teller Station, herding was no longer taught by Chukchi, whose habits of eating warble-fly larvae off reindeer's backs and guiding the herd with human urine horrified the missionary staff. Instead, Jackson arranged for Saami instructors from Norway. Heralded in newspapers across the United States as Christian, blue-eyed, literate, and civilized, they would "teach the helpless natives of the far Northwest how to take care of themselves."[72]

The lack of certainty, in the first decades of the twentieth century, was not over *whether* reindeer would make progress on the tundra, but how: What was the right kind of reindeer farm—and farmer? Under Sheldon Jackson, the program combined earthly salvation through private property with the eternal salvation of Christian conversion. To earn a herd, Iñupiaq men had to move to a mission, tend animals they were prohibited from killing so that stock could breed, were punished for eating so that stock could be sold, and were chastised for leaving untended in order to kill things they could eat. The lure was their own herd of ten or twenty reindeer—this number changed constantly—earned after a similarly capricious term of apprenticed years. And Iñupiat had to live with missionary rules for worship. In short, owning reindeer came

after performing the rituals of Christian and commercial enlightenment. Many Iñupiaq did not find this appealing; twelve years
after the program began, the majority of reindeer had not passed
to their ownership.[73] Jackson had not made Jeffersonian herders
from Iñupiat hunters.

In 1905, the Department of the Interior sent BIA agent Frank
Churchill to investigate this failure. Like Jackson, he concluded
that the reindeer had "great value . . . under proper management,
for food and clothing." However, where missions "secured a herd
of reindeer from the Government the mission got the best of the
bargain," especially after the Nome gold rush brought a booming
demand for meat. The "Eskimos are very poor indeed," he wrote,
"probably about as well off now as they ever were."[74] Instead of making Iñupiat self-sufficient, missionary education "along material and

Iñupiaq reindeer herders bringing meat to Nome. *Alaska State Archives, B.B.
Dobbs Photographs 1903–1907, ASL-P12-178.*

temporal lines has largely been a series of failures," another assessor concluded, "making the natives dependent by feeding them."[75]

Implicit in Churchill's critique was the missions' inability to
instill a functional understanding of the earthly future. Some Iñupiaq pupils might have become Christian, but they were not capitalists. Churchill, like other reformers of his generation, wanted to
separate spiritual and material growth. Religion could handle life's
cyclic rituals, the baptisms and marriages and funerals and what
came after death. The state would administer earthly progress,
managing nature's resources so that the market could value them
most efficiently. He recommended full federal oversight of the reindeer until each Iñupiaq family, and only Iñupiaq families, owned
enough to "take care of themselves and be reasonably comfortable."[76] In response, Jackson resigned in 1907. The next year, the
newly formed U.S. Reindeer Service instructed government teachers to transfer herds to Iñupiat, to Yupik on St. Lawrence Island,
and to other nations in Alaska. Reindeer ownership was now the
precursor of enlightenment, not its reward.

*

The summers when Makaiqtaq was a child were spent playing
around the half-underground sod houses at Singiq. Once, in the
long days of sun rolling on the horizon without dimming, he saw
animals grazing on the hills above, stamping flies off their patchy
coats. They were caribou, the last of the wild herds on the Seward
Peninsula. Years later, when he heard about the domestic reindeer
at Teller, he remembered their hooves and puffing breath. Makaiqtaq was a grown man by then, with a wife and an extended family
stricken by measles in 1900. Moving to a reindeer station, with its
rules and months spent away from home, would hardly help.

It was only after the Reindeer Service separated Christian salvation from market participation that Makaiqtaq—known as Thomas
Barr to the government—bought five reindeer for some fox skins

and one hundred dollars. Reindeer were now a tool for dealing with the market more on Iñupiaq terms. Makaiqtaq built a winter camp with other families at Ublasaun, a place they could seal, fish, trap, and herd over the course of a year, making all kinds of value with their work: caloric, cultural, financial. In January 1915, in deep cold, he went to the first reindeer fair. The Reindeer Service sponsored days of draft-reindeer races and butchering demonstrations and awarded prizes for sleds and herding skill. In the evenings, everyone discussed business. Makaiqtaq was not alone. By 1915, two-thirds of the seventy thousand reindeer in Alaska were owned by indigenous herdsmen.[77]

The Reindeer Service had created yeoman farmers, but reindeer yeomen were not creating profit. The local market for meat surged with the gold rush: in the first years of the twentieth century, miners were so desperate, they paid thirty cents a pound for meat. Then it ebbed, gone bust like most mines. The solution, the service reported, was "an export trade in reindeer products."[78] A pound of reindeer outside of Alaska might be worth even more than calories sold to gold prospectors. What did not pay, to the Reindeer Service's frustration, were small herds. The fine margin of energy on the tundra allows reindeer to birth, usually, a single fawn per doe each year. The average Iñupiaq herd had fifty animals. Once herders fed themselves and saved breeding stock, the remaining animals did not yield a profitable surplus of spare deer for slaughter. The small farmer would only ever be a subsistence farmer.

The Reindeer Service knew that scale mattered, because Iñupiat were not the only people marketing reindeer. Iñupiaq owners were prohibited from selling live animals to foreigners, but the same rule did not apply to reindeer retained by missions and Saami. Carl Lomen, come north during the Nome rush, saw in those swelling herds a reliable fortune. He purchased living Rangifer stock, sold paper stock in the Lomen Company, and with this capital built a vertically integrated corporation: thousands of animals herded by hired labor, run between company corrals, killed in company slaughterhouses, dispatched south in company cold-storage ships. Lomen courted national publicity to "excite sufficient curiosity in the minds of prospective customers," from restaurants and dog food companies to tanneries and the U.S. Army.[79] Thousands of pounds of reindeer meat, the surplus from his large herds, began leaving Alaska.

With Lomen's model in mind, the Reindeer Service again reformed reindeer practice: it decided to corporatize. Individual Iñupiat pooled their animals in joint stock companies. Herders were issued one share of stock per reindeer and divided annual profits proportionally. The resulting cooperatives, as they were called, were not an Iñupiaq decision; Makaiqtaq, for one, disagreed with pooled herds.[80] But the Reindeer Service believed, in theory if not in deed, that its plans furthered equality. The lesson of prior Indian policy was to extend the franchise of ownership in order to assimilate. Stock companies simply made the small-farmer ideal corporate, as tundra and market conditions demanded. It still granted Iñupiaq owners private property, and the Reindeer Service saw private property as necessary for political liberty and, eventually, equality of opportunity. Not all Iñupiaq would become rich, but any one of them might, and the rest had the ability to "secure such supplies as [modern] life demands."[81]

The assumption behind this policy was that of a fundamental human sameness, which allowed for the eventual assimilation of Iñupiat into the American body politic. But there was a second model of tundra profit by 1920s. Bringing north social Darwinist and free-market ideas, some in the Reindeer Service began to interpret economic dissimilarity as evolutionary destiny. "The Native cannot grasp the idea of a stock company," wrote one official. "It is difficult for him to understand that he owns any deer unless he can see which one he owns."[82] The universal (natural) condition of people in the marketplace was inequality, and the natural (universal) signal of inequality was race. Unlike whites, a "Native cannot see the possibilities of the reindeer business," a teacher complained, as "he has no vision. For him today is sufficient unto itself."[83]

Vision was necessary if herds were to follow William Randolph Hearst's plan and supply New York's burgeoning population with reindeer meat. The Secretary of the Interior and the press argued that such national use was possible only under white management.[84] Alaska's territorial governor agreed. "It is only through the white owners and shippers that it will be possible to add to the food supply of the country at large," he wrote, since they could find markets and investors. The export "industry must naturally fall to whites."[85] Iñupiat could be subsistence herders. They made excellent employees on white reindeer ranches, and might even supply local markets. But Iñupiat lacked "the mental capacity," one teacher wrote, to comprehend "interest or a share."[86] Growth did not come equally to all races. And if the state was to best manage growth for the nation, to provide energy for its citizens, it should not hold back the nation's natural capitalists.

In the 1920s, the two theories of Alaska's reindeer—valuable either for extinguishing Iñupiaq difference through economic assimilation or extinguishing the naturally unfit through economic competition—were in contest. The result, for Iñupiat, was more inconsistency: reindeer were under personal control, or not. Reindeer were part of Christian practice, or not. Access to their bodies was as volatile as anything on the tundra. So was the ideal vision of a reindeer owner—was he a yeoman farmer, joint-stock shareholder, or an employee of Carl Lomen? Amid this variation, Makaiqtaq and his family, and other families, adapted reindeer to their own values. To be a full Iñupiaq adult meant being able to offer reciprocal care to others; to have social power required giving gifts. Owning reindeer could be a means to that end. They bought access to imported goods or became parkas or pulled sleds. Instead of completely replacing activities foreigners interpreted as primitive—hunting seals, gathering berries, trapping—Iñupiat made herding a way to combine long-standing relationships between plants and animals and places with ownership and market relations. During the 1918 influenza pandemic, its toll so severe on the Seward Peninsula that William Oquilluk called it the "fourth disaster," reindeer fed people. The herds were a tool, one of many, for recovery—not just from the pandemic, but from all that the early decades of commerce wrought in Iñupiaq country, a way of taking new knowledge from calamity and putting it to resurgent use.

Meanwhile, the domestic reindeer followed their own motivations. Hundreds of animals might leave a valley in an afternoon to avoid biting flies. Ten thousand peeled a hillside of its lichen in a month. Around Alaska, one teacher wrote, animals from many owners mixed "because the herds are getting too big and the grazing grounds too small."[87] There were four hundred thousand domestic reindeer by the end of the 1920s. Outside the territory, people consumed 6.5 million pounds of reindeer products, most from Lomen's stock.[88] How the tundra would grow its production of meat was not quite clear, but that it would grow—that reindeer had a place in feeding the national future—was, as Arctic adventurer John Burnham observed, "a commonplace statement of the inevitable."[89]

IV.

"Inevitable" was what socialist missionaries in Chukotka understood communism to be—the natural and glorious endpoint of history. And history was supposed to end sooner, under the First Five-Year Plan. All that speed moved more Bolsheviks into Chukchi space. Ivan Druri arrived in 1929, charged with organizing Chukotka's first *sovkhoz* at Snezhnoe. The Chukchi, he found, "treated our activities with distrust and suspicion. They understood that we wanted to be *chauchu*, that is, the owners of herds, and feared us as future competitors. The poor shepherds were still under their total influence."[90] Druri started his collective with a few recruits and reindeer he bought from wealthy Chukchi on the promise of giving nine rubles per doe and twelve per bull, but he never paid. Farther north, along the Chaun and Omvaam Rivers, veterinarians and zoologists surveyed what the collectivized tundra could be expected to produce. Traveling "red tents" followed nomads across the tundra, where Bolsheviks showed films, intoning explanations over the flickering projection: this was Comrade Lenin, now dead; this is Comrade Stalin; Stalin wants new men and women, wants everyone to "raise their cultural-political level."[91]

The First Five-Year Plan also introduced a way of sorting people: not by race, as the Americans were attempting, but by their place in time. The plan demanded the USSR run, in half a decade, "the course of development that took Western Europe fifty to a hundred years," Anatolii Skachko wrote. For the Chukchi, the speed required was even faster: a millennia in a decade, as "even a thousand years ago the cultural level [of Russians] was higher."[92] Now, people were either behind—backward—or actively transforming themselves. That transformation combined material progress and personal salvation; socialism was to be a kingdom of heaven made by enlightened souls on Earth. It followed that those who chose to live in the past, like Tnayrgyn, were to blame if that kingdom came slowly, to blame for how few children were in school, or how few reindeer were in collectives. Even Bogoraz, now an old man, began to look like a saboteur, his plans for gradual Chukchi development a sign of sympathy for the past.[93] His disciples could no longer debate whether the Chukchi had classes: the lack of progress proved their existence. The tundra was backward because it was full of *kulaks* and shamans. There could be no future until every old soul was liquidated, converted to new form.

What the Chukchi saw, as the First Five-Year Plan rolled its red tents through their camps, were foreigners peering at the vegetation, prodding people, giving out pills and powders, cheating on reindeer payments, demanding that youth speak before elders and women before men, and waving their hands over reindeer herds while muttering numbers. They looked, in short, as if they cursed everything they touched.[94] Where they spoke enough Chukchi, the men and women in the tents promised the triumph of human history over natural whims, "A NEW LIFE . . . a new, healthy, cultured existence in step with peasants and workers throughout this Soviet country."[95] But this would come only if the Chukchi transformed every part of their existence—including their relationship with reindeer, the most socially powerful creature on tundra—and did so for an idea.

It was a political demand at its most basic, a demand to change the way the fruits of human labor were distributed and the nonhuman stuff of the world was possessed. It was a demand most Chukchi rejected. Families sank deeper into the tundra, keeping their herds distant from any sign of the state. One Soviet doctor complained that *kulaks* and shamans "drove teachers away like wolves drive a herd."[96] Chukchi parents explained to Bolsheviks like Tikhon Semushkin that "children need to learn to look after reindeer" and "protect the herds—therefore they cannot attend school."[97] Others, like a man listed in the Soviet records as Kirol, fled; when he met one of the red tents, he explained, "I will not go to the Soviet authority, and may it not come to me either."[98] A Chukchi shaman named Nynitnilian danced to expel the Soviets, explaining to his followers that "soon the Americans will arrive and the Russians will be gone from here."[99]

*

As the 1920s ended, the people on Alaskan land were debating how to value reindeer as part of several imagined futures: as a tool of assimilation, as a national product, as one thing in a range of options for survival. While they debated, the reindeer bred:

400,000 animals in 1929 grew to 640,000 in the early years of the next decade. The herds had a new relationship with their human minders. L. J. Palmer, a biologist at the Bureau of Biological Survey, thought Rangifer should be treated like cattle on the prairies.[100] Following his model, large herds grazed freely over the range, rather than herders moving them from one closely watched pasture to the next. Palmer concluded that such open herds were less likely to overgraze, and would liberate herders from the tedium of husbandry.[101] Basing his analysis on the emerging concept of carrying capacity, Palmer calculated that a well-managed Alaskan tundra would support three to four million animals.[102]

As reindeer multiplied, ranging across the hills and flat sea plains, animals from Iñupiaq corporations and Karl Lomen's herd mixed. By "all crowding, each pressing on the other," reindeer made ownership indistinct.[103] Who *should* own was not significantly clearer. There was the Loman Company, with its small national market—at least until 1929, when it collapsed with the rest of the American economy. And there were the Iñupiaq cooperative herds, now by Iñupiaq choice and Lomen competition more focused on distributing reindeer equitably within villages than on profits.[104] No one was pleased. Lomen believed the government meddled in the market and that the "mentality of the Eskimo is about that of a fourteen year old," with "no idea of the value of property."[105] Iñupiat reported that Lomen stole their reindeer and cheated on wages.[106] Makaiqtaq, now herding with his son Gideon, believed the open-range ideal was a government strategy to let Lomen take Iñupiaq reindeer, and with them, Iñupiaq income.[107] Everyone complained to the Department of the Interior.

The department replied with investigative committees. It undertook, in all but name, a referendum on the two ways foreigners valued reindeer in the 1930s: as tools of assimilation or as objects only valuable to the natural—meaning foreign—capitalist. The first committee sided with foreigners, citing the "disinclination of the natives, who are naturally hunters rather than herdsmen, to accept the responsibility involved in reindeer ownership and management" as a reason to support Lomen.[108] The "natural hunters" and their ally, Kivalina teacher C. L. Andrews, responded by asserting Iñupiaq rights to land, herds, and restitution for "the time [native] property has been alienated."[109]

John Collier, Franklin Roosevelt's Indian affairs commissioner, convened a second investigation. Collier was the architect of the 1934 Indian Reorganization Act, which promoted cultural pluralism, tribal self-government, and traditional economies. He concluded that herding was a customary part of Iñupiaq existence, one to which whites had no claim.[110] Lomen had to be removed from the reindeer business to preserve its "native character" and allow the industry to develop in a "native way" on "native lands." Collier's plan became law with the 1937 Reindeer Act. The Bureau of Indian Affairs bought out the Lomen enterprise and made reindeer ownership by whites illegal, to "establish and maintain for the said natives of Alaska a self-sustaining economy."[111] The U.S. government had first created a tradition in the name of assimilation, and then had to protect it as racially particular in the name of cultural preservation.

As the herds were counted and ranges allotted, the Reindeer Service also tried to make production on the tundra match New Deal production across the country. The ideal merged private property with government supervision, from range surveys and vaccination programs to research into plant growth, hoof disease, and warble flies. The state managed the tundra so that the laws of economics and biology would, as the new reindeer administrator J. Sidney Rood wrote, "give [native] owners freedom to do what they ought with regard to the rights of others." Gone was Palmer's large-herd open-range ideal. Back was exclusively Iñupiaq yeoman farming. Families without reindeer could borrow them from the government for a few years, until they took complete ownership as "individual enterprisers" who would keep "vigilant custody of such breeding stock as they can manage" out of "fear of losing money."[112] Makaiqtaq, for one, agreed with Rood; he saw domestic reindeer as originating with a father and son who bequeathed them to people who would "not sell them," but "kill of them what you require in order to live without sorrow and anxiety, but never more than that!"[113] The moral to Makaiqtaq's story was that close herding and lack of greed kept tragedy away. The moral of the Reindeer Service's version was that personal ownership guaranteed liberty and efficiency, and the market guaranteed "the rewards which herders are able to obtain from herd crops [through] supply and demand."[114] Supply and demand: the two tenets of market faith.

*

By 1930, foreigners on both sides of the Bering Strait saw reindeer as a way to reclaim useful energy from recalcitrant ground and make useful citizens from uncivilized people. In Alaska, foreigners wanted generally collectivist Iñupiat to own private property; in Chukotka, the Soviet Union tried to make the generally private Chukchi herds collective.

Within these inverted projects was a contrast between how private property and planned production imagined what kinds of beings and places were useful. The American vision had an inherent unevenness: the tundra was a different kind of productive space than the sea or the shore could ever be, because it was home to a different kind of animal. Reindeer were property. Property was supposed to make the tundra home to stable growth, to the kind of commerce that came after the unenclosed market stripped away bison and timber, or whales and walrus. Ownership made livestock valuable while they were still alive, allowing the market to think in terms of generations. Reindeer were supposed to have a future—were a thing in which marketers could *sell* futures—because their bodies were enclosed; whales and wild foxes were not.

Bolshevik foreigners brought north a vision of radical equality among people: that was the new life that inspired Semushkin and Druri, a vision of plenty so evenly distributed that all human suffering would end. With it came a radically equal approach to production: the five-year plan did not initially distinguish between kinds of animal and kinds of space, as private ownership did, but expected that anything useful to people could be collectivized. No kind of place or animal was exempt from planned increase in the 1930s. Thus, walruses were hunted collectively, foxes were farmed collectively, and reindeer were herded collectively. No body and no space could be left in the past, so all were enclosed by the Soviet ideal.

There was another difference between the inverted Soviet and American visions. In the early twentieth century, the American state separated spiritual and material conversion. Thinking about the soul's future was distant, a matter of life after death, while the material future was measured in short-term earnings and wages. Owning reindeer did not require believing in any particular vision of the soul, and being Christian did not require reindeer. Reindeer were not a requirement of any kind: Makaiqtaq could own them and Simon Paneak could ignore them. Participating in the market thus had the illusion of choice, one separate from eschatological questions. But commerce has a cosmology, binding the world into what might be sold and for how much, equating progress with growth. Owning a herd necessarily came with habits of mind. Thus, the market's way of understanding time as linear and driven by short-term material increase crept—unevenly, with deviations and adaptations—over the tundra. The Soviets were, by contrast, without artifice. Where capitalism required individuals to work their way out of material injustice alone, socialism sought to overcome such isolation whether the person felt oppressed or not, by remaking them. To be a New Man of the socialist future required transformation from the soul outward. It entailed living in a time singular in its speed. It was against the clarity of the Bolshevik vision that Nynitnilian danced.

Meanwhile, the reindeer herds streamed each autumn over hills gone red-gold, heading inland for winter; then each spring, patchy with molt and heavy with calves, back toward coasts or mountainsides over the same hills, now lit with green new growth. Each year, as the twentieth century entered its fourth decade, the herds grew. An offering of flesh to the imagination of states who saw in them history in motion: plans met, profit growing, all transforming an Arctic that seemed unchangeable except where improved by human design. For a moment, the herds gave no indication that their swelling numbers were the result of anything but the right economic form.

6

The Climate of Change

In their great herds, caribou and reindeer spread like the tributaries of a river; where the gray strands pool, they are indistinguishable at a distance from the land. It is more than an illusion. In life, as the herds paw and yank at their fodder, they churn nutrients and dead vegetation into the earth, where it rots in summer, raising the soil temperature. In the presence of scarce warmth, seeds germinate. A grazing herd, where it does not eat foliage to the quick, amplifies tundra productivity.[1] Alive, reindeer feed swarms of mosquitoes so massive, the insects can drain half a liter of blood in a day. In death, reindeer muscle becomes bears, eagles, foxes, lynx, people, ravens, wolverines, wolves. The wolf pup grows and drags down a reindeer. Around the stripped carcass, arctic poppies bud. Rangifer migration is the tundra respiring, an oscillation of energy rather than air.

There are times when the respiration of caribou and reindeer, from the coast inland and from inland coastward, falters. Across the Arctic, Rangifer herds lose thousands of animals every ten to twenty years, then recover quickly. But once or twice a century, the population collapses. A herd of half a million can be reduced to a hundred thousand in a decade. The declines have many causes: disease, slowed migration, increased predation, starvation. Ultimately, most are provoked by variations in climate. In the Arctic, the climate has historically been a complex, cyclic thing, alternating periods of slight warming and slight cooling roughly every five or six years, every decade, every two decades, every third to half a century, every eighty to ninety years, and on up to centuries. The duration and severity of seasons follow these rhythms; sometimes the warming trend of a long cycle compounds a shorter one, drawing out the beat of a hot summer into several, a cold year into three or six. Variation is a northern constant.

As Arctic land fixes less solar energy than the sea, variation amplifies the influence of scarcity. Land animals do not carry enough fat in their bodies to wait with the patience of a whale. When snow is thick, or the surface sharply iced from alternating periods of thawing and freezing, the energy needed to move and find food surpasses the energy many animals reserve in their flesh. In hot summers, caribou refuse to eat, their flanks tormented by a raging flush of insects. Cow's bodies are stressed beyond the ability to bear calves. Wolves find easy prey. Hoof disease spreads.[2] Then the climate cools again. The years of transition from a warm phase to colder often come with the most volatile weather, with late thaws that leave herds to drown in spring rivers.[3] But then, over the course of a cool decade, the caribou population surges. Migratory territories expand as fat calves mature and roam. In places, herds eat lichens and shrub down to bare earth—already, a damper on new births. Fifty to ninety years later, the climate warms. In the nineteenth century, when foreigners blamed Iñupiat for overhunting, they did not see how Rangifer herds had been in decline from European Russia to Greenland.[4] Rangifer and the species that depend on them do not only migrate through space: their numbers are unfixed in time. There is no one historical moment when the herds are not either recovering or preparing to falter.

Beringians managed these transformations by changing themselves, by alternating what they ate and where they lived. But the United States and the Soviet Union expected tame reindeer to liberate people from stochastic waves of growth and death. Domestic animals were supposed to domesticate time, allowing stable production, and, through it, progress ruled by human laws. Yet, in using reindeer to reap energy from the northern land and discipline its people, adherents to market growth and the collective plan alike embedded their economic ambitions in a world made from the wills of other species and the undulations of climate, in time that moves in cycles as much as forward.

I.

In 1932, four years after its inception, Stalin's First Five-Year Plan was declared complete. Told that "time did not wait," local officials across the Soviet Union sped it up, giving proof that socialism would not just pull even with the capitalist world, but surpass it. In the southern Soviet Union, on agricultural land, most of the acceleration came in the form of mass campaigns to appropriate grain, excise religion, liquidate class enemies, and collectivize farms. Peasants by the thousands were hungry, ill, or imprisoned.[5] The Second Five-Year Plan began with outright famine.

Socialist time had to move quickly; speed distinguished it from the market it was to vanquish. But what if that speed was terrible? Official Soviet literature offered a narrative that was both conversion guide and answer. In the standard socialist-realist plot, a spontaneous but unenlightened hero struggles against capitalist enemies, capitalist thoughts, and material suffering until he becomes conscious, able to understand the true nature of history—to resolve in communism—and his role within it. This "Long Journey" nar-

rative inspired private diaries and public reports, a script for how
to surmount the past through labor and will, to make pure, collective, and revolutionary versions of self and society.[6] And the parable
gave meaning to a dismal, even appalling present. After all, only
through privation and effort—and denouncing the unconverted—
did a person join the most heroic act in human history: that of
building the new socialist world.

Devout Bolsheviks saw the Chukchi as people needing the longest journey out of their backwardness. But the results of the First
Five-Year Plan indicated that most reindeer herders in Chukotka
had not even started. The numbers of new *kolkhozy*, collectivized
workers, socialized reindeer—the energy available to the state—all
were quantifiably, scientifically, behind the plan. Needing to catch
up with the rest of the Soviet Union, *kolkhoz* managers, secret police,
and personnel in Chukotka's stores started transforming the *byvshie
liudi*—the "former people"—by force, a "resolute struggle against
the remnants of the tribal system."[7] The past was best overcome
with resolve, by appropriating Chukchi reindeer, and by arresting
dissenters. Treating "kulaks and shamans with kindness," the party
leader in Anadyr concluded, "will make them spawn like flies. We
must seize all of them so they will not be hostile to our work."[8]

For the Chukchi, the five-year plans turned the Soviets from
something to be avoided or visited at will into danger. Wearing an
amulet now made a person a shaman, and shamans were arrested.
Families with large herds discovered they were enemies of the state
unless they gave the state their reindeer. Many Chukchi retreated
still deeper among the wide, clear rivers and lapidary hills of the
interior. Others attacked local activists and party members. Like
peasants in the southern Soviet Union, herders killed their stock
rather than give it to the state.[9] At the Second Congress of Soviets
for the Anadyr District, a Chukchi delegate, chosen for his reindeer poverty—and thus, theoretically, his Soviet sympathies—
"stabbed himself without a cry through the heart with a Chukchi

knife" and bled to death. "No one expected such a trick," wrote the party leader, who explained the suicide as the "provocation of kulaks and shamans" and buried the man as a victim of class struggle.[10]

The violence did not go unnoticed in Moscow. In 1934, Stalin ordered the "liquidation of [northern peoples'] estrangement and isolation" in order to overcome "distrust of the Center."[11] New rules let *kolkhoz* members own up to six hundred reindeer privately, rather than demanding that all animals become collective property. Soviet stores provided the only source for tea and sugar and knives; access meant joining a *kolkhoz*. By the end of 1934, Chukotka's ten collectives owned a third of the territory's estimated domestic reindeer.[12] And some Chukchi joined for reasons closer to conversion than interest in tea. Semushkin described one Chukchi, a "great political figure" named Il'mach, who lost eight hundred reindeer from his *kolkhoz* when the "shamans rustled them." After this, he asked the Soviets to "organize an education campaign, and proclaimed himself its director."[13] Il'mach was not the only Chukchi to see utility in literacy and other Soviet tools. In 1939, a boy named Victor Keul'kut was sent by his parents to begin learning to read in a tiny schoolhouse not far from Anadyr, its windows turned toward distant blue hills, the tundra reaching up their sides crimson and yellow in the autumn.

*

Iatgyrgin was sixteen years old when his family entered the Way to Communism *kolkhoz* in Beryozovo, a hundred miles southwest of where Victor Keul'kut was learning to write. In 1940, it was a small village with a school and, eventually, many tents along the Velikoi River, banks magenta with fireweed and warm enough to grow trees, close to good pasture. Iatgyrgin's family did not come willingly. In his telling, Soviet forces arrived in camp one night to arrest an elder named Gemav'e. In the shouting and confusion—

an old man, pulled from his tent—perhaps ten people were killed, including Gemav'e's three sons.[14] The police burned the tents and "took absolutely everything," Iatgyrgin remembered. "The sleds, even rope and burlap—they took every bundle." Without sleighs and draft reindeer, there was no way to move the herd to new pastures. And movement is necessary on the tundra; made immobile, families had to join the *kolkhoz*. "From the start we were crushed by the force of the authorities," Iatgyrgin recalled decades later. "Many died because we could not live with the life that was imposed on us."[15] The tundra the Soviets offered was full of hope—their idea of hope, their Long Journey into liberation. To transform, all Chukchi had to give up was their reindeer and their whole world. Eagles would no longer have their own country, mice were not people with underground houses ready to shape-shift into human hunters, and amulets could not transform from a curl of ermine hair into a live ermine and then a bear. Conversion meant losing that kind of metamorphosis. The Soviets burned Gemav'e's amulets.

Iatgyrgin's telling of collectivization at Beryozovo was not the experience of local socialists, foreign or Chukchi. In the Soviet archive, Gemav'e refused to pay taxes on his herd, making him a *kulak*. Worse, he killed the local *kolkhoz* commissioner in retaliation for his requisition of more reindeer. Gemav'e chose "the path of physical extermination of Soviets, party workers, activist-collective farmers," one Soviet historian wrote.[16] Offically, Gemav'e was shot by a group of collectivized Chukchi, who threw his corpse into the river. The *kulak*'s reindeer were given to the *kolkhoz*, becoming a quantifiable gain in the conversion of the old world into the new.

The events at Beryozovo, no matter the version, were part of a long torsion of accusations, arrests, tortures, imprisonments, and sometimes executions that began in Moscow and arrived late in Chukotka. Beginning in 1935, a political purge tinged with moral panic over disbelievers within elite party ranks spread, by 1937, to a purge of every possible sort of imperfection. What needed liquidation now was not distrust of the center, but any deviation from the true line leading to the socialist future. In Chukotka, the purges transformed collectivization from a forcible method of procuring energy to an enforceable ideological test. Those who failed it, like "comrade Karpov," went on trial for "wrecking the work of the traveling culture bases" because Chukchi refused to join. Other foreigners were charged with debauchery, excessive drinking, "leading no struggles against the *kulaks*," or any other act that prevented the creation of *kolkhozy*. Every person had to answer the question, "What have you done in the tundra?"[17] If the answer was not satisfactory, the public punishment might be imprisonment or death; the private one, the torment of failure, the journey abandoned for lack of will. If Ivan Druri could not make collectives, then Ivan Druri could not be a proper socialist.

Druri was a proper socialist. His *sovkhoz* had a bathhouse and a cabin and fourteen thousand reindeer. But *kolkhoz* managers without such herds went back to the tundra to find reindeer to save themselves and save faith. Chukchi like Iatgyrgin's family, who seemed to choose life in the past, prevented the advancement of socialism—and, therefore, the future itself. To eradicate such backwardness, new laws required Chukchi outside collectives to give the state seventy percent of their herds. School truancy became illegal after 1938, making ninety percent of nomadic children suddenly delinquent.[18] It was logic that could turn any Chukchi into a terse line in an NKVD arrest record: Karauv'e, sentenced to ten years in prison for practicing shamanism and preventing his children from joining the Komsomol. Or Vapyska, a short man scarred from smallpox, who had twenty-two reindeer and family living on the plain of the Chaun River. In May 1940, he was arrested as a saboteur. At his trial, Vapyska testified, "I do not recognize Soviet power. I alone am master on the tundra. In my camp, I will not allow the organization of a school . . . Many people are sick because the Russians travel here. Soon there will be a time when many people perish."[19] He was hundreds of miles from where Iatgyrgin's tents had been reduced to ash. Between them, the tundra was pocked with conflagrations. The conflicts, so clear and so necessary for Soviet believers, Iatgyrgin remembered as tragedy, with Chukchi digging through the snow to bury the bodies of children.

And, as with people, so too with the reindeer. The simultaneous experience of collectivization and the purges did increase the number of tundra *kolkhozy*, to twenty-one in the Anadyr *raion* by 1940. Some now functioned beyond paper declarations. But the Chukotkan herds lost over a hundred thousand animals between the start of collectivization and 1940.[20] The cause was, in part, the revolutionary climate, and in part the atmospheric one. These were warm years on the tundra.[21] But mostly, in the contest between believers in shamans' powers or Marx's prophecies, human attention strayed from the reindeer. In the breach, herds sundered. Stressed cows miscarried or bore weak fawns. Untended reindeer went feral. Migration routes were disrupted. Beds of lichen were eaten to the stone here, lay untrammeled there. Alone on the tundra, bred for traits other than wariness, domestic reindeer fell prey to growing packs of wolves.[22]

II.

In the tundra spring, wolves begin to den. A wolf pack is made of blood relations, anchored by a single breeding pair, and it is the task of this collective to rear up a new generation. As it follows the migrating Rangifer herds, the pack looks for a likely den site, a place to dig shelter for its pregnant female. Wolves bring meat to the nursing mother, and when month-old pups wobble and blink into the midsummer day, they are fed and taught by their older siblings. Wolves' gray-white bodies move in a syntax of posture, expression, voice, and tail position, used to communicate status and coordinate the hunt. A pack that stalks prey together for several seasons develops traditions around how they use each other and the surrounding land to kill.[23] Pups born in spring have to learn all these things—the value of a reindeer and the means of its death.

Wolves migrate with Rangifer through space and match their abundance in time.[24] In northwestern Alaska, the packs diminished alongside the wild herds at the end of the nineteenth century; where there had been perhaps five thousand wolves in 1850, a mere thousand remained in 1900.[25] Some ended up as pelts, trimming the parkas of whalers. Mostly, the climate and people from the sea ate the wolves' share of energy off the tundra. Thus, when domestic Rangifer arrived in North America, humans were nearly their only consumers. In the first four decades of the reindeer program, "wolves were not there," Sidney Rood wrote, with only small numbers "sighted every few years somewhere between Bristol Bay and Barrow."[26]

Then the wolves found the domestic herds. In 1925, a few scouted west toward the coast from deep in the Brooks Range.[27] A decade later, just as the Lomens were being eased out of the reindeer business, northwestern Alaska suffered what the Bureau of Indian Affairs termed "a conspicuous infestation of wolves, and alarming wolf damage."[28] A female wolf can birth half a dozen pups each summer; in two years, her young splinter into new packs, and each new pack can double in a year, if they have enough to eat.[29] Among reindeer, the eating was riotous. At Kivalina, wolves destroyed thirty-four thousand animals. The herd near Kotzebue, which had eighteen thousand reindeer in 1927, was gone in a decade.[30] The Reindeer Service described the lupine excess with horror: wolves were a menace, a scourge, a plague, an invasion.[31] Reindeer were "ripped open. Unborn fawn partly ripped out. Fawn's blood sucked."[32] Near Barrow, "wolf packs totaling over one hundred wolves each are chasing the natives," and "on one occasion the natives barely escaped with their lives."[33] By 1940, with their renewed yeoman program just taking hold, the Reindeer Service counted only a quarter million domestic Rangifer.

A year later, after the Japanese bombing of Pearl Harbor, the military started eating reindeer and stuffing life vests with reindeer hair. At the Nome Skin Sewers Cooperative Association, Iñupiaq women made reversible reindeer-hide parkas, mittens, hats, and boots for the army, earning tens of thousands of dollars for their families and a place for reindeer in national defense.[34] Wolves, for eating wartime materials, became an "ancient enemy," plotting subversion within.[35] "It's war," a teacher wrote. "The only question is how is this war to be waged?"[36] The Alaska Game Commission answered with snares, steel traps, rifles, and professional trappers hired to slaughter hundreds of wolves each year.[37] The wolf bounty jumped from ten to twenty to fifty dollars over a few decades. To assure that the "Nation's food supply is safeguarded," one reindeer manager wanted to hunt packs with machine guns.[38]

The urge to kill lasted past Japanese surrender. The Fish and Wildlife Service shot wolves from airplanes and laced pieces of blubber with strychnine into the 1950s. The market for reindeer meat in Alaska was inconsistent, and the Reindeer Service no longer believed reindeer would feed the nation, but with a growing military population in Alaska, the herds had a part in the regional future. In that future, human management of land produced wealth, and wealth allowed life to ratchet materially upward on the push-pull of supply, then demand. Remove wolves, and up the supply. Move more people to Alaska, and up the demand. Create demand, and there would be more money for reindeer owners. Market and state together would allow the tundra to grow, steadily. Unless packs interrupted supply. Domestic production on the tundra meant that it was possible both to have more reindeer than people to tend and buy them, and to pay hunters to kill the wolves that ate them.

Simon Paneak was one of the men who killed wolves within this new contradiction. Since leaving school in Barrow, Paneak

Wolves killed near Golovin, on the Seward Peninsula, winter 1941. *George C. Folger Papers, UAF-1982-5-237, Archives, University of Alaska Fairbanks.*

had been on the move, trapping furs in snow-filled valleys and up over windy passes far from Nuataaġmiut country. But around the river where he was born, the caribou were coming back in the 1930s. Paneak and a few other families tailed the herds, returning to where Tuṇŋana and Kiktuġiaq grew up with stories of grandparents "from the wolf family," who howled their return to their birth packs before dying, forming the germ of the Anaktuvuk Pass village.[39] With little money for sugar, tea, or tobacco, it was "just as in the old days," Paneak remembered, "we were living on meat." To buy ammunition, he killed "wolves, the wolf bounty being $30.00."[40] Men of his generation hunted pups in their dens and lured adults by howling.[41] The wolf bounty made some Iñupiaq participants in the reindeer economy without ever owning a herd.

Despite Paneak and other hunters, the basis of that economy had shrunk: only twenty-five thousand domestic Rangifer remained in

1950. Iñupiaq herders on the Seward Peninsula had theories about both reindeer decline and their future. Daniel Karumn described how "[a]ll [the wolves] would eat from the reindeer was the tongue, because it makes them fat."[42] Others saw lichen nibbled to the stone. The market for meat changed and changed again. Herders quarreled or left their animals to work in mines, or trap, or move with their children to school. Reindeer scattered from the torment of biting flies. These were theories born of experience on a tundra where balance was elusive. Some years, the arctic hares were so numerous, they ate all the willow, forcing reindeer to move; other years, the willows were covered in late winter ice, thwarting Rangifer teeth.[43] It was tundra where, when Clifford Weyiouanna was still a boy, his grandfather told him that the wild caribou would someday return.[44]

III.

The work of a wolf is to kill in the service of making more wolves. In bringing down a caribou calf or reindeer bull, wolves thin herds and allow lichen or willow to survive another year. A pack is one check in an arrangement never quite settled on the tundra, between photosynthetic producers and all other beings that consume them.[45]

The Chukchi did not see wolves as family, the way the Iñupiat did, but as evil beings that lived as orca whales in summer oceans and transformed into wolves to eat herds on the winter tundra.[46] It was a rare moment of agreement between Chukchi and Soviet. Wolves that "scatter the northern herds into the hills" were, from the earliest Bolshevik onward, a problem rivaling that of the Americans along the coast: both were predators.[47] Soviets were appalled, however, by how the Chukchi dealt with the packs. "The fight against the major reindeer predator—the wolf—is actually non-existent," one surveyor wrote. "The Chukchi believe that the wolf, as the primary resident of the tundra, is entitled to its share of the herds."[48]

The Soviets organized campaigns of wolf eradication. Killing wolves before they killed livestock was an old Russian practice grafted onto a new place. Less familiar were the reindeer—or, at least, the proper form their herds should assume once collectivized. The Soviets took as a given that production could be increased with proper *kolkhoz* organization, but Marx and Lenin had little to say about pastoralist husbandry. What did a Marxist reindeer do? What did a reindeer of *any* kind do? Ivan Druri spent months in hot, smoky tents, getting the "advice and help of the experienced local herders" on basic matters of reindeer breeding, migration, fodder, and disease. It was slow work. But from these "regular first-hand observations in the nomad camps," Druri wrote, specialists added biological research "to determine the pasture requirements of the reindeer during various seasons, grazing techniques, the size and the composition of the teams of the herdsmen and the state of the zoo-veterinary services."[49]

Amid the upheavals of collectivization, bureaucrats and scientists began to formulate a Soviet theory of reindeer production from Chukchi practices. They noticed that rich Chukchi had mastered a process for creating a surplus. First, they sought out the few remaining wild Rangifer and interbred domestic does with wild bulls "to improve the qualities of their reindeer."[50] Second, owners ran herds with a high ratio of females to males. Third, only large herds offered a significant surplus, as most bull calves could be killed while does were saved for breeding. And a surplus, preferably one that increased year by year, was the Soviet aspiration. A surplus could be measured in the plan, and the plan was—on the tundra, as on the shore, as anywhere—a quantifiable measure of progress on the national Long Journey to communism. In the 1940s, to help reindeer do their part in the plan, Druri wrote up the knowledge he gleaned from the Chukchi. The ideal socialist reindeer herd he described was maximally productive because it comprised many hundreds—and, optimally, thousands.[51]

The needs for those thousands—already urgent during the early

five-year plans—became more so in 1941 with the Nazi invasion far
to the west. On the tundra, Soviet bureaucrats, secret police, engineers, geologists, teachers, doctors, veterinarians—foreigners now
made up a quarter of Chukotka's population—could not expect
shipments of imported beef, pork, and sausage to keep coming.
All protein was for the front. So, it was reindeer meat that fed lend-
lease pilots flying to Alaska, construction workers, and officials
overseeing the tin-mining camps. With maximal production now
maximally critical, *kolkhozy* demanded every reindeer not yet collectivized. The "*kolkhoz* 'Forward,'" one comrade noted, "had 355
reindeer on January 1, 1941 and by January 1 1945 had 9216 head
of socialized reindeer," showing how "every year the *kolkhoz* over-
fills the plan for the development of the reindeer industry."[52] Some
Chukchi, including Victor Keul'kut—now a school graduate, working at a collective farm—joined the Red Army. Those who stayed
behind, in collectives, spent the war "fervently striving to achieve
new successes in the construction of *kolkhozy* and thus proving
again their support of our war," as the Chukotka newspaper wrote.
Collective farms sponsored a tank convoy through donations of
reindeer and rubles.[53] And they sent thousands of deer carcasses
and pounds of leather to the front.[54]

*

Away from the port towns and new military installations and patriotic *kolkhozy*, the Second World War in Chukotka was partly a civil
war. Taxes on reindeer and requisitioning provoked revolt across
the tundra. When Vapyska, the man arrested as a saboteur in 1940,
escaped prison, he convinced other families to flee Soviet wartime
demands. They were not alone. "Poor people live on the farm,
where the government collects all the profit," a man named Lyat-
ylkot told the NKVD in 1944, "but I am master of myself. Under the
reign of the Chukchi, life is better." He refused to hand over his
reindeer. During a procurement drive for the Red Army, a herder

named Trunko "categorically refused to help our country," one officer reported, and organized a raid to steal collective reindeer. The
commandant recommended using an airplane to "seize Trunko's
counterrevolutionary terrorist group" and "liquidate it" from the
tundra.[55] Five years later, Iatgyrgin returned from spring pasture
to his *kolkhoz*, Polar Star, where he found families starving. The
director had requisitioned all their meat and fish. Iatgyrgin and
others beat the director and elected a new leader. The Markovo
Red Army detachment sent soldiers to arrest the "agitators." In the
thick birches along the river, Chukchi shot at soldiers and soldiers
at Chukchi. Several elders killed themselves. Fifty people died. Iatgyrgin was imprisoned in Novosibirsk.[56]

On March 21, 1951, the regional party secretary "decided that
the time had come to establish Soviet administration on the whole
territory of Chukotka," B. M. Andronov recalled. "After all, we were
the only area in the country that still sheltered kulaks." *Kulaks* now
meant any family living away from *kolkhozy*. There were not so many
now, putting great pressure on those Chukchi who still kept clear
of the state. Fleeing and desperate, Vapyska threatened to kill his
brother if he joined a collective. Near the Omvaam River, a man
named Notanvat committed suicide rather than cede his family
and stock to a collective. His son Rul'tyl'kut became an active communist. Rul'tyl'kut was drowned by one of his father's herders, who
had sworn never to let Notanvat's children convert to the Soviet way
of being.[57]

When Iatgyrgin was released from prison in 1955, overt violence
between Soviets and Chukchi was over. The last openly practicing
shamans were in NKVD custody. Chukchi herds were socialist in
form; whether their herders were socialist in content was harder to
parse. Many families carried on rituals in private, teaching their
children at least some of the meaning behind amulets and prayers
before a helicopter came on September 1 to take them to an *inter-
nat*, or residential school. When they returned home, parents com-

plained they knew nothing of reindeer, or how to speak Chukchi properly after nine months conversing only in Russian.

But other Chukchi were party members, taking up the new rituals of filling plans and socialist celebrations.[58] A man named Otke represented Chukotka as a deputy to the Supreme Soviet. Victor Keul'kut, employed at the newspaper *Sovietskaia Chukotka* in Anadyr, found promise in writing his own Long Journey. He composed poetry about airplanes and reindeer and how "the poor / living in a *kolkhoz* together settled / on making you true, long-standing dream / that Chukchi know not a single affliction."[59] Semushkin, on a return trip to Chukotka in 1951, described the "swift changes [that] are the characteristic feature of our socialist construction," leading to "revolutionary transformations," includ-

Announcing an award for the first collective farm chief–perhaps Tymnenentynu–near Amguema, 1948. *Peter the Great Museum of Anthropology and Ethnography (Kunstkamera), Russian Academy of Sciences.*

ing roads, hospitals, and a sense of purpose. "The Soviets have awakened the Chukchi people to cultural and political life," he wrote, and "regenerated life on the cold land." One young herder told Semushkin that "a great layer of snow and ice had lain on our past life. And the Comrade Stalin helped us to break that cold layer and climb out into the sunshine . . . we are living an entirely new, interesting, and intelligent life."[60]

Perhaps the most likely way of being for Chukchi in the 1950s was to adapt old values with new. On the Omvaam River, a Chukchi man named Tymnenentynu was one of the first to join the Amguema *kolkhoz*. He also had three wives and enough personal reindeer to have influence in Chukchi terms. In 1951, old and ill, he requested to be ritually murdered by his brother, a traditional act of self-sacrifice that, with the right prayers, would bring wealth to his people. Tymnenentynu's brother was reluctant, arguing that "we live in a new time . . . and our previous laws and practices established by our ancestors are obsolete." A Soviet ethnographer intervened, horrified, explaining, "All of us, Russians and you, the Chukchi, live in a new time . . . the sick are being healed and not suffocated," and "your life . . . is necessary for the further progress of your *kolkhoz*."[61] Tymnenentynu consented to treatment rather than death—a different kind of sacrifice for a different kind of collective.

*

Tymnenentynu's *kolkhoz* was one of almost a hundred. The Soviets had their theory of herding, they had their herders, and they had over four hundred thousand reindeer on collective farms scattered across socialist land. Managed by socialist herders, not shamans, Soviet reindeer had no excuse not to be fruitful and multiply. The tundra was now under the direct supervision of scientists trained at Leningrad's Institute of Polar Agriculture and Livestock who were ready, as Rangifer specialist P. S. Zhigunov wrote, to bring northward "a new Soviet socialist culture and have

an immediately beneficial impact on the development . . . of reindeer herding."[62] Soviet socialist culture meant mapping the tundra
according to the life and death of a reindeer, from fodder to meat.
Biologists studied tundra growth, to "massively improve pastures
and enrich them with the maximum number of feed plants . . .
and cultivate methods of rational use."[63] Planners assigned each
collective a territory, and each territory prescribed "seasonal utilization" to provide optimal reindeer nutrition, and each seasonal
parcel a multiyear rotation to avoid overgrazing.[64] Veterinarians
administered vaccines for anthrax, examined hooves for disease,
dusted flies away with DDT. Zoologists studied wolf behavior.
Manuals like Ivan Druri's explained how to breed for maximal
size.[65] *Kolkhoz* workers built corrals, awnings, windbreaks, and
slaughtering facilities to reclaim all use from a dead reindeer:
the "meat, fat, lungs, heart, kidneys, blood, milk, tanned and raw
hides, wool, sinew, and horn."[66] And they killed wolves. By 1960,
the only openly violent politics left on the tundra were between
wolf packs, resurgent after years of scarce ammunition during
the war, and humans. With the goal of "total extermination," one
zoologist wrote, *sovkhozy* experimented with poison, hunting from
helicopters, traps—anything to find "the best method of eliminat-
ing the losses these predators inflict."[67]

There could be no losses, because every Soviet reindeer was
valuable. The domestic herd was just returning, in 1960, to its pre-
revolutionary size. Proving the validity of the revolution required
surpassing that number. Thus, each animal counted toward fulfilling the plan, and fulfilling the plan—pounds of meat, feet of
hide, head of live reindeer, head of bull reindeer, head of female
reindeer, number of new calves—was the central ritual of collective
success. Still certain that large herds produced the largest surplus,
local officials extended the *ukreplenie* that was closing villages on the
shoreline to the tundra. Dispersed collective farms merged; small
herds became large. *Kolkhozy*, where members collectively owned

property and set their own production quotas, were transformed into *sovkhozy*, where the state owned both. By 1960, the number of Chukchi collectives had dropped by half.[68] As measured by production, *ukreplenie* worked. "In 1961, our farm was created from two *kolkhozy*," the director of one consolidated enterprise testified. "If the *kolkhozy* did not fulfill the plans, well in the first year our *sovkhoz* met the plan across all sectors" and everyone "lives better, and are better supplied."[69]

Those supplies brought the kind of transformation dreamed of during the early five-year plans. Brigades of reindeer herders used snow machines and tank-like tractors called *vezdekhody*, or "goes-anywhere," to cross the tundra. Some dragged metal huts with them, although most herders used hide tents pulled by reindeer, to keep from disturbing tundra growth. All reported their activities to the central *sovkhoz* manager by radio.[70] Once in a place of good pasture, a few women kept camp, while four or five trained men and an apprentice worked day-long shifts in month-long rotations, watching for wolves, changing pastures, sometimes raising up an orphaned calf by hand into a camp pet.

Postwar herding tried to reduce the human nomadism necessary to tend a transient species. Men herded in shifts; women and children lived in apartment blocks in villages like Amguema and Egvekinot, in homes Soviet planners designed to be "warm, light and cozy," where "at times of rest the herders can relax in a cultured atmosphere."[71] Many families set up *yarangas* inside the largest room. Women worked in long sheds, skinning and tanning and sewing to meet *sovkhoz* plans for gloves and boots, or on fox farms. Some trained to work in the small dairy farm built outside Providenyia, milking cows and feeding them imported hay all winter. Their children spent days in school and summers at Young Komsomol camps; their husbands and fathers and brothers rotated on and off the tundra, a month at home, a month with the deer, flying back and forth by helicopter.

Because herding now required expertise in mechanics, radio operation, and veterinary protocols, and because children now grew up in school, and not on the tundra, reindeer scientists and *sovkhozy* managers concluded that "the last and decisive priority in developing reindeer herding is the task of training and re-training herders" through "compulsory apprenticeship in reindeer herding brigades . . . and through the organization of special seminars and courses."[72] The husbandry that foreigners once learned from Chukchi—Druri squatting in the *yaranga*, observing—was now taught formally. It made reindeer herding like any other sort of employment, just as Chukchi existence was supposed to look like Soviet existence anywhere, with labor structured in shifts and following production quotas "based on the projected plan of economic development" in Moscow.[73] Time on the tundra had become Soviet time, run on a factory clock, staffed by "first-rank workers of the tundra, people of a new type, who unflinchingly and every year achieve high indices in the field of reindeer breeding."[74]

Like Soviet factory work anywhere, there were problems with procurement, illiteracy, and management. Promised tundra vehicles took years to arrive. Even acquiring seal hides from sea-mammal collectives was difficult.[75] There was no radical equality in employment; *sovkhoz* managers, doctors, veterinarians, and other roles with high salaries were generally held by foreigners, who judged Chukchi as lacking necessary Russian fluency, education, and level of socialist development. Chukchi did not join the Communist Party in droves. In town, Chukchi men found it hard to marry, as women did not want a spouse gone so often to the tundra. It was easy to find alcohol. These were, to Soviet experts, temporary problems; the correct socialist form was in place, giving the "northern reindeer industry a large role in our future."[76] Socialist life would follow.

But how soon? How many reindeer were enough to secure the future? Unlike the United States, where overabundance lowered prices, demand was not a useful measure; the success of *sovkhozy* was driven not by profit, but by increasing production. State subsidies paid for any shortfall.[77] Making the future required knowing how many reindeer there could be. To answer this, Soviet range scientists began calculating the maximum production for each collective's allotted territory. For most specialists, this meant finding the tundra's carrying capacity, a fixed upper limit determined—as in the U.S.—from surveys of plant types and grazing habits, to find "the basis of correct organization."[78] But a few scientists saw the socialist future not in reaching a biological maximum, but in vanquishing the very idea of a maximum. V. Ustinov, a specialist in the Magadan land-use office, described carrying capacity as the "incorrect opinion of certain managers," and argued that reindeer numbers would continue to grow infinitely with "new forms of organizing the reindeer herd."[79] True socialist production was an escape from biology, from the cyclic constraints of birth and death. The plan would eclipse all limits on life.

IV.

Alongside the rise and fall of caribou comes the rise and fall of other living things. Arctic hare and fox populations cycle around each other. Hare eat some of the same things as reindeer, and wolves eat hares. So do golden eagles, which also eat caribou calves. These shifts between phases of density and scarcity make Beringian life precipitous. Perhaps in a centuries-long tally, there is balance, a perfect moment of a wolf dying for each wolf born, of alders sprouting for each one chewed leafless. But a human lifetime on the Beringian land is an experience of flux.

Such fluidity is not what foreigners anticipated from the domesticated tundra. Their environmental managers sought to take a world of chance and make it predictable, imminent, and part of each nation's economic formula for progress. In the United States, the tundra was supposed to be disciplined by the value the market gave reindeer and by the land's carrying capacity. In the Soviet Union, ideology supplied demand even when actual demand was amply supplied. Every collectivized reindeer had value, and every socialist herd would achieve—or perhaps even best—the tundra's maximum sustainable yield. But on both sides of the strait, once carrying capacity or market saturation or maximum production was achieved, reindeer would breed and be consumed in a continual balance set by people. On the ideal tundra, people made history by separating themselves from nature, and then rendered natural variation static. Only people were supposed to change, and do so for the better.

And people had changed, by the 1960s, through participation in the economic practices—and prophecies—of their two countries, although not to identical degrees. In Chukotka, the aspirations of Soviet herding were stable from the early 1920s through collectivization and into postwar consolidation. The tempo sped or slowed, but not the plot of the Long Journey from *kolkhoz* to *sovkhoz* and from backward to liberated. Chukchi first opposed the dictates of planned transformation, and then, after the 1950s, found in the brigades and apartment blocks a basis for enthusiasm, for writing poetry about airplanes—or at least for participation. There was prestige and meaning in the rituals of the plan. And even for the ideologically indifferent, for those Chukchi who wore amulets under their green Red Army surplus jackets and hung talismans to protect their homes and spoke Chukchi in camp, the *sovkhoz* did not vary. State investment meant even failure to meet the plan came with a salary. The socialist imperative to use every space equally meant Soviet herding was revolutionary, on the unpredictable land, for the material consistency it provided. As a result, Chukchi lives were, by the 1960s, part of Soviet time, lived around the communal labor of plan and shift.

In Alaska, the vision of what it meant to own reindeer was as

inconsistent as anything else on the tundra: Was it yeoman farming, cooperative shareholding, herding for a wage? The value of
reindeer to the market was similarly unreliable. Capitalism does
not require that every space and every person make equal profits;
it requires enough dependency on its products to ensure growth,
the aggregate total of consumption. Because consumers' value for
Rangifer was never steady, as the state hoped, they did not become
a domestic successor to wild furs and walruses and whales. Alaskan
reindeer offered no revolutionary consistency. They did not settle
time into an emergent series of profits and investments. The Reindeer Service usually interpreted this as failure, especially since most
Iñupiat chose not to herd. But for Iñupiat, living in a world where
the spirits of the dead traveled alongside men and shamans were
still rumored to kill in the 1960s, reindeer were one tool among
many for engaging with the market and living on Beringian time,
simultaneously.[80]

And where the reindeer were concerned, both systems seemed to
be working on their respective terms in the 1960s. In Alaska, there
was a slowly expanding market for reindeer meat, antlers, and
pelts.[81] Chukotka *kolkhozy* filled and overfilled Moscow's plans. On
one side of the Bering Strait, it was the state that made demands;
on the other, the market. On both, the land supplied reindeer. The
land had nothing else to do, in the view of the bureaucrats who
planned its use. With wolves exterminated, diseases treated, migration corralled, mosquitoes sprayed, and grazing regulated, Rangifer had been isolated in a space perfect for creating more Rangifer.
From this, domestic herds grew. The scale was modest in Alaska;
from the low of twenty-five thousand in the mid-1950s to forty
thousand or so a decade later. But that growth roughly matched
demand. In Chukotka, the increase was more dramatic; there were
almost six hundred thousand reindeer by 1970, finally surpassing the herds the Soviets found in the early 1920s.[82] The increase
affirmed beliefs in a rational market and in Marxist promise both.

*

And yet. Nothing exists alone on the tundra. There are always other beings, and there is always time. At first, in the 1960s, those other beings were wild Rangifer. The climate was cool in those years, and managed grazing left patches of lush pasture.[83] Humans reduced the threat of wolves. More wild calves were born, and more lived. As Clifford Weyiouanna's grandfather predicted, Alaskan caribou were back. And they began to steal domestic reindeer. One Iñupiaq herder recalled how "the caribou came in just like mosquitoes and took over everything."[84] Other domestic animals turned feral with a gust of wind, following breezes away from insects and into wild company.[85] Soviet scientist V. N. Andreev referred to the wild herds as "weeds" and called for their "complete removal from the range of domestic reindeer."[86] But there was no damming the gray rivers before they swept up tame animals.

The second beings to come, or to return, were wolves. Packs followed wild herds, developing new hunting traditions "to adapt," as one Soviet biologist noted, "and become more cautious" of traps or poison.[87] And increasingly, they found fewer traps and less poison. In the 1920s, some ecologists began theorizing that wolves provided, in Olaus Murie's words, "a certain balance between predatory species and game." Aldo Leopold wrote wolves into his land ethic.[88] In 1963, Farley Mowat's gloss on lupine ecology *Never Cry Wolf* made it popular to see packs as guardians of a natural equilibrium that humans destroyed.[89] Translated into Russian, *Never Cry Wolf* supported Soviet ecologists' observation that ungulate herds in nature preserves had grown weaker in the absence of canine predators.[90] In the United States, predation was interpreted as making individual American deer stronger by culling the weak, while the fittest survived to improve the overall stock through competition. In the Soviet Union, biologists described how wolves helped make a more wholesome, stable herd, a collective made better through struggle. In both cases, wolves righted ecological balance, and therefore had some right to exist. The right was partial, as wolf hunts continued where people and packs desired the same animals.[91] But the goal was no longer wolf extermination.

Then there was time. In the 1970s, icy springs and denning wolves caused wild Alaskan caribou to drop from nearly a quarter million animals to seventy-five thousand.[92] Iñupiaq domestic herds shrank, then grew, then shrank again in the 1990s.[93] Despite the efforts of veterinarians and herders, Chukotka's collective herds dwindled in the 1980s, losing over a hundred thousand animals.[94] A decade later, the collapse of the Soviet Union ended salaries for herders, along with fuel for helicopters and *vizdhods*, veterinary care, and imported food. Without these now-habitual tools, the herds declined to less than a hundred and fifty thousand. The regularity of Soviet life was an Arctic aberration, one the Chukchi first had to adapt to living with, then without, at "the end," one reindeer specialist wrote, "of yet another branch of human civilization."[95]

Believers in American markets and Soviet plans both took it on faith that history moved in a single direction. What made growth, what liberated people from natural impulses, was human innovation, technology, the force of socialist will, or inevitable market laws. Nature was timeless, cyclical, outside of history until it was quantified as production or consumption. But the tundra is not timeless. It is bursting with time: predators and foliage rise and fall, warm years follow cold or do not; the numbers of reindeer crash and regenerate. There was no wolf cull or vaccine, no market projection or *kolkhoz* plan that could make this riot on the tundra linear. The United States and the Soviet Union, in pinning their tundra hopes on reindeer, became dependent on an animal that would not be enclosed in their singular vision of history.

*

Beringian land is always changing, but it is hard *to* change. Iñupiaq hunters seek caribou on the tundra near Anaktuvuk Pass,
driving four-wheel all-terrain vehicles out of the village that Simon
Paneak helped found. Makaiqtaq's grandchildren have reindeer
herds, their stock becoming reindeer sausages sold on the street in
Anchorage. Seven reindeer brigades leave Amguema each spring,
following their herds to coastal pastures. For months, they live in
canvas-and-leather *yarangas*, reindeer hides spread across the floor
and lace tablecloths strung over the door to keep out mosquitoes.
None of these ways of living look identical to the way reindeer and
people lived together two hundred years ago. There are few shamans, now; the prayers are various, said in Chukchi and Iñupiaq
and English and Russian, to God and land, for Alcoholics Anonymous serenity and health. Yet, neither is everything completely
transformed. Some prayers are for caribou to give themselves. The
Amguema brigades wear reindeer skins with their jeans and, the
Soviet subsidies for petrol gone, haul their tents with geldings.
Beringians always lived at the confluence of many kinds of time:
the ebbs and flows of birds and caribou migration, the rise and fall
of a man like Ei'heli. Now these are overlaid with market demands
and the eschatology of Christian salvation and the expectations
built into Soviet infrastructure, the networks of roads and apartment blocks no longer suffused with socialist content, but still giving form to post-socialist days.

It is hard to change the tundra, but not impossible. As the twenty-
first century crawls on, humans' aggregate but uneven lust for
energy saturates the globe with levels of carbon not seen since long
before Rangifer or people existed. The Arctic climate is even more
volatile, fires in the tiaga grown large, summer growth extravagant.
In the *yarangas* near Amguema, herders brew tea and worry to each
other, in a mix of Chukchi and Russian, about late rains and early

berries and the strange new insects they see eating tundra flowers. They have already seen one branch of human civilization disintegrate; they live amid its ruins and watch to see if the market will follow. What this new climate means for Rangifer is uncertain: will they starve in deep spring snow, or grow fat in longer summers? It may make new caribou—or, at least, new caribou ways of living. Or the herds may join the inverted arc of the sixth extinction; their numbers are half what they were at the beginning of the twenty-first century, and falling.[96] And on the tundra, it has long been that, as things go with the caribou, so too with the people.

PART IV

UNDERGROUND, 1900-1980

Has man's profit been calculated quite correctly?
Isn't there something that not only has not been
but even cannot be fitted into any classification?

Fyodor Dostoevsky, *Notes from Underground*

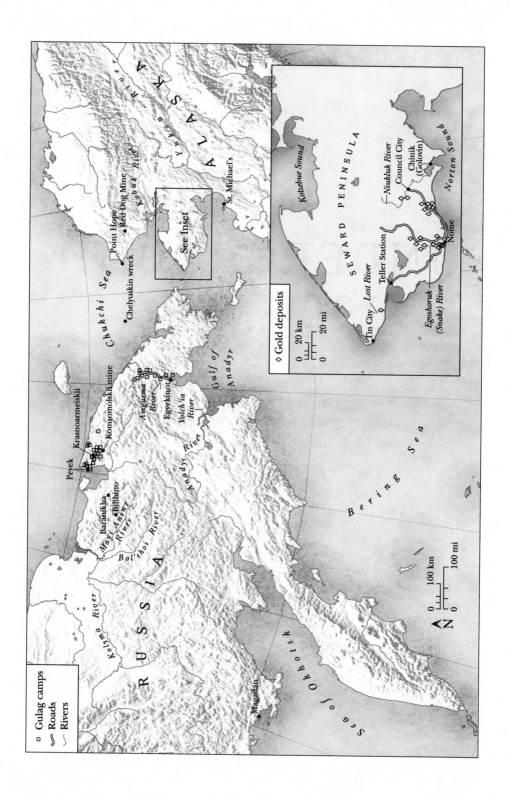

Gulag camps
Roads
Rivers

RUSSIA

ALASKA

Kolyma River

Magadan

Sea of Okhotsk

Bering Sea

Gulf of Anadyr

Anadyr River

Volch'ia River

Egvekinot

Amguema River

Bol'shoi River

Mal'yi Aniut River

Baranikha

Bilibino

Komsomolskii mine

Pevek

Krasnoarmeiskii

Chukchi Sea

Chelyuskin wreck

Point Hope

Red Dog Mine

Kobuk River

Noatak River

Yukon River

St. Michael's

See Inset

0   100 km
0   100 mi

N

SEWARD PENINSULA

Kotzebue Sound

Niukluk River

Council City

Chinik (Golovin)

Norton Sound

Nome

Teller Station

Lost River

Tin City

Egoshoruk (Snake) River

◇ Gold deposits

0   20 km
0   20 mi

7

The Unquiet Earth

I n winter, the rivers and creeks that loop down from the Beringian hills lie quiet. Some are frozen to their pebbly beds. When the sun returns, water pools overflow, jewel blue and green, on the ice. Then the streams roar. By midsummer, rivers erode their banks, opening walls of permafrost to the sun. The annual pulse of freezing and thawing, raining and running downriver, reshapes the land. Lakes form, only to have their water stolen by a stream's current. Creeks eat into the tundra, deepening their bows until they loop nearly into circles. A river in spate grates and tumbles boulders under the surface, making the water opaque, eventually spilling a plume milky with sediment into the sea.[1]

The land scraped open by rivers shows time in the vertical: the surface is the present, with the past moving downward, layer by layer. Beringia's valleys, made by ancient erosion, are colored with volcanic rock from the Jurassic, granite forged in the Cretaceous, slate from the Precambrian. Mammoth tusks and the half-foot-long incisors of extinct giant beavers emerge from river mud. Some of the land is made from long-dead living things and some from fired and compressed minerals.[2] In places, deep time has muddled these strata, mixing fossils with granite and deposits of coal, exposing veins of metal: lead, silver, tin, zinc, copper, and gold.

It was this last element that began the search for underground value in Beringia. The worth of gold is not in its utility; it contains no energy to sustain bodies or warm hearths. It is too scarce, heavy, and pliable to use for tools. It offers no shelter. Many people have died seeking it, but no person will die in its absence. The meaning and power of gold comes from the human mind, and how the human mind imagines gold's inertia. The arrangement of electrons in a gold atom precludes corrosion or tarnish. Meat rots, wood decays, and iron rusts, but gold cannot be destroyed any more than it can become something else. Its state does not change.

Permanence is the physical canvas on which human societies painted gold's value, seeing in it a manifestation of light, longevity, preciousness, beauty, royalty, eternity. Not universally: Iñupiat, Yupik, and Chukchi knew there was gold in their creeks, but saw in it little use. But Egyptians mined it, the Shang dynasty sought it, Pliny the Elder wrote about it, Columbus bore Europe to the Americas on rumors of its presence. By the turn of the twentieth century, gold inspired rushes of people to California, to Russia's Lena River, and to the Canadian Klondike, where Jack London wrote tales "of Arctic gold" and how "the lure of the North gripped the heartstrings of men."[3] For prospectors, the element's worth was clear. Gold was currency. It emerged from the ground already a monetary abstraction, valuable for its alchemic ability to become any other thing.

*

The problem of making Alaska part of America and Chukotka part of Russia, the problem of incorporating each into the world made by markets and later the world made by the plan, was the problem of enclosure. Beringian spaces and lives were supposed to follow a single set of laws and prophecies. It was a problem foreigners had confronted since Roys struck his first bowhead: the sea was never properly of a nation; the coast refused to stay still; the tundra rebelled. Beringia's underground was a different sort of challenge. Not that the earth is inert; its shifts dispersed nuggets and flakes of gold in Arctic streams. But in the short breath of a human generation, these changes are slight enough to be nearly invisible. Gold never stands up and flees the miner's pan. It does not eat or breed or scatter with changes in weather. The challenge of mining is undoing stasis, in altering the entropic results of deep time.

Changing the bones of Earth is a question of energy. Not harvesting it, but applying it, with pickax labor or steam power. Placer mines, where ores lie near the surface, needed calories to turn over gravels and mud to sift out gold. Lode mines, where metal is concentrated in veins far underground, needed power to blast away stone. From the beginning of the Nome gold rush in 1898 onward, the energy to remake Beringia was rarely local. Whether with human work or the fossilized sunlight burned in coal dredges and gasoline engines, mining reversed the outflow of Beringian energy in whale blubber, walrus fat, and reindeer meat.

Making value out of Chukotka's minerals required decisions on who owned the land and finding the energy to claw elements from it. Organizing energy and enclosure—the disposition of power and property—is the essence of politics. In Alaska and Russia at the turn of the twentieth century, the politics of mining had to do with who should rightfully benefit from gold: the individual proprietor, the corporation, the tsar, or the collective.

I.

The movement of a river through land in Beringia is a thread of energy from coast into the tundra.[4] From May to July, tens of thousands of salmon swim from the ocean: king, dog, pink, silver, red—also known as chinook, chum, humpback, coho, sockeye. Each hatched in the pebbly bed of a freshwater stream, floated as a transparent fingerling toward saltwater to grow at sea. Their twenty or forty or even one hundred pounds of muscle is power to bear each against the current, to spawn and die at the place of their hatching. Their migration carries the sea's energy far inland, into the mouth of Kotzebue Sound, up the bends of the Anadyr River, into tributaries. Some swim almost two thousand miles, if they survive the bears and wolves and eagles that pluck them from the shallows, to die over their newly lain eggs.

On the banks of Beringia's midsummer waters, Chukchi and Yupik and Iñupiat set their fish camps. As children, Constantine Uparazuck and Gabriel Adams learned to fish with nets and muskox-horn spears in the streams near the village of Chinik, on a bay on the northern edge of Norton Sound. Bent over the clear water, they knew, as their families knew, which creeks held gold.[5] They did not come to the streams for metal, but for the fish. In the long afternoons, their mothers cut away salmon heads, careful of the needling teeth, sliced down the soft belly, and pulled out the bright beads of roe. Careful with the skins, useful later for waterproof bags, they split each salmon into two sheets of flesh held together at the tail, scoring the muscle to let in air and alder smoke. Careful with the fish's soul, that it not hear people argue or see its entrails disrespected by throwing them into the river.[6] Everyone kept a watch for bears and ravens, drawn to the fish where they hung, pearly with fat, on the drying racks.

In the spring of 1898, a man named Eric Lindblom was in such a fishing camp. He was there because of gold. Newspapers from his native Sweden to his new city of Oakland were filled with stories of men becoming millionaires in an afternoon at the confluence of the Yukon and Klondike Rivers. Too poor to buy passage north—or with too little English to hear the difference between "sailor" and his profession, tailor—he hired on to a whaling ship. When the vessel put in near Teller Station for fresh water, Lindblom fled. Without food or good clothing, likely without understanding how far a mile across tundra can be, he was saved by an Iñupiaq family. They took him to Norton Sound, making camp by a winding river his hosts called Egoshoruk. Lindblom spent weeks with them as they cut salmon. Perhaps someone in the family showed him gold. Perhaps, as he claimed later, he found some himself. Or perhaps he saw nothing.

By late summer, Lindblom was near Chinik, in the trading post run by a former whaler named John Dexter. The foreign men called it Golovin. Among them was constant talk of gold: in the Klondike, in the Kobuk River, at a place up the Niukluk River called Council City.[7] Dexter gave pans to Iñupiat he knew, to check for colors when fishing and trapping. Lindblom might have heard Peter Anderson, a missionary at Golovin, say something about a find; Constantine Uparazuck and Gabriel Adams had told him they knew of creeks with gold.[8] Or maybe Lindblom talked to the boys himself. Lindblom did talk to John Brynteson and Jafet Lindeberg. Brynteson hoped to find coal, and Lindeberg came to Alaska on a U.S. government contract to tend reindeer. Together, the three men abandoned their pursuits of energy for gold.

In September, with snow already spitting down, Lindblom, Brynteson, and Lindeberg were in a small boat with Anderson, the missionary, and the boys—Uparazuck and Adams. The group sailed west toward Egoshoruk, a watercourse Lindeberg described as so "very crooked as it wandered over the tundra to the beach, we named it 'Snake River.' "[9] Who led whom? Uparazuck and Adams knew the river. Knew it, as Uparazuck's great-nephew Jacob Ahwinona explained half a century later, from experience and the "unwritten laws they passed on for generations [. . .] they knew the land, the water, the weather because they had to survive."[10] Lindblom knew nothing about survival, but might have known the river. Brynteson and Lindeberg knew rumors.

All three foreign men knew a different kind of law: the General Mining Law of 1872. Imported from the continental United States, the law allowed any citizen or person with declared interest in becoming one to claim plots 1,320 feet long by 660 feet wide containing a "valuable deposit" of minerals on public land. To the U.S. government, Alaska had been purchased from Russia for the public. The Mining Law made land American by giving it to Americans. Whether Beringians like Uparazuck and Adams were American was not entirely clear; the Organic Act, which established territorial governance in 1884, recognized Iñupiaq claims to lands "actually in their use." But with gold in the land, was fishing "use"? Without filing their own claims, Adams and Uparazuck owned nothing of what they knew.

The group saw trace gold visible even at the mouth of the Snake. After a day of slogging upstream, they found deposits so accessible, Lindeberg remembered making "wages by the most primitive mining methods—panning, rocking and sluicing."[11] In creeks they named Anvil and Dry and Glacier, they marked off claims. Lindblom staked several for himself, and claim No. 9 for Adams and No. 8 for Uparazuck.[12] In October, with real winter at their backs, the group packed nearly two thousand dollars' worth of gold flake out of the Snake River in shotgun shells.

*

News of gold broke a wave of human energy over the Seward Peninsula. Lindblom and his party tried to keep their find secret, but word trickled out of Golovin, southeast to the Klondike hopefuls at St. Michael, and onto ships bound for Seattle and San Francisco. Over the winter, the rumors brought miners from the Yukon and a failed expedition to the Kobuk River, to shiver and stake claims. In the spring of 1899, steamships bore prospectors north on clouds of coal smoke. Carl Lomen booked passage, thinking initially of gold, not reindeer. Joseph Grinnell was an aspiring zoologist. Edwin Sherzer was a railroad clerk. Seasick amid the grinding Bering Sea ice, they came north already believers in the ideas that Beringia's missionaries preached with the gospel: that wealth was liberation. Each bore hopes of spreading up rivers, and then up streams to the "great Eldorado of golden promise," as M. Clark wrote, "where auriferous sands lay waiting to pan, pick and shovel, which would make us all rich, if not millionaires."[13] Not bringing riches inland, but going inland to find riches.

To be rich in 1899 required gold. The metal backed most of Europe's currencies; in the United States, William McKinley had been president for two years by the time Lindblom fled his whaler. McKinley had campaigned on the gold standard because gold's value was inherent and its presence rare, the supply limited by nature and natural economic laws that inspired miners only in times of high demand. All this, for McKinley and his supporters, made gold-backed currency stable.[14] It also limited the quantity of money, favoring established wealth. His opponent, Democratic populist William Jennings Bryan, argued that money should represent the labor it contained; it could be made of anything and should expand in quantity alongside the growing production of America's working masses.

McKinley's victory favored one interpretation of the gospel of wealth: Andrew Carnegie's interpretation, one in which gold was money, money was naturally valuable, and value went to those whom the rules of the market and the survival of the socially fittest deemed worthy. Worth was measured in profits. Profits grew with efficiency. Efficiency required consolidation, and consolidation—

a "bigger system," as Carnegie wrote—made "bigger men, and it is by the big men that the standard of the race is raised."[15] Carnegie's "bigger system" was a corporate one. Through these jostling individual legal organisms, made up of thousands of biological organisms, the law of competition created prosperity and human perfection.[16] Just look at the railroads. At the factories. It was a reading that prophesied few owners employing many wage laborers. The freedom it offered was that of the rising tide, a force of nature that lifted all, although not equally.

Afraid of drowning amid the ice off Beringia's coast, waiting for clear weather so their ships could land, prospectors like Edwin Sherzer saw little hope in that tide. Carnegie's America was, to him, "the life of a common slave in a Railroad office," or what Jack London called the "bondage of commerce."[17] Where was the independence in labor driven not by improving an individual's property and profits, but the compulsion to serve so as not to starve? Wage labor had, since before Lincoln, been a sign of dependence and therefore of unfreedom.[18] Liberty was in working where and how a person wanted. It was a vision generated in distinction to American chattel slavery, to people who *were* property, and therefore a vision in which being even slightly unfree economically might mean being not quite white racially and utterly without rights politically. Wage work was fearsome for many reasons.

After the Civil War, industry powered by fossil fuels made wage labor more common and less temporary. To Carnegie, this made it natural. Workers were supposed to content themselves with freedom of contract, with selling hours for a wage determined by the market. But making time a commodity did not make for self-sufficiency or even, with severe depressions in the 1870s and 1890s, basic stability. As Sherzer wrote, he had "no hopes of anything in the way of salary."[19] He saw an age in which the market was free, but gilded only a few. The rest worked in "wage slavery."[20]

Emancipation for Sherzer and for many other prospectors lay

in owning enough to be self-sufficient. A frontier vision of wealth's gospel, where individuals claimed land as property and made from it profits enough for personal liberty. As Grinnell wrote in his diary, there was "the freedom of camp life and that feeling of rest after a day's work" in a "land without visible limit; a land where we are not crowded."[21] Newspapers called Alaska the last frontier, but it was also a perfect McKinley-era frontier. The land men hoped to claim was threaded with currency. The market always paid $20.67 for an ounce of gold: no tumult of changing fashion or depression. No risks of farming wheat in a year of market glut. With claim to pay dirt, "A man at least has a 'chance,'" M. Clark wrote, "and there is no chance for a poor man back in the states."[22] Mining offered to redeem capitalism by making instant capitalists.

*

At its mouth, the Snake River made a beach. Tossed here and there with kelp and the bones of sea creatures, thousands of years of water working down from the hills seeded the sand with flake gold. When Sherzer and Grinnell and their fellow prospectors waded through the surf from their ships, they walked onto a beach filled with money.

Prospectors did not recognize the wealth in the sand, at first. Miners expected gold in streams or underground veins. And as ownership was prospectors' "chance," in Clark's words, of "finding a piece of ground that will pay," the beach was unappealing because it could not legally become private property.[23] From the water to sixty feet above the high-tide line, the sand was federal territory, immune to mining claims. So, in June, the rush went first up rivers and likely creeks, the men and a few women with wooden stakes in their packs to mark off twenty-acre plots.

But how to prove ownership? The legal requirements were that one claim the land before anyone else and that one be a citizen— or have a stated public desire to become one. Who found the gold in the Snake River? Practically, all local Iñupiat. In the minds of most rushers, lured to Alaska by newspaper headlines about the "three lucky Swedes," it was Lindblom, Lindeberg, and Brynteson. Among themselves, all three men had different versions.[24] Lindblom and Lindeberg and Brynteson and Anderson and Adams and Uparazuck all owned pieces of the best creeks, according to their claims. Or not: in the winter of 1898, unsure whether the Iñupiaq boys were old enough and white enough to own land, Lindblom restaked Adams and Uparazuck's claims. Peter Anderson now held the title as a trustee.

Then came the new miners from the south. Like Lindblom, they moved stakes and filed new papers with the local mining council, often under the pretense that naturalized citizens like Lindblom were not American enough to own land. Miners from the Klondike jumped "every claim whose location bore a name ending in 'son,' 'berg' or had three consonants in a row."[25] A single mining site might be staked three or four times. By July, twelve army officers barely contained violence between claimants, rightful and otherwise.

Then, someone found gold in the sand. They left no record of the exact time or place, but within weeks, everyone knew that a ruby-red deposit of grit several feet below the surface held gold. Because the land could not be claimed, but could be worked, there was no need for legal rights, just a shovel. Making fifty or sixty dollars a day, Grinnell wrote in his diary, required only "very crude . . . 'rockers,'" time, and sweat.[26] Rockers looked something like cradles, with an open, meshed bottom: pour sand and water in the top, jostle the grit through the sieve, let the liner of felt catch the smallest flakes, and gravity and a bit of muscle freed gold from sand.

On the beach, it took little capital to make capital. All summer, shoulder to shoulder, inside and outside canvas tents, prospectors shoveled and rocked, shoveled and rocked. Some ended the season with small fortunes.[27] One prospector wrote home that he and his brother were "fast becoming property owners. Our cabin is the best on the beach."[28] Daniel Libby called the sand "a wonder and the poor man's friend."[29] Over two million dollars came from the beach in 1899. The work of water through earth over vast time made the wage slave's vision of the gold rush real.

News of the "poor man's paradise" where gold "was free to all, and the simple rocker was the miner's sole expenditure in the way of mining apparatus" filled winter newspapers from Seattle to Sweden.[30] Twenty thousand gold seekers came north in 1900, from Washington, Iowa, Nebraska, from Canada and Oregon, from as far as Scandinavia, Germany, and Britain. Some were farmers, more were fishermen and laborers, with the occasional professor or minister and many experienced miners from California and Nevada. To feed them came merchants; to sue them came lawyers; to treat their ills came doctors. Women sailed north to mine, and to sell things or selves to a town where ninety percent were men.[31] The town they called Nome, a name originating in a spelling mistake by the British Admiralty or a misunderstood Iñupiaq word.

Nome was a two-block strip along five miles of the Bering Sea coast, just above the beach. "Imagine," Sherzer wrote his fiancée, "a long stretch . . . piled high & in confusion with freight of all descriptions & tents men unloading barges & working for dear life all the time." The freight contained lumber for whole buildings. Canvas tents gave over to hotels, restaurants, dry-goods stores, a post office, a newspaper, banks—their wooden facades lining a few boardwalk streets. Anywhere without boardwalk, the mud was hip deep in the rain. Everywhere was crowded, Sherzer wrote, "with people & teams pushing, joshing & shoving."[32] Wyatt Earp opened a saloon. "Anything that one might imagine" was for sale.[33] Gambling halls relieved men of gold. So did brothels. But every bucket, board, nail, piano, can of peaches, bar of soap, chicken, pig, and human was loaded from ship to barge, from barge to shore, from shore to town. The costs of labor and fuel

inflated prices to two to five times those in Seattle.[34] Prospectors
spent millions that summer.

In return, they took from the beach only $350,000. Will McDan-
iel wrote to his parents that "the black sand tales are a fraud."[35] By
midsummer 1900, the promise of individual emancipation on the
beach—mined nearly free of gold the year before—faded against
fears of destitution. Winter would close in by October. Surviving it
required energy or currency: fuel and food to stay, money to leave.
Revenue service captains reported to Washington that thousands
were "desirous to get away now but have not the funds to procure a
passage South."[36]

The essence of boomtown growth was the exchange of money
for existence. So, to exist, miners without mines seized value where
they could. More tried claiming land, or reclaiming it; half-fictive
mining companies sold shares in stakes that did not exist. "People
staked by power of attorney; staked by agency; staked for the rela-
tives and for their friends," Edward Harrison wrote.[37] Others tried
to find value in other things. One man claimed rights to all the
fish in the Snake River. Many sold fresh water, scarce between the
Bering Sea and frozen tundra, for twenty-five cents per bucket.[38]
Some scoured the beaches for driftwood to sell for fuel. Those with
hunting skills tried for the few caribou still on the peninsula.[39] Carl
Lomen turned to farming reindeer. Another miner provided ptarmigan to a Nome store for sixty-five cents each, selling more than
two thousand in the winter of 1900–01.[40] Not a few resorted to lar-
ceny. Men lost their gold to safe deposit boxes blasted by dynamite,
or to the stupor of drugged liquor.[41]

Most used the money—some money, any money—to flee before
the sea ice closed Nome off from points south. Others stayed—to
thaw sand with scrap fires in the hopes of extracting a few grains of
beach gold, or because they had no choice. In Nome and surrounding camps, energy went missing. Woodpiles shrank. Coal vanished.
So did whiskey, potatoes, and flour. Dried fish, cached for the win-

ter in Iñupiaq camps, saved hungry foreigners.[42] Domestic reindeer disappeared. The prospect of freedom through ownership had become survival by theft.

II.

The largest ptarmigan weighs less than two pounds. In winter, they are bright white, feet covered in feathers. They eat the buds of birch and willow, making bodies so lean that even a person with the knowledge to snare them—the height to set the walrus-skin loop, the degree of tension, the most likely bushes—can starve without fatter creatures, fish or seals or whales, to eat. Iñupiat and Yupik knew not to live by bird alone. In the winter of 1900–01, Iñupiat caught them for cash, selling each for a quarter to the dealer in Nome.

Iñupiat sold other things: reindeer meat, fur boots and parkas, carved ivory, the labor of their dog teams and draft reindeer. With the encouragement of missionaries, they sold driftwood that once marked the graves of their ancestors.[43] And they made mining claims. William Oquilluk's father worked a mine. Charlie Antisarlook owned several, in addition to a reindeer herd.[44] Or did until he became one among hundreds of Iñupiat killed by the measles prospectors imported in 1900. Gabriel Adams died in the same epidemic. Across the peninsula, the disease took families in their camps and reindeer herders among their animals. Through the weeks of best summer fishing, people were too frail to set nets. Into the fall, survivors made their way to local missions or into Nome, seeking medical treatment and food. A reason to sell anything foreigners would buy.

Constantine Uparazuck survived the epidemic of 1900, mining here and there, making some money. Peter Anderson worked the claim once staked in Uparazuck's name, with fifty thousand dollars to show for his labor. Uparazuck sued Anderson in 1902, on behalf of himself and Gabriel Adams's sister. The case was settled out of court, with Anderson agreeing to pay a quarter of the profit, or five hundred dollars a year, to Uparazuck and Adams's family for twenty-five years. The Covenant Church, Anderson's employer, also sued him, arguing the gold claims were rightfully theirs. In 1904, the church brought Uparazuck to Chicago to testify about the discovery. He died, according to the legal record, of tuberculosis and was buried in Iowa, with just a photograph sent back to his family— a family that, after his death, as after Adams's death, saw little of the money their brothers and sons had put on the American map. Their shares remained in a bank in Illinois.[45]

Uparazuck was not alone in being excluded from the wealth foreigners were making on his land. Nome was essentially a segregated town, one where the local newspaper called the "Eskimo . . . a nuisance to the community and of little good to themselves," hanging "about the stores and saloons, learning plenty of vice and little good."[46] Other editorials worried about municipal funds going to Iñupiaq medical care. A missionary, with the support of the town, began convincing Iñupiat to leave Nome for a settlement called Quartz Creek, as "the struggling pioneers of northwestern Alaska should not be required to take up the heavy burden of the helpless Eskimo."[47] The experiment was a miniature version of U.S. reservation policy: segregate "the Indian at a certain stage of his development" until assimilated.[48] It was also another sign, to the Iñupiat, of how foreigners' laws and the foreigner's God did not apply universally. After all, in Nome, the sins of drink and theft—land theft, particularly—that missionaries so railed against every Sunday went on without sanction.[49]

Making land into private property is a process of reducing the claims on its resources, its waters and soils and creatures, to one legal being, human or corporate. When land is enclosed, even temporary use by others to hunt or fish or mine requires permission of the singular owner. For the U.S. government, such fixity represented progress, a critical precondition of capitalist growth. Gold was the first resource that offered to extend this progress, through a foreign settler population, in northwestern Alaska. Whaling, sealing, and walrus hunting were seasonal and transient. Reindeer farming was a tool of indigenous assimilation. The fur trade required only a few foreigners. Gold was different—what Alaskan veteran Daniel Libby saw as "but a beginning of the great and continuous flow [of wealth] that will follow for generations to come."[50]

Enclosure also required a single version of events: who found the land, who bought the deed. There was no singular history of gold discovery. But, just as Iñupiaq miners were separated from their claims and Iñupiaq families from living in Nome, Iñupiaq history was segregated from foreigners' narratives. The history of Nome gold, in the American press, was one of lucky Norwegians, not the men Jacob Ahwinona called the "three crooked Swedes" who "took advantage of the Eskimo people" by borrowing their knowledge and returning nothing. Constantine Uparazuck, in Ahwinona's telling, was murdered for his share of Anderson's settlement—an event that may not have happened, in the specifics, but which holds a general historical truth: Nome was only the latest American frontier to substantiate the freedoms of ownership through death and theft.[51]

*

After the summer of 1899, finding freedom by stealing ownership required mining hillsides and creeks. On that land, claims remained multiple and contested. In 1900, Congress tried to make the legal process easier by seating the Second Judicial Division of Alaska in Nome. Its first judge, Arthur N. Noyes, used his bench to issue injunctions on Lindblom and Lindeberg's land—now making hundreds of thousands in a season—under the pretense of examining their "alien" legal status. Noyes's cronies worked the mines while Lindblom and Lindeberg fought his ruling in court.[52]

Even after Noyes was deposed, and his indiscretions made famous in Rex Beach's novel *The Spoilers*, mines were claimed for blackmail. Others were worked by people other than their owners.[53] To mine, many prospectors discovered, required hiring a lawyer with money they did not yet have, to protect their right to work land they had not yet touched. "The future development and prospecting in Alaska is at the mercy of Lawyers, Doctors, judges, at present," a group of miners wrote to Theodore Roosevelt, noting that "for intent," a man "can not today prospect any more."[54] While they awaited their day in court, many claims were not worked at all. In 1903, twenty thousand mining sites were on file. Only five hundred saw active labor.[55]

Where they *could* mine, foreign men, a few foreign women, and a small number of Beringians hurled their energies at creek beds, tundra ponds, and the rocky corners of hills. The land absorbed their work. Outside of Nome, just moving was difficult. "You put one foot on a hummock," a miner described, "only to have it slide off into the water and muck over the top of your hip boot. You pull that leg out and hit another hummock with the other foot, which does the same."[56] Moving a mile might take two hours—three with a full pack. Feet shredded, blistered, and swelled. In the summer, the sun was hot, causing "a copious perspiration," Grinnell noted, accompanied by the "low, irritating, depressing, measly whine of the mosquito . . . there are millions!"[57] Once prospectors reached their claim, they had to build shelter, find water, and manage chores from cooking to laundry. Some found this pleasant. Sherzer wrote to his fiancée of his excitement at mastering sourdough, but admitted he was still confounded by gingerbread.[58]

Yet mining, Sherzer found, was "the hardest kind of work imaginable."[59] Panning meant hours bent over in icy water, shaking gravel in a pan. Mining deeper deposits required turning the earth inside out with a pick and spade. Grinnell recalled digging in dirt "thawed barely through its covering of moss, seldom more than six inches. The rest of the way the frozen ground was as hard as rock and had to be chipped off bit by bit." He broke his pick on a "strata of pure ice a foot thick," while "most of the way we worked through a sort of frozen muck or packed mass of unrotted vegetation." To find gold in this mess, prospectors thawed the tundra with small fires,

Miners with sluices near Anvil Creek, outside Nome, early twentieth century. Their tents are in the background. *Alaska State Archives, Alaska Purchase Centennial Collection, ca. 1764–1967, ASL-P20-064.*

"unleashing smells," Grinnell wrote, "like barnyard filth."[60] Burning meant scavenging driftwood and scrap, or packing coal from the coast. Miners pulled up the willows that fed ptarmigan to feed their fires, coughing in the acrid smoke until a patch of ground was soggy. Then they had to wash gold free. Water was often absent when miners wanted "to sluice," as William Woleben wrote, so they "had to have their water hauled to them by the barrel."[61]

All this labor trampled and stripped creek banks of their protective willows. Muddy rivulets wept into streams, then down toward the sea. Rerouted creeks dug at the roots of old mountains. Gaping holes dotted valley floors, between mounds of displaced soil. But hand-dug pits and sluicing canals worked by a lone prospector or a small team could not find most of Beringia's wealth. Time left the richest deposits far underground, where the metal's weight caught against stony berms, or in layers of gravel. Freeing that gold required transformation that eclipsed the power of human muscle.

The journal *Mining and Scientific Press* concluded that future profits would require work "on an extensive scale, either by hydraulic
means or steam shovels."[62] To mine the Seward Peninsula, people
had to become like rivers, only faster: take the slow work of ten
thousand years and do it in a single violent summer. For who wanted
to wait an eon for the golden sands to replenish?

III.

That Beringia's bones are shared on both sides of the strait is naked
to the eye. Rivers have a similar curve, mountains a telling crest
and roll. So, too, the underground. That was the hope, at least, of
a party of prospectors following a pair of Chukchi guides inland in
the summer of 1900: several Americans, some Russians, a few Chi-
nese miners hired far south, and a Polish geologist named Karol
Bogdanovich. It was a miserable expedition: wet and cold when
not hot and hazy with insects. The prospectors argued constantly.
While Bogdanovich found "signs of gold in almost every pan," the
Americans dismissed the find as mere traces.[63] They believed the
Russians planned to abandon them once gold was discovered.[64]
Bogdanovich thought the Americans were after personal fortunes,
wanting to find "where gold can be scooped with shovels."[65]

For Bogdanovich, gold was money: Russia, like the United States,
was on the gold standard. But finding gold was supposed to make
the land and its wealth imperial rather than private.[66] Legally, gold
and the Russian territory it sat within did not belong to the Chukchi
who saw it in their rivers, or to its foreign discoverers, but to the tsars.
So, too, in a sense, did human energies: each imperial subject was
born to a rank that defined whether they would labor as a peasant,
priest, merchant, or noble. To some, to the merchants and nobles,
the empire gave concessions—temporary and spatially bounded
rights—to mine. Nobles and merchants in turn hired peasants and
workers to dig and sift and sluice. State engineers and police over-

saw mines, trying to shuttle gold from ground to concessionary and state coffers without it slipping into the hands of laborers.[67] Enclosure was not a matter of personal emancipation, but imperial strategy. It did not save capitalism by making poor men rich; it saved the empire by making rich capitalists in service to the state.

In Chukotka, retired army officer Vladimir Vonliarliarskii had the imperial concession; Bogdanovich was the specialist he hired to find gold.[68] Vonliarliarskii's terms allowed him to prospect on two hundred thousand square miles, and instructed him to do so quickly. The empire worried that Americans would do to mines what they had already done to whales, walruses, and foxes: steal. Looking at Chukotka's exposed shores, the empire again felt both behind and vulnerable to the market. But with gold, there was also hope: as a pamphlet published in St. Petersburg argued, if Vonliarliarskii established a mine in Chukotka, settled Russians and Orthodox missionaries would follow "to enlighten our natives in the Christian faith and to teach them the Russian language."[69] Mining done to further the empire's "strategic ends," Ivan Korzukhin wrote, had "great moral and economic value."[70] At the turn of the twentieth century, the form of these moral ends—would Russia transcend capitalism with the peasant socialism advocated by populists, the orthodoxy of the Slavophiles, or a Marxist future?—was a matter of debate. But it started with the empire enclosing the riches of its Chukchi shore, salvaging it from the "American predators," whose trade brought only "alcohol and all sorts of useless things."[71]

Yet, Vonliarliarskii's expedition was filled with those very "predators." Vonliarliarskii believed finding gold required "foreign engineers" with experience in Beringia, and he needed "large amounts of capital. Therefore it is necessary to turn to foreign investors."[72] The empire gave him rights to treasure, but no funds for labor and supplies. So, he formed the Northeastern Siberian Company, selling stock in its only asset: the possibility of gold. John Rosene, an American by way of Norway with Alaskan shipping experience, bought the majority of shares.[73] It meant Americans and Russians were together on another exploratory venture in 1901, and in 1902, when Ivan Korzukhin lamented how the "two nations, Russian and American, get along terribly with each other."[74]

Part of the disagreement was over property. The terms of Vonliar-liarskii's concession meant that the Northeastern Siberia Company did not have alienable rights: dividing imperial land into individual claims was illegal. Rosene could not offer his employees mining titles, just a wage. With no chance of earning property, prospectors in Nome were disinclined to hire on. Experienced Russian miners were scarce so far east. Out of desperation, Rosene recruited Americans with the illegal promise of a stake in Chukotkan gold.[75]

Olaf Swenson came on the promise of such a "goldstake" before he turned to trading fur and later supplying the Soviets. He was on the Volchia River near Anadyr in 1905, when the Northeastern Siberia Company finally found creeks where, Rosen wrote, "gold showed up all over and could be picked up by the handful."[76] Rosene used dust from this Discovery strike to attract more Alaskan miners. But word of Rosene's use of foreign labor made the imperial government suspicious. So did newspaper reports in St. Petersburg that the company mistreated Chukchi and solid illegal liquor.[77] Finally, the Russian Geological Society made public the company's tactic of staking American prospectors on imperial land.[78] The empire had spent decades lamenting American theft in their waters; now the thieves had been invited inland. In 1909, the government banned foreign investment in Chukotka and declined to renew the company's concession. Gold for the empire had to avoid the "uncontrolled, most unscrupulous exploitation" of the Americans.[79]

*

Nonetheless, the Russian ministry of trade and industry wanted "the earliest possible involvement of private enterprise on the

Chukchi Peninsula" to organize the energy of extraction, and gave out new concessions, including to Vonliarliarskii's son, Aleksandr.[80] But rumors of "the unusual richness of the . . . Volchia River area," the regional mine inspector reported in 1913, were "widespread in Russia and in North America as well."[81] Ships from Vladivostok brought a few dozen hopefuls north each year. Some were peasants, hired to work at the small salmon cannery near Anadyr, only to sneak to the Discovery site. Others came under the pretense of trapping fur. They needed some reason other than prospecting; legally, only registered employees of concessionaires could work the deposit.

By 1914, there was a ragged camp of a hundred or so in the Volchia hills. "As I learned from talking personally with the gold diggers," the Anadyr mine inspector wrote, "in most cases they have neither the material resources nor sufficient knowledge of mining. They compensate with their love for the cause, their great energy and a remarkable ability to endure the most severe deprivation."[82] Most came from the Far East. Few had mining experience, although many were fishermen. Some were literate. The majority were destitute. Dozens were arrested, like "Simbirsk peasant Ivan Khrisanfov Marin," who "was found with gold" but no papers of employment, and was carrying "a notebook marked with daily production."[83] A few escaped the patrols, only to be arrested again.[84] Jafet Lindeberg's Pioneer Mining Company had ten thousand dollars in gold seized by imperial authorities for mining as a foreign agent.[85] Six peasants and two Americans were tried in Anadyr for "predatory" mining, but the magistrate concluded that the fault lay with Aleksandr Vonliarliarskii, who hired the men under false pretenses.[86]

Most of the miners evaded patrols, the "difficult terrain and harsh climatic conditions," allowing illegal workers to fade into the hills. Within a few years, miners had "many test pits," reported the head of the Anadyr post, "complete with sluicing gates. The pits are properly lined in stone, and the total length of the works is three *versts*, at the depth of two fathoms."[87] They brewed alcohol and traded it with Chukchi for food. They fished the tsars' streams. They killed reindeer by the hundreds.[88] Each autumn, the Anadyr post had to pay steamers to take any destitute miners south before winter. In 1915, the Anadyr administrator reported that "preventing the complete plunder of the mines will require a permanent armed guard of five persons." The empire sent no garrison, and so imperial gold continued to leak from Anadyr's harbor. One group of peasant miners showed ten pounds of ore around a steamship as they sailed south.[89] Another man tried to rustle nuggets out in sacks of coal.[90]

For gold to serve the empire, it had to be enclosed, sealed into the spaces and uses of the state, but enclosure takes power to make laws bind. The imperial state had little, with so few people in so vast a country. Space made Chukotka's gold expensive, as the state did not reach far enough over or under the tundra to fix wealth for itself. In the last years of the Russian Empire, what protected most of Chukotka's gold was Chukotka's earth, layering the richest strata beyond the reach of even the most desperate.

IV.

In 1903, the first coal-powered dredge began scraping up soil outside Nome. A dredge is like a small house with a chain line of toothed buckets on one end and a conveyor belt on the other, scooping gold-bearing soil and gravel at the front, dumping it into sluice boxes in the shedlike middle, blasting the rock and gold with high-pressure hoses, shaking heavy gold free of loose stone, and discarding tailings out the back.[91] Or, at least, in theory; Nome's first machine broke on the frozen ground.

Dredges were a way for people to break down mountains, to be faster than even the most torrential river. Geologic time moves so slowly, its violence is concealed, but dredges ate tons of soil and earth blasted to gravel by dynamite. This required energy: coal to make water liquid, to thaw land, and to move earth. It required technology and the expertise to run and repair motors and tracks and gears. All of this was expensive: a steam shovel on the docks in Seattle cost nearly a hundred thousand dollars, then it had to be shipped north by sea. On land, moving it cost ten to fifteen dollars per mile. Once in its river or stream, coal to power a dredge cost a hundred dollars per ton.[92]

The energy in coal power was a way of speeding up time, changing land in hours rather than generations. But the cost of collapsing epochs meant that no one would invest in dredges without guaranteed property. As Edward Harrison wrote, "there is nothing that frightens capital more easily than uncertainty of titles," without which, "many mine owners would not attempt the development of their properties."[93] But as enclosure became more certain, as claims were settled, dredges followed. And behind them came more equipment. The Pioneer Mining Company installed hydraulic lifts. Steam shovels dug through the edges of creeks into ancient beaches. "Many claims," one survey geologist wrote, "are being worked by hydraulic sluicing"—a pressurized jet of water aimed at loose rock or packed gravel to send the slurry through sluice boxes lined with mercury.[94] Steam-powered "thawers" used a coal boiler to pump warmed water into a narrow shaft, slowly melting ground through to bedrock.[95] In places, miners created fields of narrow vertical tubes sticking from the earth, each connected to a horizontal grid of pipes filled with warm water. All this water came from a massive network of ditches, cutting straight lines for miles along the edges of hills, joined in grids and parallels by roads. The first rail line, a narrow-gauge track, ran five miles from the beach to the first strike on Anvil Creek. One observer commented that the networks of ditches and tailings made the Seward Peninsula look like Mars.[96]

Most foreigners saw in this transformation a signal of miners' success in pulling currency from a land that otherwise would be "considered . . . barren and forlorn."[97] Even John Muir, elsewhere in the United States advocating for wilderness preservation, described prospectors as "a nest of ants . . . stirred up with a stick," but believed Alaska was so huge and cold that at least "the miner's pick will not be followed by the plough," with its ruinous settlers.[98] McKee wrote that "on all sides was manifest the hustling genius of the American people."[99]

Hustling genius and its piles of coal-powered slag were not the work of lucky, laboring individuals. It was the work of men who stole first the richest pieces of earth, paid lawyers to protect it, and then sold shares of it to investors to pay for equipment. It was the beach, inverted; Carnegie's vision of labor, not Jack London's, a vision in which most men earned a wage digging ditches and shoveling gravel through sluices and spraying hillsides with pressure hoses. Some of these laborers were Beringian: Nanok, from Sivuqaq, "went into hydraulic mining and earned $2.50 a day and board."[100] Gideon Barr sat for his school lessons with the children of Iñupiaq wage miners, while his father, Makaiqtaq, herded reindeer.[101] Jacob Ahwinona worked on a gold dredge. Like selling ptarmigan or fox pelts or reindeer, it was a way to draw use from what foreigners transformed.

For foreigners like Sherzer, the reality of corporate mining was a cold, remote variant of early-twentieth-century industrial unfreedom. Without prospects, most miners left. Those foreigners who remained looked at the turn of Nome events, from the promise of the beach to the reality of wage slavery, with fatalism. America everywhere was debating the proper form of capital, from the walrus coastline to Washington, D.C. In Beringia's underground, the Earth itself seemed to make a judgment: the land was recalcitrant to a lone miner's pick, the wealth spread unequally. "It is generally expected that the success of Nome as a dredging field," one observer noted, required "working the field as a consolidated enterprise."[102] Carnegie's vision seemed inevitable, as consolidating gold required consolidated energy and collective labor. In the vocabulary of options available to many Americans, the way to organize collective work was the corporation. The only kind of person who could have liberty from the underground was not an individual person, but a corporate one.

Government geologists praised the quantifiable results of corporate mining. Lindeberg's Pioneer Mining Company alone paid out hundreds of thousands in cash dividends to investors each year. Nome's fields yielded five million dollars in 1905, and over seven million the next season. And geologists saw corporations as providing stable employment, unlike the rushes.[103] Yet, some miners doubted corporate prosperity. Pay was decent around Nome—$7.50 for fifteen hours in a pit—but breakfast at a hotel in Nome cost a dollar, a ride inland to the diggings $1.50. And then there was the work itself. Arthur Olsen, employed by the Wild Goose Mining Company, described a typical day of hauling lumber in the morning, before "I was told to take a mattock and grub sod off the tundra for a dam. A mile walk to meals gives one no rest at all." The following day, Olsen "shoveled gravel till the dam broke, and all rushed out of danger," then worked a night shift where he "[s]truck a piece of hard shoveling and got fired at midnight."

"It is needless to say," he wrote in his diary, "I have a soreness and lameness after work."[104] Soreness and lameness were the results of a relatively good day. Men regularly froze fingers, broke bones, and tore their flesh.[105] They drowned, fell, or died setting dynamite. They were crushed to death in mine shafts and rockslides.

Tired of bleeding and sweating for little share in profit, workers in Nome joined mining towns across the American west and industrial laborers in the east in demanding better hours and less risk. The Nome branch of the World Federation of Miners led strikes and elected five Nome Labor Party candidates to the city council in 1906.[106] Their goals were not initially socialist. "I believe in the democracy of Andrew Jackson," one local member wrote, as "this country should be governed by the producing classes," not corporate greed.[107] But by 1912, the Socialist Party of America had Eugene Debs as a presidential candidate and an alternate vision for enclosing land. A vision that spoke to the rage of dashed prospects: for property untainted by corporate control, for worker's security in wages and conditions, for frontier freedoms. Kazis Krauczunas, who ran as a socialist in Alaska's 1912 territorial election, advocated not just the general party aims of unions and collectivism.[108] He wanted to salvage prospecting by ending corporate mining, and by making some minerals into public goods. What made the United States distinctively free, Krauczunas argued, was the common man's ownership of the frontier means of production. Alaska needed to be saved from deviant, corporate capitalism to keep it American. Otherwise, as the party's 1914 preamble stated, "Alaska, the last of the great American frontiers, the home of the pioneer, is rapidly becoming a thing of the past. The dreams of the lonely prospector are giving way to the ugly realities of wage slavery and job hunting. The nightmare of Capitalism already haunts the workers of Alaska."[109]

*

In 1922, a man named Walter Ahrns crossed from Alaska to Chukotka to join the Revkom in Anadyr.[110] During the First World War, when American socialists refused to give up the ideal of the world's workers uniting in favor of nationalism, they were arrested under the Sedition Act. By the end of the war, all of Alaska's socialist politicians were jailed or had fled.[111] In Nome, Krauczunas's call for pioneer equality was lost amid accounts of the Revkom seizing American traders' property in Chukotka and worries of the "Bolsheviks coming over to clean house."[112] Capitalism had become the American way of growth; to be against it was to be against the nation. So Ahrns left for a country where socialism was not in the past.

Across the strait, where Ahrns landed, the Bolsheviks fought for a future that transcended the alienating fetish of money, where Lenin wrote that gold would be best used to plate public toilets. The present, however, was hungry: for grain, for coal, and for technology to convert the penury of peasant labor into industrial abundance. Europe had equipment for sale and a demand for gold. In these conditions, Lenin concluded that socialism should, for a decade, sell "gold for a high price and buy cheap goods for it. Thus we must learn to howl with the wolves."[113] Bolsheviks spent the imperial bullion reserves on European military supplies, medicine, food, and machinery before the Soviets even took control of Chukotka.[114] Yet industrialization still lagged. And industry was a Bolshevik tool of enlightenment, a way to make peasant labor into proletarian labor and thus into socialist labor. Without industry, there could be no communism. There could also be no military able to resist capitalist hostilities. Creating "the economic dictatorship of the proletariat as well as its political dictatorship," Stalin told the politburo in 1927, required "temporary concessions" to foreign economic exchange.[115] Chukotka, otherwise a land of walruses and reindeer, was a source of that exchange. Gold would be the "center of gravity for [the region's] economic life."[116]

Yet, despite certainty of "colossal mineral wealth," Imperial Russia left incomplete maps and even more incomplete geological surveys.[117] When S. Sukhovii noted in 1923 that 81.02 percent of Chukotka's mining resources had yet to be explored, his precision was a fiction.[118] Two small geological expeditions in 1926 and 1928 left "the whole interior of Chukotka . . . *terra incognita*."[119] Even where the Soviets did know of gold, as around the Discovery mine, freeing it required human beings. Fewer than twenty thousand people lived in Chukotka, and most were Yupik and Chukchi, their labor necessary to make other spaces, the shore and the tundra, productively socialist.[120] The Soviet police, a local party member complained, "suffered from 'gold fever'" and did not work for the "Sovietization of our periphery."[121] So "a precondition for the devel-

opment of mining in this border region," M. Krivitsyn wrote from
Anadyr, "is undoubtedly colonization by the laboring element."[122]
The Bolsheviks needed a gold rush, to fix people to the task of
remaking their underground.

*

To fix people in space is the great act of modern state power. It
is the logic of property, marking mine from yours, and of borders, marking ours from theirs. In the United States, the underground proved easier to enclose than the sea, the shore, or the
land; with mining claims, people were fixed along the Seward
Peninsula by making stasis seem natural and voluntary. So at least
it appeared to the people of Nome in 1923, when a crowd of residents formed to witness the launch of new, "scientifically devised
ways and wholehearted means" of working placer deposits.[123]
That means was cold-water thawing. Narrow steel pipes pumped
unheated water into gold-bearing earth, raising the temperature
just enough to melt permafrost. Cheaper than steam, these new
fields of metal rods linked by water hoses joined dredges and
steam shovels. That year, Nome gold mines produced at least a
million dollars' worth.[124]

The dredges that people watched, cheering, were corporately
owned, operated by workers who no longer spoke of capitalism
as a nightmare. Around Nome, corporations had come to appear
natural, the only way forward, and what corporate capitalism did
to nature was viewed as a sign of progress. Enclosing land made
wealth. Investing that wealth in remaking more land caused
growth. Remaking land required power; money bought that power
in the form of muscles and steam-fed machinery, and then power
found money. Geologists estimated that at least five hundred million in gold remained in the Seward Peninsula.[125] Some of it was
in the slag made twenty years before by men with hand tools, still
permeated with fine gold that cold-water mining finally made prof-

itable.[126] If technology and commerce could reclaim not just waste land but the waste of the past, it had to be the future.

That future curtailed other kinds of Beringian life. Roads and short local rail lines blocked creeks. Whole stream beds disappeared amid detritus, heaps of rubble, broken flumes, and weeping canals. Open-cut placer operations chewed through three-quarters of a million cubic yards of gravel in a year.[127] Disturbed and channeled earth slid toward the sea with every thaw and rainstorm. Fish pummeled by sediments failed to spawn. Silt clouded the sun, starving algae. Productivity plummeted.[128] Although it was invisible to the triumphant residents of Nome, capitalist prosperity was in debt to the elements it rendered static and alienable, and the beings it destroyed as collateral. Where miners did the most work, Beringia's arteries of energy were bare.

The Soviet Union looked to Alaska's mining technology and envisioned not dead waters, but new life: one of collective human labor organized by the state rather than the corporation. Communism would transcend the soul-crushing forces of capital with capital's own tools. But along with their adoration for capitalism's industry, the Soviets adopted an industrial way of seeing: human freedom came from separating people's fates and souls from the Earth, and from splitting that Earth into parts useful to human development. Wise to the alienation of worker from wealth, Marxist-Leninist hopes did not dwell on how the goldfields made that wealth through theft, not just from people, but of life from rivers. Instead, the Soviets saw their future in Alaska's technology: one in which dredges and thawing points supplanted geologic time. To enable such speed was at the core of the Soviet project, an act not of destruction, but of human rebirth.

8

The Elements of Redemption

nland from the Chukchi Sea, dark mountains are covered in darker lichen. From a distance, the ridges look like folded velvet, rent here and there with vertical spines of rock. The Chukchi saw in the boulders and crags the earliest attempts of gods to make people, and the home of a terrible beast with a gaping jaw.[1] A spirit like the cold wind that keeps snow on the peaks until August. Life is small on high: a brush of fireweed on the lee of a stone, near the burrows of arctic ground squirrels. The rolling kiln of time shot the quartz and granite beneath their paws with tin. The veins are deep in hard rock, visible only where water has exposed outcroppings darker even than the lichen.

Tin is an industrial element. Malleable, resistant to corrosion, in the forge it lends liquidity and luster to baser metals. Its surface has little friction and retains oil in a lubricating slick. Tin alloys made the ball bearings of steam-powered machinery and internal combustion engines.[2] A pedestrian metal, found, by the twentieth century, in a thousand small manufactured parts, tin laced the equipment that pulled gold from Beringian earth and preserved the peaches the miners ate in their cabins. Its industrial ubiquity made it critical and valuable. With hand tools and muscle power, or industrial tools and fossil-fuel power, Americans and Soviets peeled open the land to find the stuff of cans and airplane wings, leaving similar marks on the earth: piles of tailings, dammed rivers, rerouted streams. A landscape changed not by the slow working of time, but with the rapidity of dynamite and bulldozers.

In the process, Beringian metals filled plans and made profits. Both plan and profit are ways of organizing the present and theories of the future. In Beringia, both saw in the underground only a very near future—not fish for decades to come, but metal for weeks or months. Their mode of prophecy was that of mathematics—the economic model—or the scientific laws of dialectical materialism. Proof of prophecy lay in revenue and plans fulfilled. But this did not free them from origin myths. As the twentieth-century mines exchanged the long-term future of Beringian life for short-term growth, mining in the United States and the Soviet Union also became another kind of resource, a basis for legends of capitalist freedom and socialist liberty, a way of imagining heroes made by undoing the earth.

I.

North of Chukotka's dark mountains, in October 1933, the Soviet ship *Chelyuskin* was stilled by ice, not so far from where Captain Norton wrecked eighty-one years prior. But the *Chelyuskin* was not after whales. The captain, Otto von Schmidt, was the head of Glavsevmorput, or the Main Administration of the Northern Sea Route, a state organ created in 1932 to explore and industrialize the Soviet north. It was Glavsevmorput that strung electrical wires into Yuri Rytkheu's tent in Uelen, put boilers in the Plover Bay blubber refinery, built roads, and mechanized a small fish cannery near Anadyr. Glavsevmorput pilots flew cartographic sorties over river valleys unpenned by maps. And they explored their namesake Northern Sea Route, through the Arctic Ocean from Murmansk to the Bering Strait. That was the *Chelyuskin*'s mission when it left Leningrad in July. But the pack ice north of Chukotka caught the ship. For weeks, the crew drifted with the solid sea. In February, moving ice crushed the *Chelyuskin*.[3] Schmidt—over six feet tall, bearded, and hale—had prepared his crew for the vessel's demise, unloading tents and food and the mission's radio kit. Across the Soviet Union, people listened to Schmidt's dispatches from the Chelyuskinites' ice-floe camp while Soviet pilots and dog teams attempted a rescue.

The *Chelyuskin*, from its ambitious mission to its communal challenge on the ice, was a perfect Stalin-era drama, a real-life Long Journey, in which Arctic circumstance provided every possible test of will and proved how "[n]ature subordinates herself to man when he knows how to arm himself for the fight and when he does not come out alone," as Schmidt wrote, but was "supported by the warm love of millions of citizens."[4] Coverage was constant in newspapers, radio broadcasts, and newsreels, as were stories from other Soviet Arctic expeditions of the 1930s. Stalin toasted Arctic explorers for being motivated not by capitalist profit, but the salvation of humankind; explorers toasted Stalin as "the great molder of human happiness."[5] In the immensely popular film *Seven Bold Ones*, fictional Bolsheviks saved Chukchi, discovered tin, and sacrificed for the motherland. But, real or imagined, northern Soviet feats showed the superiority of communal, enlightened struggle; if socialism triumphed in the cold, it could triumph everywhere. As the newspaper *Isvestiia* described, in the Arctic, socialist "technology has conquered nature, man has conquered death."[6]

The men and women working for Glavsevmorput on more prosaic tasks than surviving shipwreck—surveying, construction—also found a personal path to consciousness in the Arctic. Geologist M. I. Rokhlin described his time in Chukotka as living in "a 'wild untouched land,' an 'ice desert,' on the 'edge of white silence,'" but, with "work, grueling, hard, physical and mental work," he and his team "penetrated into her secrets" so that more "land will be mastered and made habitable." While camped on the northern coast, he discovered "a piece of quartz with large crystals of tin ore," a "truly sensational" find.[7] Sensational because tin was important to "the whole Soviet Union in terms of increasing the country's defenses, ensuring the successes of world labor, and raising the economic and cultural level of northern peoples."[8] Tin also brought industry, that "main engine of culture" still mostly absent in Chukotka.[9] And for Rokhlin, the work offered transformation: Chukotka's "severe working days test in every person his vitality and character," he wrote, "his capacity for action and attitude toward people, his ability to be a true Human."[10]

By the time Captain Schmidt and the *Chelyuskin* crew were rescued in April 1934, Glavsevmorput appeared ready to make Chukotka not just a piece of the Soviet project, but the best place to be Soviet: an industrial hub of heroic Arctic production. Rokhlin had his tin; other Glavsevmorput geological teams found new gold on the Bolshoi, Malyi Aniui, and Amguema Rivers.[11] But despite the description of Glavsevmorput as an "army of polar explorers" sent to attack, subdue, and conquer the Arctic, Schmidt's organization lacked the vessels necessary to supply and staff Chukotka's mines, hospitals, and electric plants.[12] The blubber refinery at Plover Bay did not even have concrete. Schmidt wrote regularly to Stalin, requesting ships, without answer. "We must strain and spend a great deal of energy to work in these difficult material conditions," one Chukotka employee wrote, "and our equipment is miserable."[13] The Soviet Union had heroes, but not enough energy to remake its underground.

*

Eighty miles from Nome, on a hillside covered in "sharp, frost-cracked rubble," geologist Frederick Fearing wrote, sat a submerged deposit of tin.[14] Below, the Lost River curled through a valley so empty of life, not even mosquitoes buzzed. A valley Iñupiat avoided because of its ghosts. But in 1913, miners began boring and blasting into the rock, drilling tunnels hundreds of feet deep to find ore. The black pebbles were refined into tin: nearly a hundred and fifty tons in a good year. Refining required importing energy. "The region is barren of timber," one geologist with the U.S. Geological Survey wrote, "so that all fuel, lumber, and mine timbers must be shipped."[15] Fossil fuels were so expensive that, in 1920, the two thousand feet of tunnels dug at Lost River were blasted using nitroglycerine, dug out with pick and shovel, and carried to the surface in buckets: a mountain remade by hand.

To undo a mountain was dangerous work. Tunnels collapsed. Mine shafts filled with water or became slides of ice. Men lost limbs to dredge gears or swinging buckets. A miner accidentally ignited sticks of blasting gelatin, blowing out his eye and tearing "the flesh from the thigh to the ankle."[16] But it was also nationally important work. The United States lacked domestic tin deposits. In 1917, the *Wall Street Journal* forecast a "tin famine."[17] After the First World War, tin-dependent airplanes and tanks became essential to the national defense. Lost River was one of the few American places where Frederick Fearing anticipated finding "oreshoots of considerable size."[18] When A. MacIntosh bought the rights to the Lost River lode in 1928, he intended to become rich by meeting a national need.

MacIntosh was bankrupt within a year. So was the country. The Great Depression had been unthinkable just a few years before, when crowds gathered around the miracle of cold-water thawing outside Nome. They had celebrated consolidated, corporate capitalism that seemed natural and prolific, a northern variant of Henry Ford's factories, wondrous for making more at less cost. But corporate capitalists spent the 1920s producing beyond what wages paid to consume. Mass consumption floated for some years on a pool of credit; corporations on speculative stock-market hope. The fall of 1929 drained both: Wall Street crashed, then banks failed, factories closed, and farms found no market for their crops. Four years later, a quarter of American workers had no employment. No wages to spend: no demand to supply. Lost River closed. Gold production on the Seward Peninsula collapsed, followed by the "disuses and obliteration of trails and roads, the closing down of stores and roadhouses and the lack of conveyances of every kind."[19] It was a small corner of a national desperation. Before 1929, a third of the United States lived in abiding poverty; after, millions more lived— or feared living—in a country where cows died for lack of feed and babies for lack of milk. It was a country where a hundred thousand Americans applied to move to the Soviet Union, fleeing a future come undone.[20]

In 1933, in one of many policies meant to save capitalism from itself and America from a revolution—communist or fascist—President Franklin Roosevelt nearly doubled the price of gold. It was not a boon for farmers, as intended. But for Alaska, as Rex Beach wrote, it brought "The Business . . . Gold Mining," amid mountains like "a haunted house" awaiting productive work to bring them alive.[21] The office of the Secretary of the Interior filled with letters of men and women wanting "to go prospecting in Alaska," as "there are no jobs to be gotten" in the contiguous states.[22] The Department of the Interior agreed; Alaska's land was full of unused value, the potential for "a rather enviable state of well-being and possibilities for commercial and industrial expansion."[23] The American north of the 1930s was not a place of heroic self-creation and historical change; it was an outlet for surviving history without growth.

It was also a place that could absorb American labor in an attempt to restart growth. Individual prospectors, once in charge of "liberating and controlling the great natural resources of Alaska," one hopeful wrote, would make "a brilliant future."[24] Roosevelt agreed, promoting in his suite of New Deal laws and agencies not just social programs, unions, and bank reform, but also a return to local self-

sufficiency. Corporate capital had undermined personal ownership, and with it, stable production. "Individual independence shall
be achieved," wrote one back-to-the land advocate, "by millions of
men and women, walking in the sunshine without fear of want."[25]

Freedom from want: the hope at the core of the New Deal. Newspapers made such freedom in Alaska seem like a matter of gump-
tion and a gold pan, which could earn prospectors "above $5 a day
shoveling and washing."[26] It was an old vision, the Nome beach
vision, where individuals made profits working for themselves.
Newspapers did not report that placer mining on the Seward Peninsula was as dependent on precipitation as Oklahoma farming—
"without rain," wrote one observer, the sluices were dry and "there
can be no work."[27] Or that mining deep lodes and frozen gravels
needed corporate investment as much as making a car. Most of the
miners who went to Nome during the Depression were like Oscar
Brown, hired to work a lode mine eighty-five feet underground in a
crawlspace where "we had to use a compass in order to be sure that
we were going in the right direction with our tunnels." He worked
"so I and my wife Ella . . . could pay our expenses."[28] He earned
enough in a summer to buy groceries for a year. Hammon Consolidated Gold Fields, Nome's largest mining conglomerate, made
enough in 1935 for "a partial repayment of the many millions of
dollars which 14,900 stockholders provided to make consolidated
operations possible."[29] Hammon's earnings were a part of a two-
million-dollar gold season. Nome's image was that of frontier salvation, of redemption by individual fortune. The reality of mining
was still wage work.

II.

Revolution requires enclosure: separation of the transformed from
the unformed, the socialists within this border, the capitalists without. But, eventually, socialist revolution was supposed to be univer-

sal, and thus enclosure temporary. First, the Bolshevik vanguard would convert Russia; then the Soviet vanguard would convert the entire world to the communist body politic. In the 1930s, Stalin pronounced the first act of enclosure complete: real, existing socialism had arrived in the Soviet Union.

Yet there were still thieves, even though no socialist should steal. There were murderers. Beyond Soviet borders, the capitalist world menaced, and its spies could be anywhere: among the peasants charged as *kulaks*, factory workers charged as wreckers, and every sort of person charged for thinking, seeming to think, or acting against the state. The NKVD arrested a steady number of such internal enemies until 1936. That year, show trials and mass arrests began in every local party, every factory, every geological expedition, every cadre trying to collectivize the tundra, in a massive purge of the impure. The truly irredeemable had to be executed, for the good of the collective. But how to save the rest?

The Soviet answer was involuntary redemption in the archipelago Aleksandr Solzhenitsyn would make famous: a system of prisons, interrogation centers, mental hospitals, and camps under the direction of the Main Camp Administration—the Gulag. Its largest island was in the Soviet northeast, run by Dalstroi, the Main Administration for Construction in the Far North.[30] Within Dalstroi, as within any part of the Gulag, redemption came from reeducation, reeducation meant learning to labor like a Soviet, laboring like a Soviet equaled feats of ever-growing production, and production converted fallen individuals into viable parts of the communist whole.[31] "The Government," a text celebrating Soviet reeducation explained, takes "a part of the Socialist plan . . . measures a tiny dose for you, and it will cure you, the criminal, with the truth of Socialism."[32] The dose was the sentence. The cure was to be reforged through labor.

Building socialism in the Gulag could mean felling timber, or pouring concrete, or digging a canal, or building a factory, or mining the underground. "Mobilizing our gold resources," one Soviet mining engineer wrote in 1931, "is absolutely necessary and timely," as the "present crisis in capitalism" was reducing the world's gold supply.[33] The Soviet Union, still dependent on foreign trade, still awaiting global revolution, needed something to feed a faltering market. Selling grain abroad was part of the answer, but Stalin and the politburo also met multiple times that year to discuss gold.[34] Geologists indicated that the Kolyma River, hundreds of miles south of Anadyr, held the most promising deposits. Dalstroi was founded to work them: to use forced labor to solve the energy problem Glavsevmorput struggled with to the north. Starting in 1932, the NKVD provided Dalstroi with tens of thousands of convicts to hurl at the ice-locked creeks and frost-covered hills along the Sea of Okhotsk.[35]

Dalstroi was, by reputation among prisoners, the worst place in the Gulag; death by hunger, disease, accident, or exposure often came before redemption.[36] It was also, by dictates of the plan, the best producer in the Gulag. Placer gold was rich on the Kolyma ground, close enough to the surface to yield ounces with only picks and shovels and pans, and even more with crude sluices and ditches. Some of the prisoners who designed Kolyma waterways had once worked for Glavsevmorput, purged for misusing funds or for insufficient devotion to revolutionary work.[37] These experts, and the sheer mass of incarcerated labor, grew Kolyma production from just over half a ton of gold in 1932 to almost thirty-seven tons in 1936.[38] Production kept climbing even as the terror deepened, leaving no one immune; Otto von Schmidt, despite his public heroics, was accused of having "gold words," but no results to show.[39] But, for every geologist sentenced to death, the purges gave two or three or five untrained men or women to the mines.[40] Enough to keep production steady. "Never, in the most feverish years of the capitalist gold rush . . . in Alaska," wrote one Dalstroi manager in

1937, "did a territory give as much gold as was produced this year in the Kolyma."[41]

Dalstroi could, with its constant supply of new muscle, manage what Glavsevmorput had not: open the northern earth to make mines produce. Soviet people were finally working with the speed of rivers. In 1939, Moscow gave Dalstroi control of Chukotka's underground.[42] Two years later, with the Red Army in existential need of tin, Gulag transports began sailing past Magadan and through the Bering Strait, "the bare rocky coast of Chukotka on the left," Valerii Iankovskii recalled, "to the right, in the haze, the distant shore of Alaska."[43]

*

Iankovskii, the son of White Russian émigrés to Korea, joined the Red Army as a translator during the Second World War, then was arrested for "helping the international bourgeoisie."[44] Aleksandr Eremin was sentenced after requesting a literate, battle-trained commanding officer while an artillery cadet in 1942. Petr Lisov, once a factory worker in Minsk, was, in his words, "arrested on account of no facts or evidence whatsoever."[45] Ivan Tvardovskii, his blacksmith father charged as a *kulak* in the early 1930s, was transported as a schoolboy to a special settlement, drafted by the Red Army, and taken as a prisoner of war in Finland, only to be arrested for dereliction of duty upon his return to the Soviet Union in 1947. Each man was seized, interrogated, sentenced, and then marched to the train, pulling east out of Moscow; days on the tracks, and then, perhaps, weeks in the Vladivostok pens before the "immense, cavernous, murky hold" of the transport ship, where, "from the floor to the ceiling, as in a gigantic poultry farm," people lived "five of them in each nine-foot-square space."[46] The ships were filled with rumors of the transport *Dzhurma*, icebound north of Chukotka not far from the *Chelyuskin*, with twelve thousand prisoners who froze or starved or ate each other before spring.[47] And, finally, the arrival in Chukotka. Inmates were sent to the camps at Egvekinot or Pevek, where "black rocks ironed flat by the wind," in Lisov's words, rose above "valleys of snow up to five meters deep."[48]

In those hills were "open-pit mines," Iankovskii recalled, where "all work is done by pick, shovel, wheelbarrow," where we "loaded [stone] and rolled it by hand on narrow rickety tracks."[49] The use of political prisoners solved the Soviet labor problem, but not other shortages. "Wood and construction material in general are absent," one Dalstroi report noted in 1941, including "sand, clay, gravel, and stone." Shipments of mining equipment landed only in the short summer. Dredges, excavators, trucks, and anything else with a motor froze in winter. In the dark hills, there was often no water to wash ore, or the water was frozen until July. Warming it required electricity, but electricity needed hydropower that functioned only with warmth.[50]

In the summer, Iankovskii washed gravel in a dredge, where he saw a prisoner sneaking small nuggets away under his tongue. In the winter, he dug by hand. "The first hole I dug three and a half meters deep in ten days. The deeper it is the warmer it seems, but is more difficult to throw out the blasted mix of rock: half falls back on your head and in your eyes."[51] Edwin Sherzer, laboring over a Nome claim almost half a century before, would have recognized this labor.

Unlike Sherzer, Iankovskii and his fellow prisoners came to Chukotka as literal wage slaves, paid a pittance or nothing at all for work they could neither decline nor flee. Not every prisoner was a miner: Tvardovskii, listed as a wood-carver on his intake form, made metal casts in the Egvekinot foundry. Aleksandr Eremin built roads and surveyed for the Chaun-Chukotka Geological Service under the direction of the tin geologist, Rokhlin. He often spent months at a time on the tundra, and eventually was allowed to live outside the camp "zone" as Rokhlin's assistant. But none of them could leave, as had most Alaska prospectors come winter. Most inmates lived in

Abandoned Gulag building on the road north out of Egvekinot, Chukotka. *Photo by author.*

stone barracks. Built for access to mine sites or road construction, rather than any place a person would choose for shelter, they sat often on ridges bare of all but reddish rock, far from even running water, where the temperature reached sixty degrees below zero. The posters on the wall "reminded us," one inmate recalled, "of Stalin's famous words: 'Work is a matter of honor, a matter of glory, a matter of valor and heroism.' "[52] For men assigned to mine, days lasted ten or twelve hours. Rations were tied to performance; the fuller the wheelbarrow, the fuller the porridge bowl. A slip from labor formation might earn a beating from the camp guards. More drastic insurrections resulted in executions. Iankovskii witnessed guards "drench still-living men with water from a hose for as long as they moved . . . squirming under the jets until they became stumps sitting in the snow."[53]

The underground itself could be deadly. From tin pits in the 1940s, Chukotka mining expanded: bauxite excavations, gold dredging, and, by 1950, a uranium mine not far from Pevek.[54] Prisoners feared lung damage from the silica they blasted loose from veins of tin, and radiation poisoning from uranium ore.[55] Deaths from accident and silicosis were frequent enough that Dalstroi declared war on them in 1953. In the same years, camp officials were routinely chastised by leadership in Moscow for their "negligent attitude toward the use of prisoners," which resulted in "wasted" laborers and unmet plans.[56] Particularly worrisome was the habit of bunking political inmates like Iankovskii with hardened criminals. In the Egvekinot camp, a Moscow inquest found "the prisoners are in two hostile groups, the so-called C and B. Each of these groups tries to subdue and influence the prisoners by extorting those who work in good faith . . . in this struggle they torment, torture and even murder each other."[57]

Guards in Chukotka responded with requests: bread, coats, doctors, more guards, more buildings. Prisoners made boots from old tires and insulated their clothes with newspapers and feathers and anything they could find. They suffered scurvy, typhus, endless dysentery. In summer, wild geese, caught flightless and molting, became camp currency.[58] "Seal, white and brown bear, hare, reindeer," Lisov wrote, "were delicacies."[59] But the meat was not constant. "Food in the camps—what, 600, 700, 800 grams of bread?" wrote Iankovskii. "It is a constant burning question: will I ever eat my fill of black bread before I die?" In the ice-rimmed confines of the bathhouse, he saw men gone "frighteningly strange: thin necks, protruding ribs and shoulder blades, and especially elbows and knees, like billiard balls."[60] Tvardovskii watched the mass grave near Egvekinot fill with "deceased prisoners dumped as a bulldozer dug a trench in advance, like dead animals. It is impossible to say how many died from the inhumane living conditions. But in that first year in Chukotka, of twelve hundred prisoners a little more than seven hundred survived."[61] Other bodies were sunk into a turquoise alpine lake.

Around its graves, the Gulag achieved that elusive task of statehood in Russian Beringia: it fixed people in space. Space enclosed in razor wire, patrolled by guards. When she was a schoolgirl, Z. I. Etuvg'e watched her Chukchi mother leave reindeer meat for the foreigners within Pevek's enclosures. She hid the food in a coal pile, where inmates sometimes left small items in return. Etuvg'e also heard days of gunfire in 1941, during an uprising that halted tin production for months and ended with dozens dead.[62] Lisov saw five men killed and eighteen wounded in an attempted escape.[63] Inside the camps, inmates passed rumors of prisoners seizing planes or crossing the ice to Alaska.[64] The Chukchi fought their own shuttering in *kolkhozy* in those same years, with their own uprisings and attempts to flee. But the land that was shelter to the Chukchi helped the state hold foreigners in the Gulag. As Iankovskii wrote, "Here in the Arctic Circle, it's hopeless. Huge expanses of bare tundra in every direction . . . the inevitable footprints in the snow. And Chukchi hunters. They receive an award for wounded fugitives."[65] The danger was mutual. Near Egvekinot, two Chukchi families sheltered a trio of escaped prisoners. Terrified they would be turned over to the police, the inmates murdered their hosts.[66]

Most prisoners labored through their sentences, collectively producing over three thousand tons of tin in 1941, nearly four thousand in 1943, and close to six thousand by 1952. In some years, the Pevek tin mines were the most productive in the country, yielding half the Soviet Union's domestic supply.[67] Dalstroi gave the Cold War nearly 170 tons of uranium.[68] But ore was only one of the things the camps planned to produce: a reformed, redeemed citizenry was the other. Gulag officials evaluated the worthiness of their inmates to rejoin the body politic by their displays of enlightenment. And just as the plan quantified time advancing, so labor toward the plan quantified personal transformation. Meeting plan, overfilling plan—those were signs of socialist fealty, along with political work and self-education. Becoming a Stakhanovite worker could earn early release. And, officially, release signaled redemption.

The experience of reformation did not, however, yield uniform personal commitment to the collective future. Some inmates, like Lisov, never recovered a sense of socialist promise; the Soviet Union became for him the Gulag, and the Gulag was "cold, hunger, abuse, humiliation and beatings."[69] Eremin, writing a decade after his release, described no fervent socialist belief in self-transformation, but found his work "hard, exhausting, but very interesting and exciting," as it gave him a chance to "observe life."[70] Tvardovskii wrote little in his memoir of Soviet ideals, but took pride in the foundry and described his fellow laborers as generally kind.[71] He was not alone in describing an ambiguous relationship with the promise of communal transformation. Camp labor was a group pursuit, but its agonies often reduced people to individual suffering, waiting for elusive salvation.

Iankovskii recalled the euphoria of his official redemption, of "walking freely for the first time in seven years . . . I walked directly through the low drooping grasses; then through a mown path on the slope of the hill running down to the blue bay . . . It was an inexpressible sense of freedom." He had a choice, like all former inmates: take a ship back to the "mainland," or work—now for pay—in the remote Southern mine. He chose to stay "in a Chukotka I fell in love with a little . . . the undulating tundra with small islands of dwarf birch," all "strung with the trails of ptarmigan, foxes, hares . . . the boundless fields of blueberries and crowberries."[72] In winter, he ate reindeer meat from the Chukchi *kolkhoz* nearby, plying young women with alcohol and listening to them recite Pushkin learned at school. He left, three years later, to join his family in Magadan. Behind him was an Earth reformed. Wheelbarrows and picks had covered hills and valleys in open trench gashes and excavation wounds. The streams along the Egvekinot road were choked with refuse and eroded soil, battering the glassine bodies of newly hatched fish.

III.

Below Beringia's mountains, in places, the tundra plain holds bowls of water to the sky. Fields of lakes and ponds, each with their own riches. Fat, pearlescent whitefish suck tiny clams from the muck. Ducks, sandhill cranes, geese, and swans nest in the reeds along their margins in spring, releasing clouds of feathers in the annual molt. In Chukotka, after 1957, their flightless bodies were no longer at risk from hungry inmates in nearby camps. That year, Nikita Khrushchev closed the northern Gulag.[73] Instead of stockades sinking into muskeg, Khrushchev promised a north populated by a new generation of workers, living in clear, insulated domes.[74] Before that space-age Arctic was built, there would be "a club, a library, a cinema" in every village. It was a new way to prove socialist competence, staff military installations, and increase production.[75]

The kind of production that Khrushchev most wanted to increase was industrial, which in Chukotka meant the exploitation of "new deposits of gold, tin, coal, and building materials . . . for the development of the country's productive forces."[76] To solve the labor problem left by the closed Gulag, Khrushchev and leaders after him made the Arctic not a place to redeem individuals for socialism, but to make socialism real for individuals. Salaries were high. By the 1960s, Anadyr, Pevek, and other mining settlements were better supplied with cognac, wine, caviar, chocolate, and imported delicacies than most urban areas. There were no queues for coats or shoes. People could buy single-family apartments. "I was making about five hundred a month," one geologist remembered. "To put that into perspective, I could eat a big lunch with three courses at the central cafeteria in Egvekinot for under a ruble."[77]

The lure worked. "The development of industry and transport in the far north," one report noted, "has produced rapid population growth in previously empty territories."[78] Chukotka's population surged from less than forty thousand people in the 1950s to more than eighty thousand twenty years later.[79] Chukchi and Yupik, more than a quarter of Chukotka's population before Khrushchev, now made up less than ten percent. Moscow sent orders to involve "small peoples" in industrial work and strengthen their collectives; this produced the consolidation that closed coastal villages and mechanized reindeer herding. But Chukchi and Yupik generally lacked the training to be geologists or surveyors, and geologists and surveyors did the most rewarded work. Preoccupation with filling the plan, one official recalled later, kept Beringian involvement from being "totally efficient."[80] Most Chukchi and Yupik stayed with their *kolkhoz*, at a remove from the restaurants and cinemas of Pevek and Egvekinot; when they did move to larger towns, they did work with little prestige or pay.

For foreigners, being a miner or a geologist offered more than a good salary and a chance to best plans. Chukotka was "a kind of spiritual oasis, an untainted paradise," one foreigner remembered.[81] It was a place for self-discovery, for the romance inspired by childhoods filled with *Chelyuskin* heroism and Jack London in translation. And there were new postwar Soviet Arctic heroes. Yuri Rytkheu's novels portrayed Chukotka as a place of elemental communism, as "ideas of social equality" and "work as the genuine measure of all things real and human" were the foundation of "the Eskimo-Chukchi philosophy . . . never formulated but practiced for centuries."[82] The Chukchi in *A Dream in Polar Fog* were guides to a pure, natural socialist self. Tikhon Semushkin's *Alitet Goes to the Hills* retold collectivization as a struggle of Soviet "real people" against American predators, in which the Soviets eventually "conquered the dead wastes" through "socialist construction in full swing."[83] And in Oleg Kuvaev's *Territoriia*, the geologist-hero had a "simple and clear life" spent "working well" in Chukotka.[84] *Territoriia* did not dramatize the labor of making a socialist self, a Long Journey as in the Stalinist Arctic, but a socialist self discovering his authentic core in nature.[85] It was a vision of Soviet life outside time, or in a timeless place: in its multiple reprints and film adaptation, the Chukotka of *Territoriia* was simultaneously modern and primordial, a real, existing romantic future.

The vision of Chukotka exported to Soviet citizens made the edge of the socialist world into the center of fulfilled socialist promises. Semushkin's Soviets exiled the market. Rytkheu's Chukchi did not live on the margins of socialist life, but were its essence. And *Territoriia*, which transplanted Dalstroi's 1949 discovery of gold near Bilibino to a later, Gulag-free time, erased from its fictional hillsides the barbed wire and stockades still present in reality. The new miners lived on the physical traces of a past other Soviets wrote into their *samizdat* narratives, the draft pieces of *The Gulag Archipelago* that passed from hand to hand through the political underground.

Kuvaev, Semushkin, and Rytkheu also described the living rivers that came before bulldozers and hydraulic washers, dredges and blasting caps. But what funded these visions of human liberation was earthly subjugation. Party official A. Riabov reported that gold production in the region in 1961 was greater than at any time in the previous seven years, and "we have overcome the standstill in the tin mining industry."[86] The Komsomolskii mine, the first large industrial gold operation, gave birth to a town of three thousand, including a "hero of socialist work" operating the region's second dredge. Mine operators were congratulated not just for tons of ore, but for "safety measures" that "decrease the number of accidents."[87] By the early 1970s, Chukotka produced nine hundred tons of gold annually and had exceeded the Eighth Five-Year Plan for tin, tungsten, and mercury.[88]

The gold was particularly useful. After Richard Nixon took the U.S. dollar off the gold standard in 1971, the market price rose. It

Gold miner posing near the Komsomolskii Mine, 1984. *Yuri Kravchenko /*
Alamy Stock Photo.

was part of an American effort to manage inflation and stagnat-
ing growth by investing in finance and services, pushing industry
increasingly outside American borders.[89] The Soviet Union tried to
manage its own productive slowdown with more industry, including gold; it became the world's second-largest exporter after South
Africa. Distant U.S. policy transformed Chukotkan earth. Around
Pevek, the land erupted in piles of broken equipment and open
trenches leaching acids. Mines turned rivers from their courses and
ripped open reindeer pastures. Chukotka's branch of the All-Union
Society for Nature Protection, which had thousands of members,
worried about rivers so polluted, "it is impossible to eat their fish,"
and urged better technology and "socialist competition in the Lenin-
ist relationship with nature," which now included the "protection of
water resources" and other environmental measures.[90] But the pre-
rogative of gold export rendered such ideals secondary. The Soviet
Union remained dependent on the market it existed to replace.
Lenin's country still had to howl with the wolves of commerce.

*

In 1951, a man named Willie Senungetuk moved to Nome. He had
grown up in Wales in the years when trapping and ivory carving
were enough to buy what a family needed. "Economic status," his
son Joseph wrote later, "depended not on monetary standards," but
in "hunting gear, larger houses . . . more storage space for food,"
and thus more ability to assist fellow villagers in lean years.[91] Such
interdependence with beings human and not survived missionary
prohibitions and the Bureau of Indian Affairs' arithmetic lessons,
the old practice of attaining leadership by providing for the community adapting to include ties to the market. But in the 1940s,
Senungetuk found the terms of that market changing. Hunting
required more equipment—outboard motors with gasoline—and
the local store now demanded cash, not fox skins. After the war,
airplanes flew between villages, allowing for regular mail and bank
access. Telephone lines arrived. Space collapsed. All of which made
currency, that thing which can move value at speed across distance,
common in villages long insulated from its use. Money changed
the terms by which providers could provide. And to be an Iñupiaq,
to be a person, was to provide. Senungetuk spoke enough English
for short conversations. He had completed the seventh grade in the
Wales BIA school. With these tools, he decided he could provide
better for his children by earning cash in Nome.

Nome had shrunk by then from its wartime bustle to a few
thousand people. This was despite the state's efforts: the army
encouraged servicemen to move north after the war, describing
"unmeasured deposits of tin, coal, mercury, antimony, copper, lead,
iron, nickel, magnesium, manganese, and platinum" and predict-
ing that "postwar prospecting will be made easier by new military
maps."[92] The metals were "of importance to the national economy
and security," in a land that would allow veterans to "renew their
spirit and forget about the turmoil of conflict," as the "pioneer

spirit that so characterized the early settlement of this country still persists."[93] But on the Seward Peninsula, pioneer spirits did not come in large numbers. With a low demand for gold immediately after the war, the "working capital for the small operator" was gone and the high costs of "repairs, equipment, and labor" remained.[94] Lost River's tin was supplanted by inexpensive imports. The only profitable mines were large, established, industrial, and owned particularly good earth.

Nome did retain something to export: the town's myth, an American version of Jack London's better-known Klondike, with its dramas of building fires and white-fanged dogs. Rex Beach's novel *The Spoilers* continued to sell, helped by a 1942 film adaptation in which John Wayne, described by a fellow miner as "a real man," woos Marlene Dietrich and saves his gold claim in a saloon brawl. It was the fourth version of *The Spoilers* to become a movie; a fifth came in 1955. Cinematic gold rushes did not feature disappointed wage workers. Instead, prospecting, as James Oliver Curwood wrote, had "its lure, its romance, its thrill," a product of work in "immeasurable spaces into which civilization had not yet come with its clang and its clamor."[95] The resource exported from Nome's postwar underground was less gold than the idea of finding it on a last frontier, where men were men, the state and its burdens of laws were absent, the Iñupiat did not exist—or existed within the narrow confines of noble savagery or savage drunkenness—and money came out of the ground. Soviet heroes envisioned a pristine nature as, in reality, they demolished rivers with their mines; Americans conquered nature that, in reality, they barely touched. That past sold.

Willie Senungetuk did not live in that past, but in a present where the most necessary currency was cash. He worked at one of Nome's mining companies, but was laid off the first winter; his wife, who sewed caribou hides, made little money as wartime demand dissipated. It was a new kind of poverty: a bad harvest year in Wales was spread equally across a village. Unemployment in Nome struck an individual family. At school, the teacher hit students, and students from different villages hit each other. A quarter of Beringians had tuberculosis. Foreigners took most of the stable, high-earning jobs and judged Beringians for their unemployment. And in Nome, where land had been claimed and sold and resold for over half a century, Iñupiat had little right to common harvests of fish or berries. Instead, one "*buys* land," Willie's son Joseph Senungetuk wrote. "So many acres . . . so many dollars." Most Iñupiat and Yupik did not have enough dollars to buy back land they had never sold and did not treat as an alienable object. The market was supposed to bring freedom; instead, it required that Iñupiat leave their villages so that they and their children might have the money to buy access to sustenance. No wonder Senungetuk saw alcohol everywhere. It was a balm against living on the meaningless, raw edge of capitalism, where "the sense of belonging and *owning* a great and marvelous land" had to be exchanged for the "white man's standards."[96]

And those standards were about to enclose more land. In 1959, the Statehood Act allowed Alaska to select 103.35 million acres of federal territory to become state property—or what one advocate called "free land," to be developed or sold away from Iñupiat and Yupik.[97] The federal government required that Alaska not claim land actively "used" by Native peoples, a statute Alaska initially ignored. William Iġġiaġruk Hensley, by then a twenty-five-year-old graduate student in Fairbanks, remembered realizing that the state was "poised to steal [our land] away from us entirely."

Hensley was not the only Beringian who was "angry," as he put it, "at the poverty we lived in, the illnesses that ravaged us," while "we had no say in what happened to us."[98] The Migratory Waterfowl Treaty made duck hunting illegal in the seasons it was most critical along the coast, leaving communities disgusted and openly breaking the law. Joseph Senungetuk grew up enraged that his father did not own the land where he fished each summer, and frustrated that his father did not expect such rights. Hensley became one of

several young Native Alaskans who went door to door in their villages, village to village in their regions, and region to region in
the state, explaining rights and impending loss. At Point Hope,
such organizing prevented the U.S. Atomic Energy Commission
from using nuclear bombs to create a deep-water harbor, a venture
named Project Chariot. In Kotzebue and Teller and around Nome,
people filed formal land claims. In 1966, the Alaska Federation
of Natives (AFN) began putting coordinated pressure on the state
and federal government to recognize indigenous sovereignty, to
reverse the conversion of land to property through theft.

Meanwhile, the federal and state governments had their own
need to settle the question of enclosure; the discovery of oil east
of the Bering Sea, at Prudhoe Bay, required a pipeline to make it
marketable. The route cut across thousands of miles of land where
Native title had never been extinguished. The AFN wanted land
protected from sale to foreigners; foreigners wanted land protected
from Native claims. After five years of debate and lobbying, President Richard Nixon signed the Alaska Native Claims Settlement
Act (ANCSA) into law.

ANCSA ended, in theory, the question of enclosure. It gave thirty-
eight million acres of land to Iñupiat, Yupik, and other Alaskan
Native nations. In exchange for extinguishing title to 325 million
additional acres, the government paid nearly a billion dollars. The
funds were disbursed through incorporated villages and regional
associations: in Beringia, the Bering Strait Regional Corporation,
the Northwest Arctic Native Association, and the Arctic Slope
Regional Corporation, with dozens of village corporations nested
within. It became the responsibility of these corporations to invest
in local businesses and operations to earn revenue for members. A
corporation too long without profit might forfeit the lands it was
created to claim. Beringians had sovereignty, had enclosed spaces
of self-determination, but not the power to exist without some participation in a world valued by dollars. The model of Iñupiat and

Yupik futures negotiated into ANCSA was, in a general sense, the same one foreigners had rushed north to escape—the model they then recreated in the capitalist underground, the model frontier myths forgot.

IV.

Beringian lakes hold a record of the past in their sediments. Meters down in the muck, caught in the bubble of a past atmosphere, are traces of years with roaring tundra fires, or heavy rains, or a distant volcano. The lakes also carry the traces of mining. Sifting Beringian earth away from gold often required using cyanide or mercury. Rending the deep ground and exposing it to air and water released sulfuric acid. The surface of the disturbed earth became toxic, and the toxins became mobile: leaching into water, drunk by animals, or absorbed through porous skin. Heavy metals dragged birds lifeless from the sky, or cleaved to the fat of fish, and then to the stomachs of people.[99] Geological elements, once locked away by geological time, now cycle through biological lives. They do so because gold, valued for its symbolic immortality, allowed people to imagine an endless, deathless chain of market growth, abstracted from all worldly matter. But all growth has a price. Mining on both sides of the Bering Strait hastened a kind of decay, deadening rivers and bleaching tundra. For people downstream, exposure to the mines reduces the time they can expect to live.

Part of the lakes' sedimentary record comes from Bilibino, a mining town not far from the Pevek camps. Once miners and geologists and engineers worked out the principles of how to apply more energy, more mechanized force, to the separation of element from surrounding strata, the market and the plan had the power to do with the Earth as they pleased. In 1973, a nuclear reactor in Bilibino began powering gold dredges and washers and the electric lights in miners' homes. The Soviet Union replaced muscle power with coal power and gasoline power and, eventually, atomic power, a great store of manmade energy to disquiet the earth. The Bilibino reactor makes radioactive waste that will take an epoch to decay. After a century of unmaking geology, humans are making their own.

To be faster than a river, to undo a mountain: these were the requirements of making value from the Beringian underground. Doing so cost energy, in rushes of labor and equipment. But it was a stable problem: the earth changes too slowly, mostly, to interfere much with human plans. A mine does not alter in the few short seasons that allow a whale to adapt to her hunter, or a reindeer to feel the agonies of a warm winter. The Arctic earth, with its cache of elements, was difficult but singular: there are only so many ways to take apart a hillside or scrape up a riverbed.

Perhaps because there was so little impediment to human desires underground, mining saw the United States and the Soviet Union at their most distinct, and most contradictory. The American gold rush brought desperate people north on the hope of liberty through personal property. Most experienced inequality that left them feeling less free. The Soviet Gulag pursued socialist freedom through imprisonment and exploitation. And, eventually, both contradictions were ignored as the underground fed a new resource, that of national myth: Chukotka as real, existing socialism, Alaska as the last frontier.

*

Chukotka is now Russia's second most productive gold region. Ten, twenty, thirty tons a year are washed out of massive open pits, stairstepping into the earth. Some deposits are leased and managed by international companies. The brutality of the Gulag, the enrichment of the state done in service to a future that never came, is now a present that enriches other states—a trajectory A. A. Siderov describes in the title of his autobiography as "from Soviet Dal-

stroi to criminal capitalism."[100] Outside the new mines are drifts of
prisoner's porridge bowls, white against the dark rock, near stone
huts with rusted window bars. None of this is visible in the 2014
film adaptation of *Territoriia*, all mountain views and clear rivers.
People in Egvekinot talk with fondness of the 1970s and 1980s,
when geologists were heroes and the state paid for vacations "to
the mainland" every year. They also tell stories of ghost men in
prisoner's quilted uniforms rising up and walking next to them, as
they pick berries, as if the underground leaches old human pain
along with mercury.

On the Alaska side, Lost River is abandoned. The Northwest Arctic Native Association runs the Red Dog Mine on the largest zinc
deposit in the world, not far from Kotzebue—like all the ANCSA
corporations, making a bargain between the present need to build
houses and employ people and keeping the land "as a fortress for
guarding our spirit, identity, traditions, language, and values," in
Hensley's words.[101] Iñupiat no longer talk of fish having souls, as
they once did on the Snake River, but they do still teach their children rituals of respect and reciprocity.[102] Around Nome, a few large
gold mines remain. And each summer, individual prospectors build
floating rigs to mine the seabed off the edge of town: the two ways
of making profit, the individual and corporate, running side by
side. Some of the prospectors make their real income not from panning gold, but from selling the idea of finding it, on the Discovery
Channel programs *Bering Sea Gold* and *Gold Rush*. Modern Linde-
bergs toil over their equipment, fight over property, and sometimes
emerge with nuggets the size of a finger. Homebuilt dredges made
to suck sand from the Bering Sea floor become heroic props, as
do old dredges brought to new and sputtering life. The drama is
in the desire—universal, in these programs—to become rich, and
the difficulty of doing so. Men wear hard hats that say "No Guts,
No Glory." They confront giant puddles and epic mud. They do not
mention mercury poisoning or regret, talking against a backdrop

of tundra, some now the property of ANCSA corporations, about men besting the earth in order to best the market.

Bering Sea Gold filmmakers do not pan over the statue of Constantine Uparazuck and Gabriel Adams that now sits in Nome's central square, erected in 2010 with funds from the Sitnasuak Native Corporation to assert a history before corporations. The earth here is always telling more than one story, from more than one time. The origin myth of Nome as a gold town exists alongside a story Jacob Ahwinona told: that his people knew of a great gold find on the Seward Peninsula. "Eskimos know where it is, but Eskimos have unwritten laws . . . you don't let out information that's not going to be good for anybody else but the greedy . . . If you're going to get something like that out, you have to share it with everybody."[103] Near Anadyr, Chukchi tell a similar story of nuggets discovered and kept secret.[104] A future where even gold resists enclosure.

PART V

OCEAN, 1920-1990

Yet is there hope. Time and tide flow wide.

Herman Melville, *Moby-Dick*

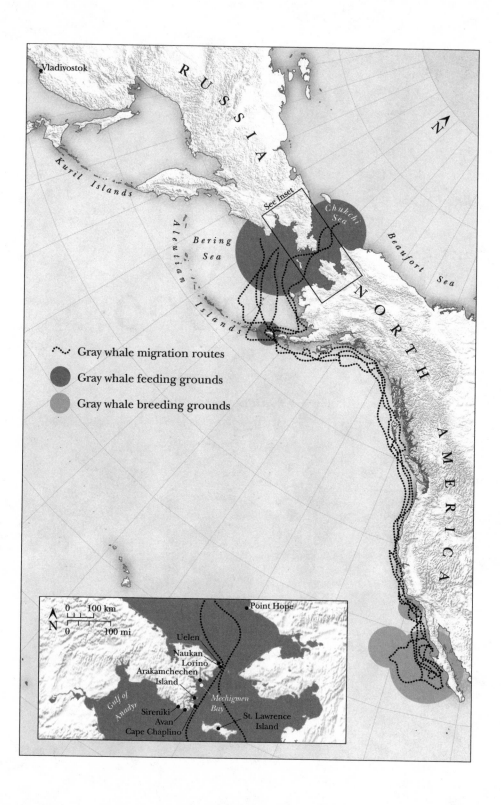

Vladivostok

R U S S I A

Kuril Islands

Aleutian Islands

Bering Sea

Chukchi Sea

See Inset

Beaufort Sea

N O R T H

A M E R I C A

⌁⌁⌁ Gray whale migration routes

⬤ Gray whale feeding grounds

⬤ Gray whale breeding grounds

Point Hope

0   100 km

N

0   100 mi

Uelen

Naukan
Lorino

Arakamchechen
Island

Gulf of
Anadyr

Mechigmen
Bay

Sireniki
Avan
Cape Chaplino

St. Lawrence
Island

9

Caloric Values

Along the eastern coast of the Pacific, the seafloor is marked in places with shallow oval depressions, arrayed in half circles like the absent petals of a massive flower. The creatures that lived here—the worms and mollusks in the mud, the open-palmed anemones, the schools of fish and pulpy squids that floated above—were scooped up into the mouth of a passing gray whale.[1] The indentations track up the coast in the wake of the animal's migration, from winters in Baja to summers north of the Bering Strait. The body of a gray whale is composed during an annual passage that runs over seven thousand miles.

The bodies made on this voyage are slow-moving, stocky, at most fifty feet long and forty tons—each triangular head mottled with barnacles; each pleated throat stopped with yellow baleen; each tail a ridge of knuckles instead of a dorsal fin. With their long flippers, gray whales make the longest migration and have the greatest attachment to the coastline of any Pacific whale, a coastal trail that intersects with the lives of other cetaceans. In the Arctic summers, grays swim in the same waters as bowheads and right whales. Along the Pacific coast, they share coves with minke whales, coming north in groups of hundreds to feast on anchovies and crustaceans, attended by million-strong flocks of seabirds. Rarely, grays might see a sei whale—a species that prefers great depths—or a fin whale breaking its winterlong fast to gorge on northern squid. In the wider North Pacific, quiet grays swim through the song of humpbacks, here and there teaching their babies to blow nets of bubbles and gulp the small fish trapped in the rising silver curtain. In lower latitudes, blue whales flap a lazy flipper off in the deep, where they sieve enough krill to become the largest animals in the Earth's history.[2] Grays swim also across the territories of sperm whales, the females caring for each other's young and teaching them the syntax of their clan, the solitary males swimming to the north, growing huge and leaving only to breed.

Whales have their habitual routes, their discrete populations; they do not socialize much across species. But the overlapping arcs of whale migration link the Beaufort and Chukchi Seas with the Bering Sea, the Bering Sea with the North Pacific basin, and on outward into the ocean as a whole. That ocean is an unsettled place, year over year. In a warm season, there are more algae and more small things ready to eat them; the floating biome expands with fish and birds and their caloric descendants. The growing and shrinking of the ice pack determines the churn of ocean water, moving sediments that are also buffeted by wind, their airy vigor directed by global shifts in atmospheric pressure.[3] In aggregate, these forces change the sea in ebbs and pulses, like tides and El Niño events. And there are more abrupt transformations, the singular shocks of volcanic eruption or tsunami. Whales are their own force. Grays alone resuspend more silt in the Pacific by eating than does the Yukon River with its thousand miles.[4] The work of making cetacean bodies changes the composition of the sea.

*

People also alter the composition of the ocean, in fishing it or running farm sediments into it or crossing it in ships. Another way is by hunting whales. Chukchi, Iñupiat, and Yupik whalers altered the density of gray whale herds for centuries. Commercial whalers reshaped the Bering Sea after 1848 by killing bowheads and right whales and gray whales to satiate the market. In the twentieth century, the Soviet Union began hunting whales to feed a vision of the future without markets at all. Socialist whaling was supposed to save Chukotka from commerce that wasted human souls and wasted whale flesh. It was a vision that began, in the 1920s, where the Soviet valuation of walruses ended: by imagining that the generation of radical new human freedom required limited hunts. But over the next quarter century, the worth of cetaceans to the Soviets shifted from local resource to national necessity, a necessity again seemingly at risk of capitalist plunder. As the scale of market demand began to harrow the world's oceans, the pace of emergent socialism also began to supersede the generational time of whales.

I.

In the decade after spring steel made baleen obsolete, market whaling in the Bering Sea dwindled, until only the American firm North Pacific Sea Products killed a few bowheads each year.[5] Whaling was again mostly Beringian. In Alaska, Yupik and Iñupiat hunted what few bowheads had endured commercial decimation, and the occasional gray whale that migrated so far northeast. Across the Bering Strait, Chukchi on Arakamchechen Island, in the village of L'uren, and north in Uvelen, pursued the survivors of the nineteenth-century commercial gray whale hunt, which had killed nearly twelve thousand bulls, nursing mothers, and their calves off Baja. Chukotkan Yupik bowhead hunters joined in kill-

ing grays, although they considered the meat's flavor unpleasant
and the whales dangerous, prone to turning on the harpooner.[6]
Energy from the sea was so diminished at the turn of the twentieth
century that any whale was better than the alternative.

By the 1910s and 1920s, gray whales were living part of each
year in what would be the Bering Sea's future. To feed demand
for meat, cosmetics, shoe polish, soap, and other products, Norwegian engineers had remade the whaling ship. Now powerful motors
propelled catcher boats with massive, explosive harpoons. Com-
pressors pumped whale carcasses with air to keep them from sinking before butchering. Evaporators supplied nearly limitless fresh
water. Refrigerators preserved meat. Boilers rendered fat from
muscle, not just blubber, making whale species passed over by the
Yankee fleet useful. Fitted with all manner of winches, pressuriz-
ers, hooks, and hoses, the new factory ships were mobile disassem-
bly lines, able to work anywhere and render any whale, no matter
how thin, how huge, how distant, or how quick, vulnerable. Or how
rare: with the permission of the Mexican government, Norwegian
whalers began hunting gray whales in Baja winters. A population
already reduced by nineteenth-century whaling to fewer than four
thousand animals flailed and tried to dive away from industrial
slaughter.[7]

The Bolsheviks, when they arrived in Chukotka, did not see
these distant deaths, or the ships doing the killing. They did witness men and women eating their walrus-hide tents. Nearly every
telegram the first Soviets sent south contained a plea for food: in
some villages because there were not enough walruses, or because
of the American "industrial-capitalist slaughter of whales."[8] The
market, Bolsheviks in Chukotka wrote, had used whales to excess
in the nineteenth century. Soviet marine biologists were particularly appalled by the practice of killing only for baleen, an act
destructive to people and whales alike, proof of capitalist rapaciousness.[9] The Committee of the North worried that the exploita-

tion had not ceased, estimating that fifty whales were still "stolen" from Soviet waters annually.[10] The result was poverty: Chukotkan collectives only harvested eight or ten bowheads each year during the 1920s, and half that many gray whales.[11] The Committee of the North advocated "protecting sea animals in the interest of safeguarding the local population," as A. Bonch-Osmolovskii wrote, "which may be achieved only by way of an international agreement."[12]

Bolsheviks in Moscow had a different idea of how to prevent capitalist theft: catch up with the market and then replace it. Imperial Russia left no whaling industry to collectivize, so in a New Economic Policy–era act of commission, the Soviet Union granted the Norwegian whaling company Vega rights to hunt with the *Comandoren-1* off Kamchatka and Chukotka in 1923. The terms of the Vega contract were meant to curb the market's irrational tendencies: Norwegians were prohibited from killing nursing female whales, and had to efficiently and completely use whale fat and meat, while also employing some Soviet citizens and paying five percent of their annual profits to Moscow.[13]

The Vega concession was unpopular among Bolsheviks in Chukotka. It was ideologically suspect, and there were worries that the Chukchi whalers employed on the *Comandoren-1* might be reporting embarrassing details of Soviet disorganization and lack of supplies. But most of all, the Norwegians were wasteful. The *Comandoren-1* killed several hundred whales annually, "enough for the natives to feed themselves for ten years," but never brought unused meat to coastal villages—something, the Committee of the North noted, even "predatory" American ships had done.[14] Such killing led to a "decrease in the whales in the coastal areas of the Chukchi Peninsula."[15] With American traders and walrus hunters now exiled from Soviet waters, Bolsheviks started blaming Norwegian "industrial-capitalist carnage" for hunger.[16] The regional worry went national in 1926, when *Pravda* reported the "strong stench" of a hundred whales "slaughtered completely senselessly, as they were unused" by the Norwegians.[17]

A year later, with NEP ending and the First Five-Year Plan imminent, Moscow terminated the Vega concession.[18] But the sense of capitalist encroachment did not end with the *Comandoren-1*'s departure from the Bering Sea. Outside the Soviet Union, the price of whale oil was on the rise. The reason, in part, was another innovation: in 1925, chemists learned how to separate the molecules that made blubber taste like whale from the molecules that made it caloric.[19] Whales could become margarine. The number of industrial ships increased from thirteen in 1925 to twenty-eight just three years later. Germany, Argentina, and Japan joined the British and Norwegians in building factory fleets. Eight, twelve, and then almost thirty thousand blue whales began dying each year, most killed in Antarctic waters.[20] The Soviets were not wrong to worry that demand could again bring commercial whaling into the Bering Sea. By the 1930s, forty percent of the margarine Britons and northern Europeans spread on their toast came from whales.[21]

*

That this new industrial whaling risked the future of every whale species was not lost on market whalers, scientists, diplomats, or anyone else familiar with the industry's past. International regulation began to seem necessary outside of Chukotka. The reasons were not those of Bonch-Osmolovskii, with his concerns about humans starving because capitalism had robbed them of blubber. The British and Norwegians saw enforced restraint as a way to protect cetacean economic worth: too many dead whales glutted the market with oil and reduced profits; too few whales drove away consumers. In the United States, whaling was a minuscule industry amid plentiful petroleum and agricultural fats; whales buttered very little bread. Cetacean value was determined for the government and the general public by the Council for the Conservation of Whales.[22] The council's members, mostly scientists from the Bureau of Biological Survey, the Smithsonian Institution, and the American Museum of Natural History, stretched the arguments of Progressive Era conservation beyond the fiscal utility. Whales, "the greatest beasts that ever lived," carried in their beings medical and evolutionary mysteries. As the council argued in one of its frequent press releases, "it would be a scientific as well as an economic catastrophe if whales should be exterminated."[23] The message reached the State Department, where in 1930, officials worried that "the indiscriminate slaughter of the kind that has been practiced in the past" would destroy cetaceans without international regulation.[24] Now, a single ship and its catcher boats could kill more whales in a season than the entire Yankee fleet had in a year.

In 1931, the League of Nations passed the Convention on the Regulation of Whaling in Geneva. The United States was a signatory, in part because of its past whaling industry—which other countries feared might only be dormant—and in part because of the influence of American marine biologists. The Soviet Union, not yet a member of the league and without a substantial whaling fleet past or present, was not a party. The convention called for research to assess whale stocks, regulations to maximize the use of each kill, and whalers to avoid hunting calves and mothers. Norway and Britain, interested in protecting their margarine, ensured that more stringent measures, such as closed seasons or formal quotas, were kept out of the agreement.[25] Gray whales, still hunted by a joint Mexican-Norwegian fleet, received no formal protection. The only ban was on bowheads and right whales, brought near extinction in the nineteenth century. In language influenced by the Bureau of Biological Survey's game laws, Yupik and Iñupiaq whalers were granted exemptions from this rule. Or they were so long as they acted as the convention assumed they should: employing "exclusively native" tools and selling no part of their kill.[26]

In the 1930s, the Yupik and Iñupiaq whalers on Alaska's coasts

only partly met the "exclusively native" ideal devised in Geneva. Iñupiaq and Yupik hunters did not use walrus-tusk harpoons, and had
not for decades. They did use motors and guns, and only abdicated
from the market because a market for baleen no longer existed
along the Bering Strait. But whales also fed people, and feeding
people with whale, the work of converting whale death to human
life, remained part of making someone a true person. In Point
Hope and Gambell and Barrow, hunting made people responsible
to the wider family of beings, human and otherwise.[27] To not maintain a relationship with whales by pursuing them was disrespectful. "If you don't hunt them," as Estelle Oozevaseuk explained of
whales and other animals, "they will just go down, dying, but if we
can hunt them, they'll multiply. That's what we Eskimos believe."[28]
Whales lingered among the ice floes to watch, to judge, and to discuss with their families whether—and to whom—they would give
over their bodies. So, Paul Silook wrote in his diary on St. Lawrence
Island in the 1930s, one day, the "wind begins to blow hard and we
hauled our whaleboats to our boat racks to have worship of whaling, which we always have."[29]

II.

A little over a hundred miles northwest, in Chukotka's Naukan,
Oleg Einetegin's childhood was also filled with whaling festivals
"being a full day long, with dancing."[30] But Einetegin would watch
these ceremonies fade over the course of his life. The first generation of Yupik and coastal Chukchi children taught in Soviet
schools joined Russian-speaking Bolsheviks and men like Mallu in
agitating for literacy, punctuality, cleanliness, women's equality—
and, in the missionary's aspiration, participation in local "groups
of the Bolshevik party."[31] The missionaries, Beringian or foreign,
had the material prestige of the socialist state behind them, and
the metaphysical prestige of a new world order, the "socialist orga-

nizations," that one convert described as "the only way to build our new life."[32] In that life, there was no space for whale kills divided by hunting prowess or age; boat captains and elders had to get "their share of the catch in the same quantity as any of the rowers," as one Soviet school teacher described, an act of socialist "leveling out."[33]

As among walrus *kolkhozy*, the transition to socialist whale hunting came without physical force, but not without loss. Festivals, as Andrei Kukilgin recalled in the 1970s, "had to be thrown out altogether," simply "because the Soviet Union had been created." Kukilgin found the activists who endorsed this policy to be "idiotic people, who did not understand at all."[34] He and others carried on their ceremonies in small, private form. Open practice was substituted for a habit of mind, an orientation toward the hunt passed from parents to children without formal display, but not without moral urgency. As Petr Tepagkaq explained decades later, in the hunting season, nobody "quarrels—whales don't like people who are angry, or greedy and mean. They go away from the shore, they don't want to meet with such people."[35]

Hunters kept themselves from anger and greed as Stalin's revolution worked to change what greed meant. As with walruses and reindeer and foxes, the deaths of whales and the transformation of their parts into quantifiable, useful things could be planned, and the plan moved socialist production to sea. The first plans, in villages like Uelen and Sireniki in 1925, were local in origin and existential in need: the emphasis was on killing enough whales to save people. But in 1928, when the First Five-Year Plan made the numerical construction of socialism a national task, Bolsheviks began discussing how much the sea off Chukotka could produce. The Committee of the North, examining past American and recent *Comandoren-1* hunting, observed that whale kills were decreasing in size "year by year, the natural result of [the] excessive slaughter of young and runty animals."[36] The committee recommended better boats, motors, and harpoons for *kolkhozy*, to assure successful hunts. But they also concluded that there were limits to numbers that people could plan on killing. Hundreds per year was unreasonable; dozens were essential. Their plan was finite, made to liberate people from want by calculating the time it took for whales to birth and grow into the forecasts of their deaths.

The Second Five-Year Plan saw the threat of regional famine wane. So too did the sense of cetacean limits. Across the Soviet Union, socialist glory was evidenced in feats of construction and increased production, each new road and factory quickening the approach of utopia. Whale killing sped up, from five or so a year to ten, fifteen, even twenty in 1934.[37] It was the weather that likely improved the hunt, not Stalin. But the increase made socialist sense; as people joined *kolkhozy*, one whale became five, five became twenty, and so the twenty whales killed this year could become fifty the next. Plans were precise: in 1932, there were 1,900 workers involved with hunting and processing sea mammals, but by 1937, there would be 2,156. Two thousand and thirty-one dead, skinned, rendered walruses would become 3,948. The number of electrical workers in Chukotka would increase from ten to 159. No one made use of "local building materials" in 1932, but 238 people would in five years.[38] The exactitude of planned production had the feel, the certainty, of science and was therefore a true guide to the future.

What moved time toward that future was industry, the factories able to "increase . . . the tempo of progress toward a prosperous, cultured life."[39] It made the industrial aspect of industrial-capitalist slaughter not just acceptable, but desirable. By the Second Five-Year Plan, Soviet planners began to think beyond Chukchi and Yupik shore whaling. Hunting from open boats was sufficient for local production—for the way people lived in the past—but, confined to "narrow coastal bases," I. D. Dobrovolskii wrote, hunters had no access to whales that congregated "in most cases outside our territorial waters."[40] If the Soviets had a modern fleet, whaling at sea would prove as amenable to fossil-fuel improvement as mining. "A massive number of baleen and sperm whales swim in the Arctic Ocean," wrote one planner, "where an industrial fleet should be sent . . . coal from Anadyr can extend the duration and radius of the voyage."[41] And whales were not just best harvested by factories; their fat, refined for "technological purposes," would help national manufacturing.[42] If their hunting ceased to be capitalist, if it was put under the command of socialist management, whales could do more than feed a few villages at the edge of the Soviet earth. They could help build a new world. As Dobrovolskii concluded, "the economy of our Union demands greater urgency in order to boost the forces of the Far East in the development of whaling."[43] Whales now lived on Moscow time.

*

Soviet factory whaling began where American whaling ended. In 1932, a repurposed American cargo ship christened the *Aleut*, attended by three Norwegian catcher boats named the *Trudfront*, *Avangard*, and *Entuziast*, left Leningrad, bound for the Bering Sea. On October 25, the fifteenth anniversary of the Russian Revolution, the crew made the Soviet Union's first pelagic whale kill, an immature fin whale.[44] "We were deeply excited," wrote B. A. Zenkovich, a biologist sailing with the *Aleut*. "Today begins a new chapter in the history of an old fishing country—Soviet whaling. We are the witnesses and active creators of the birth of the industry."[45]

In 1933, the *Aleut* began working the summer edge of the pack ice north from Kamchatka. The ship was a difficult place to live and work. Not designed to be long at sea, the *Aleut*'s tanks constantly ran short of fresh water. The engine belched coal dust that thickened whale gore to a blackish paste on deck. Inside, the ship was cramped, infested with cockroaches, and stifling; effluvia from butchering oozed in through any open porthole. Inside and out, the crew gagged on the smell.[46] They came from across the Soviet

Union; most were Russian, most could read, and most were men, but there were women, Finns, Ukrainians, Jews, Tatars, Poles, and the occasional American aboard.[47] Some were married, some got pregnant at sea, and some came with experience on fishing boats. But they were not generally people familiar with whaling, inexperience they shared with many a Yankee sailor on his first voyage out of New Bedford.

The industrial hunt was assembled from the same practical actions as its wind-powered predecessor. The *Aleut* had to find prey, kill it, and rend the carcass into constituent parts. The crew had to learn the shape of a fin whale's spout in comparison to a gray or sperm; the telltale slick of schooling krill; how seabirds flock where humpbacks feed; the protective, desperate roil of a mother whale cut off from her infant. But, unlike the commercial ships that first hunted the Arctic, the Soviet fleet was not limited to slaughtering slow animals. In the 1930s, they killed fin whales, sperm whales, humpback whales, blue whales, sometimes an orca, and the occasional right or bowhead, animals so rare, their killing "had to be regarded as an accident."[48] Gray whales now faced factory ships on both extremes of their migration: killed to sell in Baja, killed to liberate the world from selling in the Bering Sea; a fast, industrial death either way.

The industrial technology did not make whaling sure. Catcher boats were fast, but not always maneuverable enough to keep pace with the dives and turns of a fleeing whale. Zenkovich once spent six hours chasing fins in a circle, never close enough for the harpooner to fire a true shot; the only struck whale spouted blood before disappearing.[49] Industrial harpoons were charged with gunpowder and anchored to motorized winches, but, as one harpooner reported, "a whale hauled to the very prow of the ship can, with a sudden jerk, break [the cable] and flee."[50] And then there was the dismemberment. "It turns out that to kill a whale is easier than to process it," Alfred Berzin recalled. "People could not do simple

A whale being hauled aboard the *Aleut* for processing, off the
Kamchatka Peninsula, 1920s. *Popperfoto / Getty Images.*

things: turning the carcass from one side to the other during the
flensing, finding the joint to separate the head from the body, separating a spine into parts."[51]

What should become of the carcass was not yet clear. When the
catcher boats worked near Chukotka, they brought fresh whale
meat ashore; as one whaler reported, the "Eskimos know the *Aleut*
well."[52] But supplying Chukotka's regional needs was not the primary ambition of the fleet: it was supposed to manufacture nationally useful products. The *Aleut* went to sea outfitted with pressure
cookers to preserve whale meat, "which when canned has the same
quality as beef." But whale flesh putrefied quickly. As the catcher
boats learned to kill more whales, the packing line on the main
ship could not keep pace with the carcasses. Blubber spoiled within
a half day, or turned acidic in processing. There was not always the
proper equipment to boil the bones to make fertilizers.[53] Depend-

ing on the weather, the harpooner, the vessel's condition, and the size of the daily kill, the fleet might lack the "the means or opportunity to save the raw product."[54] No one thought this was ideal. "To whale effectively," Dobrovolskii wrote, required the "full utilization of the carcass of the beasts."[55] But the Stalinist revolution gave its whaling revolutionaries no time for technical ability to match ideological appetite. In the breach, much of each whale hauled rudely from the ocean dribbled back down the *Aleut*'s spillway, trailing gore behind the ship.

Despite harpoons that missed whale backs, whale backs that sank before they could be butchered, and butchery that was too slow to salvage whales for human use, the labor of slaughter did produce something to measure. Each season, the *Aleut*'s reports put the results of the catch into every possible permutation: the number of males and females of each species killed; the size of the whales; the size of the whales compared to the year previous; the size of the whales in comparison to each other; the total fat, meat, and meal produced by each species; the total fat, meat, and meal produced that year and in comparison to previous years; the quantity of raw fat and meat; the quantity of processed conserves and meal; the total number of whales killed by month, killed by location, and killed by each catcher boat. The way whales were divided put the ship over plan in the number of whales killed, but under plan for the totals of raw products—or under plan for raw products and overproducing canned meat.[56] Quantification was both irrefutable and malleable.

The only number not malleable was the total kill, and how it ranked against the planned harvest. In 1933, the *Aleut* fleet took 204 whales, well exceeding double the plan. Two years later, the number jumped to 487, well over the three hundred planned.[57] Being a whaler was a good way to be a *dvukhsotnik*, a person who overfulfilled their production quota by two hundred percent. Biologists like Zenkovich, although they warned against killing immature whales, took from their observations hopeful forecasts: fin whale harvests alone could increase by four hundred animals per year, and better knowledge of whale migrations and concentrations could increase the catch.[58]

So, the plan kept growing. In 1936, 501 whales died; the plan demanded 495. Captain A. Dudnik, aboard the *Aleut*, could proclaim that the plan had reached 101.4 percent fulfillment, and was awarded the Order of Lenin for his labors.[59] But, in the same year, he warned that plan targets needed to be curtailed, or else meeting them would be impossible, as the ice-free season was short and his equipment frail.[60] In 1937, Dudnik proved to be right: the *Aleut* failed to fill its quota. It was a terrible year to disappoint the plan. The momentum of the purges was spiraling outward from Moscow. As it had been on the tundra, underproduction at sea was an act of socialist treason. In 1938, the Eighth City Party Congress in Vladivostok pledged to fully "liquidate the consequences of sabotage and badly completed economic plans . . . by cleansing enemies of the people from the party ranks."[61] A few weeks later, Dudnik was arrested on the gangway of the *Aleut*. He spent the next six years in prison.

The purges made decreasing harvests a matter of politics, not biology. Inadequate production was blamed on wreckers and saboteurs—or it was a technological problem. "The failure of the fleet to meet the state's plan in the 1937–1940 seasons," one report noted in 1941, "is attributable solely to organizational and various other defects" that included accidents, weather, insufficient fuel and supplies, and "seemingly small things like the captains' irrational gear, which does not protect them from water."[62] When voyages met plan, it was because, as Dudnik's successor Captain Egorov put it, "the Stakhanovite collective of the whaling fleet" managed an "intensity of whale slaughter much higher than in all previous years."[63]

A decade before, whales entered the Soviet plan almost as partners in the project of transcending commercial abuse; the Committee of the North wanted to save grays and bowheads from extermination, while saving Yupik and Chukchi from exploitation. But by the late 1930s, all factors that were not human—politics, technology, planned Stakhanovite triumph—dissipated from the Soviet method of valuing cetaceans. Whales as live creatures with limits disappeared from the official records. Instead, any dead whale was a good whale, because in death, whales were proof of devotion, a material calculation of how closely the captain and crew followed the line of the plan. Almost a century before, Yankee whalers tallied up the possible future of their personal wages in their logbooks, hoping the market would give them salary; now the salary was assured and the tally was for a plan that counted, and counted toward, each whaler's active construction of a common future.

III.

There are many ways for an animal to survive the tempers of the open ocean. Jellyfish are no more than a tissue. Squids take on the color of their surroundings. Fish school by the thousands and spawn by the millions. Cetaceans' way of living requires bulk, longevity, and knowledge. Like humans, some whale species pool and share this knowledge between generations and across space. The worth of a place, the route of a migration, or the results of an action are not inherited in the genetic code, but through communication. Some of this transmission is aural. Species like humpbacks spool out their complex melodies.[64] Gray whales do not sing, but signal each other in tones so low they circumvent ambient noise. They will approach an outboard motor with curiosity, emitting sounds that match the sputtering mechanical frequency.[65] Sperm whales click and creak, sounds that young calves babble before they can articulate sense in the dialect of their clan, a vocabulary they share with thousands of other sperm across thousands of kilometers. The success of a female sperm whale in living a long, fat life filled with babies is determined by her clan, and clans can treat whales of different dialect with hostility.[66] Some of what whales sing may be the sonic form of things human cultures sculpt or forge or paint. Other sounds must be to lure, to entertain, to love, to protect, or to trumpet joy. Or to warn, to send the need for fear far into the deep.

If whales do sing songs of warning, the last years of the 1930s offered reasons for fear. International diplomacy had not curtailed their commercial persecution. Thirty or more factory ships hunted the world's oceans each year, mostly in Antarctic waters, killing whales at rates the *Aleut* could only dream of; in 1935, when the Soviets celebrated their take of two hundred fin whales, the market fleet killed over ten thousand.[67] Diplomats, scientists, and whaling industrialists met and debated, as the decade waned: Did whales deserve preservation for science or for industry? Should there be quotas assigned to nations? *Could* there be quotas, given the jurisdictional issues of international harvesting? Did whales have any value alive?[68] The whaling agreements answered yes, but whalers' actions killed thirty thousand whales in the 1935 season. With a rate of increase worthy of a Soviet plan, over forty-five thousand whales died in 1938.[69] By 1939, nearly three hundred thousand blue whales were gone from the world's oceans. They were market deaths: the *Aleut* had killed only thirteen of them. Commerical hunters turned to killing fin whales instead of blue whales, keeping oil production constant by doubling the rate of fin whale death.[70] No consumer could see or taste how the composition of their margarine had changed, or that market whaling was imperiling itself, again. And again, Smithsonian scientist Remington Kellogg wrote, "The commercial aspects [of whaling] seem to have outweighed the biological."[71]

*

In 1940, marine biologist Zenkovich wrote to Stalin in alarm: capitalists and fascists, he argued, were outpacing the *Aleut* at a time when "our country needs fat, especially fats like those from whales, with wide food and industrial applications."[72] Zenkovich wanted additional whaling ships in the North Pacific, a fleet to hunt in Antarctic waters, and shore-based stations in the Kuril Islands. The problem was not that too many whales were dying, but that not enough Soviets were their killers. His letter set the course of national ambitions; the People's Commissariat for Fisheries began studying the cost of building a whaling fleet.[73]

Soviet plans to build more ships and kill more whales were interrupted by the Second World War. There was no time or labor to build anything not directly needed by the Red Army. Commercial whalers also retreated. Factory ships joined troop convoys; catcher boats were repurposed as minesweepers. Like their crews, many did not survive the war.[74] The result was relative peace in the cetacean Antarctic. In the North Pacific, the *Aleut* did not sail in 1942 or 1943, and killed only a few whales in 1944. From pole to pole, industrial combat between humans diminished the industrial combat between humans and whales.

The decrease in whaling was not for lack of need. Whale blubber could be refined into nitroglycerine, and spermaceti, the fluid in the bulbous front of a sperm whale's skull, also had military applications. The U.S. War Productions Board requested that the American Pacific Whaling Company, one of the few commercial whaling enterprises in the U.S., produce as much oil as possible. The company complied, reporting in 1942 that, "if we don't take the whales Japan will get them."[75] The few wartime seasons when British fleets were able to hunt, they killed any whale, any time, any place, regardless of international agreements, to satiate the national "scarcity of fats and proteins."[76]

Food was even scarcer in the Soviet Union. By 1942, the German Wehrmacht occupied most of the USSR's best agricultural land. The majority of Soviet men were at war, not fishing or farming. It was a moment of productive crisis.[77] Everything, in Stalin's words, was

for the front. No species was beyond recruitment for human consumption, because it was human consumption that would "crush
the war machines of the fascist invaders and German occupiers."[78]
Fisheries experts developed recipes for seal-meat sausage, beluga
whale brisket, smoked dolphin kielbasa, and tinned baleen whale
hash. The major problem, according to the Red Army's director of
supplies for the Pacific, was the "peculiar smell of whale meat." His
solution was to "add more spice."[79]

But, for most of the war, the only Soviet people killing cetaceans were in Chukotka's collectives. These collectives, like any
in the wartime Soviet Union, were expected to "give the country
more bread, more meat, and more raw materials." Speeches about
destroying the fascists were followed by detailed production plans,
the number of dead marine mammals trailing upward toward victory.[80] Shore whaling, dismissed in the 1930s as primitive, now had
a role. "It is possible to increase the production and profitability of
maritime collectives several times over," one party expert reported
in 1941, particularly by hunting seals and "developing whaling."[81]
There was no *Aleut*, but by "multiplying the number of *dvukhsot-
niki*, and by leading in socialist competition, and in the Stakhanovite movement," Chukotkan collectives could do their part for the
motherland.[82]

Those collectives hunted "with the help of American whaling
equipment," as Naukan whaler Ankaun recalled, and relied on
harpoons with "huge shells."[83] Such gear, traded from Nome in
the early decades of the twentieth century, was derelict. In 1941,
the village of Ungazik killed its last bowhead. Hunters in Naukan
took theirs nine years later.[84] There was also little petrol or ammunition spared from combat, to use in hunting gray whales; Yupik
and Chukchi collectives killed only fifteen grays between 1941 and
1944.[85] "Here, comrades," one of Chukotka's party leaders admon-
ished in 1942, "we have extremely poor results, as the plan for sea
mammal harvests in our region is not filled . . . in 1941 it was only

72.6% complete," a percentage that had to exceed one hundred in order to "completely defeat the fascist hordes."[86]

The Second World War created massive and unmet need for energy in the Soviet Union, a sense of existential crisis more acute even than the purges: at stake was not just the rapid creation of the future, but survival in the present. By the war's end, the country had lost more than twenty million people, and many who survived were hungry. From Stalin, with his letter promising vast fat resources, down through layers of bureaucracy, to fisheries specialists with their whale meatball recipes, and eastward to Chukotkan collectives with their rusting harpoons, the value of whales was in their potential to contribute to the survival of socialism. As the war drew to a close, the official impediment to making whales feed people was technological: the Soviet Union needed to catch up and surpass capitalist-industrial whalers. Planners did not discuss limits to whale stocks in 1945, when the Red Army took possession of a German factory whaler designed for Antarctic voyages. Nor was the fate of whales an open concern as the *Aleut* relaunched in the North Pacific. The socialist aspects of whaling were also, now, in danger of outweighing the biological.

IV.

In 1946, diplomats, scientists, and industry representatives met in Washington, D.C., to negotiate regulations to prevent cetacean extinction. The United States hosted the meeting, but not out of national ambition to launch factory ships. Most whalers in America were Yupik or Iñupiat, and the whales they killed were to the Departments of Interior and State alike a regional necessity, but a federal afterthought: the U.S. had no registered commercial whale ships by 1945.[87] The industrial whaling nations were Britain and Norway, joined soon after the war by Japan. But the U.S. came out of World War II with an expanded international role, from Bretton Woods fiscal diplomacy to a military that occupied swaths of hungry Europe and Asia. And as Douglas MacArthur made clear in his message from surrendered Japan to "[g]ive me bread or give me bullets," the U.S. saw future peace depending on present welfare.[88] MacArthur restored the Antarctic factory fleet as part of Japanese reconstruction. The British wanted whale bodies to meet "critical shortage of world supplies of fats and oils." The meeting in D.C. was to plan harvests "up to estimated requirements" for calories, as long as this caused "no lasting damage to existing stocks of whales."[89] The value of cetaceans to the United States was as energy that would help guarantee "a more peaceful and happy future for mankind."[90] To assure this future, the United States convened nations with large prewar whaling programs. A Soviet delegation arrived, unexpectedly.

For whales to assist human peace and happiness, whales had to exist into the future. The United States came to the 1946 meeting under no illusion that the market, and the factory ships that served it, had any interest in the long term "perpetuation of whale stocks," in the words of Remington Kellogg.[91] The combination of demand from "increasing human populations on all kinds of natural resources," with "more efficient methods of taking and processing these resources," made the industry incapable of valuing whales alive.[92] To prevent extermination, the U.S. proposed a global conservation regime, headed by technocrats and diplomats who would establish and manage rational—meaning sustainable—human use. Making this position palatable to countries with a whaling industry, like Britain and Norway, or with industrial ambitions, like the Soviets, took many weeks and many concessions. Finally, on December 2, the Soviet Union, the United States, the United Kingdom, Norway, Japan, and an assortment of other countries signed the International Convention for the Regulation of Whaling (ICRW).

The ICRW established the International Whaling Commission (IWC), a group of scientists, diplomats, and industry representatives tasked with achieving "the optimum level of whale stocks as

rapidly as possible without causing widespread economic and nutri-
tional distress."[93] The IWC's mandate was to decide what kinds of
whales were valuable alive, what kinds were valuable dead, and who
might do the killing. Many of the rules for making these judgments
had American Progressive Era roots. Indigenous people could kill
whales to eat; scientists could kill whales to study them; no one
could kill gray whales, right whales, or whales that were pregnant
or nursing; any whale that was killed needed to be used completely;
and all whaling nations could kill a combined total of sixteen thousand blue whale units per year. A blue whale unit was equal to
one dead blue whale, or two fin whales, or two and a half humpback whales, or six sei whales, and on through the commercially
approved species.[94] No one knew if sixteen thousand blue whale
units was a sustainable annual harvest. Kellogg suspected not. But
there were national interests to consider, and it was hard to argue
against hungry countries killing whales when even the most dedi-
cated scientists had minimal knowledge of whale migration and
population. But, no matter the great pool of unknowns, the ICRW
and the multiple IWC committees it spawned codified the attempt
to make a mostly American, mostly utilitarian, generally market-
oriented but also conservation-minded way of valuing cetaceans
the global norm.

Whales were fundamentally interchangeable, by IWC logic,
subject either to industrial death—where whales became corpses
aboard factory ships that fed national markets—or indigenous
death, where whale corpses were eaten by their killers. Both were
caloric interpretations of value. Whales were energy first, and that
energy was to serve people.

*

The meeting in Washington went the way of most such meetings: bland and diplomatic, it resolved to make whales into a
dependable source of fat. In 1946, the idea that whales might value

each other—as singers, parents, clan members, caretakers, or teachers—was no more thinkable among the international bureaucrats in D.C. than was Beringians' understanding of whales giving themselves actively, with intent. In IWC terms, cetacean energy had no soul or country, no wider purpose than as human food. Caloric value was a point of agreement between the Americans and the Soviets. At the 1946 meeting, both seemed committed to managing a future for those calories. There was little signal of how radically Americans and Soviets would diverge over the next thirty years, as whales became valuable to the market only when alive and to the plan only when dead.

10

Species of Enlightenment

A whale is a culmination: of sunlight and minerals, trans- formed by photosynthesis into algae, algae into teeming banks of krill, borne upward in degrees of complexity through acts of consumption. That consumption is also produc- tive. In diving to feed and rising to breathe, whales move deep water to the surface, where plants turn its nutrients into cells. Whale digestion sends elements—iron, phosphorus—out in great plumes; the nitrogen that whale dung makes available for other organisms is greater than what spills into the sea from rivers or is fixed from the atmosphere.[1] Whales enable the conversion of energy from one species to the next, each transformation filling the sea with life.

After 1946, the Soviet factory fleet also filled the seas, the ships grasping at last what the market had grasped first: the energy of whales. It was a maritime expansion of the Soviet promise to super- sede the market and its alienating separation between labor and the value it produced. Whales were reclaimed to liberate people, not to be a fetishized commodity. But, in converting whales into production quotas, Soviet whaling made a fetish of the plan. In doing so, socialist whalers repeated the central blindness of commodity whaling; cetaceans had no legible value when embedded in the seas their vitality helped transform. On the open ocean, the moral vision of socialism stopped at the water's surface, at the line between people and the animals they stripped of a future.

I.

In 1959, Nikita Khrushchev announced at the Twenty-First Party Congress that the Soviet Union was in a new stage of history, the "period of the full-scale building of communism."[2] The authors of the Congress's seven-year plan for the "significant development of all sectors of our industry" anticipated that the "annual demand for whale fat in the Soviet Union" would exceed one hundred thousand tons.[3] Gosplan tallied what these future dead whales could become: bone meal for fertilizers, fat for margarine, grease for industry, vitamins for strong bodies, nitroglycerine for the military. Four or more new fleets were planned, in addition to the *Aleut* in the North Pacific and the *Slava* in Antarctica.[4] From pole to pole, massive central processing ships, escorted by ten or twenty or more catcher boats, were manned by crews of hundreds.

These hundreds came from across the Soviet Union, from the army and the navy, from fishing families and university programs in engineering or marine sciences. They came to do dozens of tasks: mechanics, chefs, washerwomen, doctors, dentists, radio operators, scientific personnel, shopkeepers, an editorial staff for the onboard newspaper, KGB officers, crew for cutting blubber, and trained harpooners. Yuri Sergeev dreamed as a child of "becoming a sailor, a captain," trained at a two-year civilian naval academy, and took his first job on the catcher boat *Shtorm*, where "I saw my first whale—a sperm."[5] Alfred Berzin was a marine biologist.[6] They found a floating world both different and familiar. Beyond the narrow bunks or wood-lined captain's suites, the modern factory ships were built with recognizable communal spaces: a *banya*, a cinema, a library. Crews played chess, learned to play musical instruments, had ongoing card games, kept dogs as pets, put on theatricals, and, as one sailor recalled, "attended the night school . . . as for many of us the war had kept us from any opportunity to receive secondary education."[7]

The physical conditions were sometimes distracting. Rendering whales smelled horribly. Cockroaches were so endemic that medical staff dusted DDT everywhere. Temperatures above and below deck could broil or freeze, depending on weather and mechanics. There were accidents with ropes, gunpowder, and knives, and with the drunken use of ropes, gunpowder, and knives.[8] The diet was short on fresh vegetables and long on buckwheat porridge. But crews ate more meat than most Soviet citizens, from slivers of raw whale heart to whale "steaks fried with onion, which taste like veal."[9] There were discomforts, but not so many as in the early days of the *Aleut*, and not so many more than in other Soviet factories.

As if for a factory shift, Yuri Sergeev remembered, whalers rose early. His first command as a captain, of the *Aleut* catcher boat *Avangard*, sometimes began at four in the morning, and always "the first thing—look for whales."[10] The *Avangard* was faster than any nineteenth-century ship, and its harpoons were armed with "long, sharp grenades attached to endless synthetic lines," Berzin remembered. "The harpoons cut into whales, the grenades exploded inside." If crews could find whales, they could kill them. Once dead, whales were pumped full of air until they floated like "giant pontoons on the surface," and were tagged with flags or radio receivers so that the catchers could keep hunting without losing the corpses in the waves.[11] A successful catcher could hunt for twenty-four hours

A Soviet catcher ship with a harpooned whale attached to the deck by cables, 1970s. *Greenpeace / Rex Weyler.*

at a time, and would leave a half dozen, or a dozen, or twenty whale corpses in its wake in a day. Sergeev knew a harpooner who killed three in less than half an hour.[12]

Once a whale, or three, or half a dozen from a pod were "on the flag," the catcher boats towed them to the central factory ship. Motorized winches hauled the carcasses up the spillway, slick with blood and grease, where the crew ripped them down. They had to move quickly, before the meat spoiled. "Very often our flensers have to work even harder than our whalers," one fleet captain wrote. "The blubber and water turned the deck into a skating rink," but even during storms, "they stayed there on the broad decks, flooded with the bright glare of the searchlights," until "nothing remained on deck of the mountain of blubber, meat, bones, and entrails." The parts were now in the belly of the ship, to be chopped and washed and boiled and frozen on a series of production lines, converted to bone meal, oil, vitamins, dog food, tinned meat, until all that had been a whale seemed "to melt before your very eyes."[13]

*

On the Chukchi coast, hundreds of miles west from where Sergeev captained his first catcher ship, the 1950s brought demands for better quality and quantity of blubber to villages like Uelen and Lorino. "We have whale stocks that could give ten times as much useful production in the form of fat and meat," one Chukotkan official reported, but "the number of animals fished by some collectives is far from satisfactory."[14] Marine biologist Nadezhda Sushkina described *kolkhoz* brigades hunting gray whales by firing "not less than 300–600 bullets . . . into the animal before it dies."[15] A third of the kills sank, lost under a spreading red stain. If a brigade did drag the whale to shore, it was likely small; hunters avoided grays over ten tons because "as soon as they are hit they struggle fiercely."[16] Their wooden boats were too old to chance an angry tail—or take farther out to sea after bowheads. So the fattiest whales escaped from men "overcome by feelings of fear for these giants."[17]

The answer to fear was, again, technical: the *Zvezdnyi* and the *Druzhnyi*, small factory-style catcher ships with the capacity to kill "at least 200 whales per harvest season."[18] Each summer, the ships killed gray whales in deep water and towed the corpses to shore, where a *kolkhoz* took over the butchering. Doing so allowed Chukotka's whaling *kolkhozy* to overfill their plans by 102.4, or 123, or even a triumphant 144 percent. Whales fed the foxes penned in the new farm in Lorino. Whales were refined into tallow. Whales put the collectives "on the way to achieving their socialist obligations toward the workers of Chukotka" when the *kolkhoz* " 'Lenin' took 68, 'Red Banner'—28, and 'Lenin's Way'—14."[19] By the late 1950s, fewer and fewer of the whales that died on the Soviet side of the strait were hunted by Beringians: as Petr Napaun remembered, "we did not kill whales anymore, only the whalers brought them."[20] Those whalers sometimes killed more than what twenty thousand *kolkhoz* foxes could eat; spare carcasses were dragged inland with tractors. Yupik and coastal Chukchi told their children that this was a violation of the animal's soul, which needed the sea.[21] They had to tell their children many things once taught in practice: where to find whales, how to approach them, the danger of their tails. Whaling is a bodily skill, one that became yet another thing postwar Soviet life made it difficult to translate between Yupik and Chukchi parents and their children.

There were many differences between Napaun butchering for a *kolkhoz* and Sergeev on his factory ship. Sergeev was an adult before he saw a whale; his family passed on no directions about how to sever a flipper or stories in which whales were once people. But both men worked, officially, toward the plan. The original production targets were handed down from Gosplan in Moscow, as part of the five-year plan. Between the five-year plans, there were annual plans, and within annual plans, there were quarter-year targets. The timescales by which a whale was valued shrank to a few months. Factory ships had categories within those months, for total numbers of whales each ship should kill; the total raw weight; the quantity of food-grade blubber, medicinal blubber, industrial blubber of the first grade, and industrial blubber of the second grade; the weight of meat for food, and meat for animals; the pounds of spermaceti, bone meal, and frozen liver; the number of sperm whale teeth; the grams of vitamins and ambergris. *Kolkhozy* pulled whales into meat for people, flesh for animals, blubber for refining, bones for grinding, organs for vitamins.[22] One whale could be counted dozens of ways in any given year, and new plans were reconstituted from how pieces of whale were counted the year before, often increased by a percentage ambitious enough to demonstrate progress.[23] All permutations of addition, multiplication, and division; mathematics based ultimately on acts of subtraction made invisible in the final tally: the subtraction of life from a whale and a whale from the ocean.

II.

Rendering visible the deduction of whales from the oceans was a task of the International Whaling Commission. Each year, the pelagic whaling countries—by 1960, Britain, Norway, Japan, the Netherlands, and the Soviet Union—reported how many blue whale units they killed. The Soviets added the gray whales taken by the *Zvezdnyi* and the *Druzhnyi* under the IWC indigenous exemption. From the statistics of species, size, sex, and location, IWC scientists were to assess the sustainability of industrial death and recommend future quotas "to maintain a proper balance between economic requirements and natural resources."[24]

At each IWC meeting, scientists advocated killing fewer whales. But when it came to a vote, delegates allied with their national industries ignored the recommendations. "I believe [the objections] all boiled down to what is necessary to provide a profitable operation," a U.S. participant noted, as not "a single consideration [was] based on conservation."[25] But the scientists had little recourse. The IWC could not control demand; that was set by aggregate consumers. It tried to control production, but had no enforcement power, a problem made clear when Aristotle Onassis whaled illegally in the 1950s. Any country that felt the quota was too low could leave and kill as they wished. So, for the first fifteen years of IWC meetings, the blue whale unit total barely decreased, even as fin whales— already replacing absent blue whales—shrank in size and number. Remington Kellogg worried that the IWC was presiding over "the virtual extermination of whales throughout the world."[26]

By the early 1960s, the apparent impossibility of conservation prompted some in the U.S. delegation to reconceive whale value.

Biologist John McHugh, at the Fish and Wildlife Service, argued that the "purely aesthetic view" of conserving "these majestic beasts for posterity" was irrational. Whales should be managed based on "economic objectives" and harvested like a mineral, with gold rush–style "deliberate periods of over-fishing" followed by a biologically prescribed respite.[27] McHugh was channeling a new, or renewed, line of capitalist theory. Economists like Scott Gordon and S. V. Ciriacy-Wantrup argued that conservationists ignored "the history of man's successes in discovering new resources to take the place of old."[28] It was logic familiar to nineteenth-century captains. Rational use did not require the future of whales *as* whales, only the future of the capital held temporarily in the parts of their flesh that became commodities. One way for cetaceans to compose the world run by markets was in the liquidation of an individual or species, with its corporeal revenue living on in some more profitable venture. Just look at the oil once invested in woolen mills around New Bedford. That wealth did not need whales to endure. Twentieth-century commerce still imagined that growth had no relationship with death.

In the present, the bonanza theory of killing seemed to work: whales were growing rarer and thus more expensive. Consumers looked to other kinds of fats. Facing declining profits, British and Dutch companies left the industry in 1963. By the end of the decade, the Norwegians had a lone factory ship. In Europe and the United States, edible fats now came from soy, palm, rapeseed, pigs, or cows—whale margarine had been replaced, as petroleum had replaced whale light. All that remained by the end of the 1960s was a small demand for whale meat as pet food and for sperm oil, a substance so low in friction it was needed to lubricate nuclear submarines and intercontinental ballistic missiles.[29] By then, fifty years of industrial whaling had turned more than two million whales into commodities.[30] Market pressure on those that remained was not relieved by a dawning sense of whales' worth alive, on a need to embed their slow generation into the time calculations of profit, but once again by dead whales' lack of value.

*

The Soviet Union did not end industrial whaling alongside Britain and the Netherlands: in the same years that market whalers abandoned the hunt, new socialist fleets entered the North Pacific— the *Sovetskaia Rossiia* in 1962, and the *Vladivostok* and *Dalnii Vostok* a year later.[31] It was not for lack of internal concern. Scientists from the Pacific Research and Fisheries Center (TINRO) sailed with the Soviet fleets and warned as early as 1941 that the humpback, sperm, fin, and gray whales killed on the *Aleut* were shrinking.[32] A decade later, Zenkovich worried that sperm whales were being killed too young, in "a manner which is not right and not expedient."[33] In 1959, S. Klumov informed Gosplan that whaling in the North Pacific "does not consider the state of the resource at all," leading to a "policy that is short sighted, since it will certainly lead to only one end—the rapid extermination of . . . whale stocks."[34] N. V. Doroshenko reported the new factory fleets *Vladivostok* and *Dalnii Vostok* had brought the "humpback whale population in the North Pacific and Bering Sea to a critical state," and warned that soon "it will be impossible to continue any whaling."[35] Each year, biologists told the Whaling Coordination Department within the Ministry of Fisheries of impending extinction, only to have their reports bound in string, "marked with the stamp 'secret,' then consigned to the shelves of special storage areas."[36]

Gosplan did not seal the reports of whale decline because the Soviet Union was hungry—the postwar food crises had abated. Instead, the reasons they gave to keep hunting would have been familiar to a Yankee captain in 1880: the problem was not a lack of whales, but a lack of "high speed whalers."[37] Maybe the whales had moved farther away.[38] Or new harpoons would make it possible to kill harried, canny animals.[39] Perhaps whales would not be necessary in the future, when trawlers would mechanize what had been the work of a whale into the work of industry, and harvest the calories in krill directly.[40] The value of a whale was to substantiate socialism through material increase, to prove an escalating human ability to outstrip natural limits. To imagine conversion—the transformation of one form of energy to another, or one way of being to another—as free, as liberated from the entropic tax of death, had become as much a conceit of the socialist plan as of market growth.

The transformation of people through the labor of whale transformation also had value. Killing so large an animal had always been a collective enterprise, anchored by the critical work of the harpooner. It was a combination that lent itself to labor ideals as old as the Soviet Union: Lenin described how a gifted individual could spur the collective to better production, and the resulting increase would benefit all, making socialist work "heroic, in the world-historical sense of the word."[41] In the 1960s, harpooners were singled out as such heroes, leading their crews in socialist competition.[42] Fleet newspapers ranked individual successes and productive teams, and critiqued underperformers.[43] "Comrade Kurazhagomedov has shown himself to be an excellent harpooner," the *Vladivsotok* reported in 1964, his "humility, scrupulous work, and tireless vigilance won him the praise and respect of the other whalers."[44] Flensers were challenged to keep up, to not "leave the decks for anything" in order to process more whales.[45] Sergeev recalled that, to support "collective methods of work," he distributed "equal pay to all" on his ship, a choice that "increased efficiency."[46]

Leading the competitions was the Communist Party—handing out awards, organizing celebrations, showing films, and holding discussion groups to help in "growing and tempering people."[47] On the *Vladivostok* in 1965, where over twenty percent of the crew were party members already, any "problem in implementing the state plan" could be solved by the party "mobilizing staff to implement plans through socialist pledges" and by "improving the moral and political qualities of each member of the crew," whose "daily work and trials of labor" increased party membership.[48] The end result, according to the *Dalnii Vostok* log, were catcher ships that all "successfully met the government plan, but in the lead are still those whalers who are masters of their craft."[49] And there were tangible benefits for such mastery. Our "salaries depended on production," Sergeev remembered, giving whalers an "even more stimulating factor" for work: a twenty-five-percent bonus over their base pay for meeting the plan, and over double their salary if they exceeded the plan by twenty percent.[50] Sergeev returned home rich.

Rich, and celebrated: Vladivostok and other port cities threw parties when the fleet returned, the most productive catcher boat in the lead.[51] As it had been for Khrushchev's Virgin Lands Campaign and Brezhnev's Baikal-Amur Mainline railway, the attention was national. Newspapers and radio described the importance of ambergris and whale fat, the deliciousness of whale margarine, the unctuousness of whale face cream, and the triumphant launch of new whaling vessels.[52] *Pravda* covered the victories of men like "harpooner Comrade Gnilyank, who started hunting even in stormy weather," or the "harpooner Comrade Tupikov, who mastered striking a whale at a great distance."[53] Their heroism resulted in "the successful implementation of the state plan" while making the USSR "one of the world's leading whale powers."[54]

By the time the Soviet whaling fleet trawled the oceans in force, the collective vision of labor was losing its revolutionary speed on land. Lenin's presence was constant but rote, his name on metro stops, streets, libraries, schools. Stalin had been mostly written out of the state he helped shape. Chukotka's gold geologists went north looking for a romantic past, not the luminous future that motivated early Bolsheviks. And the present Soviet Union, despite building full-scale communism, seemed to trail the capitalist world: collective farms did not produce enough grain for domestic use after 1962. The United States beat the Soviets to the moon.[55] But on a ship, with its socialist competitions and party rewards, the promise of the collective was tangible. The heroism was not in killing people or being killed in the name of the leviathan of the revolutionary state; it was in killing actual leviathans. When asked, decades after he retired, about why he spent so many years as a whaler, Sergeev answered, "Why—first, on the whaling ship, as they said at the time, there was communism."[56]

*

Communism was meant to save workers from capitalist alienation—being robbed of the value and meaning of their work and thereby made into objects, things, incapable of action. The way of salvation was labor that, on a ship, made whales into things, stripping them into quantified tallies. But industrial killing was as intimate as killing on a sailing ship, forcing crews to stare into the eyes of whales "as their resistance finally broke," before wading into the rib-vaulted body amid a rising, humid stench. Shipboard newspapers included scientific reports of cetacean intelligence, describing the adaptive communication Soviet biologists detailed from the *Aleut*'s decks. A. G. Tomilin explained how sperm whales circled in complex forms to protect their young, and noted that humpback whales called like birds to bring help when injured.[57] Such reports confirmed harpooners' observations of the "increasingly cautious behavior of whales."[58] Sailors described their prey as acting out of "love" for each other, or "to help" the wounded.[59] Zenkovich saw a female humpback that, "with danger looming over her, only pressed closer to her calf, protecting him with her body . . . she hugged the little whale, their spouts mixing" through the hours-long ordeal of killing both.[60] Some whalers recalled the empathetic toll of slaughter. "If whales could scream out in pain like people," one remembered, "we would all have gone mad."[61]

But whales did not scream. Officially, their feelings were just as mute: there was no more a place in the Soviet plan to record labor made painful by whale suffering than there had been in the commodity price of whale oil. Whales substantiated the world of their hunters by dead weight, not alive. And that weight counted even if freezers and canners malfunctioned and spoiled meat was disgorged into the sea. It counted if whales were left to suppurate in the heat of their own death. S. Klumov lamented the "outrages . . . regarding the huge loss of blubber . . . and other whaling products."[62] If commercial growth did not require that whales have a future beyond becoming a product, the socialist plan did not require that whales have a future even *as* products. So, like their past and present commercial fellows, socialist industrial whalers learned to think of whaling as "the work of hunting," in Sergeev's words, "and hunting is related to sport."[63] They used young whales as lures and to tie carcasses to their ships as "fenders" to insulate contact between vessels.[64] For objects do not suffer, even when nursing calves paddled up the slipways after their mothers' corpses, still lactating and covering the decks in milk.[65]

In that spilled milk was evidence that the plan, with its rapid increases and endless acts of division and multiplication, had no column for the time it took to make a whale. The oceans were sapped. As a result, by the 1960s, the only way to make communism on a ship was to kill any and every whale. Doing so increasingly violated the regulations of the International Whaling Commission. With the major commercial whalers no longer pressing for profits, and with multiple species of whale appearing to be near extinction, the IWC had finally lowered quotas and banned the killing of blue and humpback whales. Soviet delegates attended IWC meetings—where other nations grew suspicious that the USSR subtracted kills from their totals—and agreed to new quotas, then returned to their ships and whaled for an expanding plan. They whaled out of season; they hunted protected species; they used gray whales, meant to be indigenous sustenance, as fox food; they killed nursing females and calves and juveniles; they slaughtered whales they did not butcher and they butchered whales they did not use.

That transforming whales into lines on the plan violated international terms was known by its authors and whaling captains alike. "In total, illegal whales represented 68.3% of whales by number, and 48.6% by weight," the *Dalnii Vostok* reported in 1967. "If the fleet had strictly followed the 'Regulations' the yearly plan target would not have been fulfilled."[66] Sergeev remembered the international rules as a challenge; not meeting quota might prompt the IWC to lower the Soviet limit.[67] By then, biologists were routinely ordered off the decks when particularly rare species were killed. Such deaths were also erased from the reports sent to the IWC. KGB agents traveled with each fleet and rewrote animals killed at the wrong time, at the wrong size, or of the wrong species into legal harvests. An illegal right whale became a legal humpback; illegally small humpbacks became blue whales; too many blue whales became many sperm whales; too many small sperm whales became one large one.[68] In total, almost two hundred thousand whales disappeared from the international record, even as they appeared on Soviet tallies.[69] In the North Pacific, some of the erased whales— 145 bowheads, 149 grays—had already been rendered terribly rare by commercial whaling; the 699 right whales killed by Soviet ships pushed the species close to extinction.[70] Gone with any whale was its capacity to enrich the oceans; the energy held in the Bering Sea, as across the worlds' seas, decreased. Sunlight moved less quickly into cells. In trying to accelerate time, socialist whaling helped slow the movement of life.

*

The simultaneous public embrace of international whaling regulations and the systematic internal violation had another result. It made the communist plan enclose the seas, or at least much of the seas' cetacean energy. In the North Pacific, where Soviet whaling began, such enclosure had a long history of evading Russian grasp. It was the Americans who stole seals, walruses, and whales in the nineteenth century. It was market hunters and traders who thwarted Soviet sovereignty in the early twentieth. In the Far East, memories of these humiliations lingered. A. N. Solyanik, one of the Soviet fleet's most influential captains, grew up on stories of American predation in the Pacific. Citing the way capitalists had slaughtered walruses and bowheads in the past, Solyanik told his crews that the drive for profit made market hunters incapable of restraint.[71] His view of capitalist duplicity and rapaciousness may have been assisted by witnessing, as a delegate to the IWC in the 1950s, documentation of Aristotle Onassis's illegal hunting and the general "desire of the whaling companies to gather in every whale they can find."[72] Or, as a delegate from New Zealand noted, depleted whale stocks gave Soviets "evidence of the inability of capitalist industries to rationalize their activities."[73]

It was a theme A. A. Vakhov made national in a trilogy of novels, which began with a tragic imperial captain and ended with a Soviet factory fleet victorious over capitalist spies and diplomats whose "extensive talk" about "saving the whales from extinction" did "not fool" wise Soviet whalers.[74] Some of this language, of encroaching threat, capitalist excess, and the IWC's conservation message covering for commercial slaughter, must have been common in the Ministry of Fisheries. It was routine enough to leak into statements of a Soviet delegation that accused the United States and Canada of using regulations and cetacean science to manufacture a "land grab" in the North Pacific.[75] Soviet delegates and whaling captains alike were skeptical of IWC limits, arguing that they had privileged capitalist consumption for decades.[76] The solution was to "take at the expense of the 'American' whale population," one Gosplan official wrote, "800 additional units of baleen whales and about 1500 sperm whales," and by doing so, make socialism exist in more than one country.[77]

This, too, was a kind of socialist labor. Whaling to excess in the name of the Motherland, for some, righted the historical wrong of capitalists killing too many whales in Russian waters. It also made Soviet whaling do what much Soviet industry could not: it moved the consequences of production on Soviet lands and waters and creatures outside the country. The capitalist world, the United States in particular, was learning to send its worst pollution and industrial toxins—from the manufacture of plastics, the dyeing of cloth, the mass harvests of trees—beyond its borders.[78] The palm oil that replaced whales, after all, was grown far from Britain. The full account of commerce was paid thousands of miles away, while at home, acts cleaned the air and water and sheltered endangered species without lessening American appetites or their satiation. The market did not use less of the world, in trying to cheat death by increasing consumption. But it did move the objects of consumptive desire far away, decoupled from the deadliness of production. Soviet industry tried to cheat time by exceeding plans within Soviet borders, polluting Soviet waters, darkening Soviet atmospheres, leaching toxins into the bodies of Soviet citizens. The force of industry was confronted in honest and terrible detail in many industrial towns.[79] Whaling let Soviet feats of labor and engineering forestall the sense of political or environmental entropy. It made planned growth appear to have no cost.

III.

There is not a history yet that puts in human terms the cetacean experience of the nineteenth and twentieth centuries, this great annihilation of generations of whale minds: minds that listened as their seas grew quiet, watched as their clans shrank, fled as their families were consumed year after year in the adrenal chase, the strike, the final gouting blood. Perhaps the whales, in their songs and clicks, teach this past; perhaps they tell each other that the

peculiar and terrifying work of humans is to compose a world without whales. And perhaps they carry no such burdens. People can
and have imagined a world made better by maximal cetacean killing. The world that killing made for its survivors remains beyond
the human ken.

By the 1970s, humans were starting to imagine a world made better by killing no whales at all. In the same period that capitalist fleets
dwindled, cetacean cultural products flourished. In North America, people listened to Pete Seeger sing about whales, or whales sing
to themselves through Roger Payne's recording of humpbacks.[80]
Cetaceans on television saved humans from misadventure, and on
the theater screen saved them from nuclear annihilation.[81] More
than a decade after Soviet scientists began taking the intelligence
and vocal range of whales as fact, American researcher John Lilly
popularized the idea in the books *Man and Dolphin* and *The Mind of
the Dolphin*—although with an emphasis on interspecies communication that listed, eventually, into LSD-fueled speculation.[82] Coastal
towns began offering whale-watching tours. And, next to *Moby-Dick*,
a novel in which the pursuit of whales was a metaphor for the gap
between the human mind and knowledge of God, bookstores sold
Farley Mowat's *A Whale for the Killing*, which, like his book on wolves,
used the hunting of whales as proof of human godlessness. Why,
Mowat mused, would anyone slaughter such animals: intelligent,
peaceful, so unlike people with their technological addictions, so
able to "survive successfully as natural beings"?[83]

Living as natural beings was, in the 1970s, increasingly an American aspiration. People from middle-class suburbanites to college-
campus activists, from scientists to politicians, from hunters to
hikers, saw the world around them sliding toward "the greatest cat-
aclysm in the history of man."[84] Springs were silent. The population
was a bomb. Paradise was not made from *Cement*, as in the Soviet
novel of valorous production; it had been paved over with a park-
ing lot.[85] Astronauts showed the Earth as a lone blue marble—"a

single spaceship," in economist Kenneth Boulding's words, "without unlimited reservoirs of anything, either for extraction or for pollution, and in which, therefore, man must find his place in a cyclical ecological system."[86] Human beings had rejected this cyclical time, one in which, as environmental theologian John Claypool put it, "man was part of the animals' and plants' support system, just as they were part of his."[87] They had done so in the name of progress, which was in reality its opposite—what ecologist Paul Ehrlich termed "the rape and murder of the planet for economic gain."[88] Pollutants filled streams and bloodstreams. Nuclear capacity threatened disaster now for a geological half-life. Oil spilled, rivers caught fire, species vanished, wilderness retreated from slouching suburbs. These "were the apocalyptic facts."[89]

The apocalyptic future could be avoided by returning to the past. In that past, nature had been harmonious. This required curtailing growth—what Maine senator Edmund Muskie called an "Environmental Revolution—a commitment to a whole society . . . one of values, not ideology," and "a sense of balance."[90] This was not preservation for aesthetic enjoyment or conservation for market utility. Balance and wholeness were concepts borrowed from ecologists. In its popular form, ecology had a normative edge: nature without humans tended toward life-producing harmony, but nature as used by industrial humans upset what Rachel Carson called "the delicate balance of populations by which nature accomplishes far-reaching aims."[91] There were various ways to restore natural harmony, from the legislative—which produced the Clean Air Act, the Clean Water Act, and the Endangered Species Act—to the consumptive, which produced organic food. Industry had become synonymous with death; natural harmony with life.

Revolutions are not just material acts. They require mental reconstruction. Environmental collapse originated, in the minds of many ecological revolutionaries, with the conceptual separation of humans from nature. From this original sin, nature was bent to industrial purpose, annihilating the garden of natural harmony. Ending earthly degradation required transcending this dualism between nature and culture. Different sorts of environmentalists cast around for different methods. They adored the idea of Native Americans, moved back to the land, contemplated Gaia, called for legislation and vegetarianism. Others found salvation in whales, animals represented as innately nonviolent, nontechnical, and nondualistic. With the power of their consciousness, whales solved a "major riddle of nature and relations between species," and could teach humans to "live in harmony with Nature instead of ruthlessly plundering the seas that nurtured us."[92] Some, in this new generation of environmentalists, wanted not just to save whales, but to save people *with* whales.

Valuing whales for their transcendence was very far from the pragmatic economics of the International Whaling Commission or the Soviet concept of worth: Farley Mowat's whale was a guide to a restored natural past; the socialist whale was the raw material for a perfectly human future. But for whales to play their part in the Soviet plan, they needed not just to exist, but exist in ever-greater numbers. Yet, the number of whales killed in the twentieth century was creeping toward three million; the Soviet industrial fleets, killers of one-fifth or sixth of that total, pursued the survivors.[93] The *Dalnii Vostok* could only find a few dozen fins to kill. Half the sperm whales they harvested were pregnant or nursing.[94] The mass of whale flesh in the North Pacific was twenty percent of what it had been less than two hundred years earlier.[95] Speeding up time by killing the market's scraps had left the plan without energy.

In 1970, Gosplan reduced the annual target for the North Pacific. Two years later, after more than a decade of stalling, the Soviet Union agreed to allow IWC-affiliated international observers on their ships to record the catch.[96] Perhaps it was some sea change within Gosplan; perhaps it was so that bureaucrats at the Ministry of Fisheries could earn salaries as observers on Japanese whaling ships; perhaps it passed the blame for the inevitable slowing of Soviet whaling to capitalist outsiders. Perhaps there was simply no reason not to: it was now impossible to meet an ever-growing plan with whales. After 1972, North Pacific fleets kept their kills more or less in line with International Whaling Commission limits.[97]

Soviet whaling was whimpering toward its end. But the decline was too slow for those who valued whales transcendentally—people for whom the IWC's utilitarian policies were hopelessly corrupted by industrial ties and ignored how killing such spiritual creatures violated basic "morality," as marine biologist Victor Scheffer argued, "the simple right of the animal to live and to carry on its ancestral bloodline."[98] Whales had new and vocal advocates for these rights, from established groups like the Humane Society to the cetacean-focused Project Jonah, whose efforts helped add great whales to the American endangered species list. Advocates played humpback songs at the 1970 International Whaling Commission meeting, hoping that evidence of communication would move the Soviets to treat great whales as the "marine brother of man."[99]

*

Five years later, the Soviet whaling program was confronted by music of a different sort. That summer the *Dalnii Vostok* abandoned hunting in the Alaskan basin for lack of whales, moving south to the waters off the coast of California. On June 27, 1975, the crew on deck flensing sperm whales heard tinny, English voices singing, *We are the whales, living in the sea / Come on now, why can't we live in harmony?* Likely, few on board understood the words. When they peered over the ship's gunwales, even fewer knew why they were being hailed by guitar-playing, camera-toting men in inflatable boats. For a few strange minutes, the gore-spattered Soviet crew danced along as bearded men in wetsuits sang, *We'll make love, above the ocean floor.*[100]

The singers were activists from Greenpeace. The group began

by protesting nuclear weapons; then, inspired by Farley Mowat's descriptions of human and cetacean annihilation linked by the sperm oil that lubricated nuclear warheads, they turned to saving whales.[101] The group was varied—a photojournalist, a former Soviet prisoner, an *I Ching* mystic. Some were holistic ecologists, and others more motivated by the idea of individual cetacean rights. But by the time they confronted the *Dalnii Vostok*, they had spent a month on the *Phyllis Cormack* attempting to communicate with gray whales—by playing music or meditating—an experience that, the group's leader, Robert Hunter, recalled, had the effect "of 'converting' everyone involved into whale freaks."

Their conversion made the primary objective—to disrupt the whale fleet—morally pressing. The smell of the *Dalnii Vostok*, and the sight of blood pouring out the gunwales, was shocking. "We realized," Hunter wrote, "that here was a beast that fed itself through its anus, and it was into this inglorious hole that the last of the world's whales were vanishing—before our eyes."[102] With cameras rolling, and with the whalers no longer clapping, the Greenpeace crew tried to shelter a pod of sperms with their bodies. In the resulting confusion of roaring engines, screaming humans, spouting whales, and seeping gore, the *Dalnii Vostok* harvested two sperms. Greenpeace took away footage of a Soviet harpoon exploding into the flesh of an exhausted whale, its charge barely clearing the people trying to shelter her. Paul Watson recalled years later that his "bare hand on the whale felt the warmth of its body and the blood on my skin."[103]

For the next several years, Greenpeace pursued the Soviet fleet, using coordinates provided by the Pentagon—which thought the *Dalnii Vostok* was a surveillance front—to throw human bodies between cetaceans and the harpoon, and human cameras between the Soviet vision for whales and the American.[104] Greenpeace helped offshore the moral pollution of whaling, making the USSR look like a country out of step with history when compared to America or Britain, with their retired fleets. The capitalist past,

Greenpeace activists approaching the Soviet whaling fleet and a
harpooned sperm whale, North Pacific, 1976. *Greenpeace / Rex Weyler.*

with its millions of kills, receded behind the condemnation of present socialist hunting. But the activists also made Americans aware
of their participation, at an insulated distance, in the whale economy, as buyers of Soviet whale meat in their pet food and Japanese
sperm oil in their cars' transmissions. Anti-whaling organizations
began boycotts, trying—as the International Whaling Commission never had—to save whales by making the subtraction of their
lives visible not just to producers, but to consumers.

Among the producers, the Soviet hunters, the opprobrium of
international activists—which only increased IWC pressure to
reduce quotas or cease the hunt altogether—turned whaling from
a way of surpassing the market to a way of appearing backward.
"We were afraid of the pressure from . . . Greenpeace," one whaler
remembered. The ocean was no place for socialist heroes. It was
yet another reason to cease whaling. By the late 1970s, less than
five percent of fats in the USSR came from whales.[105] *Pravda* found

it harder to celebrate a fleet that could not fill its plans. In 1979, six years before an international industrial whaling moratorium passed the IWC, the USSR withdrew its last factory fleet from the North Pacific.

*

Enlightenment envisions a universal line from the benighted world to a better one. In the Bering Strait, capitalists tried variations on this theme, attempting regimes of private property and market participation. Communists attempted salvation by collective production. Neither vision proved particularly universal. The environmentalist claim to transcendent truth came from the extra-political, pre-culture realm of nature itself. Redemption was the result of people progressing (back) to a better world by living in ecological harmony. The moratorium on industrial whaling seemed like the triumph of this vision. Industrial societies the world over bowed to the universal veracity of environmental balance by withdrawing people from nature.

These visions were no more native to Beringia than market growth or the production plan. In the 1970s, even with many of the products of growth and plan around them, Beringians did not have the luxury of withdrawal. Whales still sustained people, physically and metaphysically. Iñupiat and Yupik hunters in Alaska killed ten or twenty bowhead whales each year. Across the strait, schooners hunted for Chukotkan *kolkhozy*, taking dozens of gray whales in the final, local enactment of plan making. With great celebration, the village of Sireniki killed a bowhead in 1972. For anti-whaling activists, Beringian whaling raised questions: Was this hunting natural enough to be harmonious? Or would all the bowheads and grays, so ravaged by commerce and commune, be killed off by tradition?

A schism opened in foreigners'—mostly Americans'—thinking about whales and humans. On the one hand were people who valued cetaceans or any other creature equally, as part of an ecological whole. Whales contributed to marine habitats at the species level, but any individual animal was unimportant, part of a larger equilibrium that included human predation. It is a position that implicated all human life in all other life; people could hunt because other animals hunted. The issue was controlling demand within biological limits.

On the other were activists who saw whales, like humans, as bearing selves—souls, even—granting each individual rights. Not beings with a country, but beings needing the protection of countries. It was an environmentalist vision that implicated all life—at least, all life intelligent enough to warrant rights—in a moral order imposed by the human mind, while asking human bodies to retreat from consuming flesh. Paul Spong, a Greenpeace activist and cetacean researcher, concluded that Yupik and Iñupiat hunters should stop hunting whales and treat them "as neighbor and friend, an object of curiosity and affection, rather than food."[106] It was a politics of reverence through abdication. There could be no hunt, no matter the hunter.

In 1977, the IWC sided with abdication, claiming the population of bowhead whales was so low, even subsistence hunts endangered the species. Their discussions, like Spong's, critiqued Iñupiat and Yupik use of technology, and dismissed Iñupiat reports of a growing number of bowheads. Iñupiaq whaler Harry Brower Sr., the youngest son of nineteenth-century captain and trader Charlie Brower, invited biologists to Utqiaġvik to monitor the bowheads. The results confirmed Iñupiaq observations. Before Congress and the IWC—sometimes in Iñupiaq, through a translator—Alaskan whalers asserted that whales were both subjects of reverence and sustenance. Whales were not and had never been objects, even after a century of market hunting; they were beings that swam up from their own country and chose to die. For whalers to refuse that gift was disrespectful, and had for many centuries meant human death from hunger.

What took precedence: animal rights or human rites? In Alaska, and eventually in Chukotka, Iñupiat, Yupik, and Chukchi hunters won the human right to enact their version of cetacean value. Or *a* version of it. Whalers had to kill whales with prescribed equipment and techniques. Each community had an annual harvest limit. Violations meant a loss of hunting privileges for five years. The quotas were initially smaller than what people needed for food, and said nothing of how bowheads would swim next to a boat, on the opposite side from the harpooner, assessing whether this group of people was worthy of its death.[107] In Beringia, whales helped set the ethical parameters of their hunting; their actions were understood by their killers as signaling their consent to die. But whales did not speak to the IWC. Its rules, like the ANCSA, were shaped by the same "Westerners" whose "greed," as Roger Silook pointed out, brought "whales nearly to extinction."[108]

IV.

A gray whale born at the end of the 1980s did not face the same risks as its parents, or its grandparents. Commercial whaling had ceased; local whaling was limited. People in Beringia killed only a few whales in each community each year. Dead whales had once been valuable as light; left alive, they had become a sign of enlightenment. After nearly a hundred and fifty years of combined capitalist and communist mass slaughter in the North Pacific, the remorseless havoc ceased. Leviathan had endured.

The leviathan that did not endure was the Soviet Union. Just over a decade after withdrawing its fleet from whaling the world's oceans, the socialist experiment withdrew itself from the world's countries. It shuddered down slowly: production, insufficient and inefficient; politics, trying on a human face, but facing humans unconvinced by its promises; industry, not making socialism, but making nature undrinkable, inedible, unbreathable. Eventually, the real-life versions of Oleg Kuvaev's geographer-heroes found pools of toxic mine runoff. Yuri Rytkheu no longer celebrated electrification, but wrote stories where whales were people and killing them left the sea "with no sign of life."[109] The Soviet plan, like ideas of market growth, assumed humans alone made time move. But market growth claimed that its movement produced only earthly progress; religion could offer anyone wanting spiritual transformation an alternate, transcendent salvation. The plan was supposed to be salvation *through* earthly progress, transcendence without death. It made the promise of utopia fragile in a present filled with shelves bare of choice and choices increasingly bare of the meaning that sustained socialist converts through the crucibles of collectivization, purges, and war.[110] In trying to make time move faster and save every living soul, socialism exhausted itself in a single generation.

In Beringia, the Soviet experiment showed to whales and other beings that socialism and capitalism could look similar, and transform the world on remarkably similar terms: both failed to recognize the timespans cetaceans live by, but learned to see those of walrus. It showed difference too: the experience of a Soviet reindeer herder, like a Soviet reindeer, was not a mirror to their counterparts in Alaska. But in the United States, the official version of the twentieth century was one entirely of divergence. Socialism withered because it was not natural; it was not natural because it had no markets; and without markets, nothing could be free.

The expiration of the Soviet Union was supposed to bring the end of history, the final answer to the great toil of working out how people should assign their energies, their notions of enclosure, their devotion. When Ronald Reagan called for Mikhail Gorbachev to "tear down this wall" between East and West Germany in 1987, that argument was explicit: "There stands before the entire world one great and inescapable conclusion: Freedom leads to prosperity. Freedom replaces the ancient hatreds among the nations with comity and peace. Freedom is the victor." Capitalist democracy was the natural end of all political struggle, and therefore universal. A comforting faith, in growth liberated from all constraint. Yet it is also a blind faith. The market, restless and global, willing to abandon places and people where growth is slow or absent, less concerned with souls than with appeasing earthly desires, still does not account for death and the time required to make life.

*

In Lorino, on Mechigmen Bay, hunters pull their boats toward the Bering Sea. A hundred years ago, people here had never heard of communism, and almost thirty years ago, people had to unhear it, unlearn the habits of that state. In 1991, the *Zvezdnyi* stopped bringing whale carcasses to shore.[111] The fox farm closed. The government stopped paying salaries. There was no fuel for the power plant. People lit their homes with seal- or whale-oil lamps.[112] Families had to piece together how to hunt from the knowledge passed down kin lines from the last active whalers. A cetacean, killed and divided on the shore, was as important in 1995 as in 1895.

In 2015, it is still important; Reagan's neat equation of freedom becoming prosperity has never quite added up to reality on this beach, or up among the old Soviet apartment blocks now painted bright colors, decorated with murals of walruses and polar bears. Communism ended suddenly because its logics of production and salvation ceased making sense. But capitalism has not started making sense here. Beringia's history suggests that it never has. Imagining endless growth and freedom from all limitations—freedom from needing whales, and what whales make of the ocean—is wrong in a practical sense. Life is so clearly made from the condition of the water, the stability of the sea ice, the presence of a gray, barnacled head. It is made from a whale choosing her time to die. The hunters start their sputtering, smoking Yamaha engines, check their ropes, and load their rifles. The whales are spouting.

Epilogue

The Transformation
of Matter

All that is solid melts into air.

Karl Marx, *The Communist Manifesto*

I n late autumn, Beringia's ravens begin to gather. They are fat and glossy after the Arctic summer, chicks grown over two feet high and ready, with their parents, to join in the company of others. Under their wings, the tundra is converting to deep red after the frost, the willows turning the course of each river and stream into loops of gilt yellow. Along the coast, the sea is rimmed with ice, the water heavy in places with slush. One day is lit by watery sun; the next will bring winter, all at once, in a blizzard. Amid the transformation of the season, the black birds cluster, patterns of ink forming and resolving in the air.

Ravens flock, but do not go south. They do not need to. The common raven, *Corvus corax*, is omnivorous and intelligent and finds ways to live not just in the Arctic, but in deserts, temperate forests, plowed fields, and cities. In the north, they inhabit every ravine's birches, every coastline's sheltering knot of spruce. They keep one rolling black eye on the world of people. It is not idle curiosity; the birds learned long ago to prospect among humans because humans make energy predictable: leaving piles of steaming carrion, racks of fish, boxes of cast-off miners' biscuits, the endless possibilities of refuse heaps. So, when the cold bears down on the land, the ravens fly to town.[1] When I chopped salmon for my dog team during my first seasons in the Arctic, the ravens would assemble a half hour before feeding time in gurgling and rasping and trilling congregations, their liquid voices my signal to start work.

From their ubiquity, Chukchi, Iñupiat, and Yupik wove ravens into their narratives of origin. The birds are both tricksters and saviors, using their wits to fetch earth for drowning people, to cast away the spirits that torment reindeer, or to kill a great whale to make land.[2] The people in Point Hope have a story about a raven that covets a skin ball, hoarded underground by a night-loving peregrine falcon. The ball holds the whole life-giving sun. Raven's plot is to free the light in order to make a new world, a better world, for human beings.[3] Liberating energy is the cause of human transformation in a story first told long before its tellers met a metal oil lamp, let alone an internal combustion engine.

*

How to take the measure of Beringia's transformations, of human plots to make new worlds? This history does not have a conclusion, as the revolutions of the long twentieth century continue into the twenty-first. Take, for example, what lies under the Chukchi Sea: millions of gallons of old sun made flesh by plants, made petroleum by time and heat and pressure, and made precious by industry. Geologists knew in the twentieth century that an oil field possibly as rich as Prudhoe Bay pooled under Beringian waters, but there was neither the technology nor the demand to attempt extraction. But in 2005, Royal Dutch Shell began buying development leases in the Chukchi and Beaufort Seas. A decade later, a half-submersible oil-drilling rig named the *Polar Pioneer* left Seattle. Shell saw in the voyage "a future of new ports, new airports and permanent rigs," able to "bind Arctic Alaska to the rest of the world."[4] Beringia seemed poised to offer up industry's most potent fuel. Environmentalists protested. "Shell helped melt the Arctic," in Bill McKibben's words, "and now they want to drill in the thawing waters."[5] Iñupiaq communities filled with oil-spill mitigation equipment and promises of employment. "The hunger for oil," Point Hope mayor Steven Oomittuk told a reporter, "our ancestors went through it before."[6]

That hunger, from the whalers of 1848 to the arrival of miners in 1898, from domestic reindeer arriving in Alaska and Bolsheviks arriving in Chukotka, from the advent of Cold War borders in 1948 to the end of Soviet factory whaling in 1979, brought foreigners to Beringia with conversion on their minds. Inspired by the promises of the industrial enlightenment, they came to make energy predictable and enclose space. They also came to make Beringia part of a linear, progressive idea of time. By the twentieth century, foreigners' temporal imagination had two variants. Commerce reduced time to the next cycle of profits, with the vague promise that general growth was the mechanism by which a better world evolved. That evolution was uneven, following trends in consumption that sometimes desired foxes and walruses and sometimes let entire villages fall outside market interest. Socialist time, wanting to use capitalism's industrial tools to supplant capitalism's inequities, promised to hasten utopia by planning a communal ascent. Soviet plans tried to speed up time everywhere and save everyone by increasing production out of every space.

Yet, as foreign ideas came to transform Beringia, those ideas were also themselves transformed. In the nineteenth century, whales thwarted commercial hunters' technology, so hunters learned to kill at a rate that undid not just bowheads, but market expectations that efficiency would lead to growth. On the sea ice, a regulated market and restricted socialist plan both recognized, eventually, the limits of walruses. Climate and wolves frustrated state attempts to make reindeer predictable. People undid

Beringian geology for gold and tin. Soviet whaling, so committed to saving human souls, proved no more able to include cetaceans in its calculations than commercial hunters, and wound down for lack of whales. As a result, what it meant to live on the shore was different from on the land; harvesting from the sea made different relationships between people and place than mining. Neither markets nor plans proved innately more rational—indeed, what was rational appears situational, as a fox asks for different relationships with people than a walrus—or better able to convert Beringia and its people to a shared, single future.[7] Across space, idea and matter combined into multiple capitalisms and multiple socialisms. The Soviet vision, generally unwilling to let any being or place exist out of planned time, expended itself more quickly than the erratic global reach of capitalism.

This has left the market, and the states that try to regulate it, as the dominant mode of foreign transformation along the Bering Strait. The revolution continues to be uneven. After six billion dollars and months of boring test wells, Shell discovered that the deposits under the Chukchi Sea were too small to legitimize the expense of work amid falling oil prices and the Arctic burdens of cold, distance, and rough seas. In the fall of 2015, the *Polar Pioneer* sailed south.

*

In 2018, I spent an afternoon watching men butcher a gray whale on a bay not far from Provideniya, on the Chukchi coast. The air was perfectly clear and the water where the whale had last been alive piercing blue. Seagulls and ravens gathered, squabbling knots of white and black, waiting for a turn with the ribs and twists of intestine. The air smelled of diesel exhaust and blood. Everything was quiet and matter-of-fact. One of the men, leaning back from the body with his long knife, dangling a cigarette, said that this whale had chosen to die by swimming up next to the harpooner. When

Hunters throwing a harpoon at a surfacing gray whale, Chukotka. *Photo by Andrey Shapran.*

the meat and blubber were cut away, two Soviet-era trucks dragged it across the pebbly spit to sit among the bones of other whales.

A year before, people told me the same thing—the choice of death—about a bowhead whale on St. Lawrence Island. In less explicit terms, this was how I was taught to hunt caribou on the Gwitchin tundra. You live here by never boasting about the number of animals that died, and by giving meat to people without any. You live here by not offending the beings that make your life possible. You live here because other lives give themselves to you. To articulate the act of consumption, of taking energy this way, is not romantic. It is a political assertion. The politics of the gift, like all politics, are a vision of time. A whale or a caribou giving itself holds open a future where today's recipient—the killer—will be called upon to give. A reciprocal ethics, acknowledging that all life shifts between consuming and providing. Commodities make no such demands.

These ways of relating to animals and places have altered over the past two hundred years. But then, change is a millennia-long Beringian tradition.[8] Before foreigners came, societies invented new ways to make homes and meaning, and to learn, in William Oquilluk's telling, from disaster. After foreigners came, Beringians took on, as Sadie Brower Neakok explained, a "way of life [that] is sort of two-fold: knowing the white man's way and then our traditional Eskimo ways were instilled in us."[9] Foreigners wanted everyone to live in the same time. Many Beringians are committed to living in more than one: that of the market, and those of caribou, fish, seals, and dozens of other beings and places.

To live even partly on the market's terms, however, requires money. In Gambell, on St. Lawrence Island, there is paid work with the Native Corporation, at the store, post office, school, and clinic. Men sell carved ivory pieces and artifacts excavated from their ancestors' trash piles in the brief season when tourists come to watch migrating sandhill cranes and other birds. But many families have no consistent income, in a village where heat and electricity can run over two thousand dollars per month. A can of tomatoes and a box of spaghetti at the store—when the planes can stock it—cost almost twenty dollars. Hunting requires gasoline and bullets. There are not enough homes, or materials to repair them. Walking among Gambell's rows of houses in 2017, a summer full of whale blubber and fresh fish and children hanging off the back of four-wheelers with glee, I kept remembering Joseph Senungetuk's words from the 1970s. Foreigners promised "over and over again," he wrote, "that there will be changes made for the better, 'in due time.' Again we ask: Give or Take a Century—when is 'due time?' "[10]

Foreigners tend to see poverty in Gambell, or anywhere in Beringia, in two ways. The first assumes progress is a fact, that material increase is deferred but inevitable: get a job, and join the good life! In this vision, Beringians are often critiqued for not changing enough, or too slowly. In the second, foreigners see Yupik, Iñupiat, and Chukchi as fallen from a perfect, unchanging past, one free of wars and defined by natural harmony. They are then judged for deviating from a state that never existed. Both views assess Beringians according to their place on a continuum of universal history: if they are poor it is temporary; or, if they assert customary relationships with, say, the bowhead, they cannot be *real* relationships because modernity corrupts tradition. A whale cannot give itself to people in a motorboat.

Both judgments assume modernity blots out all else, erasing the salience of living values that predate, endure, and sometimes reject ideas of worth imported by states and market relations. Hunting whales or picking berries have meanings that survived the alienation of colonialism. And both judgments elide how, fifty years after Joseph Senungetuk wrote, the assurances of missionaries and bureaucrats—convert to a life of plenty and liberty!—remain forestalled, at best, or duplicitous. Capitalism makes the freedoms of profit for some through theft from others. It steals energy—in human labor, in whale bodies, in submarine oil deposits—and lifetimes. Not everyone can be a thief, even in *due time*. Beringians, with long experience of being robbed, have reason to think that foreigners' *better* will never come.

Sixty miles across the sea from Gambell, the kind of time promised for most of the twentieth century will also never arrive. Ureliki was built by the Soviet military, over a Yupik village, into a place people tell me was a thriving, happy town. No one lives here now. The sense of life abandoned mid-stride, mid-sentence, is everywhere: among the piles of coal ready for the electric plant; in the garage, with its doors open, awaiting vehicles for repair; in the apartments, with wallpaper and high ceilings visible through broken windows. In 1988, people celebrated the October Revolution and went to work, an entire civilization of concrete and military prowess and murals of socialist triumph solid around them. Three years later, it was gone: The Soviet Union, in collapse, had no need of Ureliki. In the lifespan of an arctic fox, its population had

Gray whale bones and fresh carcass with seagulls, Chukotka.
Photo by author.

moved on. Three decades later, fireweed grows amid half-built, deserted structures and bursts through sagging roofs. Ureliki is eerily beautiful and vitally alive, as ruins are converted into soil.

This, perhaps more than anything, is the measure of human transformations in Beringia: they are ongoing, but impermanent, and overrun by other life. The nature of history when nature is part of what makes it is cacophony: not harmonious but revealing both a linear *uqaluktuaq* story and many cyclical *unipkaaq*, converging. We all live in more than one time, even if we are taught to refuse the idea. The evidence is all around us, in the layered world: a mossy, decaying mission store in Gambell, built near an ancient whale-butchering place, across from a row of tidy new homes. Or, as I saw in Lavrentiya, a house with Soviet concrete walls, but a roof made of walrus hide so fresh, it smelled.

*

The ravens called to us from shore in the autumn, out on the river to pull up the salmon nets. It was on the river, my hands in the fish gore, that my hosts explained—patiently, for I was young and not disposed to think of endings—that I was likely in the last generation to see this river, to fish these salmon, in this way. Salmon are trawled aggressively at sea, and they do not like warm water. The twentieth century had just ended, but in the Arctic, change was already imminent. I had come by then to love a place that could kill me in a moment's carelessness. It was also a place that I, in the course of living the life I knew as normal, the life of engines and electric lights, was helping erode.

I remember looking out over the tundra. There is a particular light where the sun comes down bright through the clouds on a far hill, a bloom of green. It is like a thousand other moments where the sensory immediacy of the north cuts to the quick. The cracking-spark sound of the spruce fire starting in a canvas tent on a morning so cold, everything touched by breath is rimed in frost. The loamy smell of the air among great whale jaws, where they crumble into a beach—some ripe with recent death, others chalk-white with age. The sound of a caribou exhaling in panic before the gunshot. The mouthfeel of bowhead, the raw, black skin crunching slightly, the fat dense and springy. The thrum of fear behind the breastbone, when the bear lifts her head from among the willows. To live here is to be very clear on the debts of the flesh. There I was, lifting fish from the river to make them into food, with muscles fed on caribou and berries. There I have been since, hands slippery with walrus fat, or cooking the gray whale that fed me, one summer, for a week. That is the contradiction of existing in Beringia: in order to live, something, some being, is always dying. As in the Iñupiaq legend, where the raven takes the sun from the falcon and they fight, battling a pattern of dark and light into the land and the sky. Looking at this, raven concludes that there cannot only be light, or life: such a world would be sterile.

There is no exit from this contradiction. Humans are of places; we sit deep in them and cannot help but change them. To be alive means taking up our place in a chain of conversions. It is not optional. We are embarked. But to where? Scale matters, in such things. Foreigners introduced new scales—shortening the horizon of imagined time to the next sale or next plan, while expanding the gauge of appetite. A hundred whales became a thousand, ten thousand. More harvest in the short term would bring the Promised Land sometime—next year? In a decade?—while separating the act of living, of consuming, from dying. Some ways of imagining the future require more energy than others, and the industrial enlightenment was particularly covetous. Fossil fuels freed the use of energy from human toil, allowing human history to seem separate from the rest of time. It wrote concern for cyclical life out of most calculations of value; cycles, after all, have a peak and a decline, a season for birthing and for dying. They invoke mortality. Ideas of ever-increasing growth emphasize the life phase, as if we as a social body are permanent adolescents, hungry and rising, immortal. This made possible a new idea of liberty, released from the constraints of the matter that made us, and from the precariousness of being.

The irony of the attempt is that it has made being human—and being walrus, seal, reindeer, tiny mollusk—more precarious. Beringians have lived through what William Oquilluk called the four disasters, and may be facing a fifth; already, Shishmaref and Kivalina and Lorino are at risk of eroding into a sea no longer tempered from storms by sea ice. In 2013, in an echo of the disastrous 1870s, Gambell was hungry; the ice too far off and unstable to hunt walruses. With assistance insufficient, the village had a PayPal site for donations. In February 2019, the air temperature at the North Pole was above freezing. Ice rotted in the midwinter dark under a bubble of warm air. There was open water between the Diomede Islands, a place where whalers once waited until June to find clear passage. Inland, the creeping absence of cold kills black spruce as the permafrost loosens beneath their roots.

Not all beings struggle; the bowheads are having fat babies, and ravens expand their range, using equipment built for oil exploration as substitutes for nesting trees. For much Arctic life, the future is uncertain to a new degree. The cyclical *unipkaaq* is changing. What happens when not three warm seasons worry a caribou herd, but thirty in a row? When walruses must birth on beaches rather than their floating coast? And what of the iceless shores where polar bears now meet grizzlies and between them breed strange new creatures: perhaps fit for a warmer age, perhaps unfit for any.

My Gwitchin host father told me on a visit a few years ago, only half-joking, that foreigners had brought the end of a world to his people a century ago. Then it was missionaries and measles and decimated species, but now climate change will take the end of a world south.[11] The planet without Beringia's cold has existed before, and great and plentiful life existed along with it, but never in the experience of *Homo sapiens*. The sea ice, while it seems altogether elsewhere, moderates the extremity of storms and regulates the global circulation of air and water, keeping the climate stable. This stability underwrote the agrarian and industrial ideals foreigners brought here, ideals that Beringia's changeability helped shape into particular expressions at sea, on shore, on the land. Now the ideologies of the twentieth century, in trying to make the world home to universal rules of growth and using fossil fuel to do so, have made the world profoundly less stable. As a consequence, Beringia might—should its icy shape continue to corrode—by sheer force of disastrous presence reshape ideas everywhere in the twenty-first century.

Historians are reticent to predict the future, but two things speak out from Beringia's past. One is the inconsistency between human desire and material outcome. People are only part of what shapes action. The other is that Big Oil will return to drill, eventually, if it is permitted to, and if we ask it with our demand for energy; the market, after all, is not external to us but the aggregate of action. The first requires recognizing the limits of human choice; the second our power: the energy that sustains us is made by other beings, but energy is also what we put into the world, with our labor and thought; it demarcates what matters as we transform matter. In doing so, we cannot decide all of what will come to pass, but we can decide what we value, the scales on which we conceive life and consume death. "The continuous work of the imagination," Barry Lopez wrote from Gambell thirty years ago, is "to bring what is actual together with what is dreamed."[12] What do we dream now, in our global masses? Imagining another politics, one not so covetous of all energy and so bent on the fictions of enclosure, one not so blind to our place in the family of things, might be a start. We can still wager on the world we wish to compose.

ACKNOWLEDGMENTS

The years I have spent learning to tell this story have been a gift I do not always feel worthy of receiving. Beringia consented to have me there; I hope this book reciprocates in some small way all it has given.

And I hope I have lived up to Stanley Njootli's teaching; his wit and wisdom kept me alive from my first years in the Arctic on. To Maureen Vittrekwa also: you have been with these thoughts from the beginning.

Yuri Slezkine guided this book—before it was a book—with seriousness and humor, and is alone among advisors in never thinking it crazy. Brian DeLay enriched my understanding of U.S. history. Ryan Tucker Jones sent help from every corner of the Pacific. Alexei Yurchak lent me an anthropologist's perspective. I owe special thanks to the careful reading given the manuscript by Jochen Hellbeck, Kate Brown (all that is solid indeed melts!), Paul Sabin, Holly Case, Robert Self, Sarah Besky, and Ethan Pollock. Many other people read and commented: Robert Chester, Daniel

Sargent, Joseph Kellner, Alan Roe, Chris Casey, Erica Lee, Tehila Sasson, Joshua Reid, Alexis Peri, Yana Skorabogotov, Jacqui Shine, Rebecca Nedostop, Faiz Ahmed, Emily Owens, Nancy Jacobs, anonymous readers, members of the Berkeley Kruzhok, the Berkeley Borderlands Writing Group, the Brown Legal History Workshop, and the Brown Modern European Working Group. Any lingering errors are my own.

So many archivists, colleagues, and friends made my research possible. Peter Schweitzer gave me the initial contacts to work in Chukotka. Eduard Zdor, Gennady Zelensky, Anastasiia Yarzutkina, Vladimir Bichkov, Alex Vykvyragtyrgyrgyn, Kolya Ettyne, and Vladimir Nazarov made me welcome and showed me wonders. In Magadan, I was helped by Maksim Brodkin, Olga Gdurdovna, Liudmila Khakhovskaia, and Anatolii Shirokov. Elena Mikaelovna made me a Vladivostok Thanksgiving. In Moscow, archivists at GARF, RGAE, and Memorial managed not to laugh when I asked about a place that is the butt of many a Soviet joke. Mark Procknik at the New Bedford Whaling Museum has been an amazing guide. In Alaska, I have many debts, among them Anders Apassingok Sr. and his family, Sue Steinacher, Eddie Ungott, Iver Campbell, Annie Weyiouanna, George Olanna, Percy Nayokpuk, and Corey Ningeulook. Lisa Ellanna gave me amazing bowhead meat. For guidance, I am grateful to Julie Raymond-Yakoubian, Henry Huntington, and Laura Eerkes-Medrano. All this travel was funded by a Brown University Salomon Fellowship, the Institute at Brown for Environment and Society, a Fulbright-Hays DDRA, a Javits Fellowship, the Berkeley Institute for International Studies, and a Mellon-ACLS Dissertation Completion Grant.

My editor, Alane Mason, elevated my prose and tamed my worst habits. My agent, Don Fehr, made the book I could only dream of in graduate school a reality. Helmut Smith saw what could be long before I did. Sofija Podvisocka saved me with research assistance. Elizabeth Rush has been a friend and guide. Molly Roy made maps from my incoherent desires. Critical passages were composed in the Chair of the Five East Poets Society amid a glorious dog rumpus. Murphy made sure I never wrote alone. To have composed the first draft and survived revisions without Peggy O'Donnell's companionship across hundreds of single-track miles (or just hundreds of miles) is unthinkable.

This book would have never been without parents who taught me to love words, heed the living world, and let me leave for the Arctic at eighteen. And to the person who has moved my books across country, bought me cases of Grenache, endured my absences, and never let me feel my obsessions were a burden: without you, Alex, there is no life I can imagine.

A NOTE ON SOURCES

Like any history, this book emerges from the shards of knowledge the past left to the present. I used three main kinds of sources, and each has a history of how it came to be.

The first consists of Beringians' histories. Some of these emerge where Beringian voices were recorded in early ethnographic and state records. Others are taken from Yupik, Iñupiat, and Chukchi oral traditions; histories that, to generalize, distinguish between the recent past—say, five generations back—and a deeper, more mythical time. People born in the early twentieth century thus described life before and after foreigners were a regular presence. Most of this generation died before I came to Beringia, but many gave their words to compendia I found critical, among them Igor Krupnik's work in Chukotka in the 1970s and 1980s; Ernest Burch Jr.'s field notes from Iñupiaq nations from the 1960s to the 1990s; and the Yupik oral histories edited by Anders Apassingok in the 1980s. Literate cultures have long dismissed such oral knowledge as incapable of transmitting the past with accuracy. I see it, following its practitioners, as containing an argument about knowledge itself. Rather than a singular, written-down object, Beringian traditions are polyvocal, collaborative, and vital to survival. My method is indebted to this practice, in which many voices, sometimes contradictory, come to the listener (here, the reader)—who, in deliberating over variation, becomes a participant in deciding and passing on what is useful to the future.

Second, this book uses local, regional, and national records from Imperial Russia, the United States, and the Soviet Union to give shape to state ambitions and troubles. In addition, to access foreigners' lived engagement with Beringia, I used memoirs, letters, and diaries. On some subjects, I used memoirs written some decades after the fact, if I could triangulate them with contemporary accounts. In writing about the Gulag and Soviet whaling, for example, I used accounts written before and after the Soviet collapse where the versions from both concurred.

Finally, this book bases some of its descriptions of Beringia on scientific materials, often alongside indigenous oral knowledge and personal observation. Thus, this is a history that uses science, not a history of science. But to tell a history in which the songs of whales and the shapes of stones and all things in between—the spotted hawk swooping by—are part requires leaning on all ways of explaining song, stone, or swoop. I learned in Beringia that any tool helpful to survival is worth using, no matter its origin. In that spirit, this book uses any tool helpful to putting into one language a place with many, and into words things that do not speak human tongues.

NOTES

NARA CA	National Archives and Records Administration, San Francisco, CA
NHA	Nantucket Historical Association, Nantucket, MA
NBWM	New Bedford Whaling Museum Research Library, New Bedford, MA
PPL	Providence Public Library, Providence, RI
RGAE	Rossiiskii gosudarstvennyi arkhiv ekonomiki, Moscow
RGIA DV	Rossiiskii gosudarstvennyi istoricheskii arkhiv Dal'nego Vostoka, Vladivostok
SI	Smithsonian Institution Archives, Washington, DC
TsKhSDMO	Tsentr khraneniia sovremennykh dokumentov Magadanskoi oblasti, Magadan
UAA	University of Alaska Archives and Special Collections, Anchorage, AK
UAFOHP	University of Alaska Fairbanks Oral History Program

PERIODICAL ABBREVIATIONS

DAC	*Daily Alta California*, San Francisco, CA
Dk	*Dalnevostochnii kitoboi*, onboard newspaper of the *Sovetskaia Rossiia*
GV	*Gazeta Vladivostok*, Vladivostok
HG	*Hawaiian Gazette*, Honolulu, HI
NN	*Nome Nugget*, Nome, AK
NTWN	*Nome Tri-Weekly Nugget*, Nome, AK
NYT	*New York Times*, New York, NY
Ook	*Okhota i okhotnich'e khoziaistvo*, Moscow
PCA	*Pacific Commercial Advertiser*, Honolulu, HI
SCh	*Sovetskaia Chukotka*, Anadyr
SFC	*San Francisco Chronicle*, San Francisco, CA
Ss	*Sovetskii sever*
TF	*The Friend*, Honolulu, HI
TP	*The Polynesian*, Honolulu, HI
WP	*Washington Post*, Washington, DC
WSL	*Whalemen's Shipping List and Merchant's Transcript*, New Bedford, MA

PROLOGUE: THE MIGRATION NORTH

1. For orthographic simplicity, I am eliding the linguistic distinction between Siberian Yupik, in Chukotka and on St. Lawrence Island, and mainland Alaska Yup'ik, and using Yupik (rather than Yupiit and Yupiget respectively) as plurals.

2. G. E. Fogg, *The Biology of Polar Habitats* (Oxford: Oxford University Press, 1998), 27–29. My thinking on energy here is drawn particularly from William Cronon, *Nature's Metropolis: Chicago and the Great West* (New York: W. W. Norton, 1991), chap. 4; Richard White, *The Organic Machine* (New York: Hill and Wang, 1995); and Ryan Tucker Jones, "The Environment," in *Pacific Histories: Ocean, Land, People,* ed. David Armitage and Alison Bashford (New York: Palgrave Macmillan, 2014), 121–42.

3. Deserts are the exception; for biomass differences, see F. Stuart Chapin III, Pamela A. Matson, and Peter Vitousek, *Principles of Terrestrial Ecosystem Ecology* (New York: Springer, 2011), 175–80.

4. It is in the nineteenth century that these historical traditions enter the written record. On the nature of stories, see Asatchaq and Tom Lowenstein, *The Things That Were Said of Them: Shaman Stories and Oral Histories of the Tikiġaq People* (Berkeley: University of California Press, 1992), introduction, and B. Bodenhorn, "'People Who Are Like Our Books': Reading and Teaching on the North Slope of Alaska," *Arctic Anthropology* 34, no. 1 (January 1997): 117–34.

5. I owe these ideas to indigenous teachers in the Arctic, beginning with Stanley Njootli and the experience of the land he gave me. I wish to acknowledge these as my primary intellectual debts; following Zoe Todd, "An Indigenous Feminist's Take on the Ontological Turn: 'Ontology' Is Just Another Word for Colonialism," *Journal of Historical Sociology* 29, no. 1 (March 2016): 4–22. In more academic work, my thinking overlaps with that of Timothy Mitchell in *Rule of Experts: Egypt, Techno-Politics, Modernity* (Berkeley: University of California Press, 2002), 19–53; intent in Linda Nash, "The Agency of Nature or the Nature of Agency," *Environmental History* 10, no. 1 (January 2005): 67–69; the embeddedness of humans in Tim Ingold, *The Perception of the Environment: Essays in Livelihood, Dwelling, and Skill* (London: Routledge, 2000); and the copious ontology of Jane Bennett, *Vibrant Matter: A Political Ecology of Things* (Durham, NC: Duke University Press, 2010).

6. On "balance," see Emma Marris, *Rambunctious Garden: Saving Nature in a Post-Wild World* (New York: Bloomsbury, 2011) and the debate in *Conservation Biology* 28, no. 3 (June 2014).

7. Quoted in *The Earth Is Faster Now: Indigenous Observations of Arctic*

Environmental Change, ed. Igor Krupnik and Dyanna Jolly (Fairbanks: ARCUS, 2002), 7.

CHAPTER 1: WHALE COUNTRY

1. Lloyd F. Lowry, "Foods and Feeding Ecology," in *The Bowhead Whale*, ed. John J. Burns, J. Jerome Montague, and Cleveland J. Cowles (Lawrence, KS: Society for Marine Mammology, 1993), 203–38; Joe Roman et al., "Whales as Marine Ecosystem Engineers," *Frontiers in Ecology and the Environment* 12, no. 7 (September 2014): 377–85; Craig R. Smith, "Bigger Is Better: The Role of Whales as Detritus in Marine Ecosystems," in James A Estes et al., *Whales, Whaling, and Ocean Ecosystems* (Berkeley: University of California Press, 2006), 286–302; N. J. Niebauer and D. M. Schell, "Physical Environment of the Bering Sea Population," in J. J. Burns et al., *The Bowhead Whale*, 23–43; Committee on the Bering Sea Ecosystem, *The Bering Sea Ecosystem* (Washington, DC: National Academy Press, 1996), 28–71. On endowing this whale with character, see Bennett, *Vibrant Matter*, 119–21.

2. Lowry, "Foods and Feeding Ecology," 222–23.

3. D. A. Croll, R. Kudela, and B. R. Tershy, "Ecosystem Impact of the Decline of Large Whales in the North Pacific," in Estes et al., *Whales, Whaling*, 202–14.

4. A. M. Springer et al., "Sequential Megafaunal Collapse in the North Pacific Ocean: An Ongoing Legacy of Industrial Whaling?" *Proceedings of the National Academy of Sciences of the United States of America* 100, no. 21 (October 14, 2003): 12223–28 and A. Sinclair, S. Mduma, and J. S. Brashares, "Patterns of Predation in a Diverse Predator-Prey System," *Nature* 425 (September 18, 2003): 288–90.

5. The technique used to age whales gives a range for this individual between 177 and 245 years; I am using the average. John Craighead George et al., "Age and Growth Estimates of Bowhead Whales (*Balaena mysticetus*) via Aspartic Acid Racemization," *Canadian Journal of Zoology* 77 (1999): 571–80, and Amanda Leigh Haag, "Patented Harpoon Pins Down Whale Age," *Nature* 488 (June 19, 2007): doi:10.1038/news070618-6.

6. Lewis Holmes, *The Arctic Whalemen, or Winter in the Arctic Ocean* (Boston: Thayer and Eldridge, 1861), 84. Thomas Norton recounted the wreck of the *Citizen* to Holmes, the ship's logs having been lost.

7. Holmes, *Arctic Whalemen*, 119.

8. Tom Lowenstein, *Ancient Land, Sacred Whale: The Inuit Hunt and Its Rituals* (New York: Farrar, Straus, and Giroux, 1993), 116.

9. See Ann Fienup-Riordan, *Eskimo Essays: Yup'ik Lives and How We See Them* (New Brunswick, NJ: Rutgers University Press, 1990), 66–67, and Chie Sakakibara, "*Kiavallakkikput Agviq* (Into the Whaling Cycle): Cetaceousness and Climate Change Among the Iñupiat of Arctic Alaska," *Annals of the Association of American Geographers* 100, no. 4 (2010): 1003–12.

10. Edith Turner, "American Eskimos Celebrate the Whale: Structural Dichotomies and Spirit Identities among the Iñupiat of Alaska," *TDR* 37, no. 1 (Spring 1993): 100.

11. Charles Campbell Hughes, "Translation of I. K. Voblov's 'Eskimo Ceremonies,'" *Anthropological Papers of the University of Alaska* 7, no. 2 (1959): 78; and Anders Apassingok, Willis Walunga, and Edward Tennant, eds., *Sivuqam Nangaghnegha: Siivanllemta Ungipaqellghat / Lore of St. Lawrence Island: Echoes of Our Eskimo Elders*, vol. 1, *Gambell* (Unalakleet, AK: Bering Strait School District, 1985), 205–7, 223.

12. Asatchaq and Lowenstein, *Things That Were Said*, 116.

13. Anders Apassingok et al., eds., *Sivuqam Nangaghnegha: Siivanllemta Ungipaqellghat / Lore of St. Lawrence Island: Echoes of Our Eskimo Elders*, vol. 3, *Southwest Cape* (Unalakleet, AK: Bering Strait School District, 1989), 157.

14. Anders Apassingok et al., eds., *Sivuqam Nangaghnegha: Siivanllemta Ungipaqellghat / Lore of St. Lawrence Island: Echoes of Our Eskimo Elders*, vol. 2, *Savoonga* (Unalakleet, AK: Bering Strait School District, 1987), 145.

15. SI, Henry Bascom Collins Collection, Unprocessed Box 3, File: Collins 1930.00A, pp. 4–5. Ceremonies varied and partly secret, so any description is incomplete and local.

16. Apassingok et al., *Southwest Cape*, 15. See also Igor Krupnik and Sergei Kan, "Prehistoric Eskimo Whaling in the Arctic: Slaughter of Calves or Fortuitous Ecology?" *Arctic Anthropology* 30, no. 1 (January 1993): 1–12. The description of whaling here is compiled from Stoker and Krupnik, "Subsistence Whaling," in J. J. Burns et al., *The Bowhead Whale*, 579–629; James W. VanStone, *Point Hope: An Eskimo Village in Transition* (Seattle: University of Washington Press, 1962); Carol Zane Jolles, *Faith, Food, and Family in a Yupik Whaling Community* (Seattle: University of Washington Press, 2002); Ernest S. Burch, Jr., *The Iñupiaq Eskimo Nations of Northwest Alaska* (Fairbanks: University of Alaska Press, 1998).

17. Peter Whitridge, "The Prehistory of Inuit and Yupik Whale Use," *Revista de Arqueologia Americana* 16 (1999): 108.

18. Lowenstein, *Ancient Land*, 160–61.

19. Apassingok et al., *Gambell*, 237.

20. Tom Lowenstein, *Ultimate Americans: Point Hope, Alaska, 1826–1909* (Fairbanks: University of Alaska Press, 2008), 3.

21. Semen Iena, quoted in Igor Krupnik and Michael Chlenov, *Yupik Transitions: Change and Survival at the Bering Strait, 1900–1960* (Fairbanks: University of Alaska Press, 2013), 211. See also Apassingok et al., *Savoonga*, 125.

22. John Kelly, quoted in Lowenstein, *Ultimate Americans*, 3.

23. Lowenstein, *Ancient Land*, 84.

24. Sue E. Moore and Randall R. Reeves, "Distribution and Movement," in J. J. Burns et al., *The Bowhead Whale*, 313–86.

25. Stoker and Krupnik, "Subsistence Whaling," 592–94.

26. Alexander Starbuck, *A History of the American Whale Fishery from Its Earliest Inception until the Year 1876* (Waltham, MA: Self-published, 1878), 155–56n. On eating whale, Nancy Shoemaker, "Whale Meat in American History," *Environmental History* 10, no. 2 (April 2005): 269–94.

27. "Plant Watering and Sulphering," *Evening Bulletin* (San Francisco), May 20, 1886; untitled article, *Atchison (KS) Daily Globe*, January 12, 1898; other uses summarized from Zephaniah Pease and George Hough, *New Bedford, Massachusetts: Its History, Industry, Institutions and Attractions* (New Bedford, MA: New Bedford Board of Trade, 1889).

28. David Moment, "The Business of Whaling in America in the 1850s," *Business History Review* 31, no. 3 (Autumn 1957): 263–64.

29. Lance E. Davis, Robert E. Gallman, and Karin Gleiter, *In Pursuit of Leviathan: Technology, Institutions, Productivity, and Profits in American Whaling, 1816–1906* (Chicago: University of Chicago Press, 1997), 521.

30. Herman Melville, *Moby-Dick* (Boston: C. H. Simonds, 1922), 36–37.

31. Jeremiah Reynolds, *Address, on the Subject of a Surveying and Exploring Expedition* (New York: Harper and Brothers, 1836), 264.

32. John Quincy Adams, "President's Message," *Niles' Register*, Baltimore, MD, December 10, 1825.

33. Reynolds, *Address, on the Subject*, 196.

34. "On the Expediency of Authorizing an Exploring Expedition, by Vessels of the Navy, to the Pacific Ocean and South Seas," March 21, 1836, *American State Papers: Naval Affairs*, 4:868.

35. Starbuck, *A History*, 3.

36. "On the Expediency," 867.

37. On whale taxonomy, see D. Graham Burnett, *Trying Leviathan: The Nineteenth-Century New York Court Case That Put the Whale on Trial and Challenged the Order of Nature* (Princeton, NJ: Princeton University Press, 2007).

38. Edward S. Davoll, *The Captain's Specific Orders on the Commencement of a*

Whale Voyage to His Officers and Crew (New Bedford, MA: Old Dartmouth Historical Sketch Number 81, 1981), 7.

39. NBWM, Logbook of the *Nimrod* (Ship), ODHS 946, p. 96.

40. Sailors were not listed in most logs by race, although the descriptions in the *Seaman's Register* in New Bedford give some sense of their origins. For more, Margaret S. Creighton, *Rites and Passages: The Experience of American Whaling, 1830–1870* (New York: Cambridge University Press, 1995), 121–23; Nancy Shoemaker, *Native American Whalemen and the World: Indigenous Encounters and the Contingency of Race* (Chapel Hill: University of North Carolina Press, 2015), and W. Jeffery Bolster, *Black Jacks: African American Seamen in the Age of Sail* (Cambridge, MA: Harvard University Press, 1998).

41. Joan Druett, ed., *"She Was a Sister Sailor": Mary Brewster's Whaling Journals 1845–1851* (Mystic, CT: Mystic Seaport Museum, 1992), 337. "Kanaka" referred to indigenous Pacific Islanders; for a history, see Gregory Rosenthal, *Beyond Hawai'i: Native Labor in the Pacific World* (Berkeley: University of California Press, 2018), chap. 3.

42. Walter Nobel Burns, *A Year with a Whaler* (New York: Outing Publishing, 1913), 12, 13.

43. John Jones diary, in Stuart Frank, *Meditations from Steerage: Two Whaling Journal Fragments* (Sharon, MA: Kendall Whaling Museum, 1991), 23–24.

44. NBWM, Logbook of the *Eliza F. Mason* (Ship), ODHS 995, p. 25.

45. Stuart M. Frank, *Jolly Sailors Bold: Ballads and Songs of the American Sailor* (East Windsor, NJ: Camsco Music, 2010), 340, 338.

46. Quoted in Druett, *Sister Sailor,* 344.

47. Stuart M. Frank, *Ingenious Contrivances, Curiously Carved: Scrimshaw in the New Bedford Whaling Museum* (Boston: David Godine, 2012).

48. NBWM, Logbook of the *Lydia,* KWM 132, p. 59.

49. Holmes, *Arctic Whalemen,* 271–72.

50. NBWM, Logbook of the *Nimrod* (Ship), ODHS 946, p. 112.

51. *WSL,* January 9, 1849.

52. BL, Charles Melville Scammon Papers, P-K 206, vol. 1, pp. 102–3 and *WSL,* February 6, 1849.

53. *TP,* November 4, 1848. News of Roys's discovery appeared in marine journals across the world by 1849; see John Bockstoce, *Whales, Ice, and Men* (Seattle: University of Washington Press, 1986), 24.

54. Lowenstein, *Ancient Land,* xix–xx; Hal Whitehead and Luke Rendell, *The Cultural Lives of Whales and Dolphins* (Chicago: University of Chicago Press: 2015), 83–84, 184–85.

55. Druett, *Sister Sailor*, 372.

56. Druett, *Sister Sailor*, 385–87. On the 1849 season, see Bockstoce, *Whales, Ice, and Men*, 94–95.

57. Logbook of the *Ocmulgee*, July 25, 1849, quoted in Arthur C. Watson, *The Long Harpoon: A Collection of Whaling Anecdotes* (New Bedford, MA: Reynolds Printing, 1929), 49.

58. The average oil yield varies depending on the calculations used. The numbers here are from Harston H. Bodfish, *Chasing the Bowhead: As Told by Captain Harston H. Bodfish and Recorded for Him by Joseph C. Allen* (Cambridge, MA: Harvard University Press, 1936), 95; Charles M. Scammon, *The Marine Mammals of the North-Western Coast of North America* (San Francisco: John H. Carmany, 1874), 52; and Bockstoce, *Whales, Ice, and Men*, 95.

59. *WSL*, July 12, 1853; William Fish Williams, "The Voyage of the *Florence*, 1873–1874," in *One Whaling Family*, ed. Harold Williams (Boston: Houghton Mifflin, 1963), 370.

60. Davoll, *Captain's Specific Orders*, 8.

61. NBWM, Logbook of the *Saratoga* (Ship), KWM 181, p. 124.

62. W. N. Burns, *Year with a Whaler*, 60.

63. NBWM, Logbook of the *Saratoga* (Ship), KWM 181, p. 87.

64. PPL, B. F. Hohman Collection, *Cornelius Howland* (Ship) 1867–1870, folder 1.

65. NBWM, Logbook of the *Frances*, ODHS 994, p. 99.

66. David Wilkinson, *Whaling in Many Seas, and Cast Adrift in Siberia: With a Description of the Manners, Customs and Heathen Ceremonies of Various (Tchuktches) Tribes of North-Eastern Siberia* (London: Henry J. Drane, 1906), 113.

67. James F. Munger, *Two Years in the Pacific and Arctic Oceans and China* (Fairfield, WA: Ye Galleon Press, 1967), 66.

68. NBWM, Logbook of the *Frances*, ODHS 994, p. 97.

69. NBWM, Logbook of the *Roman 2nd* (Ship), KWM 176, p. 170.

70. Scammon, *Marine Mammals*, 58. Logbooks, whalers' memoirs, and the whalers' newspaper the *Whalemen's Shipping List and Merchant's Transcript* consistently refer to whales by the barrels and/or pounds of baleen they produced.

71. Ellsworth West, *Captain's Papers: A Log of Whaling and Other Sea Experiences* (Barre, MA: Barre Publishers, 1965), 13.

72. Eliza Azelia Williams, "The Voyage of the *Florida*, 1858–1861," in H. Williams, *One Whaling Family*, 77.

73. E. A. Williams, "Voyage of the *Florida*," 194.

74. West, *Captain's Papers*, 13.

75. Scammon, *Marine Mammals*, 42, 54; Charles H. Stevenson, "Fish Oils, Fats and Waxes," in *U.S. Fish Commission Report for 1902* (Washington, DC: Government Printing Office, 1903), 177–279, 189.

76. NBWM, Logbook of the *Saratoga*, KWM 180, p. 225.

77. Scammon, *Marine Mammals*, 294.

78. W. N. Burns, *Year with a Whaler*, 147.

79. West, *Captain's Papers*, 14.

80. H. Williams, *One Whaling Family*, 196.

81. NBWM, Logbook of the *Frances*, ODHS 994, p. 45.

82. W. N. Burns, *Year with a Whaler*, 203; W. F. Scoresby quoted in Dick Russell, *Eye of the Whale: Epic Passage from Baja to Siberia* (New York: Simon & Schuster, 2001), 602.

83. Herbert L. Aldrich, *Arctic Alaska and Siberia, or, Eight Months with the Arctic Whalemen* (Chicago: Rand, McNally, 1889), 33. See also Wilkinson, *Whaling in Many Seas*, 113. On animal pain in the nineteenth century; see Harriet Ritvo, *The Animal Estate: The English and Other Creatures in Victorian England* (Cambridge, MA: Harvard University Press, 1987); Janet M. Davis, *The Gospel of Kindness: Animal Welfare and the Making of Modern America* (New York: Oxford University Press, 2016).

84. See, for example, Scammon, *Marine Mammals*, 25, 78; Henry Cheever, *The Whale and His Captors* (New York: Harper and Brothers, 1853), 135.

85. Scoresby, quoted in Russell, *Eye of the Whale*, 602.

86. Jones in Frank, *Meditations from Steerage*, 24.

87. Lowenstein, *Ultimate Americans*, 23.

88. Date of foreign contact varied, from the seventeenth century in parts of Chukotka to the mid-nineteenth for parts of Alaska. On the nineteenth-century trade, see John R. Bockstoce, *Furs and Frontiers in the Far North: The Contest among Native and Foreign Nations for the Bering Strait Fur Trade* (New Haven, CT: Yale University Press, 2009). For the early contact period in Chukotka, see N. N. Dikov, *Istoriia chukotki s drevneishikh vremen do nashikh dnei* (Moscow: Mysl, 1989), pt. 1.

89. Frederick Beechey, *Narrative of a Voyage to the Pacific and Bering's Strait, to Cooperate with the Polar Expeditions; Performed by His Majesty's Ship "Blossom," . . . . in the Years 1825, 26, 27, 28,* (London: Colburn and Bentley, 1831), 2: 284. *TP*, November 4, 1848, references Beechey directly.

90. Druett, *Sister Sailor*, 379.

91. Druett, *Sister Sailor*, 382.

92. "Letters About the Arctic No. VIII, At Sea Dec. 15 1852," *WSL*, June 28, 1853.

93. Druett, *Sister Sailor*, 380.

94. Druett, *Sister Sailor*, 373, 378.

95. Journal of Eliza Brock, May 25, 1854, voyage of the *Lexington* (Ship), NHA PMB #378.

96. *WSL*, December 24, 1850.

97. "Speech of Mr. Seward," *New York Daily Times*, July 31, 1852.

98. GWBWL, Logbook of the *Hibernia* (Ship), Log 82a, 1868–1869, pp. 55, 57, 58, 60. Bockstoce (in *Whales, Ice, and Men*, 101–2) first identified this pattern of whale evasion causing decreased commercial success.

99. NBWM, Logbook of the *William Baylies* (Steam bark), ODHS 955, p. 81.

100. *WSL*, November 25, 1851.

101. Wilkinson, *Whaling in Many Seas*, 106. See also Bodfish, *Chasing the Bowhead*, 126, 94.

102. Arthur James Allen, *A Whaler and Trader in the Arctic: My Life with the Bowhead, 1895–1944* (Anchorage: Alaska Northwest Publishing Company, 1978), 98.

103. NBWM, Logbook of the *Saratoga* (Ship), KWM 180, pp. 192–93.

104. Frank, *Jolly Sailors Bold*, 339.

105. Holmes, *Arctic Whalemen*, 46.

106. Holmes, *Arctic Whalemen*, 137, 115.

107. Douglas A. Woodby and Daniel B. Botkin, "Stock Sizes Prior to Commercial Whaling," in J. J. Burns et al., *The Bowhead Whale*, 390–93.

CHAPTER 2: WHALE FALL

1. Spencer Apollonio, *Hierarchical Perspectives in Marine Complexities: Searching for Systems in the Gulf of Maine* (New York: Columbia University Press, 2002).

2. Bockstoce, *Whales, Ice, and Men*, 346.

3. NBWM, Logbook of the *Nassau* (Ship), ODHS 614, p. 81.

4. NBWM, Logbook of the *Saratoga* (Ship), KWM 180, p. 11.

5. Aldrich, *Arctic Alaska*, 49; "The Commerce in the Products of the Sea," S. Misc. Doc. No. 33, 42nd Cong., 2nd Sess. (1872), 33.

6. NBWM, Logbook of the *Nimrod* (Ship), ODHS 946, p. 105.

7. *PCA*, December 15, 1859.

8. M. E. Bowles, "Some Account of the Whale-Fishery of the N. West Coast and Kamschatka," *TP*, October 2, 1845.

9. Scammon, *Marine Mammals*, 215.

10. *TF*, October 15, 1850.

11. As Ryan Jones argues in the *Empire of Extinction: Russians and the North Pacific's Strange Beasts of the Sea, 1741–1867* (New York: Oxford University Press, 2014), the North Pacific was where modern understandings of extermination originated.

12. W. N. Burns, *Year with a Whaler*, 70.

13. Melville, *Moby-Dick*, 433–34.

14. "Letter from the Arctic by a Foremast Hand," *PCA*, October 28, 1858.

15. N. V. Doroshenko, "Gladkie kity Okhotskogo moria (istoriia promysla, sovermennoe sostoianie)" in A.B. Yablokov and V.A. Zemsky, *Materilay sovetskogo kitoboinogo promysla (1949–1979)* (Moscow: Tsentr ekologicheskoi politiki Rossii, 2000), 32.

16. Aldrich, *Arctic Alaska*, 22–23.

17. Bodfish, *Chasing the Bowhead*, 33.

18. "We Left Not One Minute Too Soon," *PCA*, November 18, 1871.

19. "The Reasons Why the Arctic Fleet Was Abandoned," *WSL*, November 14, 1871.

20. Bodfish, *Chasing the Bowhead*, 90.

21. *WSL*, December 22, 1863.

22. NBWM, Logbook of the *Nimrod* (Ship), ODHS 946, p. 230–31.

23. See Christopher Jones, *Routes of Power: Energy in Modern America* (Cambridge, MA: Harvard University Press, 2014), 109–15.

24. Pease and Hough, *New Bedford*, 25–26.

25. Starbuck, *A History*, 109–10.

26. Bockstoce, *Whales, Ice, and Men*, 205.

27. *Vanity Fair*, April 20, 1861, p. 186.

28. *WSL*, July 2, 1861.

29. *WSL*, January 14, 1879.

30. Pease and Hough, *New Bedford*, 32–35.

31. Classified ad, "Corsets and Skirts," *New York Daily News*, June 7, 1856; Valerie Steele, *The Corset: A Cultural History* (New Haven, CT: Yale University Press, 2001).

32. Pease and Hough, *New Bedford*, 32.

33. Waldemar Bogoras [Vladimir Bogoraz], *The Chukchee* (1904–09; repr., New York: Johnson Reprint Corp., 1971), 651.

34. Bogoras, *The Chukchee*, 651.

35. The Russian-Chukchi wars included alliances between the Russians, Yukagir, and Koryak against a coalition of Yupik and Chukchi. See I. S. Vdovin, *Ocherki istorii i etnografii Chukchei* (Moscow and Leningrad: Nauka, 1965), 106–35, and Bogoras, *The Chukchee*, 682–97.

36. RGIA DV F. 702, Op. 1, D. 275, L. 1. "Aliens" is an imperfect translation of *inorodtsy*—a word that means both "foreign" culturally and "indigenous" geographically.

37. O. V. Kotzebue, *A Voyage of Discovery into the South Sea and Beering's Straits, for the Purpose of Exploring a North-East Passage, Undertaken in the Years 1815–1818*, (London: Longman, Hurst, Reese, Orme, and Brown, 1821), 1: 262.

38. Bockstoce, *Furs and Frontiers*, 16.

39. Bogoras, *The Chukchee*, 19.

40. Apassingok et al., *Gambell*, 213.

41. There was some trade with private ships from Hawaii in the early 1850s; see Bockstoce, *Furs and Frontiers*, 267–73.

42. APRCA, Dorothea Leighton Collection, Box 1, Folder 3: Koyoyak, p. 17.

43. PPL, Captain B. F. Hohman Collection, Journal of the *Cornelius Howland* (Ship), 1868–1870, pp. 83–84. For a full discussion of these incidents, see Bockstoce, *Furs and Frontiers*, 277–280.

44. Edward William Nelson, *The Eskimo about Bering Strait: Extract from the Eighteenth Annual Report of the Bureau of American Ethnology* (Washington, DC: Government Printing Office, 1900), 299.

45. NBWM, Logbook of the *John Howland*, KWM 969, p. 268.

46. "Letter about the Arctic," *WSL*, July 4, 1853, and NBWM, Logbook of the *Frances*, ODHS 994, p. 52.

47. Bockstoce, *Furs and Frontiers*, 312–15.

48. Bogoras, *The Chukchee*, 711–12.

49. Wilkinson, *Whaling in Many Seas*, 279.

50. Bockstoce, *Whales, Ice, and Men*, 346–47 and Woodby and Botkin, "Stock Sizes," 390–91 and 402–4 on estimating past bowhead populations.

51. *WSL*, December 31, 1872.

52. *WSL*, January 10, 1865.

53. APRCA, Dorothea Leighton Collection, Box 1, Folder 3.2: Koyoyak, pp. 100–102.

54. W. N. Burns, *Year with a Whaler*, 151. On the politics of alcohol trading among whalers, see Lowenstein, *Ultimate Americans*, chap. 6.

55. APRCA, Ernest S. Burch Jr. Papers, Series 5, Box 226, File H88-2A-1, Mamie Mary Beaver interview, p. 2.

56. Ernest Burch Jr, *Social Life in Northwest Alaska* (Fairbanks: University of Alaska Press, 2006), 113–14; Igor Krupnik, *Pust govoriat nashi stariki: rasskazy aziatskikh eskimosov-iupik, 1975–1987* (Moscow: Institut Naslediia, 2000), 361; and Peter Schweitzer, "Spouse-exchange in North-eastern Siberia: On Kinship and Sexual Relations and Their Transformations," in Andre Gingrich, Siegfried Haas, Sylvia Haas, and Gabriele Paleczek, eds., *Kinship, Social Change and Evolution: Proceedings of a Symposium Held in Honour of Walter Dostal*, Wiener Beiträge zur Ethnologie und Anthropologie 5 (Horn, Austria: Berger, 1989): 17–38.

57. In chapter 9 of *Ultimate Americans*, Lowenstein makes clear that rape and spouse exchange were quite different categories.

58. Ejnar Mikkelsen, *Conquering the Arctic Ice* (London: Heinemann, 1909), 310.

59. Bogoras, *The Chukchee*, 610.

60. Robert Strout, "Sketch of the Performance," GWBWL, Collection 210, vol. 2, p. 109.

61. Extract from the Report of the Cruise of the Revenue Cutter *Bear*, December 4, 1913, NARA MD RG 48 CCF 1907–1936, File 6-6, p. 2.

62. Bockstoce, *Whales, Ice, and Men*, 277.

63. Druett, *Sister Sailor*, 186.

64. "Massacred Whalers," *SFC*, October 27, 1891.

65. Bogoras, *The Chukchee*, 41.

66. John W. Kelly, *English-Eskimo and Eskimo-English Vocabularies* (Washington, DC: U.S. Bureau of Education, 1890), 21. The full impact of syphilis in this period is difficult to extrapolate, but the dynamics seem similar to what Stephen Hackel describes in *Children of Coyote, Missionaries of Saint Francis: Indian-Spanish Relations in Colonial California, 1769–1850* (Chapel Hill: University of North Carolina Press, 2005).

67. RGIA DV F. 702, Op. 1, D. 127, L. 6. See also RGIA DV F. 702, Op. 1, D. 1401, L. 68.

68. Bogoras, *The Chukchee*, 297, 460.

69. Krupnik and Chlenov, *Yupik Transitions*, 25.

70. Burch Jr., *Iñupiaq Eskimo Nations*, 48–49. For detailed community-level impacts of the famines in this period, see Krupnik and Chlenov, *Yupik Transitions* for Chukotka and nearby islands and Burch Jr.'s *Iñupiaq Eskimo Nations* for a large portion of the Alaska coastline.

71. APRCA, Dorothea Leighton Collection, Box 2, Folder 45, p. 6. In *Yuuyaraq: The Way of the Human Being* (Fairbanks: Alaska Native Knowledge Network, 1996), Harold Napoleon argues that alcohol is a way of dealing with the traumatic aftermath of epidemic disease.

72. APRCA, Ernest S. Burch Jr. Papers, Series 5, Box 226, Folder H88-2B-7, Tommy Lee (Ambler) interview, p. 15.

73. Mikkelsen, *Conquering the Arctic Ice*, 373.

74. *WSL*, April 8 1872. See also "Shipmaster," *TF*, March 1, 1872.

75. Patrick Henry Ray, "Ethnographic Sketch of the Natives of Point Barrow," *Report of the International Polar Expedition to Point Barrow, Alaska, in Response to the Resolution of the House of Representatives of December 11, 1884*, pt. III (Washington, DC: Government Printing Office, 1885), 37–60.

76. W. N. Burns, *Year with a Whaler*, 174.

77. *Hawaiian Star*, January 31, 1902. Agassiz was a frequent visitor to Hawaii, and must have spoken to the fate of cetaceans at one of his public lectures in the mid-1880s.

78. "Scarcity of Whalebone," *Hawaiian Star*, April 25, 1892.

79. "The Whaling Fleet: Interesting Statistics on the Trade," *SFC*, November 10, 1889.

80. "For the Honorable Secretary of the Interior in Behalf of the Northern Alaska Eskimos," Conrad Seim, p. 19, NARA CA RG 48, M430, Roll 9.

81. "Scarcity of Whalebone," *San Francisco Call*, April 25, 1892.

82. PPL, Nicholson Whaling Log Collection, no. 674, Logbook of the *William Baylies*, 1887, p. 48; Logbook of the *William Baylies*, 1892, p. 362. John A. Cook noted at least thirty whaleboats being used on the Chukchi coast by 1900—see *Thar She Blows* (Boston: Chapman and Grimes, 1937), 147.

83. APRCA, Ernest S. Burch Jr. Papers, Series 5, Box 226, Files H88-2A-36, Harold Downey interview, p. 1.

84. Lowenstein, *Ultimate Americans*, 135–136, 110.

85. Bockstoce, *Furs and Frontiers*, 333.

86. Bockstoce, *Whales, Ice, and Men*, 201.

87. APRCA, Ernest S. Burch Jr. Papers, Series 5, Box 220, File: Kivalina, Clinton Swan interview, p. 42. On this labor, see Mark S. Cassell, "Iñupiat Labor and Commercial Shore Whaling in Northern Alaska," *The Pacific Northwest Quarterly* 91, no. 3 (2000): 115–23.

88. J. G. Ballinger Report 191, NARA MD RG 48, Central Classified File 1907–1936, File 6-6.

89. Lowenstein, *Ultimate Americans*, 83–84.

90. Edward Nelson, quoted in Lowenstein, *Ultimate Americans*, 108.

91. RGIA DV F. 702, Op. 1, D. 313, L. 13, 69.

92. M. Vedenski, "O neobkhodimosti okhrany kitovogo i drugikh morskikh promyslov v nashikh severo-vostochnykh vodakh," *Priamurskie vedomosti* 11 (1894): 11.

93. RGIA DV F. 702, Op. 1, D. 275, L. 1.

94. RGIA DV F. 702, Op. 1 D. 1401, L. 61.

95. RGIA DV F. 702, Op. 1, D. 275, L. 1.

96. RGIA DV F. 702, Op. 1, D. 313, L. 32.

97. RGIA DV F. 702, Op. 1, D. 275, L. 1.

98. Reynolds, *Address, on the Subject*, 67.

99. NBWM, Logbook of the *Eliza F. Mason* (Ship), ODHS 995, p. 51.

100. C. L. Hooper to the Secretary of the Interior, 1880; NARA CA RG 26, M-641, Roll 1.

101. W. N. Burns, *Year with a Whaler*, 165; Calvin Leighton Hooper, *Report of the Cruise of the U.S. Revenue Steamer* Thomas Corwin *in the Arctic Ocean, 1881* (Washington, DC: Government Printing Office, 1884), 41.

102. Harrison G. Otis, "Report of Special-Agent Otis upon the Illicit Traffic in Rum and Fire-arms," in "Letter from the Secretary of the Trea-

sury," S. Exec. Doc. No. 132, 46th Cong., 2d Sess. (March 30, 1880), p. 46.

103. Doroshenko, "Gladkie," 33.

104. *Seal and Salmon Fisheries and General Resources of Alaska*, (Washington, DC: U.S. Government Printing Office, 1898), III: 565.

105. Lonny Lundsten et al., "Time-Series Analysis of Six Whale-Fall Communities in Monterey Canyon, California, USA," *Deep-Sea Research Part I: Oceanographic Research Papers* 57, no. 12 (December 2010): 1573–84; A. J. Pershing et al., "The Impact of Whaling on the Ocean Carbon Cycle: Why Bigger Was Better," *PLoS ONE*, August 26, 2010, doi: 10.1371/journal.pone.0012444.

106. "Editorial," *SFC*, August 15, 1899.

107. Charles Brower, *Fifty Years Below Zero: A Lifetime of Adventure in the Far North*. (New York: Dodd, Mead, 1942), 242–243.

108. Harry Brower Sr. and Karen Brewster, eds., *The Whales, They Give Themselves* (Fairbanks: University of Alaska Press, 2005), 136, 160.

CHAPTER 3: THE FLOATING COAST

1. Bering Sea ecosystem and ice descriptions taken from Shari Fox Gearheard et al., *The Meaning of Ice: People and Sea Ice in Three Arctic Communities* (Hanover, NH: University Press of New England, 2013); Lyudmila S. Bogoslovskaya and Igor Krupnik, eds., *Nashi ldy, snega i vetry: Narodnye i nauchnye znaniia o ledovykh landshaftakhi klimate Vostochnoi Chukotki* (Moscow: Russian Heritage Institute, 2013); E. Sakshaug, "Primary and Secondary Production in the Arctic Seas," in *The Organic Carbon Cycle in the Arctic Ocean*, ed. Rüdiger Stein and Robie Macdonald (Berlin: Sperger, 2004), 57–81; Alan M. Springer, C. Peter McRoy, and Mikhail V. Flint, "The Bering Sea Green Belt: Shelf-Edge Processes and Ecosystem Production," *Fisheries Oceanography* 4, no. 3–4 (September 1996): 205–23; Christopher A. North et al., "Deposit-feeder Diet in the Bering Sea: Potential Effects of Climatic Loss of Sea Ice-related Microalgeal Blooms," *Ecological Applications* 24, no. 6 (September 2014): 1525–42; Clara Deal et al., "Large-scale Modeling of Primary Production and Ice Algal Biomass within Arctic Sea Ice in 1992," *Journal of Geophysical Research* 116 (July 2011): doi: 10.1029/2010JC006409.

2. APRCA, Dorothea C. Leighton Collection, Box 3, Folder: Paul Silook, pp. 72–73.

3. Bogoras, *The Chukchee*, 492.

4. Ekaterina Rubtsova, *Materialy po yazyku i folkloru eskimosov (Chaplinskii dialect) Pt. 1* (Moscow: Izd-vo AN SSSR, 1954), 290–91.

5. Lyudmila Bogoslovskaya et al., *Maritime Hunting Culture of Chukotka: Traditions and Modern Practices* (Anchorage: National Park Service, 2016), 30.

6. Apassingok et al., *Gambell*, 133.

7. Bogoras, *The Chukchee*, 387, 405–6.

8. Waldemar Bogoras [Vladimir Bogoraz], "The Eskimo of Siberia," in *Memoirs of the American Museum of Natural History: The Jesup North Pacific Expedition, vol. 8, pt. III, The Eskimo of Siberia*, ed. Franz Boaz (New York: Leiden, 1913), 446.

9. Magdaline Omiak, in *Ugiuvangmiut Quliapyuit / King Island Tales: Eskimo History and Legends from Bering Strait*, Lawrence D. Kaplan and Margaret Yocom, eds. (Fairbanks: University of Alaska Press, 1988), 51.

10. Bogoras, *The Chukchee*, 315–16; S. Ia. Serov, "Guardians and Spirit Masters of Siberia," in *Crossroads of Continents: Cultures of Siberia and Alaska*, ed. William Fitzhugh and Aron Crowell (Washington, DC: Smithsonian Institution Press, 1988), 245.

11. Aron L. Crowell and Estelle Oozevaseuk, "The St. Lawrence Island Famine and Epidemic, 1878–80: A Yupik Narrative in Cultural and Historical Context," *Arctic Anthropology* 43, no. 1 (2006): 1–19.

12. Nikolay Galgawyi, quoted in Bogoslovskaya et al., *Maritime Hunting Culture*, 24.

13. W. N. Burns, *Year with a Whaler*, 193.

14. NBWM, Logbook of the *Trident* (Bark), KWM 192, p. 56.

15. Charles Madsen, *Arctic Trader* (New York: Dodd, Mead, 1957), 205–06.

16. PPL, Nicholson Whaling Log Collection 181, *Cornelius Howland*, p. 270, and William Fish Williams, "The Destruction of the Whaling Fleet in the Arctic Ocean 1871," in H. Williams, ed., *One Whaling Family*, 226.

17. Scammon, *Marine Mammals*, 178–79. See also Madsen, *Arctic Trader*, 198, and W. F. Williams, "Destruction of the Whaling Fleet," 227.

18. Wilkinson, *Whaling in Many Seas*, 94.

19. Hooper, *Report of the Cruise*, 46.

20. Bodfish, *Chasing the Bowhead*, 21; W. F. Williams, "Destruction of the Whaling Fleet," 226; PPL, Nicholson Whaling Log Collection 181, *Cornelius Howland*, p. 295.

21. Hooper, *Report of the Cruise*, 46, and W. F. Williams, "Destruction of the Whaling Fleet," 226–27.

22. Howard A. Clark, "The Pacific Walrus Fishery," in George Brown Goode ed. *The Fisheries and Fishery Industries of the United States, vol. 2, sec. 5*, ed. George Brown Goode (Washington, DC: Government Printing Office, 1887), 316.

23. H. A. Clark, "Pacific Walrus Fishery," 316.

24. John Muir, *The Cruise of the* Corwin (Boston: Houghton Mifflin, 1917), 142–43.

25. PPL, Nicholson Whaling Log Collection 599, *Sea Breeze*, p. 77.

26. PPL, Nicholson Whaling Log Collection 181, *Cornelius Howland*, p. 297.

27. H. A. Clark, "Pacific Walrus Fishery," 315.

28. John R. Bockstoce and Daniel B. Botkin, "The Harvest of Pacific Walruses by the Pelagic Whaling Industry, 1848–1914," *Arctic and Alpine Research* 14, no. 3 (August 1982): 183–88, and Francis Fay, Brendan P. Kelly, and John L. Sease, "Managing the Exploitation of Pacific Walruses: A Tragedy of Delayed Response and Poor Communication," *Marine Mammal Science* 5, no. 1 (January 1989): 1–16.

29. APRCA, Dorothea C. Leighton Collection, Box 1, Folder 3, p. 37.

30. Harry DeWindt, *Through the Gold Fields of Alaska to Bering Strait* (London: Chatto and Windus, 1899), 191; Aurel Krause and Arthur Krause, *To the Chukchi Peninsula and to the Tlingit Indians 1881/1882: Journals and Letters by Aurel and Arthur Krause* (Fairbanks: University of Alaska Press 1993), 58.

31. Krupnik and Chlenov, *Yupik Transitions*, 24–25.

32. The population decline between 1800 and 1890 in Chukotka was roughly fifty percent; in northwestern Alaska, the decrease was from about five thousand people to around one thousand in the same period; see Krupnik and Chlenov, *Yupik Transitions*, 36–37; Burch, *Iñupiaq Eskimo Nations*, 325.

33. Bogoras, "Eskimo of Siberia," 433–34.

34. APRCA, Dorothea C. Leighton Collection, Box 1, Folder 3, pp. 35–36.

35. Crowell and Oozevaseuk, "St. Lawrence Island Famine," 11–12.

36. Bogoras, *The Chukchee*, 492, 731.

37. Patrick Henry Ray, *Report of the International Polar Expedition to Point Barrow, Alaska* (Washington, DC: Government Printing Office, 1885), 48.

38. Bogoras, *The Chukchee*, 731.

39. *WSL*, April 9, 1872.

40. John Murdoch, "Natural History," in P. H. Ray, *Report of the International*, 98.

41. Ebenezer Nye, *Republican Standard* (New Bedford, MA), August 2, 1879.

42. "The Poor Whalers," *SFC*, November 24, 1883.

43. On this dynamic, see Arthur McElvoy, *The Fisherman's Problem: Ecology and Law in the California Fisheries, 1850–1980* (Cambridge, UK: Cambridge University Press, 1986), and Cronon, *Nature's Metropolis*, chap. 4.

44. *WSL*, February 6, 1849.

45. Bogoras, *The Chukchee*, 535, 581; Aldrich, *Arctic Alaska*, 50; Krupnik and Chlenov, *Yupik Transitions*, 86–87. Quwaaren is spelled, variously, as Kuwar, Kuva'r, Kohar, Kohorra, Goharren, and Quarry.

46. RGIA DV F. 702, Op. 1, D. 313, L. 3.

47. A. H. Leighton and D. C. Leighton, "Eskimo Recollections of Their Life Experiences," *Northwest Anthropological Research Notes* 17, nos. 1/3 (1983), 159.

48. Bockstoce, *Furs and Frontiers*, 322.

49. APRCA, Ernest S. Burch Jr. Papers, Series 5, Box 227, File H88-2D-1, Robert Cleveland interview, April 9, 1965, p. 6.

50. Lowenstein, *Ultimate Americans*, 94.

51. Bogoras, *The Chukchee*, 23.

52. Asatchaq and Lowenstein, *Things that Were Said*, 169.

53. Bogoras, *The Chukchee*, 62.

54. Bockstoce, *Furs and Frontiers*, 342; William Benjamin Jones, *Argonauts of Siberia: A Diary of a Prospector* (Philadelphia: Dorrance, 1927), 113–14, 119.

55. For expansion before Peter the Great, see Yuri Slezkine, *Arctic Mirrors: Russia and the Small Peoples of the North* (Ithaca, NY: Cornell University Press, 1994), 11–41, and after, 80–129. On furs, Janet Martin, *Treasure of the Land of Darkness: The Fur Trade and Its Significance for Medieval Russia* (Cambridge, UK: Cambridge University Press, 1986).

56. Waldemar Jochelson, *The Koryak* (New York: American Museum of Natural History, 1913), 802, 803.

57. Veniamin, Arkhiepiskop Irkutskii i Nerchinskii, *Zhiznennye voprosy pravoslavnoi missii v Sibiri* (St. Petersburg: Kotomka, 1885), 7. On fur policy, see RGIA DV F. 702, Op. 1, D. 1401, L. 80. For hunting laws, see, N. F. Reimers and F. R. Shtilmark, *Osobo okhraniaemye prirodnye territorii* (Moscow: Mysl, 1978), 24–26.

58. M. V. Nechkina, ed., *"Russkaia Pravda" P.I. Pestelia i sochineniia, ei predshestvviushchie* (Moscow: Gosudarstvennoe izdatelstvo politicheskoi literatury, 1958), 142. On the image of Siberia, Mark Bassin, "Inventing Siberia: Visions of the Russian East in the Early Nineteenth Century," *American Historical Review* 96, no. 3 (1991): 763–94.

59. RGIA DV F. 702, Op. 1, D. 313, L. 3.

60. RGIA DV F. 702, Op. 1, D. 1401, L. 68; RGIA DV F. 702, Op. 1, D. 275, L. 20; Slezkine, *Arctic Mirrors*, 107.

61. RGIA DV F. 702, Op. 1, D. 313, L. 3.

62. A. A. Resin, *Ocherki inorodtsev russkago poberezhia Tikhago Okeana* (St. Petersburg: A. C. Suvorovna, 1888), 68.

63. RGIA DV F. 702, Op. 1, D. 1401, L. 1.

64. K. P. Pobedenotsev, *Pisma Pobedonostseva k Aleksandru III*, tom I (Moscow: Novaia Moskva, 1925), 84.

65. RGIA DV F. 702, Op. 1, D. 127, L. 2; RGIA DV F. 702, Op. 1, D. 275, L. 1.

66. *Papers Relating to the Bering Sea Fisheries* (Washington, DC: U.S. Government Printing Office, 1887), 103.

67. Harrison Thornton, *Among the Eskimos of Wales, Alaska 1890–93* (Baltimore: Johns Hopkins Press, 1931), 3, 232.

68. "Treaty with Russia (To Accompany Bill H. R. No. 1096)" H. Report No. 37, 40th Cong., 2nd Sess. (May 18, 1868), pp. 1:12–13.

69. G. W. Bailey, quoted in Bockstoce, *Furs and Frontiers*, 327.

70. Otis, "Report of Special-Agent Otis," 46.

71. Kathleen Lopp Smith and Verbeck Smith, eds., *Ice Window: Letters from a Bering Strait Village, 1892–1902* (Fairbanks: University of Alaska Press, 2001), 139.

72. Smith and Smith, *Ice Window*, 55.

73. APRCA, Saint Lawrence Island Journals Microfilm, Vol 1: William Doty, p. 25.

74. APRCA, Ernest S. Burch Jr. Papers, Series 3, Box 74, file "California Yearly Meeting of Friends," Journal of Friends Mission Journal, November 27, 1899.

75. APRCA, Ernest S. Burch Jr. Papers, Series 3, Box 74, file "California Yearly Meeting of Friends," Journal of Friends Mission, March 23, 1901; March 24, 1901, and Summary of Traditions Broken in 1900–1901.

76. Martha Hadley, *The Alaskan Diary of a Pioneer Quaker Missionary* (Mount Dora, FL: Self-published, 1969), 183.

77. Sheldon Jackson to W. Harris, January 11, 1904, NARA CA RG 48, M-430, Roll 10.

78. George Thornton Emmons, *Condition and Needs of the Natives of Alaska*, S. Doc. No. 106, 58th Cong., 3d Sess. (1905), p. 8.

79. William Oquilluk, *People of Kauwerak: Legends of the Northern Eskimo*, 2nd ed. (Anchorage: Alaska Pacific University Press, 1981), 125–27.

80. Sheldon Jackson, quoted in Lowenstein, *Ultimate Americans*, 37. That Jackson saw the same event as Oquilluk narrates is an educated guess on my part.

81. APRCA, Ernest S. Burch Jr. Papers, Series 3, Box 74, file "California Yearly Meeting of Friends," Journal of Carrie Samms, October 13, 1897. See also T. L. Brevig, *Apaurak in Alaska: Social Pioneering among the Eskimos*, trans. and ed. J. Walter Johnshoy (Philadelphia: Dorrance, 1944).

82. RGIA DV F. 702, Op. 1, D. 313, L. 3.

83. RGIA DV F. 702, Op. 1, D. 1401, L. 1.

84. Smith and Smith, *Ice Window*, 152.

85. Lowenstein, *Ultimate Americans*, 120.

86. RGIA DV F. 702, Op. 1., D. 720, L. 9; *NN*, July 5, 1905.

87. RGIA DV F. 702, Op. 2, D. 229, L. 300; Bogoras, *The Chukchee*, 62–63.

88. E. C. Pielou, *A Naturalist's Guide to the Arctic* (Chicago: University of Chicago Press, 1994), 272, 284–86; A. Angerbjorn, M. Tannerfeldt, and S. Erlinge, "Predator–prey Relationships: Arctic Foxes and Lemmings," *Journal of Animal Ecology* 68 (1999): 34–49.

89. Smith and Smith, *Ice Window*, 215.

90. Hadley, *Alaskan Diary*, 87.

91. Miners to Secretary of the Interior, July 11, 1899, NARA CA RG 48, M-430, Roll 6.

92. Sheldon Jackson to W. T. Harris, December 6, 1899, NARA CA RG 48, M-430, Roll 6.

93. Alfred Brooks, *Blazing Alaska's Trails* (Fairbanks: University of Alaska Press, 1953), 74.

94. George Bird Grinnell, *A Brief History of the Boone and Crockett Club* (New York: Forest and Stream, 1910), 4.

95. Henry Fairfield Osborn, "Preservation of the Wild Animals of North America," in *American Big Game in its Haunts: The Book of the Boone and Crockett Club*, ed. George Bird Grinnell (New York: Forest and Stream, 1904), 349–73, 356–57.

96. Theodore Roosevelt, "Opening Address by the President," in *Major Problems in American Environmental History*, ed. Carolyn Merchant (Boston: Houghton Mifflin, 2005), 321. On efficiency, see Samuel Hays, *Conservation and the Gospel of Efficiency: The Progressive Conservation Movement, 1890–1920* (Cambridge, MA: Harvard University Press, 1959).

97. Osborne, "Preservation," 352.

98. M. Grant, "The Vanished Game of Yesterday," in *Hunting Trails on Three Continents: A Book of the Boone and Crockett Club*, ed. George Bird Grinnell, Kermit Roosevelt, W. Redmond Cross, and Prentiss N. Gray (New York: Windward House, 1933), 2.

99. Madison Grant to Andrew J. Stone, March 11, 1902, quoted in James Trefethen, *Crusade for Wildlife: Highlights of Conservation in Progress* (Harrisburg, PA: Stackpole, 1961), 139. On progressive conservation, see Douglas Brinkley, *The Wilderness Warrior: Theodore Roosevelt and the Crusade for America* (New York: HarperCollins, 2009) and Ian Tyrrell, *Crisis of the Wasteful Nation: Empire and Conservation in Theodore Roosevelt's America* (Chicago: University of Chicago Press, 2015). Conflict between

conservationists and locals was common; see Karl Jacoby, *Crimes against Nature: Squatters, Poachers, Thieves and the Hidden History of American Conservation* (Berkeley: University of California Press, 2001) and Theodore Catton, *Inhabited Wilderness: Indians, Eskimos, and National Parks in Alaska* (Albuquerque: University of New Mexico Press, 1997).

100. 35 Cong. Rec., H3840–47 (April 8, 1902). On the game law, see Ken Ross, *Pioneering Conservation in Alaska* (Boulder: University Press of Colorado, 2006), 116–34, and Donald Craig Mitchell, *Sold American: The Story of Alaska Natives and their Land, 1867–1959* (Hanover, NH: University Press of New England, 1997), 150–92.

101. *Eskimo Bulletin* V (May 1902), 3.

102. "Alaska Indians Starving," *NYT*, October 8, 1903.

103. Senate Subcommittee of Committee on Territories, *Conditions in Alaska*, S. Rep. No. 282, 58th Cong., 2d Sess. (1904), pt. 2, p. 149 and pt. 1, p. 29.

104. John Backland October 9, 1914, NARA MD RG 22, Reports 1869–1937, Entry 91.

105. Report of the *Bear*, 1911, NARA MD RG 48, CCF 1907–1936, File 6-12.

106. RGIA DV F. 702, Op.1, D. 127, L. 2.

107. RGIA DV F. 702, Op.1, D. 275, L. 24.

108. RGIA DV F. 702, Op.1, D. 127, L. 2.

109. John Bockstoce, *White Fox and Icy Seas in the Western Arctic: The Fur Trade, Transportation, and Change in the Early Twentieth Century* (New Haven, CT: Yale University Press, 2018), 110–11.

110. Krupnik and Chlenov, *Yupik Transitions*, 94–103, quote from 96.

111. William R. Hunt, *Arctic Passage* (New York: Scribner, 1975), 267.

112. RGIA DV F. 702, Op. 1, D. 313, L. 69.

113. RGIA DV F. 702, Op. 2, D. 206, L. 344.

114. RGIA DV F. 702, Op. 2, D. 229, L. 300–301.

115. Anastasia Yarzutkina, "Trade on the Icy Coasts: The Management of American Traders in the Settlements of Chukotka Native Inhabitants," *Terra Sebus: Acta Musei Sabasiensis*, Special Issue: Russian Studies from Early Middle Ages to the Present Day (2014): 361–84.

116. Madsen, *Arctic Trader*, 188.

117. Olaf Swenson, *Northwest of the World: Forty Years Trading and Hunting in Northern Siberia* (New York: Dodd, Mead, 1944), 95; "Walrus Catch Largest Known," *Los Angeles Times*, October 1, 1915.

118. Madsen, *Arctic Trader*, 215.

119. Igor Krupnik, *Pust govoriat*, 24. Records for this period are incomplete; Yupik recall walrus numbers declining until about 1920. James Brooks, "The Pacific Walrus and Its Importance to the Eskimo Economy," *Trans-*

actions of the North American Wildlife Conference 18 (1953): 503–10. Russia reported U.S. kills in the thousands. RGIA DV F. 702, Op. 2, D. 229, L. 278.

120. RGIA DV F. 702, Op. 7, D. 85, L. 141.

121. RGIA DV F. 702, Op. 1, D. 1401, L.61.

122. RGIA DV F. 702, Op. 7, D. 85, L. 141.

123. GARF F. 3977, Op. 1, D. 811, L. 125; GAPK F. 633, Op. 4, D. 85, L. 41.

124. E. Jones to Secretary of Commerce, January 16, 1914; S. Hall Young to the New York Zoological Society, January 12 1914; and A. W. Evans to Secretary of the Interior, July 30, 1913; all in NARA MD RG 22: Wildlife Service Reports 1869–1937, Entry 91.

125. RGIA DV F. 702, Op. 1, D. 275, L. 16; RGIA DV F. 702, Op. 2, D. 229, L. 282; Madsen, *Arctic Trader,* 97.

126. GAPK F. 633, Op. 4, D. 85, L. 42.

127. GARF F. 3977, Op. 1, D. 811, L. 125; Joseph Bernard, "Local Walrus Protection in Northeast Siberia," *Journal of Mammalogy* 4, no. 4 (November 1923): 224–27, 227.

128. James Ashton, *Ice-Bound: A Traveler's Adventures in the Siberian Arctic* (New York: Putnam, 1928), 127–28.

129. Swenson, *Northwest of the World,* 9–11.

130. ChOKM, Tikhon Semushkin Collection, "Predvaritelnye materialy po administrativno-upravlencheskoi strukture na Chukotke, sovremennomu sovetskomu stroitelstvu i perspektivam," p. 34.

CHAPTER 4: THE WAKING ICE

1. The Macaulay Collection, Cornell University Library, recordings no. ML120323, ML120370, and ML129690.

2. Vivian Senungetuk and Paul Tiulana, *A Place for Winter: Paul Tiulana's Story* (Anchorage: Ciri Foundation, 1987), 21; Macaulay Library recordings no. ML128122 and ML128121.

3. Senungetuk and Tiulana, *Place for Winter,* 21.

4. Hajo Eicken, "From the Microscopic, to the Macroscopic, to the Regional Scale: Growth, Microstructure and Properties of Sea Ice," in *Sea Ice: An Introduction to its Physics, Chemistry, Biology and Geology,* ed. David Thomas and Gerhard Dieckmann (Oxford, UK: Blackwell Science, 2003), 22–81.

5. Senungetuk and Tiulana, *Place for Winter,* 15.

6. Gerhard Dieckmann and Hartmut Hellmer, "The Importance of Sea Ice: An Overview," in Thomas and Dieckmann, *Sea Ice,* 1–21.

7. N. A. Zhikharev, ed., *Pervyi revkom Chukotki 1919–1920: Sbornik dokumentov i materialov* (Magadanskoe knizhnoe izdatelstvo 1957), 38, 20.

8. Zhikharev, ed. *Pervyi revkom*, 33.

9. RGIA DV F. R-2336, Op. 1, D. 17, L. 11; Zhikharev, *Pervyi revkom*, 24. On the revolution in Chukotka, see N. N. Dikov, *Ocherki istorii Chukotki s drevneishikh vremen do nashikh dnei* (Novosibirsk: Nauka, Sib. Otd-nie, 1974), 146–64 and N. A. Zhikharev, *Ocherki istorii Severo-Vostoka RSFSR, 1917–1953* (Magadan: Magadanskoe knizhnoe izdatelstvo, 1961), 37–69.

10. Tenth Party Congress, quoted in Slezkine, *Arctic Mirrors*, 144. On the committee, see *Arctic Mirrors*, chaps. 5 and 6.

11. Vladimir Bogoraz, "Podgotovitelnye mery k organizatsii malykh narodnostei," *Sovetskaia Aziia* 3 (1925): 48.

12. V. Lenin, *Polnoe sobranie sochinenii* (Moscow: Politizdat, 1958–65), 41: 245–46.

13. *KPSS v rezoliutsiiakh i resheniiakh s"ezdov, konferentsii I plenumov TsK, vol. 2, 1917–1922* (Moscow: Izdat.pol. lit., 1983), 367.

14. B. I. Mukhachev, *Borba za vlast sovetov na Chukotke (1919–1923): Sbornik dokumentov i materialov* (Magadan: Magadanskoe Knizhnoe Izdatelstvo, 1967), 124.

15. Mukhachev, *Borba za vlast*, 133.

16. RGIA DV F. R-2413, Op. 4, D. 1798, L. 52.

17. APRCA, Oscar Brown Papers, Box 1, p. 20–24.

18. P. G. Smidovich, introduction to N. Galkin, *V zemle polunochnogo solntsa* (Moscow: Molodaia gvardiia, 1929), 6.

19. RGIA DV F. R-2333, Op. 1, D. 128, L.372. See also RGIA DV F. R-623, Op. 1, D. 36, L. 1.

20. Mukhachev, *Borba za vlast*, 104.

21. GARF F. 3977, Op. 1, D. 881, L. 126.

22. RGIA DV F. R-4559, Op. 1, D. 1, L. 117 and 118.

23. GARF F. 3977, Op. 1, D. 11, L. 19.

24. GARF F. 3977, Op. 1, D. 811, L. 129b.

25. GAPK F. 633, Op. 5, D. 43, L. 6, 6.

26. RGIA DV F. R-2413, Op. 4, D. 629, L. 5.

27. RGIA DV F. R-2413, Op. 4, D. 629, L. 5.

28. Leighton and Leighton, "Eskimo Recollections," 59.

29. Swenson, *Northwest*, 172–74.

30. GARF F. 3977, Op. 1, D. 11, L. 17.

31. Roger Silook, in *Gifts from the Ancestors: Ancient Ivories of Bering Strait*, ed. William W. Fitzhugh, Julia Hollowell and Aron L. Crowell (Princeton: Princeton University Press, 2009), 217.

32. Simon Paneak, *In a Hungry Country: Essays by Simon Paneak*, ed. J. M. Campbell (Fairbanks: University of Alaska Press, 2004), 34.

33. Leighton and Leighton, "Eskimo Recollections," 252.

34. Leighton and Leighton, "Eskimo Recollections," 80–81.

35. Napaaq, also known as Florence Nupok, was a talented artist. See Suzi Jones, ed., *Eskimo Drawings* (Anchorage: Anchorage Museum of Art, 2003), 137–156.

36. Leighton and Leighton, "Eskimo Recollections," 165. Quote is from Koneak, another Gambell resident.

37. APRCA Charles Lucier Collection, Box 3, File 3-18, Jack Tiepelman, p. 1.

38. Leighton and Leighton, "Eskimo Recollections," 158.

39. Oquilluk, *People of Kauwerak*, 131; Brevig, *Apaurak in Alaska*, 158. I have heard this idea expressed by people throughout the Arctic.

40. Oquilluk, *People of Kauwerak*, 128.

41. Asatchaq and Lowenstein, *Things That Were Said*, 193–95.

42. *Report of the Commissioner of Education, 1925* (Washington, DC: Government Printing Office, 1925), 28.

43. Gambell teacher quoted in Charles C. Hughes, *An Eskimo Village in the Modern World* (Ithaca, NY: Cornell University Press, 1962), 190.

44. Riggs to the Secretary of Agriculture, November 11, 1919, p. 11; NARA MD RG 126, CCF 1907–1951, File 9-1-33.

45. Memo to Education Department Employees, August 25, 1920, NARA MD RG 48, CCF 1907–1936, File 6-13. The classic work on this subject is Louis Warren, *The Hunter's Game: Poachers and Conservationists in Twentieth-century America* (New Haven, CT: Yale University Press, 1997).

46. Bockstoce, *White Fox*, 19.

47. Frank Williams to E. W. Nelson, December 21, 1921, NARA MD RG 22, Entry 162.

48. Frank Dufresne, quoted in Mitchell, *Sold American*, 187.

49. Chief of Bureau to Frank Dufresne, February 7, 1923, NARA MD RG 22, Entry 162.

50. H. Liebes & Co. to Department of Fisheries, September 22, 1923, NARA MD RG 22, Entry 162.

51. Apassingok et al., *Savoonga*, 175.

52. F. G. Ashbrook, *Blue Fox Farming in Alaska* (Washington, DC: Department of Agriculture, 1925), 16.

53. Ashbrook, *Blue Fox Farming*, 1. Most of the farms were on Alaskan islands; see Sarah Isto, *The Fur Farms of Alaska: Two Centuries of History and a Forgotten Stampede* (Fairbanks: University of Alaska Press, 2014).

54. Wilfred Osgood, *Silver Fox Farming* (Washington, DC: Government Printing Office, 1908), 45.

55. Adam Leavitt Qapqan, UAFOHP, Project Jukebox, IHLC Tape 00058, Section 5.

56. Isto, *Fur Farms of Alaska*, 70.

57. Bockstoce, *White Fox*, 212–13.

58. Bogoslovskaya et al., *Maritime Hunting Culture*, 27.

59. GARF F. 3977, Op. 1, D. 809, L. 17.

60. ChOKM, Matlu, *Avtobiografiia (Rasskaz Matliu)*, Coll. N. 5357.

61. Anatolii Skachko, "Problemy severa," *Ss* no. 1 (1930): 15–37, 33.

62. RGIA DV F. R-2413, Op. 4, D. 974, L. 109.

63. RGIA DV F. R-2413, Op. 4, D. 629, L. 107.

64. GARF F. 3977, Op. 1, D. 11, L. 40.

65. Krupnik and Chlenov, *Yupik Transitions*, 230–32.

66. Krupnik, *Pust govoriat*, 267.

67. B. M. Lapin, *Tikhookeanskii dnevnik* (Moscow: Federatsiia, 1929), 36.

68. L. N. Khakhovskaia, "Shamany i sovetskaia vlast na Chukotke," *Voprosy istrorii* no. 4 (2013): 113–28, 121.

69. L. S. Bogoslovskaya, V. S. Krivoshchekov, and I. Krupnik, eds., *Tropoiu Bogoraza: Nauchnye i literaturnye materialy* (Moscow: Russian Heritage Institute-GEOS, 2008), photo 1-41.

70. Anders Apassingok, personal communication, July 2017.

71. Krupnik and Chlenov, *Yupik Transitions*, 113–14.

72. Peter Schweitzer and Evgeniy Golovko, "The 'Priests' of East Cape: A Religious Movement on the Chukchi Peninsula during the 1920s and 1930s," *Etudes/Inuit/Studies* 31, no. 1–2 (2007): 39–58.

73. ChOKM, Tikhon Semushkin Collection, "Predvaritelnye materialy," 34. Krupnik and Chlenov also describe this incident in *Yupik Transitions*, 233–34.

74. Walrus harvest tallies from Igor Krupnik and Ludmila Bogoslovskaya, *Ecosystem Variability and Anthropogenic Hunting Pressure in the Bering Strait Area* (Washington, DC: Smithsonian Institution, 1998), 109. See also Francis H. Fay and C. Edward Bowlby, *The Harvest of Pacific Walrus, 1931–1989* (Anchorage: U.S. Fish and Wildlife Technical Report, 1994), 20. All fox numbers in this section from GARF F. 3977, Op. 1, D. 819, L. 15–17.

75. GARF F. 3977, Op. 1, D. 11, L. 40.

76. RGIA DV F. R-2413, Op. 4, D. 974, L. 115v.

77. RGIA DV F. R-2413, Op. 4, D. 974, L. 108, 115b.

78. GARF F. A-310, Op. 18, D. 329, L. 51; GAMO F. P-12, Op. 1, D. 14, L. 8;

GARF F. 3977, Op. 1, D. 423, L. 13; RGIA DV F. R-2413, Op. 4, D. 974, L. 128.

79. Yuri Rytkheu, *Reborn to a Full Life* (Moscow: Novosti Press, 1977), 52.

80. Norman Whittaker to Clifford C. Presnall, January 22, 1945, NARA MD RG 22, Entry P-285.

81. Vladimir Tiyato in Krupnik, *Pust govoriat*, 143–44.

82. William Iġġiaġruk Hensley, *Fifty Miles from Tomorrow: A Memoir of Alaska and the Real People* (New York: Farrar, Straus and Giroux, 2009), 67.

83. Rytkheu, *Reborn*, 55.

84. Margaret Seeganna, in Kaplan and Yocom, *Ugiuvangmiut Quliapyuit*, 25.

85. *Smoke Signals* quoted in Dorothy Jean Ray, *Eskimo Art: Tradition and Innovation in North Alaska* (Seattle: University of Washington Press, 1977), 55; Don Foster to Peter Mayne, June 23, 1949, NARA AK RG 75, Decimal File 997.4.

86. John L. Buckley, *The Pacific Walrus: A Review of Current Knowledge and Suggested Management Needs* (Washington, DC: Government Printing Office, 1958), 2. On World War II spending, see Stephen Haycox, *Alaska: An American Colony* (Seattle: University of Washington Press, 2002), 257–72.

87. Albert Heinrich to Clifford Presnall, March 20, 1945, NARA MD RG 22, Entry P-285; J. Murie to FWS Director, January 28, 1945, NARA MD RG 22, Entry P-285.

88. "Protection of Walruses in Alaska," H. Report No. 883, 77th Cong., 1st Sess. (June 28, 1941), p. 2.

89. Brooks, "Pacific Walrus and Its Importance," 506.

90. Clifford Presnall to Norman Wittaker, January 4, 1945. NARA MD RG 22, Entry P-285.

91. GARF F. R-5664, Op. 46, D. 1137, L. 2.

92. GAMO F. P-22, Op. 1, D. 122, L. 4, 81.

93. GAMO F. P-22, Op. 1, D. 213, L. 71.

94. Copies of the permissions are in NARA AK RG 75, Mission Correspondence 1935–1968.

95. Krupnik and Chlenov, *Yupik Transitions*, 250.

96. Krupnik, *Pust govoriat*, 499.

97. "Alaska: America's Greatest Wealth of Untapped Resources," 1947, NARA MD RG 48, CCF 1937–1953, p. 10. For Native participation in World War II, see Holly Guise, "World War Two and the First Peoples of the Last Frontier: Alaska Native Voices, Indigenous Equilibrium Theory, and Wartime Alaska 1942–1945" (PhD diss., Yale University, 2018).

98. APRCA, Ernest S. Burch Jr. Papers, Series 3, Box 74, File: Henry Geist, p. 9.

99. Michael Krauss, "Crossroads? A Twentieth-Century History of Contacts across the Bering Strait," in *Anthropology of the North Pacific Rim*, ed. William W. Fitzhugh and Valerie Chaussonnet (Washington, DC: Smithsonian Institution Press, 1994), 365–79.

100. A. Day to Office of Indian Affairs, November 30, 1944, NARA DC RG 75, CCF 1940–1957.

101. C. Sullivan to Claude Hirst, September 17, 1936, NARA AK RG 75, Alaska Reindeer Service Administrative Correspondence 1934–1953.

102. B. Lafortune to Claude Hirst, August 18, 1939, NARA AK RG 75, Alaska Reindeer Service Administrative Correspondence 1934–1953. See also F. A. Zeusler to Claude Hirst, August 19, 1936.

103. John Buckles to Durward Allen, December 1, 1953, NARA MD RG 22, Entry P-285; Untitled Report, no author or page numbers, 1946; NARA MD RG 22, Entry 246.

104. Hensley, *Fifty Miles*, 76, 78, 72–73.

105. Joan Naviyuk Kane, *A Few Lines in the Manifest* (Philadelphia: Albion Books, 2018), 20.

106. Senungetuk and Tiulana, *Place for Winter*, 38–40.

107. Yuri Rytkheu, *Liudi nashego berega* (Leningrad: Molodaia gvardiia, 1953), 2.

108. GAMO F. P-22, Op. 1, D. 659, L. 9. On failed construction and the state, see Nicolai Ssorin-Chaikov, *The Social Life of the State in Subarctic Siberia* (Stanford, CA: Stanford University Press, 2003).

109. Yuri Rytkheu, *From Nomad Tent to University* (Moscow: Novosti Press, 1981), 26.

110. Krupnik and Chlenov, *Yupik Transitions*, 271; Tobias Holzlehner, "Engineering Socialism: A History of Village Relocations in Chukotka, Russia," in *Engineering Earth: The Impacts of Megaengineering Projects*, ed. S. D. Brunn (Dordrecht, Netherlands: Springer, 2011), 1957–73.

111. Rytkheu, *Reborn*, 70.

112. Nina Akuken, quoted in Krupnik and Chlenov, *Yupik Transitions*, 274–75.

113. Krupnik, *Pust govoriat*, 218.

114. E. E. Selitrennik, "Nekotorye voprosy kolkhoznogo stroitelstva v Chukotskom natsionalnom okruge," *Sovetskaia etnografiia* no. 1 (1965): 13–27, 16.

115. Krupnik and Chlenov, *Yupik Transitions*, 282–83.

116. GAChAO R-23, Op. 1, D. 51, L.61.

117. GARF F. A-310, Op. 18, D. 191, L. 10.

118. GAMO F. P-12, Op. 1, D. 84, L. 107.

119. Rytkheu, *From Nomad Tent*, 20.

120. Mikhail M. Bronshtein, "Uelen Hunters and Artists," *Études/Inuit/Studies* 31, No. 1–2 (2007): 83–101.

121. Francis H. Fay, *Pacific Walrus Investigations on St. Lawrence Island, Alaska* (Anchorage: Alaska Cooperative Wildlife Unit, 1958), 4.

122. Albert Reed to General Commissioner for Indian Affairs, August 12, 1947, NARA AK RG 75, Juneau Area Office 1933–1963, File 920.

123. Bogoslovskaya et al, *Maritime Hunting Culture*, 87.

124. Francis H. Fay, "Ecology and Biology of the Pacific Walrus, *Odobenus Rosmarus Divergens Illiger*," *North American Fauna* LXXIV (1982): 171–72; G. C. Ray, J. McCormick-Ray, P. Berg, and H. E. Epstein, "Pacific Walrus: Benthic Bioturbator of Beringia," *Journal of Experimental Marine Biology and Ecology* no. 330 (2006): 403–19.

125. S. E. Kleinenberg, "Ob okrane morzha," *Priroda* no. 7 (July 1957), trans. D. E. Sergeant, *Fisheries Research Board of Canada Translation Series No. 199* (Montreal: Fisheries Research Board, 1959), 5.

126. RGAE F. 544, Op. 1, D. 32, L. 13.

127. RGAE F. 544, Op. 1, D. 32, L. 13.

128. RGAE F. 544, Op. 1, D. 60. L. 3. "Conservation" is an American term—the Soviets generally used "nature protection."

129. The organization was renamed the International Union for the Conservation of Nature in 1956.

130. RGAE F. 544, Op. 1, D. 32, L. 1. On international ties, see Douglas Weiner, *A Little Corner of Freedom: Russian Nature Protection from Stalin to Gorbachev* (Berkeley: University of California Press, 1999), 261–82.

131. Kleinenberg, "Ob okrane," 5.

132. Kleinenberg, "Ob okrane," 5.

133. Krupnik and Bogoslovskaya, *Ecosystem Variability*, 109.

134. This argument goes against much early environmental history, which emphasized communism as more destructive than capitalism; see, for example, Murray Feshbach, *Ecological Disaster: Cleaning Up the Hidden Legacy of the Soviet Regime* (New York: Twentieth Century Fund Press, 1995); Paul Josephson, *The Conquest of the Russian Arctic* (Cambridge, MA: Harvard University Press, 2014). For accounts with more nuance, see Andy Bruno, *The Nature of Soviet Power: An Arctic Environmental History* (New York: Cambridge University Press, 2016); Stephen Brain, *Song of the Forest: Russian Forestry and Stalinist Environmentalism 1905–1953* (Pittsburgh: University of Pittsburgh Press, 2011), and Alan Roe, "Into Soviet Nature: Tourism, Environmental Protection, and the Formation of Soviet National Parks, 1950s–1990s" (PhD diss., Georgetown University, 2016).

135. Anonymous, quoted in Anna Kerttula, *Antler on the Sea: The Yupik and Chukchi of the Russian Far East* (Ithaca, NY: Cornell University Press, 2000), 139; Fay and Bowlby, *Harvest of Pacific Walrus*, 3.

136. Fay, Kelly, and Stease, "Managing the Exploitation," 5.

CHAPTER 5: THE MOVING TUNDRA

1. Pielou, *Naturalist's Guide*, 86–98.

2. Valerius Geist, *Deer of the World: Their Evolution, Behavior, and Ecology* (Mechanicsburg, PA: Stackpole, 1998), 315–36; B. C. Forbes and T. Kumpula, "The Ecological Role and Geography of Reindeer (*Rangifer tarandus*) in Northern Eurasia," *Geography Compass* no. 3 (2009): 1356–80. Sleepwalking caribou are a personal observation.

3. Valerius Geist, "Of Reindeer and Man, Human and Neanderthal," *Rangifer* 23, Special Issue no. 14 (2003): 57–63. Vladimir Pitulko, "Ancient Humans in Eurasian Arctic Ecosystems: Environmental Dynamics and Changing Subsistence," *World Archeology* 30, no. 3 (1999): 421–36.

4. Ernest Burch Jr., *Caribou Herds of Northwest Alaska, 1850–2000* (Fairbanks: University of Alaska Press, 2012), 148.

5. Leonid Baskin, "Reindeer Husbandry / Hunting in Russia in the Past, Present and Future," *Polar Research* 19, no. 1 (2000): 23–29. Igor Krupnik, *Arctic Adaptations: Native Whalers and Reindeer Herders of Northern Eurasia*, trans. Marcia Levenson (Hanover, NH: University Press of New England, 1993), 166–68.

6. Marcy Norton, "The Chicken or the *Iegue*: Human-Animal Relationships and the Columbian Exchange," *American Historical Review* 120, no. 1 (February 2015): 28–60; and Tim Ingold, "From Trust to Domination: An Alternative History of Human-Animal Relations," in *Animals and Human Society: Changing Perspectives*, ed. Aubrey Manning and James Serpell (London: Routledge, 2002), 1–22.

7. Krupnik, *Arctic Adaptations*, 161.

8. Bogoras, *The Chukchee*, 71–73, 84.

9. On the pastoralist shift, see I. Gurvich, "Sosedskaia obshchina i proizvodstvennye obedineniia malykh narodov Severa," in *Obshchestvennyi stroi u narodov Severnoi Sibiri*, ed. I. Gurvich and B. Dolgikh (Moscow: Nauka, 1970), 384–417 and I. S. Vdovin, "Istoricheskie osobennosti formirovaniia obshchestvennogo razdeleniia truda u narodov Severo-Vostoka Sibiri," in *Sotsialnaia istoriia narodov Azii* (Leningrad: Nauka, 1975), 143–57.

10. This paragraph is drawn from Krupnik, *Arctic Adaptations*, chaps. 4 and 5; I. S. Vdovin, *Ocherki istorii*, 15–22; and Bogoras, *The Chukchee*,

73–90. The human population in 1600 was probably around two thousand, and reached almost nine thousand by the end of the 1800s, when growth stabilized.

11. L. M. Baskin, *Severnyi olen: Upravlenie povedeniem i populiatsiiami olenevodstvo okhota* (Moscow: KMK, 2009), 182–88.

12. Bogoras, *The Chukchee*, 44–45.

13. Bogoras, *The Chukchee*, 371 (quote), 322–23, 643.

14. Eigil Reimers, "Wild Reindeer in Norway—Population Ecology, Management, and Harvest," *Rangifer Report*, no. 11 (2006): 39.

15. APRCA, Ernest S. Burch Jr. Papers, Series 3, Box 124, File "Western Arctic Herd Sequence," no page numbers.

16. Descriptions of Iñupiat hunting summarized from APRCA, Charles V. Lucier Collection, Box 3, Folder: Buckland Ethnographic Notes, 3–4; and Burch, *Iñupiaq Eskimo Nations*. References to caribou migrations come from Burch's *Caribou Herds*, 67–91.

17. APRCA, Ernest S. Burch Jr. Papers, Series 3, Box 75, File: 1965 A-Series, Regina Walton Interview, pp. 50–51; Burch, *Iñupiaq Eskimo Nations*, 45.

18. Burch, *Caribou Herds*, 119.

19. APRCA, Charles V. Lucier Collection, Box 3, Folder: Buckland Ethnographic Notes 3–4 and APRCA, Ernest S. Burch Jr. Papers, Series 5, Box 227, Folder H88-2B-9, p. 23.

20. Edwin S. Hall Jr., *The Eskimo Storyteller: Folktales from Noatak, Alaska* (Knoxville: University of Tennessee Press, 1975), 78–79, 211; APRCA, Charles V. Lucier Collection, Box 3, Folder: Deering Ethnography 3-9; Nicholas J. Gubser, *The Nunamiut Eskimos: Hunters of Caribou* (New Haven, CT: Yale University Press, 1965), 200.

21. Christopher Tingook, in APRCA, Ernest S. Burch Jr. Papers, Series 3, Box 124, "Western Arctic Herd Sequence," no page numbers. The expedition to find John Franklin bought caribou in the 1850s, as did the Western Union Telegraph Expedition in the late 1860s, and the International Polar Year crew in the 1880s. See Bockstoce, *Furs and Frontiers*, 144–46 and Burch, *Caribou Herds*, 120–21.

22. Burch, *Iñupiaq Eskimo Nations*, 107.

23. Henry Dall, *Alaska and Its Resources* (Boston: Lee and Shepard, 1897), 147; Nelson, *The Eskimo about Bering Strait*, 229; Charles Townsend, "Notes on the Natural History and Ethnology of Northern Alaska," in M. A. Healy, *Report of the Cruise of the Revenue Marine Steamer* Corwin *in the Arctic Ocean in the Year 1885* (Washington, DC: Government Printing Office, 1887), 87; and John Murdoch, *Ethnological Results of the Point Barrow Expedition* (1892; repr. Washington, DC: Smithsonian Institution Press, 1988), 267–68.

24. Burch, *Caribou Herds*, chaps. 4 and 5; Burch, *Iñupiaq Eskimo Nations*, 47, 374. Research on how the dynamics of animal populations and ecological stress contribute to dependency on European goods and ideas has a rich historiography; see, for example, Richard White's classic *The Roots of Dependency: Subsistence, Environment and Social Change among the Choctaws, Pawnees, and Navajos* (Lincoln: University of Nebraska Press, 1988); Marsha Weisiger's *Dreaming of Sheep in Navajo Country* (Seattle: University of Washington Press, 2011), and Hackel's *Children of Coyote*.

25. APRCA, Ernest S. Burch Jr. Papers, Series 3, Box 97, Serial File on Caribou Data, Entry 105, 79, 14; and File: Seward Peninsula, Interview with Gideon Barr, p. 1.

26. Linda Ellanna and George Sherrod, *From Hunters to Herders: The Transformation of Earth, Society and Heaven among the Iñupiat of Beringia* (Anchorage: National Park Service, 2004), 45.

27. Summarized from Oquilluk, *People of Kauwerak*. The third disaster might have been the result of the Mount Tambora eruption; Lisa Navraq Ellanna, personal communication, July 2017.

28. APRCA, Ernest S. Burch Jr. Papers, Series 3, Box 124, "Northeast Coast: Caribou, Informant: Simon Paneak," no page numbers.

29. W. N. Burns, *Year with a Whaler*, 149.

30. This was Horace Greeley's opinion, which was harsher than most (*New York Daily Tribune*, April 11, 1867). The lack of agricultural potential was an issue even for Alaska's boosters; see Charles Sumner, *Speech of Hon. Charles Sumner of Massachusetts on the Cession of Russian America to the United States* (Washington, DC: Congressional Globe Office, 1867), 33.

31. M. A. Healy, "Destitution among the Alaska Eskimo," *Report of the Federal Security Agency: Office of Education* (Washington, DC: Government Printing Office, 1906), 1: 1097.

32. W. E. Nelson, *Report upon Natural History Collections Made in Alaska between the Years 1877 and 1881* (Washington, DC: U.S. Army Signal Service, 1887), 285.

33. Paul Niedieck, *Cruises in the Bering Sea*, trans. R. A. Ploetz (New York: Scribner, 1909), 115. The degree to which Native hunting caused the caribou decline is not settled, and is part of a longstanding debate around the "ecological Indian." Richard Stern et al. argue against overhunting in *Eskimos, Reindeer and Land*, Bulletin 59, December 1980 (Fairbanks: Agricultural and Forestry Experiment Station, School of Agriculture and Land Resources Management, University of Alaska Fairbanks, 1980), 14. Burch contends that overhunting with rifles was the primary cause of the crash. Given that the late nineteenth century

saw a decline in Rangifer around the Arctic, it seems to me that hunting compounded climatic pressures. In this sense, caribou echo bison on the Great Plains, although without the habitat destruction, settlers, and proximity to industrial markets; see Andrew C. Isenberg, *The Destruction of the Bison: An Environmental History, 1750–1920* (New York: Cambridge University Press, 2000) and Theodore Binnema, *Common and Contested Ground: A Human and Environmental History of the Northwestern Plains* (Toronto: University of Toronto Press, 2004), chaps. 1 and 2.

34. Healy, "Destitution," 1097.

35. Sheldon Jackson, *Introduction of Domestic Reindeer into Alaska: Preliminary Report of the General Agent of Education for Alaska to the Commissioner of Education* (Washington, DC: Government Printing Office, 1891), 4–5.

36. On Jackson, see Roxanne Willis, *Alaska's Place in the West: From the Last Frontier to the Last Great Wilderness* (Lawrence, KS: University Press of Kansas, 2010), 24–25 and Stephen W. Haycox, "Sheldon Jackson in Historical Perspective: Alaska Native Schools and Mission Contracts, 1885–1894," *Pacific Historian* 26 (1984): 18–28.

37. Sheldon Jackson, "Education in Alaska," S. Exec. Doc. No. 85, 49th Cong., 1st Sess. (1886), p. 30.

38. S. Jackson, *Introduction of Domestic Reindeer*, 9.

39. S. Jackson, *Introduction of Domestic Reindeer*, 7.

40. Townsend, "Notes on the Natural History," 88.

41. Helen Hunt Jackson, *A Century of Dishonor* (Boston: Roberts Brothers, 1881), 1.

42. Sheldon Jackson, *Preliminary Report of the General Agent for Alaska* (Washington: Government Printing Office, 1890), 10.

43. Townsend in S. Jackson, *Report on Introduction of Domestic Reindeer into Alaska with Maps and Illustrations*, Sen. Doc. No. 22, 52nd Cong., 2d Sess. (1893), 34.

44. Some anthropologists argue that on the Seward Peninsula, caribou herds did not decline enough to cause hardship or emigration; see Dean Olson, *Alaska Reindeer Herdsmen: A Study of Native Management in Transition* (Fairbanks: University of Alaska, Institute of Social Economic and Government Research, 1969), 20, and Dorothy Jean Ray, *The Eskimos of Bering Strait, 1650–1898* (Seattle: University of Washington Press, 1975), 112–13.

45. Sheldon Jackson, *Report on Introduction of Domestic Reindeer into Alaska 1894* (Washington, DC: Government Printing Office, 1895), 58.

46. RGIA DV F. 702, Op. 1, D. 682, L. 13; S. A. Buturlin, *Otchet upolnomochennago Ministerstva vnutrennykh del po snabzheniiu prodovolstvem v 1905 godu, Kolymskago i Okhotskago kraia* (St. Petersburg: Tipografaia Minis-

terstva vnutrennikh del, 1907), 70–72; RGIA DV F. 702, Op. 3, D. 160, L. 13.

47. Baron Gerhard Maydell, *Reisen und forschungen im Jakutskischen gebiet Ostsibiriens in den jahren 1861–1871* (St. Petersburg: Buchdruckerei der K. Akademie der wissenschaften, 1893–96); Bogoras, *The Chukchee*, 73, 706–708.

48. RGIA DV F. 702, Op. 3, D. 414, L. 87.

49. RGIA DV F. 702, Op. 1, D. 682, L. 3, 4, 5a; RGIA DV F. 702, Op. 3, D. 414, L. 89.

50. RGIA DV F. 702, Op. 1, D. 682, L. 93. As of 1911, only one school not on the coast or at the administrative and trading hubs of Anadyr and Markovo, where many of the pupils were cossacks, was in operation.

51. RGIA DV F. 702, Op. 3, D. 160, L. 13–14, quote: 40.

52. RGIA DV F. 702, Op. 1, D. 682, L. 45, 62; RGIA DV F. 702, Op. 3, D. 160, L. 33.

53. RGIA DV F. 702, Op. 1, D. 682, L. 25. Necrobacillosis, a bacterial infection of the hooves, is the most common disease among reindeer in northeastern Eurasia and is prevalent when warm, damp conditions allow the bacteria to breed. Damaged hooves are also more susceptible. See K. Handeland, M. Moye, B. Borgsjo, H. Bondal, K. Isaksen, and J.S. Agerholm, "Digital Necrobasillosis in Norwegian Wild Tundra Reindeer (*Rangifer tarandus tarandus*)" *Journal of Comparative Pathology* 143, no. 1 (July 2010): 29–38. On decline, see RGIA DV F. 702, Op. 3, D. 563, L. 147–148; Krupnik, *Arctic Adaptations*, 173–175.

54. Bogoras, *The Chukchee*, 347.

55. Vladimir Bogoraz, quoted in Yuri Slezkine, *Arctic Mirrors*, 148. For an overview of Bogoraz's life, see Sergei Kan, " 'My Old Friend in a Dead-end of Empiricism and Skepticism': Bogoras, Boas, and the Politics of Soviet Anthropology of the Late 1920s–Early 1930s," *Histories of Anthropology Annual* 2, no. 1 (2006): 33–68.

56. RGIA DV F. R-2411, Op. 1, D. 66, L. 195.

57. GARF F. 3977, Op. 1, D. 225, L. 188.

58. T. Semushkin, *Chukotka*, in *Izbrannye proizvedeniia v dvukh tomakh, t. 2* (Moscow: Khudozhestvennaia literatura moskva 1970), 210.

59. Semushkin, *Chukotka*, 144.

60. Semushkin, *Chukotka*, 37, 36.

61. V. S. Flerov, ed., *Revkomy Severo-vostoka SSSR (1922–1928 gg.) Sbornik dokumentov i materialov* (Magadan: Magadansokoe knizhnoe izdatelstovo, 1973), 196.

62. GARF F. A-310, Op. 18, D. 88, L. 42.

63. Galkin, *V zemle polunochnogo*, 160.

64. RGIA DV F. R-4315, Op. 1, D. 32, L. 11.

65. RGIA DV F. R-623, Op. 1, D. 36, L. 8.

66. Slezkine, *Arctic Mirrors*, 239.

67. Semushkin, *Chukotka*, 36.

68. Flerov, ed. *Revkomy Severo-vostoka*, 196–97.

69. Counts of reindeer vary somewhat, and all are estimates. The total of 556,000 domestic head in 1926–27 given by I. S. Garusov is about average—see *Sotsialisticheskoe pereustroistvo selskogo i promyslovogo khoziaistva Chukotki 1917–1952* (Magadan: Magadanskoe knizhnoe izdatelstvo, 1981), 81.

70. GARF F. 3977, Op. 1, D. 716, L. 24.

71. GAMO F. 91, Op. 1, D. 2, L. 94.

72. "Herders of Reindeer," *WP,* July 1, 1894. See also Willis, *Alaska's Place in the West*, 31.

73. Stern et al., *Eskimos, Reindeer and Land*, 25–26.

74. Frank Churchill, *Reports on the Condition of Education and School Service and the Management of Reindeer Service in the District of Alaska* (Washington, DC: Government Printing Office, 1906), 37, 36, 39.

75. Walter Shields, Report Superintendent N.W. District, June 30, 1915, p.10–11, NARA DC RG 75, General Correspondence 1915–1916, Entry 806.

76. Churchill, *Condition of Education*, 46.

77. On Makaiqtaq, see Department of the Interior, *Report on the Work of the Bureau of Education for the Natives of Alaska, 1914–1915* (Washington, DC: Government Printing Office, 1917), 72–85; Ellanna and Sherrod, *From Hunters to Herders*, chap. 3. On Native ownership, see U.S. Bureau of Education, *Report on Work of the Bureau of Education for the Natives of Alaska 1913–1914* (Washington, DC: Government Printing Office, 1917), 7.

78. Bureau of Education, *Report on the Work of the Bureau . . . 1914–1915*, 8.

79. Carl Lomen, *Fifty Years in Alaska* (New York: D. McKay Co, 1954), 148.

80. Ellanna and Sherrod, *From Hunters to Herders*, 54–55.

81. Bureau of Education, *Report on the Work of the Bureau . . . 1914–1915*, 52.

82. NARA AK RG 75, Alaska Reindeer Service Historical Files, File: History-general, 1933–1945, "Quotations," p. 32.

83. APRCA, Fosma and Sidney Rood Papers, Box 2, Erik Nylin Annual Report from Wales 1922–1923.

84. Hunt, *Arctic Passage*, 219; "Reindeer to Help the Meat Supply," Newspaper clipping, June 15, 1914, NARA MD RG 48, CCF 1907–1936, file: 6-2/6-4; Lewis Laylin to Hon. James Wickersham, March 12,

1913, NARA AK RG 75, Alaska Reindeer Service Historical Files, File: History-general, 1933–1945.

85. Report of the Governor of Alaska, *Reports of the Department of the Interior*, vol. 2 (Washington DC: Government Printing Office, 1918), 519.

86. NARA AK RG 75, Alaska Reindeer Service Historical Files, File: History-general, 1933–1945, "Quotations," p. 32.

87. Unalakleet Teacher Wellman, Annual Report 1922–1923, NARA AK RG 75, Alaska Reindeer Service Historical Files, File: History-general, 1933–1945.

88. Olson, *Alaska Reindeer Herdsmen*, 14.

89. John B. Burnham, *The Rim of Mystery: A Hunter's Wanderings in Unknown Siberian Asia* (New York: Putnam, 1929), 281.

90. I. Druri, "Kak byl sozdan pervyi olenesovkhoz na Chukotke," *Kraevedcheskie zapiski* XVI (Magadan, 1989), 9.

91. RGIA DV F R-2413, Op.4, D. 967, L. 13.

92. A. Skachko, "Ocherednye zadachi sovetskoi raboy sredi malykh narodov Severa," *Ss*, no. 2 (1931) 5–29, 20.

93. Kan, " 'My Old Friend,' "; Slezkine, *Arctic Mirrors*, 189.

94. GARF F. A-310, Op. 18, D. 88, L. 44; RGIA DV F. R-4315, Op. 1, D. 32, L. 3, 10.

95. GARF F. 3977, Op. 1, D. 225, L. 5.

96. Semushkin, *Chukotka*, 299.

97. D. I. Raizman, "Shaman byl protiv," in Bogoslovskaya et al., *Tropoiu Bogoraza*, 95–101, 100.

98. GARF F. A-310, Op. 18, D. 88, L. 43.

99. Quoted in L.N. Khakhovskaia, "Shamany i sovetskaia vlast na Chukotke" *Voprosy Istorii* 4 (2013): 112–127, 117.

100. Isaac Andre Seymour Hadwen and Lawrence Palmer, *Reindeer in Alaska* (Washington DC: Government Printing Office, 1922), 69.

101. Lawrence Palmer, *Raising Reindeer in Alaska* (Washington, DC: USDA Miscellaneous Publication No. 207, 1934), 23–31.

102. Hadwen and Palmer, *Reindeer in Alaska*, 4.

103. NARA AK RG 75, Alaska Reindeer Service Historical Files, File: History-general, 1933–1945, "Quotations," p. 13.

104. Stern et al., *Eskimos, Reindeer and Land*, 26.

105. Carl Lomen, 1931 testimony in *The Eskimo* 11, no. 4 (October 1994), 1.

106. Reindeer Committee Report of 1931, in *United States v. Lomen & Co.*, April 17, 1931, NARA DC RG 75, CCF 1907–1939.

107. Ellanna and Sherrod, *From Hunters to Herders*, 60–61.

108. Survey of the Alaska Reindeer Service, 1931–1933, p.2, NARA AK RG 75, Alaska Reindeer Service Historical Files, File: Reports 1933.

109. C. L. Andrews, Protest against Action of Investigators in Reindeer Survey, p. 7, NARA MD RG 126, CCF 1907–1951, File 9-1-33.

110. Kenneth R. Philip, "The New Deal and Alaskan Natives, 1936–1945," in *An Alaska Anthology: Interpreting the Past*, ed. Stephen W. Haycox and Mary Childer Mangusso (Seattle: University of Washington Press, 1996), 267–86.

111. House of Representatives, "Alaska Legislation: Hearing before the Committee on the Territories," 75th Cong., 1st. Sess. (June 15 and 22, 1937), 2.

112. J. Sidney Rood, *Narrative Re: Alaska Reindeer Herds for Calendar Year 1942, with Supplementary Data* (Nome: U.S. Bureau of Indian Affairs Alaska, 1943), 151.

113. Gideon Barr, quoted in Ellanna and Sherrod, *From Hunters to Herders*, 48.

114. Rood, *Narrative Re: Alaska Reindeer*, 151.

CHAPTER 6: THE CLIMATE OF CHANGE

1. J. Olofsson, S. Stark and L. Oksanen, "Reindeer Influence on Ecosystem Process in the Tundra," *Oikos* 105, no. 2 (May 2004): 386–96; Johan Olofsson et al., "Effects of Summer Grazing by Reindeer on Composition of Vegetation, Productivity, and Nitrogen Cycling," *Ecography* 24, no. 1 (February 2001): 13–24; Heidi Kitti, B. C. Forbes and Jari Oksanen, "Long- and Short-term Effects of Reindeer Grazing on Tundra Wetland Vegetation," *Polar Biology* 32, no. 2 (February 2009): 253–61; Forbes and Kumpula, "The Ecological Role and Geography of Reindeer," 1356–80.

2. Krupnik, *Arctic Adaptations*, 143–47; Anne Gunn, "Voles, Lemmings and Caribou—Population Cycles Revisited?" *Rangifer* 23, Special Issue no. 14 (2003): 105–11; J. Putkonen and G. Roe, "Rain-on-snow Events Impact Soil Temperatures and Affect Ungulate Survival," *Geophysical Research Letters* 30, no. 4 (February 2003), DOI: 10.1029/2002GL016326; Baskin, "Reindeer Husbandry," 23–29. The classic work on Arctic population cycles is Christian Vibe, "Arctic Animals in Relation to Climatic Fluctuations," *Meddelelser om Grønland* 170, no. 5 (1967).

3. Liv Solveig Vors and Mark Stephen Boyce, "Global Declines of Caribou and Reindeer," *Global Change Biology* 15, no. 11 (November 2009): 2626–33.

4. Vibe, "Arctic Animals," 163–79; Krupnik, *Arctic Adaptations*, 143–48.

5. On collectivization, see Yuri Slezkine, *The House of Government: A Saga*

of the Russian Revolution (Princeton: Princeton University Press, 2017), chap. 12 and Stephen Kotkin, *Stalin: Waiting for Hitler* (New York: Penguin, 2017) chap. 2.

6. Katarina Clark, *The Soviet Novel: History as Ritual* (Bloomington: University of Indiana Press, 1981), 10–17; Jochen Hellbeck, *Revolution on My Mind: Writing a Diary under Stalin* (Cambridge, MA: Harvard University Press, 2006), introduction. The phrase "Long Journey" is adapted from Slezkine, *Arctic Mirrors*, 292.

7. RGIA DV F. R-2413, Op. 4, D. 974, L. 66.

8. RGIA DV F. R-2413, Op. 4, D. 629, L. 93.

9. Dikov, *Istoriia Chukotki*, 211; Garusov, *Sotsialisticheskoe*, 130–32. Such slaughter was common across the Soviet Union; see Bruno, *The Nature of Soviet Power*, chap. 4.

10. TsKhSDMO F. 22, Op. 1, D. 2, L. 35.

11. Stalin, quoted in Viktor Grigorevich Vasilev, M. T. Kiriushina and N. A. Menshikov, *Dva goda v tundre* (Leningrad: Izd-vo Glavsevmorputi, 1935), 3.

12. Dikov, *Istoriia*, 212–13.

13. RGAE F. 9570, Op. 2, D. 3483, L. 31.

14. Iatgyrgin interview in Z. G. Omrytkheut, "Ekho Berezovskogo vosstaniia: Ochevidtsy o sobytiiakh 1940 i 1949 gg," in Bogoslovskaya et al., *Tropoiu Bogoraza*, 91–92. Vladislav Nuvano argues that the murderer was a Koryak refugee in Chukotka—personal communication, May 2014.

15. Iatgyrgin in Omrytkheut, "Ekho Berezovskogo," 91.

16. Garusov, *Sotsialisticheskoe*, 131. The above account is taken from Garusov.

17. RGAE F. 9570, Op. 2, D. 3483, L. 17, 14, 15, 64.

18. GAChAO. F. R-16, Op. 1, D. 13, L. 34–41.

19. Raizman, "Shaman byl protiv," 95–96, quote from 100.

20. Decade-by-decade averages of Chukotka's domestic reindeer are from Patty Gray, "Chukotkan Reindeer Husbandry in the Twentieth Century," in *Cultivating Arctic Landscapes: Knowing and Managing Animals in the Circumpolar North*, ed. David Anderson and Mark Nutall (New York: Berghahn Books, 2004), 143.

21. K. R. Wood and J. E. Overland, "Early 20th Century Arctic Warming in Retrospect," *International Journal of Climatology* 30, no. 9 (July 2010): 1269–79.

22. Wolves might have been on the increase earlier; in 1928, the Soviets issued a bounty. See GAChAO F. R-2, Op. 1, D. 2, L. 19.

23. *Tradition* is the word used by L. David Mech and Rolf O. Peterson to describe how packs hunt; see "Wolf-Prey Relations" in *Wolves: Behavior, Ecology, and Conservation*, ed. L. David Mech and Luigi Boitani (Chi-

cago: University of Chicago Press, 2003), 131–57. For wolf mental processes, see L. David Mech, "Possible Use of Foresight, Understanding, and Planning by Wolves Hunting Muskoxen," *Arctic* 60, no. 2 (June 2007): 145–49. The rest of this paragraph is summarized from Mech and Boitani, ed., *Wolves: Behavior, Ecology, and Conservation*, 1–34, 66–103, 161–92; Marco Musiani et al., "Differentiation of Tundra/Taiga and Boreal Coniferous Forest Wolves: Genetics, Coat Color, and Association with Migratory Caribou," *Molecular Ecology* 16, no. 19 (October 2007): 4149-70; and Gary Marvin, *Wolf* (London: Reaktion Books, 2012), 11–34.

24. A. T. Bergerud, Stuart N. Luttich, and Lodewijk Camps, *The Return of the Caribou to Ungava* (Montreal: McGill-Queens University Press, 2008), 10; Layne G. Adams et al, "Population Dynamics and Harvest Characteristics of Wolves in the Central Brooks Range, Alaska," *Wildlife Monographs* 170, no. 1 (2008): 1–18.

25. Burch, *Caribou Herds*, 53.

26. APRCA, Fosma and Sidney Rood Papers, Box 1, J. Sidney Rood, "Alaska Reindeer Notes," p. 1.

27. Reindeer Supervisor, May 1925, NARA AK RG 75, Alaska Reindeer Service Historical Files, File: History-general, 1933–1945. There were scattered reports of wolves in 1909, but concern mounts after 1925.

28. Brief Statement Regarding the Wolf Problem on Reindeer Ranges, May 18, 1940, NARA DC RG 75, BIA CCF 1940–1957, File: 43179.

29. National Research Council, *Wolves, Bears and Their Prey in Alaska* (Washington, DC: National Academy Press, 1997), 49.

30. Sidney Rood, Message to Association of Bering Unit Herds, April 8, 1943, NARA AK RG 75, Alaska Reindeer Service Historical Files, File: History-general, 1933–1945.

31. On foreigners' conceptions of wolves, see K. S. Robisch, *Wolves and the Wolf Myth in American Literature* (Reno, NV: University of Nevada Press, 2009), and Jon Coleman, *Vicious: Wolves and Men in America* (New Haven, CT: Yale University Press, 2006).

32. Report from Wainwright, AK, July 9, 1936, NARA AK RG 75, Reindeer Service Decimal Correspondence, File: Predators, 1936–1937.

33. G. Collins to S. Rood, March 24, 1937, NARA AK RG 75, Reindeer Service Decimal Correspondence, File: Predators, 1936–1937.

34. Jennifer McLerran, *A New Deal for Native Art: Indian Arts and Federal Policy, 1933–1943* (Tuscon, AZ: University of Arizona Press, 2009), 107.

35. Russell Annabel, "Reindeer Round-Up," NARA AK RG 75, Reindeer Service Decimal Correspondence, File: General Correspondence 1901–1945.

36. Noatak Teacher to Mr. Glenn Briggs, January 25, 1937, NARA AK RG 75, Reindeer Service Decimal Correspondence, File: Predators, 1936–1937.

37. Ross, *Pioneering Conservation*; Donald McKnight, *The History of Predator Control in Alaska* (Juneau: Alaska Department of Fish and Game, 1970), 3, 6–8. These numbers are for all of Alaska.

38. Press Release, Fish and Wildlife Service, December 1, 1941, NARA MD RG 126, CCF 1907–1951; Sidney Rood to Major Dale Gaffney, January 21, 1941, NARA AK RG 75, Reindeer Service Decimal Correspondence, File: Predators, 1940–1941.

39. APRCA, Ernest S. Burch Jr. Papers, Series 5, Box 220, File: Kivalina, Jimmy and Hannah Hawley interview, p. 35; see also Hall, *Eskimo Storyteller*, 167–68, 296–98.

40. Paneak, *In a Hungry Country*, 88, 89.

41. Gubser, *Nunamiut Eskimos*, 266–67.

42. Dan Karmun, UAFOHP Project Jukebox, Tape H2000-102-05, Section 4. See also NARA AK RG 75, Hollingsworth to Area Director Juneau, January 12, 1951, Alaska Reindeer Service Decimal Correspondence, File: Reindeer by-products, misc. 1951.

43. Krupnik, *Arctic Adaptations*, 157–58.

44. Clifford Weyiouanna, UAFOHP Project Jukebox, Tape H2000-102-22, Section 2.

45. The relationship between wolves and ecosystem regulation is debated; for an overview, see Emma Marris, "Rethinking Predators: Legend of the Wolf," *Nature* 507 (March 13, 2014): 158–60.

46. Bogoras, *The Chukchee*, 323.

47. Mukhachev, *Borba za vlast*, 64–65.

48. GARF F. A-310, Op. 18, D. 88, L. 86. Wolf extermination had a long tradition in Russia, and aggression toward humans was apparently more common than in North America; see Will N. Graves's idiosyncratic *Wolves in Russia: Anxiety through the Ages* (Calgary, AB: Detselig, 2007) and Ian Helfant, *That Savage Gaze: Wolves in the Nineteenth-Century Russian Imagination* (New York: Academic Studies Press, 2018). M. P. Pavlov argues that the Russian desire to exterminate wolves goes back at least to the mid-nineteenth century—*Volk* (Moscow: Agropomizdat, 1990), 9–10.

49. Druri, "Kak byl sozdan," 7; P. S. Zhigunov, ed., *Reindeer Husbandry*, trans. Israel Program for Scientific Translations (Springfield, VA: U.S. Department of Commerce, 1968), 177. Baskin argues ("Reindeer Husbandry," 25) that Soviet scientists across the north were dependent on local knowledge as they developed reindeer science.

50. F. Ia. Gulchak, *Reindeer Breeding*, trans. Canadian Wildlife Service (Ottawa: Department of the Secretary of State, Bureau for Translations, 1967), 26.

51. Druri's manual *Olenevodstvo* was published in 1955 and 1963 (Moskva: Izdatelstvo selkhoz literatury, zhurnalov i plakatov, 1963), 39. See also Baskin, *Severnyi olen*.

52. GARF F. A-310, Op. 18, D. 369, L. 10.

53. *SCh*, February 5, 1944.

54. GARF F. A-310, Op. 18, D. 369, L. 3.

55. GAMO F. P-22, Op. 1, D. 180, L. 1, 2.

56. Omrytkheut, "Ekho Berezovskogo," 91–94; Vladislav Nuvano, "Tragediia v selakh Berezovo i Vaegi 1940 i 1949gg," in Bogoslovskaya et al., *Tropoiu Bogoraza*, 85-90; Nuvano, personal communication May 2014.

57. B. M. Andronov, "Kollektivizatsiia po-Chukotski" in Bogoslovskaya et al., *Tropoiu Bogoraza*, 103 (quote), 106. Andronov was a senior security officer in the MGB (another iteration of the internal police) and hints that Rul'tyl'kut was an informant for the security services.

58. Chukchi party membership stayed under twenty percent of Chukotka's total. See Patty Gray, *The Predicament of Chukotka's Indigenous Movement: Post-Soviet Activism in the Russian Far North* (Cambridge, UK: Cambridge University Press, 2005), 97.

59. Victor Keul'kut, *Pust stoit moroz* (Moscow: Molodaia gvadiia, 1958), 44.

60. Tikhon Semushkin, *Alitet Goes to the Hills* (Moscow: Foreign Language Publishing House, 1952), 12, 13.

61. V. G. Kuznetsova, quoted in E. A. Davydova, "'Dobrovolnaia smert' i 'novaia zhizn' v amguemenskoi tundre (Chukotka): Stremlenie ukhoda v mir mertvykh Tymenenentyna," *Vestnik arkheologii, antrpologii i enografii* 4, no. 31 (2015):131–32. See this article for the full case.

62. GARF F. A-310, Op. 18, D. 682, L. 25.

63. RGAE F. 8390, Op. 1, D. 2385, L. 36.

64. Zhigunov, *Reindeer Husbandry*, 187.

65. See, for example, Zhigunov, *Reindeer Husbandry*; Gulchak, *Reindeer Breeding*; Druri, *Olenevodstvo*; E. K. Borozdin and V. A. Zabrodin, *Severnoe olenevodstvo* (Moscow: Kolos, 1979). See also RGAE F. 8390, Op. 1, Del, 2385, L. 35–39.

66. GARF F. A-310, Op. 18, D. 682, L. 48.

67. Zhigunov, *Reindeer Husbandry*, 324. See also V. M. Sdobnikov, "Borba s khishchnikamiin," in *Severnoe olenevodstvo*, ed. P. S. Zhigunov (Moscow: Ogiz-Selhozgiz, 1948), 361.

68. Gray, "Chukotkan Reindeer Husbandry," 143. Gray points out that Chukotka was an experimental region for the move from *kolkhoz* to *sovhkoz*. Caroline Humphrey argues that *sovkhozy* were seen as a more advanced mode of socialist production; see *Marx Went Away— But Karl Stayed Behind* (Ann Arbor: University of Michigan Press, 1998), 93.

69. GAChAO F. R-20, Op. 1, D. 43, L. 6.

70. Zhigunov, *Reindeer Husbandry*, 82; V. Kozlov, "Khoziaistvo idet v goru," in *30 let Chukoskogo natsionalnogo okruga* (Magadan: Magadanskoe Knizhnoe Izdatelstvo, 1960), 65–69.

71. GAChAO F. R-23, Op. 1, D. 51, L. 35.

72. GARF F. A-310, Op. 18, D. 682, L. 30.

73. Zhigunov, *Reindeer Husbandry*, 85.

74. Gulchak, *Reindeer Breeding*, 260–61.

75. GAChAO F. R-2, Op. 1, D. 37, L. 88–90.

76. GARF F. A-310, Op. 18, D. 682, L. 28. On experts, see Slezkine, *Arctic Mirrors*, 350–52.

77. Baskin, "Reindeer Husbandry," 27; Igor Krupnik, "Reindeer Pastoralism in Modern Siberia: Research and Survival during the Time of the Crash," *Polar Research* 19, no. 1 (2000): 49–56.

78. Gulchak, *Reindeer Breeding*, 191.

79. V. Ustinov, *Olenevodstvo na Chukotke* (Magadan: Magadanskoe Knizhnoe Izdatelstvo, 1956), 18, 93.

80. APRCA, Ernest S. Burch Jr. Papers, Series 5, Box 228, File: NANA, Selawik, p. 25; Gubser, *Nunamiut Eskimos*, 151.

81. Stern et al., *Eskimos, Reindeer and Land*, 64–68.

82. Gray, "Chukotkan Reindeer Husbandry," 143.

83. David R. Klein and Vladimir Kuzyakin, "Distribution and Status of Wild Reindeer in the Soviet Union," *Journal of Wildlife Management* 46, no. 3 (July 1982): 728–33; David R. Klein, "Conflicts between Domestic Reindeer and their Wild Counterparts: A Review of Eurasian and North American Experience," *Arctic* 33, no. 4 (December 1980): 739–56.

84. Tom Gray, UAFOHP, Project Jukebox, Tape H2000-102-17, Section 11. See also APRCA, Ernest S. Burch Jr. Papers, Series 3, Box 75, File 1965B, p. 106.

85. Clifford Weyiouanna, UAFOHP, Project Jukebox, Tape H2000-102-22, Section 6.

86. V. N. Andreev, *Dikii severnyi olen v SSSR* (Moscow: Sovetskaia Rossiia, 1975), 71.

87. Sdobnikov, "Borba s khishchnikamiin," 361.

88. Olaus Murie quoted in Ross, *Pioneering Conservation*, 287. See also

Adolph Murie, *The Wolves of Mount McKinley* (Washington, DC: National Park Service, 1944).

89. Graves, *Wolves in Russia*, 59; Marvin, *Wolf*, 144–46; Ken Ross, *Environmental Conflict in Alaska* (Boulder: University of Colorado Press, 2000), 49–75.

90. K. P. Filonov, *Dinamika chislennosti kopytnykh zhivotnykh i zapovednost. Okhotovedenie.* (Moscow: TsNIL Glavokhota RSFSR and Lesnaia promyshlennost, 1977), 88–89. See also Wiener, *A Little Corner of Freedom*, 374–97. For a sample of Soviet debates over wolf culling, see O. Gusev, "Protiv idealizatsii prirody," *Ook* 11 (1978): 25–27; S. S. Shvarts, *Dialog o prirode* (Sverdlovsk: Sredne-uralskoe knizhnoe izdatelstvo, 1977); A. Borodin, "Usilit borbu s volkami," *Ook* 7 (1979): 4–5; G. S. Priklonskii, "Rezko sokratit chislennost" *Ook* 8 (1978): 6; A. S. Rykovskii, "Volk – vrag seroznyi," *Ook* 7 (1978): 8–9; Y. Rysnov, "Ne boites polnostiu unichtozhit volkov," *Ook* 9 (1978): 10; and V. Khramova, "Borba s volkami v viatskikh lesakh," *Ook* 12 (1974): 44.

91. McKnight, *History of Predator Control*, 8; Ross, *Environmental Conflict*, 49–77; D. I. Bibikov, *Volk: Proiskhozhdenie, sistematika, morfologiia, ekologiia* (Moscow: Akademia nauk, 1985), 562–71; Coleman, *Vicious*, chap. 9.

92. Monte Hummel and Justina Ray, *Caribou and the North: A Shared Future* (Toronto: Dundurn Press, 2008), 85.

93. Jim Dau, "Managing Reindeer and Wildlife on Alaska's Seward Peninsula," *Polar Research* 19, no. 1 (2000): 75–82; C. Healy, ed., *Caribou Management Report of Survey-Inventory Activities 1 July 1998–30 June 2000* (Juneau: Alaska Department of Fish and Game Project 3.0, 2001).

94. Gray, "Chukotkan Reindeer Husbandry," 143.

95. Igor Krupnik, "Reindeer Pastoralism." The Zadorin quote appears on p. 50.

96. Kyle Joly et. al., "Linkages between Large-scale Climate Patterns and the Dynamics of Arctic Caribou Populations," *Ecography* 34, no. 2 (April 2011): 345–52; D. E. Russell, A. Gunn, S. Kutz, "Migratory Tundra Caribou and Wild Reindeer," *Arctic Report Card 2018*, http://www.arctic.noaa.gov/Report-Card.

CHAPTER 7: THE UNQUIET EARTH

1. Pielou, *Naturalist's Guide*, 47–61.

2. R. W. Boyle, *Gold: History and Genesis of Deposits* (New York: Van Nostrand Reinhold, 1987). For the Seward Peninsula, see C. L. Sainsbury, *Geology, Ore Deposits and Mineral Potential of the Seward Peninsula, Alaska,*

U.S. Bureau of Mines Open-File Report 73-75, 1975. For Chukotka, see A. V. Volkov and A. A. Sidorov, *Unikalnyi zolotorudnyi raion Chukotki* (Magadan: DVO RAN 2001).

3. Jack London, "In a Far Country," in *Klondike Tales* (New York: Modern Library, 2001), 24.

4. I am indebted to Richard White's *Organic Machine* for this understanding of rivers.

5. Jacob Ahwinona, "Reflections on My Life," in *Communities of Memory: Personal Histories and Reflections on the History, Culture, and Life in Nome and the Surrounding Area* (Nome, AK: George Sabo, 1997), 17–18.

6. Julie Raymond-Yakoubian and Vernae Angnaboogok, "Cosmological Changes: Shifts in Human-Fish Relationships in Alaska's Bering Strait Region," in Tuomas Räsänen and Tania Syrjämaa, *Shared Lives of Humans and Animals: Animal Agency in the Global North* (New York: Routledge, 2017), 106–7.

7. APRCA, Hazel Lindberg Collection, Box 3, Series 1, Folder 52: Jafet Lindeberg, p. 7. In 1866–67, Daniel Libby found evidence of gold; in 1897, on the advice of John Dexter, who operated a small silver mine in the Omilak Mountains, began prospecting at Melsing Creek. Libby convened the first miner's council on the Seward Peninsula. See Terrence Cole, *Nome: City of the Golden Beaches* (Anchorage: Alaska Geographic Society, 1984), 11–24.

8. Jeff Kunkel, with assistance from Irene Anderson, *The Two Eskimo Boys Meet the Three Lucky Swedes*, commissioned by the elders and board of the Sitnasuak Native Corporation (Anchorage: Glacier House, 2002), 11. In another version of this story, Mary Antisarlook showed Lindeberg gold—Charles Forselles, *Count of Alaska: A Stirring Saga of the Great Alaskan Gold Rush: A Biography* (Anchorage: Alaskakrafts, 1993), 13.

9. APRCA, Hazel Lindberg Collection, Box 3, Series 1, Folder 52: Jafet Lindeberg, p. 7–8.

10. Ahwinona, "Reflections," 17–18.

11. APRCA, Hazel Lindberg Collection, Box 3, Series 1, Folder 52: Jafet Lindeberg, p. 7–8.

12. Kunkel, *Two Eskimo Boys*, 13.

13. M. Clark, *Roadhouse Tales, or, Nome in 1900* (Girard, KS: Appeal Publishing, 1902), 14.

14. See Katherine Morse, *The Nature of Gold: An Environmental History of the Klondike Gold Rush* (Seattle: University of Washington Press, 2010), 16–39. For the gold standard, see Catherine R. Schenk, "The Global Gold Market and the International Monetary System," in *The Global Gold Market and the International Monetary System from the Late 19th Century to*

the Present: Actors, Networks, Power, ed. Sandra Bott (New York: Palgrave Macmillan, 2013), 17–38.

15. Andrew Carnegie, *The Gospel of Wealth* (New York: The Century Co., 1901), 94.

16. For an overview of this period, see Richard White, *The Republic for Which It Stands* (New York: Oxford University Press, 2017), 831–54; on capitalism, see David Montgomery, *Citizen Worker: The Experience of Workers in the United States with Democracy and the Free Market during the Nineteenth Century* (Cambridge, MA: Harvard University Press, 1993).

17. Edwin B. Sherzer, *Nome Gold: Two Years of the Last Great Gold Rush in American History, 1900–1902*, ed. Kenneth Kutz (Darien, CT: Gold Fever Pub, 1991), 27. See also M. Clark, *Roadhouse Tales*, 95; London, "In a Far Country," 24.

18. My analysis here is drawn from White, *Republic for Which*, 237–39.

19. Sherzer, *Nome Gold*, 27.

20. M. Clark, *Roadhouse Tales*, 95. Politically, many of the gold rushers espoused views along the populist spectrum—see Charles Postel, *The Populist Vision* (New York: Oxford University Press, 2007); Robert Johnston, *The Radical Middle Class: Populist Democracy and the Question of Capitalism in Progressive-Era Portland, Oregon* (Princeton, NJ: Princeton University Press, 2003).

21. Joseph Grinnell, *Gold Hunting in Alaska*, ed. Elizabeth Grinnell (Elgin, IL: David C. Cook, 1901), 90, 13. For the idea of freedom, see Paula Mitchell Marks, *Precious Dust: The American Gold Rush Era, 1848–1900* (New York: William Morrow, 1994), 372–73 and Morse, *Nature of Gold*, 117–25.

22. M. Clark, *Roadhouse Tales*, 95.

23. M. Clark, *Roadhouse Tales*, 95.

24. *NN*, January 1, 1900. Unable to determine who found gold first, the newspaper printed multiple versions of this story.

25. Rex Beach, "The Looting of Alaska," *Appleton's Booklovers' Magazine*, January-May 1906: 7.

26. Grinnell, *Gold Hunting*, 89.

27. "At Least $400,000," *Nome News*, October 9, 1899.

28. Jeff Kunkel, ed., *Alaska Gold: Life on the New Frontier, 1989–1906, Letters and Photographs of the McDaniel Brothers* (San Francisco: California Historical Society, 1997), 87.

29. APRCA, Memoirs and Reminiscences Collection, Box 3, Daniel Libby to H. R. Mac Iver, October 25, 1899, p. 4.

30. "More Rosy Tales of the Golden Sands on Beaches at Cape Nome," *SFC*, September 12, 1899.

31. James H. Ducker, "Gold Rushers North: A Census Study of the Yukon and Alaska Gold Rushes, 1896–1900," in Haycox and Mangusso, *Alaska Anthology*, 206–21.

32. Sherzer, *Nome Gold*, 25.

33. L. H. French, *Nome Nuggets: Some of the Experiences of a Party of Gold Seekers in Northwestern Alaska in 1900* (New York: Montross, Clarke and Emmons, 1901), 34.

34. Edward S. Harrison, *Nome and the Seward Peninsula: History, Description, Biographies* (Seattle: Metropolitan Press, 1905), 58.

35. Kunkel, *Alaska Gold*, 141.

36. Captain of the Steamer *Perry* to the Secretary of the Treasury, June 23, 1900, NARA AK RG 26, M-641, Roll 8. See also Lieutenant Jarvis to the Secretary of the Treasury, September 5, 1899, NARA AK RG 26, M-641, Roll 8.

37. E. S. Harrison, *Nome and the Seward Peninsula*, 53.

38. Sherzer, *Nome Gold*, 45; M. Clark, *Roadhouse Tales*, 36; Lanier McKee, *The Land of Nome: A Narrative Sketch of the Rush to Our Bering Sea Gold-Fields, the Country, Its Mines and Its People, and the History of a Great Conspiracy 1900–1901* (New York: Grafton Press, 1902), 32.

39. Miners noticed the caribou population on the Seward Peninsula was still almost nonexistent—McKee, *Land of Nome*, 97; M. Clark, *Roadhouse Tales*, 155.

40. M. Clark, *Roadhouse Tales*, 89.

41. "Chloroformed and Robbed of $1,300," *Nome Chronicle*, November 17, 1900; "Knock Out Drop Was Employed," *Nome Chronicle*, September 29, 1900; "Stole Muther's Safe," *Nome Gold Digger*, November 1, 1899.

42. Sherzer, *Nome Gold*, 38; some mistook caches of food left at wintering sites as free for the taking. See Senate Subcommittee of Committee on Territories, *Conditions in Alaska*, pt. 2, p. 159; E. S. Harrison, *Nome and the Seward Peninsula*, 31.

43. APRCA, Ernest S. Burch Jr. Papers, Series 3, Box 74, file "California Yearly Meeting of Friends," Martha Hadley Report.

44. *Nome Daily News*, August 2, 1900.

45. Kunkel, *Two Eskimo Boys*, 17, 22–25.

46. Quoted in Mitchell, *Sold American*, 144.

47. *NN*, November 12, 1904. For a history of Quartz Creek, see Mitchell, *Sold American*, 146–48.

48. *NN*, August 12 1903.

49. Ellanna and Sherrod, *From Hunters to Herders*, 54.

50. APRCA, Memoirs and Reminiscences Collection, Box 3, Folder 53: Manuscript by Daniel Libby, p. 4.

51. Ahwinona, "Reflections," 18. See also Kunkel, *Two Eskimo Boys*, 19–20.

52. Cole, *Nome*, 79–90.

53. Case 102, NARA AK RG 21, M-1969, Roll 4.

54. Ed Wilson to President Theodore Roosevelt, October 4, 1901, NARA MD RG 126, Office of Territories Classified Files 1907–1951, File 9-120. The letter was signed by almost fifty miners.

55. Senate Subcommittee of Committee on Territories, *Conditions in Alaska*, pt. 2, 176.

56. M. Clark, *Roadhouse Tales*, 13.

57. Grinnell, *Gold Hunting*, 12.

58. See Sherzer, *Nome Gold*, 42–43; see also APRCA, William J. Woleben Papers, Transcript of Diary 1900, p. 4, and Grinnell, *Gold Hunting*, 96. The gender dynamics in Nome were similar to those in other rush towns—see Susan Lee Johnson, *Roaring Camp: The Social World of the California Gold Rush* (New York: W. W. Norton, 2000), chaps. 2 and 3.

59. Sherzer, *Nome Gold*, 37.

60. Grinnell, *Gold Hunting*, 88.

61. APRCA, William J. Woleben Papers, Transcript of Diary 1900, p. 21.

62. Otto Halla, "The Story of the Nome Gold Fields," *Mining and Scientific Press*, March 1, 1902, p. 116.

63. K. I. Bogdanovich, *Ocherki Chukotskogo poluostrova* (St. Petersburg: A. S. Suvorin, 1901), 19.

64. This is from a secondhand account by Jane Woodworth Bruner, "The Czar's Concessionaires: The East Siberian Syndicate of London; A History of Russian Treachery and Brutality," *Overland Monthly* 44, no. 4 (October 1904): 411–22, 414–15.

65. Bogdanovich, *Ocherki Chukotskogo*, 34.

66. Ivan Korzukhin, *Chto nam delat s Chukotskim poluostrovom?* (St. Petersburg: A. S. Suvorin, 1909), 27–28.

67. For an overview of tsarist mining law, see Michael Melancon, *The Lena Goldfields: Massacre and the Crisis of the Late Tsarist State* (College Station, TX: Texas A&M University Press, 2006), 28–32, 40–46.

68. V. Vonliarliarskii, *Chukotskii poluostrov: ekspeditsiia V. M. Vonliarliarskogo i otkrytie novogo zolotonosnogo raiona bliz ust'ia r. Anadyria, 1900–1912 gg.* (St. Petersburg: K. I. Lingard, 1913), 21–26.

69. Anonymous, *Zabytaia okraina* (St. Petersburg: A. S. Suvorin, 1902): 60–62 (Thomas Owen identifies—correctly, I think—Ivanov as the author); "Chukchi Gold: American Enterprise and Russian Xenophobia in the

Northeastern Siberia Company," *Pacific Historical Review* 77, no. 1 (February 2008): 49–85.

70. Korzukhin, *Chto nam delat,* 27–28.

71. RGIA DV F.702, Op. 7, D. 85, L. 141.

72. Vonliarliarskii, *Chukotskii poluostrov,* 14.

73. Owen, "Chukchi Gold," 60–65.

74. Ivan A. Korzukhin, *Chukotskii poluostrov* (St. Petersburg: Yakor, 1907), 3–4. Other versions of these trips are in W. B. Jones, *Argonauts of Siberia,* 70–71, and Lucile McDonald, "John Rosene's Alaska Activities, Part I," *The Sea Chest: Journal of the Puget Sound Maritime Historical Society* 10 (March 1977): 107–21, 114. McDonald's articles contain verbatim quotes from Rosene's lost memoir.

75. Swenson, *Northwest of the World,* 8, 13.

76. Lucile McDonald, "John Rosene's Alaska Activities, Part II," *The Sea Chest: Journal of the Puget Sound Maritime Historical Society* 10 (June 1977): 131–41, 138. See also RGIA DV F. 1370, Op. 1, D. 4, L. 119.

77. McDonald, "John Rosene's . . . Part II," 138; Swenson, *Northwest of the World,* 17–18.

78. Konstantin N. Tulchinskii, "Iz puteshestviia k Beringovomu prolivu," *Izvestiia Imperatorskogo Russkogo geografi cheskogo obshchestva* 42, vypusk 2–3 (1906): 521–79. His report is analyzed in RGIA DV F. 1370, Op. 1, D. 4, L. 131–144.

79. N. Tulchinskii, quoted in Vdovin, *Ocherki istorii,* 261.

80. RGIA DV F. 702, Op. 2, D. 324, L. 8.

81. RGIA DV F. 1005, Op. 1, D. 220, L. 7.

82. RGIA DV F. 1008, Op. 1, D. 16, L. 31. Most of the miners were members of the peasant estate, or *soslovie.* A few were from the *raznochintsy* (literally, people of various ranks). There is little other information about their origins.

83. RGIA DV F. 1008, Op. 1, D. 16, L. 117.

84. RGIA DV F. 1008, Op. 1, D. 16, L. 27–28. Numbers of arrests are hard to find, as some Chukotka records burned.

85. Preston Jones, *Empire's Edge: American Society in Nome, Alaska 1898–1934* (Fairbanks: University of Alaska Press, 2007), 87. Ruthmary McDowell remembered her father's friends organizing a party to prospect in Chukotka between 1906 and 1913, only to be exiled—APRCA, Ruthmary McDowell Papers, Box 1, Folder 32, p. 1.

86. RGIA DV F. 702, Op. 2, D. 324, L. 34–36. See also RGIA DV F. 702, Op. 2, D.285, L. 9–15.

87. RGIA DV F. 1005, Op. 1, D. 220, L. 114, 84. A *verst* is about two-thirds of a mile.

88. RGIA DV F. 702, Op. 3, D. 563, L. 147–148.

89. RGIA DV F. 1005, Op. 1, D. 220, L. 84 (quote), 8, 7.

90. RGIA DV F. 1008, Op. 1, D. 16, L. 117. Some local officials were clearly sympathetic with the miners; l. 31.

91. APRCA, Reed Family Collection, Subseries 3, Box 14, Leonard Smith, "History of Dredges in Nome Placer Fields," no page numbers.

92. Alfred H. Brooks, "Placer Mining in Alaska," in *Contributions to Economic Geology 1903*, ed. S. F. Emmons and C. W. Hayes (Washington, DC: Government Printing Office, 1904), 43–59; Halla, "Story of the Nome Gold Fields," 116.

93. E. S. Harrison, *Nome and the Seward Peninsula*, 69.

94. Brooks, "Placer Mining in Alaska," 53.

95. E. S. Harrison, *Nome and the Seward Peninsula*, 271.

96. Cole, *Nome*, 99.

97. McKee, *Land of Nome*, 28.

98. S. Hall Young, *Alaska Days with John Muir* (New York: Fleming H. Revell, 1915), 210–11; John Muir, *Our National Parks* (1902; repr. Madison: University of Wisconsin Press, 1981), 12.

99. McKee, *Land of Nome*, 105.

100. Leighton and Leighton, "Eskimo Recollections," 58.

101. Ellanna and Sherrod, *From Hunters to Herders*, 55–57. See also Senate Subcommittee to Committee on Territories, *Conditions in Alaska*, 107, 203; Mikkelsen, *Conquering the Arctic Ice*, 377; DeWindt, *Through the Gold Fields*, 32–33.

102. APRCA, Smith, "History of Dredges," no page numbers. The trend toward corporate mergers was a national one; see Richard White, *Railroaded: The Transcontinentals and the Making of Modern America* (W. W. Norton & Company, 2011); Charles Perrow, *Organizing America: Wealth, Power, and the Origins of Corporate Capitalism* (Princeton, NJ: Princeton University Press, 2002); and Olivier Zunz, *Making America Corporate, 1870–1920* (Chicago: University of Chicago Press, 1990).

103. Alfred Brooks, "The Development of the Mining Industry," United States Geological Survey Bulletin No. 328 (Washington, DC: Government Printing Office, 1909), 31. See also Theodore Chapin, "Placer Mining on the Seward Peninsula," United States Geological Survey Bulletin No. 592 (Washington, DC: Government Printing Office, 1914), 385.

104. APRCA, June Metcalfe Northwest Alaska Collection, Box 1, Series 1, Folder 17: Arthur Olsen Diary, 1906–1907, p. 10–13, 31.

105. *Report of the Mine Inspector for the Territory of Alaska to the Secretary of the Interior for the Fiscal Year Ended June 30, 1914* (Washington: Government Printing Office, 1914), 10–12.

106. The World Federation of Miners was an official syndicate of the International Workers of the World, the most radical of the unions. For strikes, see P. Jones, *Empire's Edge*, 58, 72–74, 82.

107. "Labor Ticket Will Be in the Field," *NTWN*, March 8, 1906; "Radical Change Is Wanted By People," *NTWN*, March 20, 1906; *NTWN*, April 4, 1906; and *NN* November 5, 1908.

108. Joseph Sullivan, "Sourdough Radicalism: Labor and Socialism in Alaska, 1905–1920," in Haycox and Mangusso, *Alaska Anthology*, 222–37. For the broader context, see Thomas Andrews, *Killing for Coal: America's Deadliest Labor War* (Cambridge, MA: Harvard University Press 2010) and Mark T. Wyman, *Hard Rock Epic: Western Miners and the Industrial Revolution, 1860–1910* (Berkeley: University of California Press, 1979).

109. "Preamble and Platform, Socialist Party of Alaska, 1914," quoted in Sullivan, "Sourdough Radicalism," 224.

110. Reports of John Creighton, reproduced in James Thomas Gay, "Some Observations of Eastern Siberia, 1922," *Slavonic and East European Review* 54, no. 2 (April 1976): 248–61, 251.

111. *Nome Industrial Worker*, December 13, 1915. Socialists in Alaska met a similar fate to socialists around the United States; see Eric Foner, "Why Is There No Socialism in the United States?" *History Workshop*, no. 17 (Spring 1984): 59–80.

112. UAA, Wilson W. Brine Papers, Box 1, File: letters 1923, Letter of June 28, 1923. See also *NN*, June 19, 1920.

113. V. Lenin quoted in Siegfried G. Schoppe and Michel Vale, "Changes in the Function of Gold within the Soviet Foreign Trade System Since 1945–46," *Soviet and Eastern European Foreign Trade* 15, no. 3 (Fall 1979): 60–95, esp. 61.

114. RGAE, F. 2324, Op. 16, D. 43, L. 74. For Soviet debates about trade and currency, see Oscar Sanchez-Sivony, *Red Globalization: The Political Economy of the Soviet Cold War from Stalin to Khrushchev* (New York: Cambridge University Press, 2014), 33–37; Alec Nove, *An Economic History of the U.S.S.R.* (London: Penguin, 1989), 147–53; R. A. Belousov, *Ekonomicheskaia istoriia Rossii XX vek* (Moscow: Izdat, 2000), 2: 371–77.

115. Stalin's statement is translated in full in Michal Reiman's *The Birth of Stalinism: The U.S.S.R. on the Eve of the "Second Revolution"* (Bloomington: Indiana University Press, 1987), 128–33.

116. I. L. Iamzin and V. P. Voshchinin, *Uchenie o kolonizatsii i pereseleniiakh* (Moscow: Gosizdat, 1926), 222.

117. RGIA DV F. R-2333, Op. 1, D. 128, L. 375.

118. S. Sukhovii, "Kamchatskie bogatstva i ovladenie imi gosudarstvom," *Ekonomicheskaia zhizn Dalnego Vostoka*, no. 1 (1923): 15–17.

119. A. I. Kaltan, "Otchet po obsledovaniiu Chukotskogo poluostrova 1930/1931 g.," reprinted in Bogoslovskaya et al., *Tropoiu Bogoraza*, 330, and V. T. Pereladov, "Otkrytie pervoi promyshlennoi rossypi zolota na Chukotke," in Bogoslovskaya et al., *Tropoiu Bogoraza*, 283.

120. Niobe Thompson, *Settlers on the Edge: Identity and Modernization on Russia's Arctic Frontier* (Vancouver: University of British Columbia Press, 2008), 4–5.

121. RGIA DV F. R-2350, Op. 1, D. 26, L. 23. Such private mining activity appears to have been common in the Far East—A. I. Shirokov, *Gosudarstvennaia politika na Severo-Vostoke Rossii v 1920–1950-kh gg.: Opyt i uroki istorii* (Tomsk: Izd-vo Tom., 2009), chap. 2. In this period, the state gave concessions to local prospectors, but all gold had to be turned over to the state—RGIA DV F. R-2333, Op. 1, D. 256, L.1–2.

122. RGIA DV F. R-2333, Op. 1, D. 128, L. 376.

123. "All Nome Attends Yuba Launching," *NN,* June 2, 1923.

124. P. Jones, *Empire's Edge*, 95.

125. Alfred Brooks et al., "Mineral Resources of Alaska, Report on Progress of Investigations in 1914," United States Geological Survey Bulletin No. 622 (Washington, DC: Government Printing Office, 1915), 69; Alfred Brooks et al., "Mineral Resources of Alaska, Report on Progress of Investigations in 1919," United States Geological Survey Bulletin No. 714-A (Washington, DC: Government Printing Office, 1921), 10.

126. APRCA, Janet Virginia Lee Papers, Box 4: Photographs, and APRCA, Smith, "History of Dredges," no page numbers.

127. J. B. Mertie, Jr., "Placer Mining on Seward Peninsula," United States Geological Survey Bulletin No. 662 (Washington, DC: Government Printing Office, 1917): 455.

128. On ecosystem impact, see Erwin E. Van Nieuwenhuyse and Jacqueline D. LaPerriere, "Effects of Placer Gold Mining on Primary Production in Subarctic Streams of Alaska," *Journal of the American Water Resources Council* 22, no. 1 (February 1986): 91–99; A. M. Miller and R. J. Piorkowski, "Macroinvertebrate Assemblages in Streams of Interior Alaska Following Alluvial Gold Mining," *River Research and Applications* 20, no. 6 (November 2004): 719–31; James B. Reynolds, Rodney C. Simmons, and Alan R. Burkholder, "Effects of Placer Mining Discharge on Health and Food of Arctic Grayling," *Journal of the American Water Resources Association* 25, no. 3 (June 1989): 625–35; and David M. Bjerklie and Jacqueline D. LaPerriere, "Gold-Mining Effects on Stream Hydrology and Water Quality, Circle Quadrangle, Alaska," *Journal of the American Water Resources Association* 21, no. 2 (April 1985): 235–42.

CHAPTER 8: THE ELEMENTS OF REDEMPTION

1. Bogoras, *The Chukchee*, 285, 14.

2. For an overview, see Mats Ingulstad, Espen Storli, and Andrew Perchard, "The Path of Civilization Is Paved with Tin Cans," in *Tin and Global Capitalism, 1850–2000: A History of the "Devil's Metal,"* ed. Mats Ingulstad, Espen Storli and Andrew Perchard (New York: Routledge, 2014), 1–21 and Ernest Hedges, *Tin and Its Alloys* (London: Royal Society of Chemistry, 1985).

3. John McCannon, *Red Arctic: Polar Exploration and the Myth of the North in the Soviet Union 1932–1939* (New York: Oxford University Press, 1998), 61–70, 119–127.

4. Otto Schmidt's foreword in Lazar Brontman, *On the Top of the World: The Soviet Expedition to the North Pole, 1937* (London: Victor Gollancz, 1938), xi–xiii.

5. Ivan Papanin, *Life on an Ice Floe*, trans. Helen Black (New York: Messner, 1939), 36. On new coverage, see Karen Petrone, *Life Has Become More Joyous, Comrades: Celebrations in the Time of Stalin* (Bloomington: University of Indiana Press, 2000), chap. 3.

6. Quoted in McCannon, *Red Arctic*, 84.

7. M. I. Rokhlin, *Chukotskoe olovo* (Magadan: Magadanskoe knizhnoe izdatelstvo, 1959), quotes from 59, 20, 21, and 51.

8. Speech quoted in N. N. Dikov, *Istoriia Chukotki*, 199.

9. RGAE F. 9570, Op. 2, D. 3483, L. 6.

10. Rokhlin, *Chukotskoe olovo*, 58.

11. Volkov and Sidorov, *Unikalnye zolotorudnye*, 7.

12. McCannon, *Red Arctic*, 57–59.

13. RGAE F. 9570, Op. 2, D.3483, L. 59.

14. Frederick C. Fearing, "Alaska Tin Deposits," *Engineering and Mining Journal* 110, no. 4 (July 24, 1920): 154–58, 154.

15. Brooks et al., "Mineral Resources of Alaska . . . 1914," 88 (quote), 373.

16. Fearing, "Alaska Tin," 155. More dangers of lode mining, this time for gold, are described by Oscar Brown: APRCA, Oscar Brown Papers, Box 1, pp. 40–41.

17. "Threatened Tin Famine," *Wall Street Journal*, June 2, 1917.

18. Fearing, "Alaska Tin," 158.

19. APRCA, Reed Family Papers, Series: Irving Mckenny, Subseries: Land and Mineral Survey Records, Box 13, File: Seward Peninsula – General, "Report on Conditions on the Seward Peninsula in 1929," no page numbers.

20. David Kennedy, *Freedom from Fear: The American People in Depression and*

Fear, 1929–1945 (New York: Oxford University Press, 1999), 164. This section is drawn from Kennedy, chaps. 1, 2, and 6.

21. Rex Beach, *Cosmopolitan* magazine, 1936, quoted in Kim Heacox, *John Muir and the Ice that Started a Fire: How a Visionary and the Glaciers of Alaska Changed America* (Guilford, CT: Lyons Press, 2014), 198–99.

22. J. A. Nadeau to Roosevelt, May 29, 1935, NARA MD RG 126, CCF 1907–1951, File: 9-1-16. Many of the letters in the 1930s reference the article by Rex Beach in *Cosmopolitan.*

23. Harry Slattery to Mr. Bachelder, August 3, 1936, NARA MD RG 48, CCF 1907–1936, File: 9-1-4 General.

24. Letter to Harold Ickes, January 25, 1934, NARA MD RG 48, CCF 1907–1936, File 1-270, Alaska General 1933.

25. Henry Anderson, "The Little Landers' Land Colonies: A Unique Agricultural Experiment in California," *Agricultural History* 5, no. 4 (October 1931): 142. Also see Willis, *Alaska's Place in the West,* 48–70.

26. "Alaska Reviving Placer Mining," *WP,* December 14, 1930. See also "Alaska Missed by Depression," *Los Angeles Times,* December 14, 1933; "Boom Sighted for Alaska," *Los Angeles Times,* October 8, 1936.

27. Charlotte Cameron, *A Cheechako in Alaska and Yukon* (London: T. Fisher Unwin, 1920), 264. See also Alfred Brooks et al., "Mineral Resources of Alaska, Report on Progress of Investigations in 1916," United States Geological Survey Bulletin No. 662 (Washington, DC: Government Printing Office, 1918), 451, and APRCA, Reed Family Papers, Series: Irving Mckenny, Subseries: Land and Mineral Survey Records, Box 11, File: Correspondence—B. D. Stewart, 1929–1938 and Box 13, File: Seward Peninsula—General.

28. APRCA, Oscar Brown Papers, Box 1, pp. 39–40.

29. *Nome Daily Nugget,* December 1, 1936.

30. Dalstroi was the largest entity in the Gulag system; see David Nordlander, "Capital of the Gulag: Magadan in the Early Stalin Era, 1929–1941," (PhD diss., University of North Carolina, 1997), 136.

31. Steven Barnes argues that the ideal of redemption in the camps must be taken seriously—see *Death and Redemption: The Gulag and the Shaping of Soviet Society* (Princeton, NJ: Princeton University Press, 2011), 57–68. He shares this orientation with Oleg Khlevniuk, *The History of the Gulag: From Collectivization to the Great Terror,* trans. Vadim A Staklo, ed. David Nordlander (New Haven, CT: Yale University Press, 2004) and Lynne Viola, *The Unknown Gulag: The Lost World of Stalin's Special Settlements* (New York: Oxford University Press, 2007). Jeffery Hardy argues that reeducation and social redemption were part of larger global trends: *The Gulag after Stalin: Redefining Punishment in Khrushchev's Soviet*

Union, 1953–1964 (Ithaca, NY: Cornell University Press, 2016). I follow Barnes's approach over works that emphasize pure political repression or economic need. For examples of these, see Galina Ivanova, *Istoriia GULAGa, 1918–1958: sotsialno-ekonomicheskii ipolitico-pravovoi aspekty* (Moscow: Nauka, 2006) and Anne Applebaum, *Gulag: A History* (New York: Doubleday, 2003).

32. *Belomor,* a book celebrating the use of forced labor, quoted in Barnes, *Death and Redemption,* 14.

33. GAMO F. R-23, Op. 1, D.1, L. 168.

34. Nordlander, "Capital of the Gulag," 72–73; on the Depression era in Soviet policy, see Sanchez-Sibony, *Red Globalization,* chapter 1.

35. Nearly a million people passed through Kolyma between 1932 and 1953. See A. I. Shirokov, *Gosudarstvennaia politika,* 203–4, 326; I. D. Batsaev and A. G. Kozlov, *Dalstroi i Sevvostlag OGPU-NKVD CCCR v tsifrakh I dokumentakh* (Magadan: RAN DVO, 2002), 1:6, 1:15; V. G. Zeliak, *Piat metallov Dalstroia: Istoriia gornodobyvaiushchei promyshlennosti Severo-Vostoka v 30-kh–50-kh gg. XX v.* (Magadan: Ministerstvo obrazova-niia i nauki RF, 2004), 293; and Nordlander, "Capital of the Gulag," 312–13.

36. Accounting for death in the Kolyma camps is difficult; see Khlevniuk, *History of the Gulag,* 320–23. Batsaev and Kozlov (*Dalstroi i Sevvostlag* 1: 6) estimate 130,000 people died in the Kolyma before 1951. This total does not include those killed during mass executions, ten thousand or more of whom were shot in 1937–1939—see Khlevniuk, *History of the Gulag,* 170–71.

37. Sergei Larkov and Fedor Romanenko, *"Vragi naroda" za poliarnym kru-gom* (Moscow: Paulson, 2010), 21–162. For the camps during the purges, see Shirokov, *Gosudarstvennaia politika,* 190–200.

38. I. D. Batsaev, *Ocherki istorii magadanskoi oblasti nachalo 20kh—seredina 60kh gg XX* (Magadan: RAN DVO, 2007), 59, and Shirokov, *Gosudarst-vennaia politika,* chap. 3.

39. RGAE F. 9570, Op. 2, D. 3483, L. 6.

40. The rate of gold production increase did slow; see Batsaev, *Ocherki isto-rii magadanskoi oblasti,* 64.

41. Quoted in Alexandr Kozlov, "Pervyi director," *Politicheskaia agitatsiia,* nos. 17–18 (September 1988): 27–32.

42. Chaunskii Raisovet, 11 January 1942, in *Sovety severo-vostoka SSSR (1941–1961 gg.): sbornik dokumentov i materialov,* chast 2, ed. A. I. Krushanov (Magadan: Magadanskoe knizhnoe izdatelstvo, 1982), 55–56. On early mining in Chukotka, see Shirokov, *Gosudarstvennaia politika,* 243, and Zeliak, *Piat metallov,* 81.

43. V. Iu. Iankovskii, *Dolgoe vozvrashchenie: Avtobiograficheskaia povest* (Iaro-slavl: Verkhne-Volzh. kn. izd-vo, 1991), 55.

44. Iankovskii, *Dolgoe vozvrashchenie*, 4–5.

45. MSA, F. 1, Op. 2, D.2701: Petr Lisov Papers, L. 33.

46. Michael Solomon, *Magadan* (New York: Vertex, 1971), 85.

47. Tales of the *Dzhurma* were common enough by the late 1940s to enter into historians' accounts, although the authors note the stories could not be substantiated. Martin Bollinger claims that the *Dzhurma* could not have been in the Arctic Ocean in 1934 because Dalstroi did not yet own the vessel; see *Stalin's Slave Ships: Kolyma, the Gulag Fleet, and the Role of the West* (Westport, CT: Praeger, 2003), 65–74.

48. MSA, F. 1, Op. 2, D.2701: Petr Lisov Papers, L. 47; GARF F. 9414, Op. 1d, D.197, L. 2; and GARF F. 9414, Op. 1d, D.161, L. 4.

49. Iankovskii, *Dolgoe vozvrashchenie*, 57, 59.

50. GAMO F. R-23, Op. 1, D.1145, L. 45 (quote), 48; GARF F. 9401, Op. 2, D.235, L. 243.

51. Iankovskii, *Dolgoe vozvrashchenie*, 74, 57, 59 (quote).

52. I. I. Pavlov, *Poteriannye pokoleniia* (Moscow: SPb., 2005), 87.

53. Iankovskii, *Dolgoe vozvrashchenie*, 66.

54. Zeliak, *Piat metallov*, 213–14.

55. V. F. Grebenkin, "Raduga vo mgle," *Petlia: Vospominaniia, ocherki, doku-menty*, ed. Iu. M. Beledin (Volgograd, 1992), 242; John Lerner, *Prosh-chai, Rossiia!: Memuary "amerikanskogo shpiona*," trans. I. Dashinskogo (Kfar Habad: Yad HaChamisha Press, 2006), 334–35.

56. GAMO F. R-23, Op. 1, D.5501, L. 19–22, 1.

57. GARF F. 8131, Op. 37, D.4477, L. 9.

58. MSA, F. 2, Op. 1, D.263: Alexandr Eremin Papers, L. 61.

59. MSA, F. 1, Op. 2, D.2701: Petr Lisov Papers, L. 33. Malnutrition in the camps varied by location and time; supplies were generally better by the 1950s.

60. Iankovskii, *Dolgoe vozvrashchenie*, 56, 64.

61. I. T. Tvardovskii, *Rodina i chuzhbina: Kniga zhizni* (Smolensk: Posokh: Rusich, 1996), 265. See also MSA, F. 2, Op. 1, D.263: Alexandr Eremin Papers, l. 54. I have found no precise numbers for deaths in the Chu-kotka camps.

62. Raizman, "Shaman byl protiv," 101; GAMO F. R-23, Op. 1, D.5210, Ll. 12–13.

63. MSA, F. 1, Op. 2, D.2701: Petr Lisov Papers, l. 35.

64. MSA, F. 2, Op. 1, D.263: Alexandr Eremin Papers, l. 50; Dalan (V. S. Iakovlev), *Zhizn i sudba moia: Roman-esse* (Iakutsk: Bichik, 2003), 158; A. A. Zorokhovich, "Imet silu pomnit: Rasskazy tekh, kto proshel

ad repressii," *Moskva rabochii* (1991): 199–219, 210. I have found no accounts of escapees reaching Alaska.

65. Iankovskii, *Dolgoe vozvrashchenie*, 65.

66. MSA, F. 2, Op. 1, D.263: Alexandr Eremin Papers, l. 50.

67. John Thoburn, "Increasing Developing Countries' Gains from Tin Mining," in Ingulstad et al., *Tin and Global Capitalism*, 221–39, 225.

68. Zeliak, *Piat metallov*, 291, 295.

69. MSA, F. 1, Op. 2, D.2701: Petr Lisov Papers, l. 35.

70. MSA, F. 2, Op. 1, D.263: Alexandr Eremin Papers, l. 56.

71. Tvardovskii, *Rodina i chuzhbina*, 265–66.

72. Iankovskii, *Dolgoe vozvrashchenie*, 82, 102.

73. Dikov, *Istoriia Chukotki*, 291

74. *Soviet News*, February 12, 1962.

75. GARF F. A-259, Op. 42, D.8340, L. 7, 14.

76. GARF F. A-259, Op. 42, D.8339, L. 50, 10.

77. Quoted in Thompson, *Settlers on the Edge*, 47. On conditions in Chukotka generally, see Thompson, *Settlers on the Edge*, 46–50; A. I. Ivanov, *Lgoty dlya rabotnikov severa* (Moscow: Yuridicheskaya Literatura, 1991); and L. N. Popov-Cherkasov, *Lgoty i preimushchestva roabochim i sluzhshashim* (Moscow: Yuridicheskaya Literatura, 1981).

78. RGAE F. 8390, Op. 1, D.2790, L. 13.

79. Thompson, *Settlers on the Edge*, 4–5.

80. S. I. Balabanov interview with Yuri Slezkine, quoted in *Arctic Mirrors*, 339.

81. Ukrainian mining engineer, quoted in Thompson, *Settlers on the Edge*, 64.

82. Yuri Rytkheu, *Sovremennye legendy* (Leningrad: Sovetskii pisatel, 1980), 213. See also Semushkin, *Chukotka*; Rytkheu, *A Dream in Polar Fog*, trans. I. Yazhbin (New York: Archipelago Books, 2005).

83. Semushkin, *Alitet Goes to the Hills*, 12.

84. Oleg Kuvaev, *Territoriia*, (Moscow: Izdatelstvo Ast, 2016), 182. For a discussion of the versions of Kuvaev's novel, see V. V. Ivanov, *Kuvaevskaia romanistika: Romany O. Kuvaeva "Territoriia i 'Pravila begstva': Istoriia sozdaniia, dukhovnoe i khudozhestvennoe svoeobrazie* (Magadan: Kordis, 2001). Thompson (*Settlers on the Edge*, 68–70) discusses the importance of Kuvaev for his informants.

85. There were many mining novels, including, G. G. Volkov, *Bilibina: Dokum. Povest o pervoi Kolymskoi ekspeditsii 1928–1929 gg.* (Magadan: Kn. izd-vo, 1978), Volkov, *Zolotaia Kolyma: Povest khudozhnik M.Cherkasov* (Magadan: Knizhnoe izd., 1984), and E. K. Ustiev, *U istokov zolotoi reki* (Moscow: Mysl, 1977). Memoirs of geologists also proliferated;

see, G. B. Zhilinskii, *Sledy na zemle* (Magadan, Magadanskoe kn. izdatelstvo, 1975) and N. I. Chemodanov, *V dvukh shagakh ot Severnogo poliusa. Zapiski geologa.* (Magadan: Magadanskoe kn. izdatelstvo 1968).

86. *SCh* January 27, 1961.

87. GAChAO, F. R-130, Op. 1, D.54, L. 18. This file contains multiple reports and measures to decrease mining injuries.

88. Dikov, *Istoriia Chukotki*, 336–39; A. A. Siderov, "Zoloto Chukotkii" (1999), manuscript in author's possession.

89. Quinn Slobodian, *Globalists: The End of Empire and the Birth of Neoliberalism* (Cambridge, MA: Harvard University Press, 2018), chap. 7, and Andy Bruno, *Nature of Soviet Power*, chap. 5.

90. GAChAO, F. R-143, Op. 1, D. 4, L. 38, 2–3. On nature protection, see Weiner, *Little Corner of Freedom*.

91. Joseph Senungetuk, *Give or Take a Century: An Eskimo Chronicle* (San Francisco: Indian Historian Press, 1971), 108.

92. "Alaska: Our Northern Outpost," *Armed Forces Talk* 218: 7, NARA MD RG 126, Office of Territories CF, 1907–1951, File: 9-1-22.

93. "Supporting Materials for Alaska Development Administration Legislation," p. 9, NARA MD RG 126, Office of Territories CF, 1907–1951, File: 9-1-60; "Our Last Frontiers: How Veterans and Others Can Share Them," Department of the Interior Pamphlet, NARA MD RG 126, Office of Territories CF, 1907–1951, File: 9-1-22.

94. "Northwestern Alaska: A Report on the Economic Opportunities of the Second Judicial Division, 1949," p. 2, NARA MD RG 126, Office of Territories CF, 1907–1951, File 9-1-60.

95. James Oliver Curwood, *The Alaskan: A Novel of the North* (New York: Grosset and Dunlap, 1922), 42, 12.

96. Senungetuk, *Give or Take a Century*, 106.

97. House of Representatives, "Alaska Statehood Hearings," 83rd Cong., 1st Sess. (April 1953), 80–86.

98. Hensley, *Fifty Miles*, 111, 124.

99. On mining impact, see Lorne E. Doig, Stephanie T. Schiffer, and Tarsten Liber, "Reconstructing the Ecological Impacts of Eight Decades of Mining, Metallurgical, and Municipal Activities on a Small Boreal Lake in Northern Canada," *Integrated Environmental Assessment and Management* 11, no. 3 (July 2015): 490–501; K. Kidd, M. Clayden, and T. Jardine, "Bioaccumulation and Biomagnification of Mercury through Food Webs," in *Environmental Chemistry and Toxicology of Mercury*, ed. Guanglian Liu, Yong Cai, and Nelson O'Driscoll (Hoboken NJ: Wiley, 2011); R. Eisler, "Arsenic Hazards to Humans, Plants, and

Animals from Gold Mining," *Review of Environmental Contamination and Toxicology* 180 (2004): 133–65; D.B. Donato et al., "A Critical Review of the Effects of Gold Cyanide-Bearing Tailing Solutions on Wildlife," *Environment International* 33, no. 7 (October 2007): 974–984; and R. Eisler, "Mercury Hazards from Gold Mining to Humans, Plants, and Animals," *Review of Environmental Contamination and Toxicology* 181 (2004): 139–98.

100. A. A. Siderov, *Ot Dalstroia SSSR do kriminalnogo kapitalizma* (Magadan: DVO RAN, 2006).

101. Hensley, *Fifty Miles*, 174.

102. Raymond-Yakoubian and Angnabookgok, "Cosmological Changes," 107–9.

103. Ahwinona, "Reflections," 19.

104. A. Vykvyragtyrgyrgyn, personal communication, August 2018.

CHAPTER 9: CALORIC VALUES

1. Mary Nerini, "A Review of Gray Whale Feeding Ecology," in *The Gray Whale:* Eschrichtius Robustus, ed. Mary Lou Jones, Steven L. Swartz, and Stephen Leatherwood (Orlando, FL: Academic Press, 1984), 423–50; and Mary Lou Jones and Steven L. Swartz, "Gray Whale: *Eschrichtius robustus*" in *Encyclopedia of Marine Mammals*, ed. William F. Perrin, Bernd Wursig, and J. G. M. Thewissen (London: Academic Press, 2009), 503–11.

2. T. A. Jefferson, M. A. Webber, and R. L. Pitman, eds., *Marine Mammals of the World: A Comprehensive Guide to Their Identification* (Amsterdam: Elsevier, 2008), 47–50 and 59–65; P. K. Yochem and S. Leatherwood, "Blue Whale *Balaenoptera musculus* (Linnaeus, 1758)" in *Handbook of Marine Mammals, Vol. 3: The Sirenians and Baleen Whales*, ed. S. H. Ridgway and R. Harrison (London: Academic Press, 1985), 193–240; Whitehead and Rendell, *Cultural Lives*, 92–95.

3. Phyllis J. Stabeno et al., "Physical Forcing of Ecosystem Dynamics on the Bering Sea Shelf," in *The Sea: Volume 14B: The Global Coastal Ocean*, ed. Allan R. Robinson and Kenneth Brink (Cambridge, MA: Harvard University Press, 2006), 1177–1212; Bodil A. Bluhm and Rolf Gradinger, "Regional Variability in Food Availability for Arctic Marine Mammals," *Ecological Applications* 18, issue sp2 (March 2008): S77–S96; J. J. Walsh and C. P. McRoy, "Ecosystem Analysis in the Southeastern Bering Sea," *Continental Shelf Research* 5 (1986): 259–88; N. C. Stenseth et al. "Ecological Effects of Climate Fluctuations," *Science* 297, no. 5585 (August 23, 2002): 1292–96.

4. K. R. Johnson and C. H. Nelson, "Side-scan Sonar Assessment of Gray Whale Feeding in the Bering Sea," *Science* 225, no. 4667 (September 14, 1984): 1150–52. On whales in their environment, see Joe Roman et al., "Whales as Marine Ecosystem Engineers"; Croll, Kudela, and Tershy, "Ecosystem Impact"; and P. Kareiva, C. Yuan-Farrell, and C. O'Connor, "Whales Are Big and It Matters," in Estes et al., *Whales, Whaling*, 202–14 and 379–87.

5. GAPK F. 633, Op. 4, D. 85, L. 35–37.

6. On gray whale ferocity, see Krupnik, *Pust govoriat*, 159, 168, 174–175, and Scammon, *Marine Mammals*, 29. On Alaska and Chukotka hunting, William M. Marquette and Howard W. Braham, "Gray Whale Distribution and Catch by Alaskan Eskimos: A Replacement for the Bowhead Whale?" *Arctic* 35, no. 3 (September 1982): 386–94; and Igor Krupnik, "The Bowhead vs. the Gray Whale in Chukotkan Aboriginal Whaling," *Arctic* 40, no. 1 (March 1987): 16–32.

7. Serge Dedina, *Saving the Gray Whale: People, Politics, and Conservation in Baja California* (Tucson, AZ: University of Arizona Press, 2000), 21.

8. RGIA DV F. R-2413, Op. 4, D. 39, L. 165. On hunger: GARF F. 3977, Op. 1, D. 811, L. 68b and RGIA DV. F R-2413, Op. 4, D. 1798, L. 12.

9. GAPK F. 633, Op. 7, D. 19, L. 53–70.

10. GARF F. 3977, Op. 1, D. 423, L. 79.

11. Harvest totals in these years remain incomplete; see Krupnik, "The Bowhead vs. the Gray Whale," 23–25.

12. GARF F. 3977, Op. 1, D. 11, L. 19.

13. GAPK F. 633, Op. 5, D. 3, L. 57–61. See also GAPK F. 633, Op. 7, D. 19, L. 20–21; F. 633, Op. 5, D. 3, L. 39–45.

14. GARF F. 3977, Op. 1, D. 423, L. 79; GAPK F. 633, Op. 5, D. 3, L. 72. Mamonov, the director of fisheries in the Far East, dismissed these reports, believing killing whales took too much work to use nothing of the carcass; L. 73.

15. RGIA DV F. R-2413, Op. 4, D. 39, L. 165.

16. RGIA DV F. R-2413, Op. 4, D. 39, L. 165; GAPK F. 633, Op. 7, D. 19, L. 54.

17. GAPK F. 633, Op. 5, D. 3, L. 72. See also GAPK F. 633, Op. 7, D. 19, L. 71–72.

18. GAPK F. 633, Op. 7, D. 19, L. 71.

19. Kurkpatrick Dorsey, *Whales and Nations: Environmental Diplomacy on the High Seas* (Seattle: University of Washington Press, 2014), 21–22.

20. Dorsey, *Whales and Nations*, 291–92. There is a growing body of literature on twentieth-century whaling, including Dorsey, *Whales and Nations*, D. Graham Burnett's *The Sounding of the Whale: Science and*

Cetaceans in the Twentieth Century (Chicago: University of Chicago Press, 2012); Frank Zelko, *Make it a Green Peace!: The Rise of Countercultural Environmentalism* (New York: Oxford University Press, 2013), Jun Morikawa, *Whaling in Japan: Power, Politics, and Diplomacy* (New York: Columbia University Press, 2009), and Jason Colby, *Orca: How We Came to Know and Love the Ocean's Greatest Predator* (New York: Oxford University Press, 2018). There is a tendency to celebrate (mostly) elite (mostly) white men; an exception is Joshua Reid's *The Sea is My Country: The Maritime World of the Makahs* (New Haven, CT: Yale University Press, 2015).

21. Undated letter, Leonard Carmichael to Robert Murphy, SI RU 7165, Box 23, Folder 6.

22. Dorsey, *Whales and Nations*, 40–45.

23. "The Value of Whales to Science," SI RU 7170, Box 10, Folder: "Information—Whale Press Releases."

24. Robert Philips to Wilbur Carr, September 19, 1930, NARA MD RG 59, Department of State Decimal File 1930–1939, File 562.8F1. On the economics of whale fat, see Mark Cioc, *The Game of Conservation: International Treaties to Protect the World's Migratory Animals* (Athens: Ohio University Press, 2009), 132–33.

25. Cioc, *Game of Conservation*, 128.

26. Convention for the Regulation of Whaling, Geneva, 1931

27. Jolles, *Faith, Food, and Family*, 314–16.

28. Estelle Oozevaseuk, quoted in Fitzhugh et al. *Gifts from the Ancestors*, 206.

29. APRCA, Otto W. Geist Collection, Series 5, Box 9, Folder 40: Paul Silook Diary 1935 (?), p. 7.

30. Oleg Einetegin, in Krupnik, *Pust govoriat*, 172.

31. ChOKM, Matlu, *Avtobiografiia (Rasskaz Matliu)*, Coll. N. 5357.

32. RGIA DV F. R-2413, Op. 4, D. 974, L. 115v.

33. Katerina Sergeeva, "V Urelikskom natssovete (Bukhta Provideniia)," *Ss* 1 (1935): 95–101, 97.

34. Andrei Kukilgin, in Krupnik, *Pust govoriat*, 266–67.

35. Petr Teregkaq, quoted in Bogoslovskaya et al., *Maritime Hunting Culture*, 104.

36. GARF F. 3977, Op. 1, D. 423, L. 79.

37. Krupnik and Bogoslovskaya, *Ecosystem Variability*, 109–10. The species-level data from this period is not clear; N. B. Shnakenburg estimated that forty percent of the whales killed between 1923 and 1932 were grays—"Kitovyi promysel na Chukotke," *Tikhookeanskaya zvezda* 259 (1933): 3.

38. GARF F. 3977, Op. 1, D. 819, L. 70, but such planning documents are thick on the archival ground.

39. GARF F. 5446, Op. 18, D. 3404, L. 3.

40. GAPK F. 633, Op. 5, D. 43, L. 27.

41. GARF F. 3977, Op. 1, D. 819, L. 37.

42. GARF F. 3977, Op. 1, D. 11, L. 40.

43. GAPK F. 633, Op. 5, D. 43, L. 28.

44. October 25 is the Russian Revolution's anniversary, according to the Julian calendar. Viacheslav Ivanitskii, *Zhil otvazhnyi kapitan* (Vladivostok: Dalnevostochnoe knizhnoe izdatelstvo, 1990), 88–94.

45. B. A. Zenkovich, *Vokrug sveta za kitami* (Moscow: Gosudarstvennoe izdatelstvo geograficheskoi literatury, 1954), 47.

46. See A. A. Berzin, "The Truth about Soviet Whaling," trans. Yulia Ivashchenko, *Marine Fisheries Review* 70, no. 2 (2008): 4–59, 9–10; GAPK F. 1196, Op. 1, D. 227, L. 91–92.

47. GAPK F. 1196, Op. 1, D. 227, L. 10–14.

48. GAPK F 1196, Op. 1, D. 212, L. 5. Sums of whale kills from Y. V. Ivashchenko, P. J. Clapham, and R. L. Brownell Jr., "Soviet Catches of Whales in the North Pacific: Revised Totals," *Journal of Cetacean Research and Management* 13, no. 1 (2013): 59–71.

49. Zenkovich, *Vokrug sveta*, 130–32.

50. GAPK F. 1196, Op. 1, D. 221, L. 12.

51. Berzin, "The Truth about Soviet Whaling," 10.

52. GAPK F. 1196, Op. 1, D. 227, L. 27.

53. GAPK F. 1196, Op. 1, D. 1, L. 18, 19–20; Berzin, "Truth about Soviet Whaling," 10–12.

54. GAPK F. 1196, Op. 1, D. 212, L. 1.

55. GAPK F. 633, Op. 5, D. 43, L. 28.

56. See, for example, GAPK. F. 1196, Op. 1, D. 226, L. 12–15; GAPK F. 1196, Op. 1, D. 4, L. 2-7. This accounting is in every annual report, however, and usually goes on for dozens of pages.

57. Plan numbers from GAPK F. 1196, Op. 1, D. 3, L. 64b–65; harvest totals in Ivashchenko et. al., "Soviet Catches," 63. Ivashchenko and Clapham have done the important work of adding up Soviet catch totals.

58. GAPK F. 1196, Op. 1, D. 207, L. 64, 32–33; GAPK F. 1196, Op. 1, D. 4, L. 116

59. GAPK F. 1196, Op. 1, D. 3, L. 65, 64b.

60. GAPK F. 1196, Op. 1, D. 1, L. 9b.

61. Ivanitskii, *Zhil otvazhnyi kapitan*, 129.

62. GAPK F. 1196, Op. 1, D. 9, L. 269.

63. RGAE F. 8202, Op. 3, D. 1132, L. 108.

64. Ryuji Suzuki, John Buck, and Peter Tyack, "Informational Entropy of Humpback Whale Songs," *Journal of the Acoustical Society of America* 119 No. 3 (March 2006): 1849–66; Whitehead and Rendell, *Cultural Lives,* 84–97.

65. Marilyn Dahlheim, H. Dean Fisher, and James Schempp, "Sound Production by the Gray Whale and Ambient Noise Levels in Laguna San Ignacio, Baja California Sur, Mexico," in M. L. Jones, et al., *The Gray Whale,* 511–41.

66. T. M. Schultz et al., "Individual Vocal Production in a Sperm Whale (*Physeter macrocephalus*) Social Unit," *Marine Mammal Science* 27, no. 1 (January 2011): 148–66, and Whitehead and Rendell, *Cultural Lives,* 146–58.

67. Dorsey, *Whales and Nations,* 291–92.

68. Discussions of international whaling meetings are from SI RU 7165, Box 3, Folder 6, "London—International Whaling Commission 1937"; SI RU 7165 Box 5, Folder 5, "London—International Whaling Conference, 1938"; and SI RU 7156, Box 5, Folder 2, "London—International Whaling Conference 1939—U.S. Delegation Correspondence."

69. Dorsey, *Whales and Nations,* 291–92. For the full debate, see Dorsey, *Whales and Nations,* chap. 2; and Burnett, *Sounding of the Whale,* 330–36.

70. Catch numbers from R. C. Rocha Jr., P. J. Clapham, and Y. V. Ivashchenko, "Emptying the Oceans: A Summary of Industrial Whaling Catches in the 20th Century," *Marine Fisheries Review* 76, no. 4 (2014): 37–48.

71. "ICW 1938 /19/fifth session," SI RU 7165 Box 5, Folder 5, p. 2.

72. GARF F. 5446, Op. 24a, D. 614, L. 3–4.

73. GARF F. 5446, Op. 24a, D. 614, L. 11.

74. Dorsey, *Whales and Nations,* 97.

75. M. A. Lagen to Chas. E. Jackson, April 13, 1942, SI RU 7165 Box 6, Folder 4. The U.S. also used Norwegian factory vessels to hunt sperm whales in secret in 1941; see Dorsey, *Whales and Nations,* 97.

76. "The Future of Whaling," 1945, p. 4, NARA MD RG 43, Entry 242.

77. On wartime and postwar hunger, see Wendy Goldman and Donald Filtzer, eds., *Hunger and War: Food Provisioning in the Soviet Union during World War II* (Bloomington: Indiana University Press, 2015).

78. GAChAO F. R-23, Op. 1, D. 7, L. 36.

79. RGAE F. 8202, Op. 3, D. 1166, L. 35–36, quote: 104.

80. GAChAO F. R-23, Op. 1, D. 7, L. 13, 36 (quote), 37. GAMO F. P-22, Op. 1, D. 94, L. 185–187.

81. GAMO F. P-22, Op. 1, D. 94, L. 177.

82. GAChAO F. R-23, Op. 1, D. 7, L. 13.

83. Ankaun, in *Naukan i naukantsy: rasskazy naukanskikh eskimosov,* V. Leonova, ed. (Vladivostok: Dalpress, 2014), 20.

84. Krupnik "The Bowhead," 26–27.

85. GAChAO F. R-23, Op. 1, D. 7, L. 19–20.; Krupnik and Bogoslovskaya, *Ecosystem Variability,* 109–110.

86. GAMO F. P-22, Op. 1, D. 94, L. 182, 186.

87. "Leviathan's Decline and Fall," NARA MD RG 43, Entry 242.

88. Quoted in Walter LaFeber, *The Clash: U.S.-Japanese Relations Throughout History* (New York: Norton, 1997), 260.

89. "Draft Comments for US Delegation, November 9, 1945," NARA MD RG 43, Entry 242.

90. "Address of the Honorable C. Girard Davidson, November 26 1946," NARA MD RG 43, Entry 246.

91. Kellogg to Secretary of State, undated, NARA MD RG 43, Entry 242.

92. "Sanctuaries as a Conservation Measure," November 1945, NARA MD RG 43, Entry 242.

93. International Convention for the Regulation of Whaling, adopted in Washington, DC, December 2, 1946, p. 1.

94. On diplomacy, see Burnett, *Sounding of the Whale,* chaps. 4 and 5, and Dorsey, *Whales and Nations,* chap. 3. The Blue Whale Unit predated the IWC, and was first used to regulate oil production; see Johan N. Tonnessen and Arne Odd Johnsen, *The History of Modern Whaling* (Berkeley: The University of California Press, 1982), 313–14.

CHAPTER 10: SPECIES OF ENLIGHTENMENT

1. W. K. Dewar et al., "Does the Marine Biosphere Mix the Ocean?" *Journal of Marine Research* 64 (2006): 541–51; J. Roman and J. J. McCarthy, "The Whale Pump: Marine Mammals Enhance Primary Productivity in a Coastal Basin," *PLoS ONE* (October 11, 2010): DOI: 10.1371/journal. pone.0013255; Roman et al., "Marine Ecosystem Engineers."

2. Khrushchev quoted in Ronald Grigor Suny, *The Soviet Experiment: Russia, the USSR, and the Successor States* (New York: Oxford University Press, 1998), 407.

3. GARF F. A-262, Op. 5, D. 8259, L. 1.

4. On Soviet whaling in the Antarctic, see Y. Ivashchenko, P. Clapham, and R. Brownell, "Soviet Illegal Whaling: The Devil and the Details," *Marine Fisheries Review* 73, no. 3 (2011): 1–19, and Y. Ivashchenko and P. Clapham, "A Whale of a Deception," *Marine Fisheries Review* 71, no. 1 (2009): 44–52.

5. Y. Sergeev, "Dolgii put k mechte," in *Antarktika za kormoi . . . o kitoboiakh*

dalnevostochnikakh, ed. V. P. Shcherbatiuk (Vladivostok: Izdatelstvo Morskogo gosudarstvennogo universiteta imeni admirala G.I. Nevelskogo, 2013), 62–168, 62, 69–70.

6. Valentina Voronova, "Kitoboi Yuri Sergeev," *Zolotoi Rog*, no. 38 (May 20, 2010), 22.

7. Anna Berdichevskaia, "Proshchai, Antarkitka, i prosti," *Iug*, November 30, 2006.

8. GAPK F. 666, Op. 1, D. 990, Ll. 98–116; GAPK F. 666, Op. 1, D. 983, Ll. 3–14; "Skolko zhe mozhno zhdat," *Dk*, December 1, 1967; First Mate P. Panov, "Eto kasaetsia vsekh," *Dk*, January 12, 1968; "Poleznaia vstrecha," *Dk*, January 26, 1968; "Sudovoi Mekhanik," *Dk*, October 22, 1967; Berzin, "Truth about Soviet Whaling," 3–4; Vladimir Verevkin, "Gorzhus, chto byl kitoboem," *GV*, September 19, 2008; and Berdichevskaia, "Proshchai, Antarkitka, i prosti." The account of industrial whaling that follows draws from the logs of both North Pacific vessels, and from ships working in Antarctica.

9. Zenkovich, *Vokrug sveta*, 73.

10. Sergeev, "Dolgii put k mechte," 103.

11. Berzin, "Truth about Soviet Whaling," 30–31. See also Iosif Benenson, *Kitoboi i kitoboitsy*, no page numbers, 2011. Manuscript in author's possession.

12. Sergeev, "Dolgii put k mechte," 106.

13. A. Solyanik, *Cruising in the Antarctic: An Account of the Seventh Cruise of the SLAVA Whaling Flotilla* (Moscow: Foreign Languages Publishing House, 1956), 58–59, 57.

14. GAChAO F. R-23, Op. 1, D. 51, L. 178.

15. N. N. Sushkina, *Na puti vulkany, kity, ldy* (Moscow: Gosudarstvennoe izdatelstvo geograficheskoi literatury, 1962), 99.

16. Andrei Kukilgin, in Krupnik, *Pust govoriat*, 159.

17. GAChAO F. R-23, Op. 1, D. 51, L. 179.

18. GAChAO F. R-23, Op. 1, D. 23, L. 44.

19. GAChAO F. R-23, Op. 1, D. 51, L. 178 (on overfilled plans), 14, 152.

20. Napaun, in Krupnik, *Pust govoriat*, 164.

21. Eduard Zdor, personal communication, May 2014; GAChAO F. R-23, Op. 1, D. 51, L. 179.

22. See, for example, "Vypolnenie plana po pererabotke syrtsa i vypuska produktsii za 1964 god (*Dalnii Vostok*)," document in author's possession; GAPK F. 666, Op. 1, D. 1001, Ll. 38–46; "Svedeniia o vypolnenii plana po vyrabotke produktsii k/f *Vladivostok* za 1968 god," document in author's possession; GAPK F. 66, Op. 1, D. 1033, Ll. 9–25. The list of these annual reports could go on and on—every voyage produced hundreds of pages.

23. On plans, see Ivashchenko et al., "Soviet Illegal Whaling," 4–6, and I. F. Golovlev, "Ekho 'Misterii o kitakh'," in Yablokov and Zemsky, 16.

24. IWC Verbatim Record 1958, Tenth Meeting Document XIII, p. 2.

25. IWC Verbatim Record 1963, 15/17, p. 68.

26. Transcript of 1959 IWC meeting, SI, RU 7165, Box 32, Folder 5.

27. John McHugh to Remington Kellogg, December 10, 1962, SI RU 7165, Box 27, Folder 1.

28. Scott Gordon, "Economics and the Conservation Question," *Journal of Law and Economics* 1 (October 1958): 110–21, esp. 111. Burnett also associates McHugh's view with Gordon and Ciriancy-Wantrup—see Burnett, *Sounding of the Whale*, 511–12.

29. Dorsey, *Whales and Nations*, 194, 235.

30. Rocha et al., "Emptying the Oceans," 40. I am subtracting here the rough total of Soviet kills to 1969.

31. The *Sovetskaia Rossiia* whaled the North Pacific from 1962 until 1965, the *Vladivostok* from 1963 to 1978, the *Dalnii Vostok* from 1963 to 1973 and 1978 to 1979, and the *Slava* from 1966 until 1969. The *Aleut* retired in 1967.

32. GAPK F. 1196, Op. 1, D. 9, Ll. 55–56.

33. Y. Ivashchenko, P. Clapham, and R. Brownell, "Scientific Reports of Soviet Whaling Expeditions in the North Pacific, 1955–1978," *Publications, Agencies and Staff of the U.S. Department of Commerce*, Paper 127 (2006), 6. Alfred A. Berzin smuggled these documents out of TINRO archives, which remain closed.

34. GARF F. A-262, Op. 5, D. 8259, L.8.

35. Ivashchenko et al., "Scientific Reports," 10.

36. Berzin, "Truth about Soviet Whaling," 6.

37. GARF F. A-262, Op. 5, D. 8259, L. 21.

38. GAPK F. 666, Op. 1, D. 1001, L. 7, 15.

39. GAPK F. 666, Op. 1, D. 991, L. 55; GAPK F. 1196, Op. 1, D. 9, L. 269.

40. Berzin, "Truth about Soviet Whaling," 52. The Soviet Union did attempt to harvest some krill in Antarctica.

41. V. I. Lenin, *How to Organize Competition* (Moscow: Progress Publishers, 1964), 408. On postwar labor, see Donald Filtzer, *Soviet Workers and Late Stalinism: Labour and the Restoration of the Stalinist System after World War II* (New York: Cambridge University Press, 2002); on ideological dissipation, see Alexei Yurchak, *Everything Was Forever, Until It Was No More: The Last Soviet Generation* (Princeton, NJ: Princeton University Press, 2006).

42. GAPK F. 666, Op. 1, D. 991, L. 42.

43. "V Bazovom komitete," *Dk*, January 12, 1968.

44. GAPK F. 666, Op. 1, D. 982, L. 66.

45. Solyanik, *Cruising in the Antarctic*, 60.

46. Sergeev, "Dolgii put k mechte," 131.

47. "Krepkii splav," *Pravda*, October 24, 1964; B. Revenko and E. Maslov, "O razhdelshchikakh kitov," in Shcherbatiuk ed, *Antarktika za kormoi*, 362–364, 363.

48. GAPK F. 666, Op. 1, D. 990, L. 118.

49. GAPK F. 666, Op. 1, D. 991, L. 42.

50. Sergeev, "Dolgii put k mechte," 131. On salaries, Ivashchenko et al., "Soviet Illegal Whaling," 4.

51. *Dk*, September 28, 1967; Verevkin, "Gorzhus, chto byl kitoboem."

52. "Kratkie novosti," *Pravda*, January 15, 1961; "Bagatstva okeana— Rodine," *Pravda*, October 24, 1963; "Zolotoi kashalot," *Pravda*, January 16, 1967; "Bogatye ulovy" *Pravda*, April 2, 1965.

53. "V dalekoi Antarktike," *Pravda*, May 5, 1955.

54. "Krepkii splav," *Pravda*, October 24, 1964; A. Oliv, "Antarkticheskii promysel vchera i segodnaia" in Shcherbatiuk, *Antarktika za kormoi*, 364–65.

55. Aaron Hale-Dorrell, *Corn Crusade: Khrushchev's Farming Revolution in the Post-Stalin Soviet Union* (New York: Oxford University Press, 2019).

56. Voronova, "Kitoboi Yuri Sergeev," 22.

57. Benenson, *Kitoboi i kitoboitsy*; A. G. Tomilin, "O golose kitoobraznykh i vozmozhnosti ego ispolzovaniia dlia ratsionalizatsii promysla morskikh mlekopitaiushchikh," *Rybnoe khoziaistvo* no. 6 (June 1954): 57–58.

58. G. Veinger, "Nezvanyi gost," *Dk*, May 9, 1968; quote from GAPK F. 666, Op. 1, D. 983, L. 10.

59. Berzin, "Truth about Soviet Whaling," 47.

60. Zenkovich, *Vokrug sveta*, 159–61; see also Berzin, "Truth about Soviet Whaling."

61. Berdichevskaia, "Proshchai, Antarkitka, i prosti."

62. Ivashchenko et. al., "Scientific Reports," 8. On waste, see Golovlev, "Ekho 'Misterii o kitakh,'" 20–21; Berzin, "Truth about Soviet Whaling," 15–25; E. I. Chernyi, "Neskolko shtrikhov k portretu sovetskogo kitoboinogo pormysla," in Yablokov and Zemsky, *Materialy sovetskogo kitoboinogo promysla*, 26; and N. V. Doroshenko, "Sovetskii promysel bliuvalov, serykh i gladkikh (grenlandskikh i iuzhnykh iaponskikh) kitov v Severnoi Patsifike v 1961–1979 gg," also in *Materialy sovetskogo kitoboinogo promysla*, 96–103.

63. Sergeev, "Dolgii put k mechte," 131.

64. An example of fender whales: GAPK F. 1196, Op. 1, D. 9, L. 47.

65. Voronova, "Kitoboi Yuri Sergeev," 22; Berzin, "Truth about Soviet Whaling," 26.

66. Appendix to Ivashchenko, et al., "Soviet Illegal Whaling," 19.

67. Sergeev, "Dolgii put k mechte," 133.
68. Berzin, "Truth about Soviet Whaling," 54; Golovlev, "Ekho 'Misterii o kitakh,'" 15–18. E. I. Chernyi, "Neskolko shtrikhov," 28.
69. Ivashchenko et. al., "Soviet Illegal Whaling," 17.
70. Ivashchenko, et. al., "Soviet Catches," 63.
71. Golovlev, "Ekho 'Misterii o kitakh,'" 14–15.
72. IWC Verbatim Record 1959, Eleventh Meeting, Document XIV, p. 25.
73. IWC Verbatim Record 1958, Tenth Meeting, Document XIII, p. 83.
74. A. A. Vakhov, *Fontany na gorizonte* (Khabarovsk: Khabarovskoe knizhnoe izdatelstvo, 1963), 141. The first in this series is *Tragediia kapitana Ligova* (Magadan: Oblastnoe knizhnoe izdatelstvo, 1955), and the second, *Shtorm ne utikhaet* (Magadan: Magadanskoe knizhnoe izdatelstvo, 1957). See also Petr Sazhin's novella *Kapitan Kiribeev* (Moscow: Khudozhestvennaia literatura, 1974).
75. "Minutes of the Scientific Committee Meeting, May 30 1952," SI RU 7165, Box 14, Folder 1.
76. "Statement of the Delegation of the Soviet Union," February 10, 1967. SI RU 7165 Box 28, Folder 1. Most internal policy debates about whaling remain closed, or, as E. I. Chernyi speculates, have been destroyed.
77. GARF F. A-262, Op. 5, D. 8259, L. 7.
78. See, for example, David N. Pellow, *Resisting Global Toxics: Transnational Movements for Environmental Justice* (Cambridge, MA: MIT Press, 2007).
79. See Bruno, *Nature of Soviet Power*, chap. 5.
80. Scott McVay, "Can Leviathan Endure so Wide a Chase?" *Ecologist* 1, no. 16 (October 1971): 5–9.
81. *Flipper*, the 1963 film and later television series, and the 1973 movie *The Day of the Dolphin*.
82. Zelko, *Make it a Green Peace*, 185–89 and Burnett, *Sounding of the Whale*, chap. 6.
83. Farley Mowat, *A Whale for the Killing* (1972; repr. Vancouver: Douglas and McIntyre, 2012), 39.
84. Paul Ehrlich, "Eco-Catastrophe!" *Ramparts* (September 1969): 24–28, 28.
85. I draw here, variously and partially, from Hal Rothman, *The Greening of a Nation?: Environmental Politics in the United States Since 1945* (Fort Worth, TX: Harcourt Brace College Publishers, 1998); Adam Rome, *The Genius of Earth Day: How a 1970 Teach-in Unexpectedly Made the First Green Generation* (New York: Hill and Wang, 2010); Zelko, *Make it a Green Peace*; and Paul Sabin, *The Bet: Paul Ehrlich, Julian Simon, and Our Gamble over the Earth's Future* (New Haven, CT: Yale University Press, 2013).
86. Kenneth E. Boulding, "The Economics of the Coming Spaceship

Earth," in *Environmental Quality in a Growing Economy: Essays from the Sixth RFF Forum*, ed. Henry Jarrett (Baltimore: Johns Hopkins University Press, 1966), 9.

87. John Claypool quoted in Adam Rome, *Genius of Earth Day*, 176.

88. Ehrlich, "Eco-Catastrophe!" 28.

89. John Claypool quoted in Adam Rome, *Genius of Earth Day*, 178.

90. Edmund Muskie, *Congressional Record—Senate*, vol. 120, pt. 9 (April 23, 1974): 11324–27. For disagreements with Muskie, see Rome, *Genius of Earth Day*, 135–37, and Sabin, *The Bet*.

91. Rachel Carson, *Silent Spring* (1962; repr. New York: Houghton Mifflin, 2002), 57. On ecology and its popularization, see Donald Worster, *Nature's Economy: A History of Ecological Ideas* (Cambridge, UK: Cambridge University Press, 1994), and Sharon Kingsland, *Evolution of American Ecology 1890–2000* (Baltimore: Johns Hopkins University Press, 2005).

92. Peter Morgane, "The Whale Brain: The Anatomical Basis of Intelligence," in *Mind in the Waters: A Book to Celebrate the Consciousness of Whales and Dolphins*, comp. Joan McIntyre (New York: Scribner, 1974), 93.

93. Rocha, et. al, "Emptying the Oceans," 42–45.

94. Ivashchenko et al., "Scientific Reports," 20–22.

95. Bete Pfister and Douglas Demaster, "Changes in Marine Mammal Biomass in the Bering Sea/Aleutian Islands Region before and after the Period of Commercial Whaling," in Estes et al., *Whales, Whaling*, 116–133.

96. IWC Verbatim Record 1971, Meeting 23, pp. 25–27.

97. Ivashchenko et al., "Soviet Catches," 64–70.

98. Victor Scheffer, "The Case for a World Moratorium on Whaling," in McIntyre, *Mind in the Waters*, 230.

99. McVay, "Can Leviathan Endure?," 6–7, 9.

100. Robert Hunter, *Warriors of the Rainbow: A Chronicle of the Greenpeace Movement 1971–1979* (Amsterdam: Greenpeace International, 1979), 192.

101. Rex Weyler, *Song of the Whale* (Garden City, NY: Anchor/Doubleday 1986), 114–19.

102. Hunter, *Warriors of the Rainbow*, 177, 207.

103. Paul Watson, "What I Learned the Day a Dying Whale Spared My Life," *The Guardian*, January 9, 2013.

104. Zelko, *Make it a Green Peace*, 285–86.

105. Viktor Serdiuk, "Poslednii kitoboi," in Shcherbatiuk, *Antarktika za kormoi*, 201–04. Quote appears on p. 203.

106. Paul Spong, "In Search of a Bowhead Policy," *Greenpeace Chronicles* (November 1978), 2.

107. George Noongwook et al., "Traditional Knowledge of the Bowhead Whale (Balaena mysticetus) around St. Lawrence Island, Alaska," *Arctic* 60, no. 1 (March 2007): 47–54.

108. Roger Silook, quoted in Milton Freeman, *Inuit, Whaling, and Sustainability* (London: Altamira Press, 1998), 171.

109. Yuri Rytkheu, "When the Whales Leave," *Soviet Literature* 12 (1977): 3–73.

110. On the Soviet collapse, see Slezkine, *The House of Government,* chap. 33, and Joseph Kellner, "The End of History: Radical Responses to the Soviet Collapse," (PhD diss.: University of California Berkeley, 2018).

111. Nina Vovna, interviewed by Sue Steinacher, 2000, transcript in author's possession.

112. Sergey Vykovsyev, interviewed by Sue Steinacher, 2000, transcript in author's possession.

EPILOGUE: THE TRANSFORMATION OF MATTER

1. William Boarman and Bernd Heinrich, "*Corvus corax*: Common Raven," in *The Birds of North America,* no. 476, ed. Alan Poole and Frank Gill (American Ornithologists' Union, 1999): 1–32, and personal observation.

2. For examples, see Kira Van Deusen, *Raven and Rock: Storytelling in Chukotka* (Seattle: University of Washington Press, 1999), 21–23 and 102–4; Hall, *Eskimo Storyteller,* 93–95, 347–48, 447–49; and Lowenstein, *Ancient Land,* 3–6; 65–66.

3. Lowenstein, *Ancient Land,* 65–70.

4. McKenzie Funk, "The Wreck of the Kulluck," *NYT,* December 30, 2014.

5. 350.org, "Bill McKibben Responds to White House Decision on Arctic Drilling," press release, May 11, 2015, https://350.org/press-release/bill-mckibben-responds-to-white-house-decision-on-arctic-drilling/.

6. William Yardley and Erik Olsen, "Arctic Village Is Torn by Plan for Oil Drilling," *NYT,* October 11, 2011.

7. This runs counter to a common theme in Soviet histories, including Martin Malia, *The Soviet Tragedy: A History of Socialism in Russia 1917–1991* (New York: Free Press, 1994) and Stephen Kotkin, *Magnetic Mountain: Stalinism as Civilization* (Berkeley: University of California Press, 1995), that see the Soviet experiment as doomed by its lack of markets. Many environmental histories of the Soviet Union sharpen this point, starting with Douglas Weiner's *Little Corner of Freedom* and Paul Joseph-

son's *Conquest of the Russian Arctic*. John McNeill sees both socialist and capitalist development as having similar consequences in *Something New under the Sun: An Environmental History of the Twentieth Century* (New York: W. W. Norton, 2000), a view shared with Dipesh Chakrabarty, "The Climate of History: Four Theses," *Critical Inquiry* 35, no. 2 (Winter 2009): 197–222. Kate Brown critiques both systems in *Plutopia: Nuclear Families, Atomic Cities, and the Great Soviet and American Plutonium Disasters* (New York: Oxford University Press, 2013).

8. B. Bodenhorn, "It's Traditional to Change: A Case Study of Strategic Decision-Making," *Cambridge Anthropology* 22, no. 1 (2001): 24–51.

9. Sadie Brower Neakok, quoted in Brower and Brewster, *The Whales, They Give Themselves*, 172.

10. Senungetuk, *Give or Take a Century*, 163.

11. See also Kyle Powys Whyte, "Indigenous Science (Fiction) for the Anthropocene: Ancestral Dystopias and Fantasies of Climate Change Crises," *Environment and Planning E: Nature and Space* 1, no. 1–2 (March–June 2018): 224–42.

12. Barry Lopez, *Arctic Dreams* (New York: Vintage, 1986), 414.

INDEX

Note: Material in illustrations is indicated by *italic* page numbers. Endnotes are indicated by n after the page number.